Liberty in Absolutist Spain

The Johns Hopkins University Studies in
Historical and Political Science
108th Series (1990)

1. *Liberty in Absolutist Spain:*
The Habsburg Sale of Towns, 1516–1700
Helen Nader

Liberty in Absolutist Spain

The Habsburg Sale of Towns,
1516–1700

Helen Nader

The Johns Hopkins University Press
Baltimore and London

This book was brought to publication with the generous assistance of the Program for Cultural Cooperation between the Spanish Ministry of Culture and North American Universities.

Softshell Books edition, 1993

The Johns Hopkins University Press
2715 North Charles Street
Baltimore, Maryland 21218-4319
The Johns Hopkins Press Ltd., London

Library of Congress Cataloging-in-Publication Data
Nader, Helen. 1936–
Liberty in absolutist Spain: the Habsburg sale of towns,
1516–1700 / Helen Nader.
p.   cm.—(The Johns Hopkins University studies in
historical and political science: 108th ser., 1)
Includes bibliographical references.
ISBN 0-8018-3850-9.—ISBN 0-8018-4731-1 (pbk.)
1. Municipal government—Spain—Castilla y León—
History. 2. Municipal incorporation—Spain—Castilla y
León—History. 3. Municipal charters—Spain—Castilla y
León—History. 4. Castilla y León—History, Local.
5. Spain—Politics and government—1516–1700.
I. Title. II. Series.
JS6320.C296N33   1990   89-24503
320.8'0946'2—dc20   CIP

A catalog record for this book is available from the British Library.

Contents

Illustrations

Figures

Maps

Preface

Every author owes much to individuals and institutions whose moral and financial support make research possible. I owe more than most because of the generosity of the support I have received. I also owe an explanation, however, because the research did not turn out the way I designed and described it to funding institutions. This book began in 1976 as a study of how nobles managed their landed estates, which produced most of Castile's wealth in the age of Spanish grandeur. As I analyzed the records of fifteen noble estates, many aspects of the agrarian economy emerged, including costs and benefits of grain, olive oil, and wine production in various regions. This was a result I had hoped for and for which I had received fellowship support. The topic of the book kept changing, however, because my research revealed that nobles limited their managerial activities to livestock breeding and selling. Noble lords were not making the important decisions about crop production. Town councils made those decisions and initiated large-scale capital development to improve agricultural production.

After writing chapters on each of these topics, I began drafting an introduction explaining the political and legal constraints on the nobility's involvement in crop production. By the summer of 1983 the introduction had reached 150 typewritten pages, and I knew I was in trouble. I had spent years researching and writing about nobles and farmers, but their economic decisions could be explained only within the context of an implicit legal reality: every noble estate was a town. When I compared noble estates with royal and ecclesiastical estates, I found them to be organized in the same way. The Castilian agrarian economy functioned through a municipal administration that is virtually forgotten today. In order to understand the relationship between noble lord and town council, I needed to learn more about Castilian towns.

During the next four years I alternated between moments of high excitement as enigmas gave way to answers and deep despair as I realized how many topics still need research. Two years of reading Spanish and Latin American urban history yielded some surprising observations. We know a great deal about Castile's cities, particularly in the north, in the Middle Ages but very little after 1500. Small towns and villages are almost unknown during any period.

The lack of published information about small towns and villages presented difficulties in identifying some of the places I had researched. Sometime in 1985, while trying to locate a few of these small towns on modern maps, I recognized a familiar shape. The outline of the noble estate for which I had accumulated the largest amount of archival material, Estremera, had not changed in two hundred years. Estremera's municipal boundaries on the Spanish government's 1972 maps appeared identical to a drawing that the Estremera town council submitted to the royal government in 1752 (compare map 7 and fig. 5). The modern boundaries also fit the verbal description that an earlier Estremera town council had provided in response to a royal questionnaire in 1580. Other modern towns that I chose at random and traced back showed the same continuity. When I stepped back and looked at municipal boundaries as a whole, I began to see a pattern that seemed a revelation: there are no unincorporated spaces between towns. The municipal boundaries of Castilian cities and towns fit together as tightly as the pieces of a jigsaw puzzle. This suggested that all the agricultural land of Castile is incorporated in municipalities (see fig. 1).

If the spatial and legal relationships between Castilian towns and their farmland already had been fixed in the Middle Ages, I could incorporate my findings about noble estates into the history of small towns. Though the story of Castile's towns during the last four hundred years would still be static, many enigmas might be resolved. I tested this idea by comparing two rich sources of information for New Castile: the responses that Estremera and hundreds of other municipal councils gave to the royal questionnaire distributed between 1575 and 1580, known as the *Relaciones topográficas*, and the responses of the same councils to the 1752 survey known as the Catastro del marqués de la Ensenada. Contrary to my expectations, many municipalities went through significant transformations between the two surveys. For example, most of the towns in the 1575–80 survey had been villages without municipal boundaries in 1500, and nearly all passed from the royal domain to noble estates or from ecclesiastical estates into the royal domain between 1530 and 1752. The demand for change came from unlikely poles of the political power spectrum—small villages and the royal treasury. Both supported a royal policy of selling charters of township, a policy that historians have long studied at the treasury level. The number and impact of changes I encountered at the local level required nothing less than a redefinition of the society itself. I decided to abandon the estate management research results, retaining just a few sentimental favorites, in order to focus on the towns.

The results of the new approach have been as much a surprise to me as they may be to other specialists in Spanish history. Like most historians, I assumed that rigid Castilian attitudes in the Habsburg centuries caused Spain's decline, and so I had begun the research looking for stagnation and resistance to change. I found instead the strengths and ingenuity of a society changing and reshaping itself at a dizzying pace. Rather than powerless and inarticulate peasants, I encountered the astute arguments

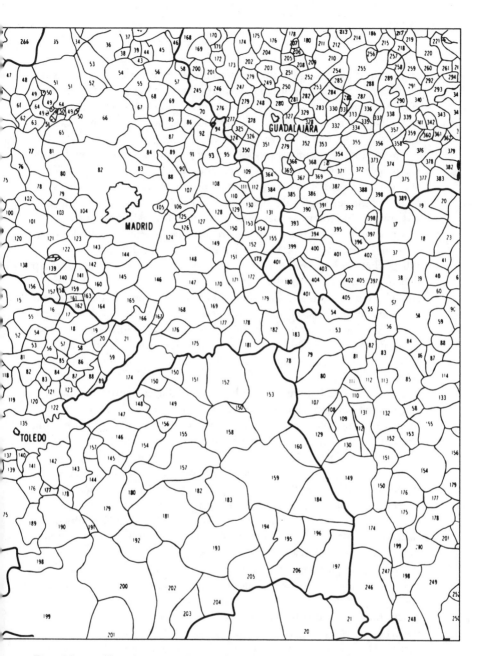

Fig. 1. Municipal boundaries, 1972. Reprinted from José Manuel Casas Torres, *España: Atlas e índices de sus términos municipales*, 2 vols. (Madrid, 1969), vol. 2, plate 8.

and pungent rhetoric of farmers adept in the discourse of municipal government. At every stage of the research I looked for flawed and oppressive
relationships but found spirited town and village councils stoutly exercising
and increasing their powers of self-administration—and lords and monarchs helping them to do it. Habsburg Castile was a much more varied
and dynamic society than we imagined.

The rule of autonomous towns over subject villages was so obvious to
the people of Castile that they simply took it for granted except when it
was being changed or disputed. Their silence shapes both the chronological
focus and the geographical scope of this book. Though a continuous feature
of Castilian life from the medieval reconquest through most of the nineteenth century, the process of town formation became most visible between
1516 and 1700, when the Habsburg kings made township available to any
village that could raise the money. The sale of town charters led to sharp
debates between the royal government and city councils and to bitter
struggles between villages and their ruling towns. These antagonisms en-
gendered legal briefs, treatises, and petitions, creating a volume of paperwork unknown before the Habsburg period. Buried in these thousands
of pages of legal formulae and bureaucratic repetition, local conditions
and aspirations emerge, expressed in the words of the local citizens themselves.

I begin with a handful of late bloomers, villages whose essential first
stage in the development as a Castilian municipality—that revealing moment when the founding citizens elected their first municipal officers and
the land passed into the hands of the municipal council—occurred on
the eve of the Habsburg period. I present these events from the point of
view first of the ordinary citizens, then of the noble lord, and finally
of the monarch. After that, I bring to the foreground specific instances of
the change from village to town. Finally, I explore some consequences
of town liberty on the citizens themselves by displaying the subsequent
decisions that towns made in exercising their new judicial and economic
powers and tax collection responsibilities.

Because my purpose is to describe institutional developments and administrative processes that have not been discussed previously, my greatest
concern is to make the municipality as comprehensible as possible. The
functioning of an institution so pervasive and unquestioned can best be
discerned by observing the activities of specific municipalities over a long
period of time. Only after we understand the natural internal development
of individual towns and villages can we begin to see how all of these
municipal cells fit together. To that purpose, I set aside for a later volume
the analysis of Castile's cities because it grew so large that it threatened
to overwhelm everything else. I also omit most of the noble estates that
formed the original research base of this book in order to highlight a

variety of municipalities: towns scattered throughout Castile; towns in the three classic categories of jurisdiction—royal (*realengo*), ecclesiastical (*abadengo*), and lay (*solariego*); and towns whose economic activities covered the full range from mining to grain farming. Nevertheless, in the interest of providing some sense of continuity and a representative focal point for tracing change over time, I present vignettes from the history of the noble estates with which I am most familiar, those of the marquises of Mondéjar.

I hope that these new perceptions and questions will seem a worthwhile result of the generous support I received for the original project. I am deeply grateful for fellowships from the John Simon Guggenheim Foundation, the National Endowment for the Humanities, the Woodrow Wilson Center for International Scholars, and the Tinker Foundation. The Food Research Institute at Stanford University, the Arizona Center for Medieval and Renaissance Studies at Arizona State University, and the Woodrow Wilson Center for International Scholars at the Smithsonian Institution all provided stimulating working environments while I was a fellow or research scholar at their institutions. Indiana University supported my research and writing efforts with a sabbatical leave and research grants. Silvia Arrom, Ann Carmichael, Christopher Cokinos, Marsha Cotton, Leila Johnson, and Fareed Nader selflessly read and responded to early drafts of some chapters; their penetrating questions and challenges contributed much to the evolution of this book.

My deepest thanks and warm feelings go to the citizens of many small towns in New Castile, particularly in the Alcarria region of Guadalajara Province. Mayors, town councilmen, notaries, municipal secretaries, shopkeepers, farmers, shepherds, and priests all interrupted their daily work to lead me to a hard-to-find spot in the countryside, show me how grain, wine, and olive oil were stored, and refer me to the local specialists in logging, esparto weaving, or cheesemaking. The phenomenal memory of local individuals has been of invaluable assistance in explaining regionalisms in vocabulary, enigmatic proverbs, and municipal traditions. Above all, I appreciate the precautions town officials took before permitting me to consult their municipal archives: their stewardship has preserved irreplaceable documents for hundreds of years.

A Note on Translation
and Place-Names

"Town" and "liberty" are not words usually associated with the Spanish Habsburg empire. They are rarely mentioned in the many books written about Spain. Yet they were common terms of government among Castilian rulers and taxpayers. By using them as the basic terminology for Spanish municipal government I am trying, not to introduce new vocabulary, but to remain faithful to the premodern meaning of words that are used more loosely today. The process of converting a village into a town had a special vocabulary that disappeared with the practice itself. The monarchy used several verbs for the act of separating a village from the jurisdiction of its ruling town or city. I try to retain the emotional overtones of these verbs, as well as their specificity, by using "liberate" for *liberar,* "exempt" for *eximir,* and "dismember" for *dismembrar.* I translate the word *villazgo* as "township" when it refers to the status of town and "charter" when it refers to the grant conferring that status.

Throughout this book I translate *ciudad* as "city," *villa* as "town," and *lugar* or *aldea* as "village." Even though all of these Spanish terms are still used today, they had specific legal meanings in the sixteenth and seventeenth centuries that were lost as the institutions themselves disappeared. In the Middle Ages a city (*ciudad*) held special status as a city-state not subject to royal jurisdiction in its internal affairs. A town (*villa*) was independent of any other municipality but subject to the king or some other lord.[1] At times, the word *lugar* was used in the same way as it is today, as any "place" or small settlement, but in official contexts the word *lugar* referred to a village that was located within the municipal boundaries of a city or town and legally subject to its council. I use the Spanish word *pueblo* in its specific legal sense in the early modern period for any municipality with a functioning municipal council, regardless of its legal status. The term *despoblado* referred to a municipality whose council no longer functioned even if its fields continued to be farmed.

A *vecino* was a citizen of a specific city, town, or village, in contrast to noncitizens, who were temporary or permanent residents (*residentes* and *moradores*).[2] In census terminology, *vecino* referred to the head of the citizen household, so that a village of fifteen households was said to have fifteen *vecinos.* Today, Spaniards are citizens of the nation, and *vecino* has been reduced to the meaning of co-resident or neighbor, without political or legal connotations. Each Castilian, in addition to being a citizen by birthright of a municipality, was a subject (*vasallo*) of the monarch. Castilians who were citizens of ecclesiastical or seignorial towns were also subjects (*vasallos*) of the town's lord (*señor*).

In the Habsburg period, municipal judges of cities, towns, and villages were called *alcaldes ordinarios* officially and just *alcaldes* in daily usage. The modern *alcalde* has no judicial authority, and so the modern word is usually translated as "mayor." An appellate judge was called *alcalde mayor*. Though the appellate judge resided in a city or town, he was appointed by the lord or king and was not an officer of the municipality itself.

By using this English vocabulary consistently, I hope to avoid some of the confusion that might result from using the Spanish words themselves. Spaniards do not confuse *ciudad* and *villa* in their daily conversation, but some important histories of Habsburg Spain are written in French, which translates both *ciudad* and *villa* as *ville*.[3] In modern English we use the word "villa" for a large and imposing country residence—just the opposite of the Castilian *villa*. The medieval English *vill* may have been equivalent to the Castilian *villa*, but this raises another layer of possible confusion between "village" and *vill*.[4]

Several villages (*lugares*) and towns (*villas*) changed their name during the Habsburg centuries, usually as a result of the sale process described in this book. Others employed variant spellings, such as *Fontanar* and *Hontanar*. Some villages used qualifiers to distinguish them from other places of the same name, such as the modern Gárgoles de Arriba and Gárgoles de Abajo, whose sixteenth-century names were Gárgoles de Suso and Gárgoles de Yuso.[5] Frequently villages employ two versions of their name—such as Aldea del Monte and San Juan del Monte—within the same document. In other cases, an old medieval name seems to hang on in local tradition simply because it lends itself to amusing speculation; the people of Villanueva de la Cañada, for example, remember that their town once was called La Despernada. In the text of this book, I use the twentieth-century place-name as it appears on topographic maps published by the Instituto Geográfico Nacional.

Wherever possible, I quote, translate, or paraphrase from published sources that are available to readers who might not have access to the archives. Where published sources could not be found, I provide my English translation or paraphrase of an unpublished document, with my transcription of the manuscript in the notes. I hope this will allow specialists to refer back to the documents and judge for themselves the significance of town liberty in the history of Castile.

Liberty in Absolutist Spain

Introduction

One of the extraordinary royal fundraising schemes in sixteenth-century Europe was the seizure and sale of church property. In England Henry VIII and Elizabeth I dissolved monasteries and sold the property to private buyers.[1] In the Holy Roman Empire both Protestant and Catholic states appropriated monastic and episcopal property to finance their wars against each other and strengthen their own internal governments.[2] In Spain the Habsburg kings sold towns and villages belonging to military orders, monasteries, and the archbishop of Toledo. Some European monarchs extended the same process to secular jurisdictions. In England the monarchy sold crown lands.[3] In Naples and Castile the Habsburg rulers stripped the cities of municipal territory in order to convert their subject villages into salable towns.[4]

In most parts of Europe the sales transferred large expanses of land to new owners whose economic self-interest guaranteed loyalty to the regime. The monarchs, particularly in the Protestant countries, gained the political support of new owners, which took the place of support from the church. In effect, the rulers bought the loyalty of the aristocracy by giving them the opportunity to buy church estates.

In Spain the consequences were much more complicated. For the political administration of the monarchy the most significant result was the proliferation of jurisdictions. While rulers in other countries consolidated their power with the support of a few newly empowered purchasers, in Castile the monarchy sold so much to so many different buyers, both individual and corporate, that the effect was the opposite of consolidation: the Habsburg monarchs in Castile fragmented local administration, creating hundreds of newly autonomous towns. Yet, ironically, the long-term benefit to the monarchy was the same, for newly chartered towns were intensely loyal to the monarchy that had liberated them from the control of cities and older towns.

These results derived from a fundamental characteristic of Castilian society: there was no distinction between urban and rural. All the land of Castile was incorporated in the municipal boundaries of cities and towns, which were the territorial divisions of the monarchy. Throughout the medieval centuries Castilian kings had organized newly conquered territory into municipalities. The conquering kings delegated royal jurisdiction to the new city and town councils and granted them municipal territories that included farmland, woods, water sources, and pasture. When subject villages developed within the municipal boundaries of the cities and towns during the fourteenth and fifteenth centuries, kings excised villages and land from the ruling municipal council, elevated each village to the status of a town and gave the new town to a loyal military or ecclesiastical supporter. The Habsburg kings introduced an innovation by converting this traditional Castilian process of town formation into a cash transaction.

We are faced with one of the paradoxes of Castilian history, an absolutist monarchy inextricably associated with municipal liberty. The operative passages of the royal charters granting township stated, typically:

I, Philip, king of Castile, in consideration of the services [in cash] you have rendered to me, full knowingly and willingly make use of my royal absolute power to liberate you, the village of X, from the city of Y and make you a free town for and over yourself.

The innovation of selling town charters to villages succeeded because it satisfied the needs of both subjects and rulers. The drive for town liberty rose out of popular expectations of self-government: every village aspired to be liberated from the jurisdiction of its ruling town or city and become a town of its own with authority over its own farmland, even if the cost was high. The rulers needed cash to finance their foreign wars: Charles V, Philip II, and Philip IV all were graciously pleased to grant township to their deserving subjects, for a price.

The effects of these sales on the royal finances have been studied by some of Spain's greatest economic historians, who have demonstrated that the sales brought in enough money at crucial moments to satisfy the king's creditors and enable him to negotiate new war loans.[5] And, significantly, the sales did not appreciably diminish income from the royal jurisdiction, because the territories sold were not historically part of the royal domain. They were ecclesiastical or city jurisdictions incorporated into the royal domain specifically for the purpose of sale.

Charles V began with the towns of the religious military orders of Santiago, Calatrava, and San Juan, transferring towns from the military orders into the royal domain and then selling them to royal officials and nobles. Philip II seized much of the archdiocese of Toledo, elevated its villages to townships, incorporated the new towns into the royal domain, and then sold them to the highest bidder, converting them into seignorial towns. When individual buyers were lacking, Philip II and Philip IV extracted villages from their ruling towns and cities and sold charters of township to the villages themselves, making them royal towns. If towns objected to being sold into a nobleman's jurisdiction, they could exercise their option of returning to the royal jurisdiction by submitting a competing bid (*tanteo*) matching the price that the new lord had paid to the royal treasury. Philip IV found a way to profit from seignorial jurisdictions, too.

Lords traditionally granted township to their villages gratis; Philip IV now required a royal license for such a transformation and exacted a fee from the village for the license.

Despite the months and years that might elapse in negotiations between the royal treasury and prospective buyers, the consequences of town sales could fall upon the citizens themselves with startling suddenness. Some towns went through the ceremonies of alienation from an ecclesiastical jurisdiction, incorporation into the royal domain, transfer to a noble buyer, and reconstitution as a seignorial town all within the space of three or four days. Even the transformation from village to town could be accomplished in a few hours. A village judge could awake one morning holding authority to try only petty cases punishable with small fines, receive the charter of township from the royal council at noon, and retire at night as a town judge with the power of capital punishment.

The phenomenon touched every corner of the kingdom, and at a level that affected most peoples' daily lives. The monarchy sold towns and township in all parts of Castile, from the Asturias and Basque regions in the Atlantic north to Seville, Granada, and Murcia in the Mediterranean south. The new towns tended to be small, ranging from thirty-seven to nine hundred households, and represented the basic administrative unit of Castilian government. The small villages and towns, with their democratic town meetings and annually elected municipal judges and councils, were the urban norm. More than 80 percent of Castilians lived in towns and villages. Cities, a distinct legal category in Castile, were not sold by the Habsburgs, nor were they the urban norm; of Castile's more than fifteen thousand municipalities only about thirty were cities, and they were home to only 20 percent of the Castilian population.[6]

The long-term effect of the sales was the repeated fracturing of large municipalities into numerous small towns. Increasing the number of towns fragmented local administration, because it changed the legal status of many of Castile's most ubiquitous municipalities, the villages. Villages (lugares) in Castile did not have the authority to administer themselves; they were subject to towns and cities. Towns (villas), like cities, were self-administering. In 1500, at the beginning of the Habsburg period, a majority of the municipalities in New Castile—about 60 percent—were villages; in 1700, at the end of the Habsburg sales, more than 75 percent of the municipalities were towns (for the persistence of these fractured boundaries as late as 1972 see fig. 1). We tend to equate absolutism with centralization, but in Spain the kings invoked their royal absolute power to decentralize administration.

This redistribution of authority did not necessarily work to the disadvantage of the monarchy. Royal power and local self-government augmented each other. The royal government exercised its political authority in Castile through town and city councils in an administrative structure that linked towns directly to the monarchy but not with each other. Whereas a village could litigate and act only through its ruling city or town, all cities and towns acted as agents of the monarchy. Each fragmentation, therefore, created more towns to act as royal agents. Kings and lords had everything to gain from their subjects' self-administration and knew it. The lord who liberated a village from one of his seignorial towns and granted it a charter of township created two town councils to administer his seignorial jurisdiction instead of one. The queen embroiled in a civil war could entice a village to rebel against its ruling town whose noble lord opposed her by promising the village a charter of township. With one stroke, she diminished the extent of her opponent's seignorial jurisdiction and increased the number of towns loyal to her. Such proliferation of autonomous municipal jurisdictions over the course of centuries resulted in an ever higher density of royal and seignorial authority throughout the realm, administered by ever smaller towns.

Castilians and their rulers did not regard this development of municipal independence as incongruous with royal absolutism. Monarchical governments measured their grandeur not only by the extent of their territory but also by the number of administrative units and subjects under their rule. A judge of the Council of Castile at the end of the sixteenth century claimed that there were 32,000 municipalities in all of Spain and that "the greatness of the Council of Castile" derived from the fact that it was the royal supreme court to which half of those municipalities—the 15,760 Castilian cities, towns, and villages—brought their appeals cases. The 16,000 municipalities in the non-Castilian parts of Spain did not take their appeals to a single supreme court but divided their appeals among the high courts of Catalonia, Aragon, and Valencia.[7] Castile was a monarchy of municipalities; the more towns the greater the realm. A noble estate was a cluster of towns; the more towns the greater the lord.

This, at least, was what Castilians said in the Habsburg period. Villagers seeking town charters addressed their kings as partners with shared responsibilities and a mutual fate. They argued that villages, because they lacked the autonomy of towns, could not achieve the happiness and prosperity that were the source of the monarch's reputation and power. In hundreds of petitions, Castilian taxpayers recited the familiar litany: the village judge's insufficient judicial powers tarnished the monarch's reputation as the fount of justice, a declining village population diminished the realm, uncultivated land impoverished the royal treasury.

For example, in 1625 the village of Villamanta explained how its lack of township adversely affected the king (see map 1).[8] The village was separated from its ruling town of Casarrubios by more than two leagues of wilderness (monte) in which there had occurred many violent incidents,

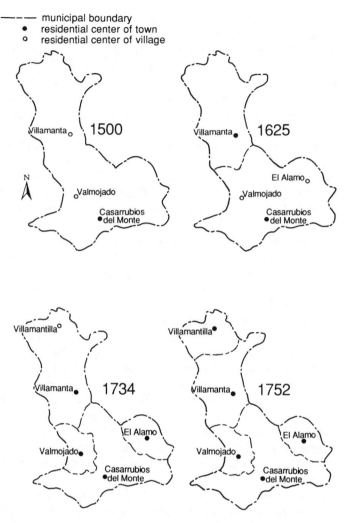

Map 1. Development of the Villages in the Town of Casarrubios del Monte, 1500, 1625, 1734, and 1752

including robberies and murders, and by dangerous arroyos, which flooding made impassable in winter, preventing the villagers from appearing before the Casarrubios town judge, with a resultant loss of their lawsuits. For this reason and because of the harassment and injustices they suffered daily from the town judges, the village judge being arrested for trivial reasons and village citizens fined and accused purely for the profit of the town officials, the village had lost population. Of the 300 households it once had had, only 160 remained, because many villagers, not wanting to see their children suffer and live under the threat of being ruined, married outside the jurisdiction of the town of Casarrubios. And so despite the village's abundant resources for provisioning the royal court in Madrid, most of its fields were abandoned and uncultivated for lack of population, thus contributing to the bankruptcy of the royal treasury.

The people of Villamanta were not being entirely frank in explaining the reasons for their population decline; they shaped their history to satisfy the monarchy's legal theory justifying these transformations from village to town. Fifty years earlier, in 1576, Villamanta reported that its population had declined from 300 to 250 households in just twenty years. They explained that many citizens had died in epidemics, especially an epidemic in 1557.[9] But this information would not have helped their petition in 1625, although the intervening years, especially 1598 through 1601, had been marked by some of the most serious epidemics in Castilian history. Becoming a town would not affect the death rate, yet the villagers needed to persuade the king that by making them a town he would stem their population decline and thereby fulfill the royal mission of populating the realm. So they blamed the demographic collapse of their village on political oppression at the hands of the town council of Casarrubios del Monte.

For all these reasons, Villamanta's citizens petitioned to be made a town. Their lord, the count of Casarrubios, regarded the petition favorably and offered to join in the petition if necessary. The Cortes approved the petition and recorded it as a model for other seignorial villages seeking town charters. King Philip IV invoked his royal absolute power to grant the charter of township to Villamanta. Village citizen, noble lord, the Cortes, and king all believed that what was good for the village was good for the monarchy.

If this perception that an absolute monarch's reputation rested on the happiness of his subjects seems startling, it is nevertheless simply the obverse of the truism beloved by kings and queens that all the subjects of a monarchy shared in the ruler's fortunes. The queen who defeated a political rival freed her subjects from local injustice. A king's victory in war redounded to the glory of the entire kingdom. A royal bankruptcy trickled down to impoverish the taxpayers. Crown and town formed a single body that flourished or withered as one.

The real tension in this society was not between monarch and nobles nor between lord and subjects but between municipalities and, especially, between towns and their own subject villages. City and town councils usually administered their municipal territory to the advantage of their own citizens and to the disadvantage of the villagers, who resented the town's legal authority and economic control over them. By transforming the process of town formation into a cash transaction, the Habsburg rulers transferred the initiative to the villages. Villages that sought to remedy their disadvantages now could take the lead in becoming autonomous royal towns by submitting a bid to the royal treasury. From the point of view of the ruling town, a village that sought to become a town became the enemy, because a town could not exist within the territory of another municipality—by definition it had to have an autonomous municipal territory of its own, which could only be carved out of the territory of its ruling town. The successful bid (tanteo), by gaining autonomy for one village, increased tensions between the remaining villages and their ruling city or town council.

Charles V took advantage of this tension to raise capital from the cities by playing villages against their ruling councils; he offered to sell township to villages and then allowed the ruling cities to offer more money if the emperor would promise not to change the status of their villages. In 1537 the village of Linares petitioned the emperor to be liberated from the city of Baeza and be given a charter of township, but the city of Baeza outbid Linares, receiving from Charles a guarantee that the city would never be deprived of its subject villages or territory. Thirty years later Philip II accepted a higher bid from Linares and revoked his father's promise to the city, explaining that the guarantee to Baeza had proved "most noxious and prejudicial to Linares by depriving it of the hope of being liberated and separated from the jurisdiction of the city, leaving it in perpetual subjection." Furthermore, he continued, the city of Baeza, believing that Linares could never be granted autonomous jurisdiction, had treated the village badly. In order to correct this injustice, the king explained, he used his royal absolute power to break the previous guarantee to Baeza and give Linares the status of a town "free and exempt from the city."[10]

Given a choice between Castile's cities, whose representatives in the Cortes were resisting tax increases, or hundreds of villages willing to pay cash for independence from cities and towns, Castilian monarchs naturally favored the villages. The loudest voices objecting to the process of fragmentation, therefore, were those of the oldest cities and towns, who complained bitterly of being stripped of territory and subject population. The conflicts in this society were between municipal competitors for the same resources, not between subjects and their royal or noble lords.

This is not the way we think of Spain. A monarchy that decentralizes its authority is extremely difficult for us to conceptualize, and more so in Castile, which has a reputation for authoritarian government and oppressive social relations. In the sixteenth and seventeenth centuries the Habsburg kings in Spain certainly provided every opportunity to put the negative aspects of absolute monarchy to the test. They claimed absolutist powers, engaged in foreign wars almost incessantly, and then faced the equally burdensome task of suppressing tax revolts in Catalonia and the Basque regions. Yet, even with high taxes and decentralized government, after the Comunero Revolt in 1521–22 Castile experienced no major rebellions, and we are hard pressed to find even minor ones. We do not have to look far beyond Castile to find bloody uprisings, regicides, tax revolts numbering in the hundreds, and other disturbances during the sixteenth and seventeenth centuries.

Why was Castile exempt? Scholars have suggested various possible reasons: a resident monarch, charity during hard times, social control by a locally powerful aristocracy.[11] For most historians of Spain, Castile's domestic calm suggests a passivity that contrasts unfavorably with the aggressiveness of the Catalans and Basques. The availability and efficiency of town liberties provides a powerful additional explanation. Even the smallest and most humble village could gain freedom from its ruling city or town by subsidizing an absolute monarchy.

Liberty from the rule of another municipality fulfilled the highest aspirations of Castilian political life. Personal liberty was not at issue, for Castilians had a long tradition of free personal status; sixteenth-century Castile had no serfs, no forced labor service, no demesne farms or manor houses. This point is well known, though it seems to need frequent restatement.[12] The ways in which Castilians exercised their personal liberty in public life, in contrast, have received little attention from modern historians. Historians of the Spanish Middle Ages have described the municipal institutions established in the cities during the age of reconquest.[13] Although these institutions declined after the thirteenth century, María del Carmen Carlé has detected new types of municipal councils in the fifteenth century.[14] These municipal governments, particularly in small towns and villages, remained the principal means through which Castilians exercised personal liberty in the sixteenth through the nineteenth centuries. Democratic self-government was the ideal and often the practice in Castilian towns; citizens in town meetings made the most important decisions, and elected town judges and councilmen daily administered justice, taxation, and the local economy.[15] This strong tradition of town democracy by a free people is generally believed to be a British trait, not Spanish, yet it shaped both the political and the economic life of most of Castile's people.

The urban nature of the countryside also shaped Castilian political administration. Cities and towns were the monarchy's basic unit of territorial administration. There were no regional governments in Castile, no provinces, no intendencies, no royal territorial governors. Each city and town council corresponded with the royal court directly, speaking on behalf of its citizens and its subject villages. When a village became a town, it, too, corresponded directly with the royal court and exercised the monarchy's delegated judicial powers. There was no court-country rift in Castile, but a unitary structure linking royal court directly to country town.

The economy was shaped by the fact that all the territory of Castile was incorporated into municipalities. City and town councils owned and managed the land. The councils allocated house lots and farm fields to their citizens, regulated the rotation of crops and grazing, determined who could put new land to the plow, and used the profits from municipal assets to pay royal taxes and seignorial dues collectively on behalf of the citizens. Agricultural life was urban life, and the success or failure of the agrarian economy depended on wise management of the municipal territory by city and town councils.

The Castilians' famed litigiousness might be seen as a sign of their confidence in their capacity for self-administration and their essential faith that the monarch or lord was not the enemy. Without a remote and centralized government meddling in their daily lives, and with local control of justice, land, and taxation, Castilians had a sense that they managed their own affairs. People do not need to resort to violence if they already control their daily lives or if they believe they can acquire that control through purchase. The Habsburg sale of church and royal towns and villages made the acquisition of local self-administration a lively possibility.

Yet the extension of autonomy and municipal territory to smaller and smaller municipalities has never received systematic study. Spaniards did not just forget this aspect of their own history in a fit of absent-mindedness, nor did the knowledge of Castile's municipal history fade with disuse; a powerful new royal government worked assiduously for years to discredit local autonomy. While municipal traditions remained deeply embedded in local government, the attitudes of the royal government changed drastically in the eighteenth century when the Bourbons replaced the Habsburgs as the ruling dynasty. The new dynasty turned against the municipalities and gradually dismantled the power of Castile's local institutions. At the same time, the Bourbons encouraged Castilians to rewrite their history to obliterate the memory of the municipality as the home of Castile's democratic tradition. The Bourbons were so successful in this campaign that historians today consistently misinterpret both the economy and the politics of Castile in the Habsburg period. Modern categories of study, such as feudalism, centralization, or capitalism, obscure the fundamental importance of the Castilian municipality as the basic territorial unit of the monarchy. In some cases, modern reformers have plucked incorrect impressions of the most elementary aspects of economic life, such as inheritance law or the private ownership of land, from romantic novels or political ideologies. Social science models that assume these incorrect impressions to be part of the historical record seriously distort the beliefs and activities of Castilians before the Bourbon period.

The polemical rewriting of Castilian municipal history began during the eighteenth century in the heat of Bourbon reforms. When the French Bourbons inherited the thrones of Spain in 1700, they found the power and independence of Spanish municipalities intolerable.[16] There were no intermediaries between the municipal councils and the royal council, no royal constraints on municipal autonomy. The kings addressed decrees to "all the cities, towns, and villages of our realms" because there were no other administrative units to implement royal policy. Furthermore, the economic centrality of municipal ownership of the land made the cities and towns tempting objects for reform by the Bourbons' finance ministers.

The Bourbons began a long campaign to create provinces as an intermediate level of royal jurisdiction over the cities and towns.[17] The count of Floridablanca proposed a division of the realm into provinces, but the project sank in the complexity of Castile's fragmented jurisdictions.[18] By the end of the eighteenth century the Bourbon government had achieved significant changes: they had established new taxes and abolished old ones, installed intendants in the Castilian cities to supervise the collection of royal taxes by the towns, stripped municipal judges of much of their power, and forced town councils to submit their land management to royal inspection.[19] But no political reorganization into provinces had been accomplished.[20] The new compilation of royal law published in 1805, the *Novísima recopilación*, depended on the traditional municipal administration and ordered "the pueblos whose judges have jurisdiction in the first instance," that is, all cities, towns, and villages, to implement the new code.[21] By the end of the century the monarchy's financial situation was such that the Bourbons, too, began to grant town liberty in exchange for cash.[22]

With the resurgence of the Cortes as a political force during the Napoleonic invasion, the first Spanish constitution, drawn up by the revolutionary Cortes of Cádiz in 1812, promised a territorial division: "A more convenient division of Spanish territory shall be made by a constitutional law as soon as the political circumstances of the nation permit."[23] In 1833 political circumstances permitted publication of a royal decree in which Isabel II created forty-nine provinces. These units interposed between municipal and royal governments did not supersede the powers of the town councils, because these provinces were simply electoral units of the Cortes.[24] After another half-century of proposals, the constitution of 1876 asserted in principle that provinces were the administrative units of the centralized nation, and in 1892 legislation finally provided provincial governments with powers over the municipalities.[25] Thus it is only in the twentieth century that municipalities have been subordinate to provincial governments in Castile.[26]

In the long and acrimonious debates leading to the constitution of 1876, politicians on both sides used the history of Castilian municipal traditions as a weapon of persuasion and propaganda. Representatives to the Cortes defended the tradition of autonomous municipalities that, they claimed, had given the Cortes its power in earlier centuries. Antonio Sacristán y Martínez wrote a history of medieval municipalities in order to demonstrate that with the disappearance of municipal statutory independence and equality, "political liberty, daughter of municipal autonomy, received a fatal blow." Nineteenth-century liberals rejected the argument that municipalities were an obstacle to the formation of a modern nation-state. On the contrary, they believed that the municipality was "the birthplace of love of country and love of liberty. The exercise of political liberty is incomprehensible without the direct participation of citizens in the government of the country, and from this general principle we cannot exclude the municipality, eternal basis on which nationalities are founded."[27]

Sacristán y Martínez and his liberal colleagues in the Cortes lovingly studied the democratic tradition of town meeting. Yet they were well aware that the Bourbon rulers associated town democracy with rebellion: in 1808 the declaration of war against the Napoleonic government had been issued on behalf of all Spaniards by the judge of Móstoles, a town of three hundred households near Madrid that had bought its liberty in the sixteenth century. During Fernando VII's repression of liberals in the 1820s, these deputies could not safely speak about the heroic role of towns in the guerrilla war against the French invaders. Instead they romanticized the medieval towns that had defied earlier foreign intruders; the Comunero revolt against the Habsburgs especially attracted nineteenth-century liberals as a surrogate for municipal resistance to Bourbon centralization. Madrid in the 1870s enjoyed a revival of Golden Age theater in which good town judges, in the name of the king, exercised their judicial authority against injustice and tyranny.

The liberals' opponents, who believed that suppression of municipal autonomy and a division into provinces were necessary in order to create a modern nation-state, also rewrote Spanish history. In the heyday of town liberty during the Habsburg centuries, loyal sons had recorded the triumphant moments and charms of their hometowns by writing histories of individual cities and towns. In the late nineteenth century these gave way to provincial studies in which advocates of the centralized nation-state rewrote the history of Castile. Cayetano Rosell directed a grand project to publish a general history of Spain province by province.[28] For the first time, there appeared histories of provinces, bibliographies of works composed by native sons of provinces, descriptions of provincial spots of interest, eulogies of the medicinal benefits of natural springs in various provinces, biographies of the famous sons of provinces, and provincial statistics.[29] For most students of Spanish history this massive campaign to erase the memory of municipal independence succeeded to such effect that its vocabulary itself disappeared.

For historians the effect of this nineteenth-century rewriting of Spanish medieval history has been to blur or even obliterate the memory of Castile's earlier political administration. Urban historians today study only the cities—the upper extreme of the continuum of municipalities—as instruments of the monarchy's local administration. This distorts our understanding of Castilian political norms, because cities were too large to maintain the democratic town meeting or even the annually elected town council.

Studies of cities pass over small-town Castile, the site and context of daily life for the vast majority of Castilians until the twentieth century. That is because Castilian history has been written from the point of view of the cities, yet cities were, of necessity, antagonistic toward township, which deprived them of their dependent villages and municipal territory. When these studies bring in the small towns and villages, they come as an afterthought, as the passive or violent victims of decisions and actions taken at the top. The traditional focus on the superstructure leaves us with only the vaguest hints of the administrative structure and activities of the great mass of the population.

Most historians of Castilian administration, when finally they come to the municipality, cite a chapter on cities published by M.-J. Gounon-Loubens more than a century ago. Gounon-Loubens recognized the national preeminence of the Cortes cities in taxation and in acclaiming the sovereign[30] but not their role as administrators of the surrounding countryside, nor did he mention towns or villages. His purpose in this chapter was to describe Castile's cities in relation to the royal councils and other national institutions as part of the Habsburg Europe-wide system. Because he focused on royal government, he overlooked much of the local administration. Modern historians of the cities, if they pursue institutional history at all, accept this narrow focus.[31] The pioneer urban historians of Castile have followed this model. Bartolomé Bennassar's study of Valladolid in the sixteenth century confines itself to the residential nucleus (caserío) of Valladolid proper and does not address Valladolid's administrative role in the royal government. Furthermore, despite the broad scope of the book's subtitle, the author dismisses as trivial the relationship between Valladolid and its villages.[32] Bennassar's study ignores the crucial point that the city or town council was the residual owner and effective manager of the surrounding farmland, including its subject villages. Carla Rahn Phillips made the first successful marriage of city and subject villages in her demographic and economic study of Ciudad Real in the Habsburg centuries, and this same approach is now bearing fruit in the first studies of major cities—Segovia and Cordoba—and their subject villages.[33]

Just as urban historians isolate cities from their supporting land and villages, rural historians cut villages off from their ruling cities. David Vassberg's overview, our most important study of Castilian rural economy and society to date, for example, describes the farm community's struggle to gain or retain access to communal lands, without distinguishing between village and autonomous town nor addressing the relationship between subject village and ruling city. Michael Weisser's essay on rural society describes in vivid terms the dysfunctional relationship between the twenty-two villages in the Montes de Toledo and the ruling city council of Toledo.[34] Weisser, extrapolating from the Montes de Toledo to all of Castile, posits a seventeenth-century origin for twentieth-century agrarian revolt. Yet his conceptual and scholarly choices limit both his analysis and his conclusions. The dysfunction he describes was a consequence of the peculiar legal status of the Montes de Toledo rather than a typical relationship between country and city. The Montes de Toledo was not part of the municipal territory incorporated by the city's royal charter (fuero); it was a section of royal land that the city council purchased more than a century after the conquest and thereafter owned and managed as the city council's corporate assets (propios).[35] Far from being typical, the legal status, and therefore the economic and political resources, of the Montes de Toledo were unique in Castile. Villages within the city's statutory jurisdiction, in contrast, displayed much more independence and self-sufficiency, as Salvador de Moxó noted.[36] Hilario Casado's research on the region around the city of Burgos, where the city-village legal relationships were the norm for Castile, draws a strikingly different picture from that sketched by Weisser.[37] Casado describes people making a living within the traditional legal and administrative framework. Leading citizens of the city buy property in the villages and years later move there. Families prosper in the business of farming and move to the city. Farmers market their agricultural produce in distant towns and bring back merchandise for sale in their home villages. Although Casado's study stops in 1528, just before the period when the Habsburg kings transformed Castilian society by selling townships, it displays a society in constant change throughout the fifteenth and early sixteenth centuries, a robust agricultural economy in the last years of the fifteenth century, and the continuing importance and solidarity of the rural municipality. Above all, Casado demonstrates the interplay between city and village, perfectly conjoined and profoundly interrelated.

These historians advance our understanding of the agricultural economy and village society, placing Castile in the forefront of what Roger Manning has called "the most important trend in early modern European history and social history in the past quarter century—the growing appreciation of the overwhelmingly rural nature of the diverse societies and economies of Europe."[38] Casado has gone farther, showing us that "the divisions between the two worlds, urban and rural, were permeable and in many cases very confused."[39] These concepts are fundamentally different from our traditional view of Castilian agrarian society, yet they have been found to explain other parts of Europe in the same centuries.

The European context sets the stage for what I propose to illustrate in this book—the overwhelmingly urban nature of the countryside and the connection between small country towns and absolute monarchy. In studying the towns and villages of Castile I follow the lead of both contemporary and ancient guides. A modern historian of Eastern Europe, Jerome Blum, sketched a procedure for comparing the internal structures of rural towns that shapes my organization of the data for Castile.[40] For understanding the interrelationship between the monarchy and the Castilian municipality, my guide is Aristotle. In discussing the polis, Aristotle said, "In this subject as in others the best method of investigation is to study things in the process of development from the beginning."[41]

There are, of course, many histories of Spanish towns; these have been written for centuries by enthusiastic native sons whose access to oral tradition and knowledge of the local environment make their works invaluable for the modern professional historian.[42] Historians of medieval Spain have always known the value of these local and legal histories and have used them to great advantage. The American historian Heath Dillard, for example, has used municipal law codes and local histories in drawing a broad picture of women's lives and activities in medieval cities and towns.[43] In order to find discussions of the internal development of towns and villages, therefore, we turn to the historical tradition that focuses on the legal history of individual municipalities. Historians of law have described all the legal institutions of individual cities and towns during and after the reconquest of the thirteenth century.[44] A model of the genre, and one that has been fundamental to the conceptualization of this book, is the legal history of Madrid's municipal government during the Middle Ages by Rafael Gibert.[45] Most notably, Gibert extended his research beyond Madrid into comparative studies of citizenship and liberty in other Castilian towns.[46]

Strangely, no one has directed a study specifically at the legally organized municipality as the focus of social and political existence after 1500. For historians of the Habsburg and modern periods, changing legal status and administrative powers of Spanish towns remain an aspect of life that was obvious and yet untouched by scholarship.[47] Historians of modern Spain produce broad and cogent studies of the reforms attempted by the royal government, particularly the royal treasury, yet these studies of the central administration do not reach out to the towns and villages.[48]

The most sweeping attempts at assessing the state of the Castilian countryside in the Habsburg period are studies based on a survey questionnaire circulated by Philip II between 1575 and 1580. This survey, popularly known as the *Relaciones topográficas*, provides a broad range of information from over five hundred towns and villages in New Castile. The royal government instructed each municipal council to delegate two well-informed and intelligent citizens to make responses (*relaciones*) to the questionnaire. The citizens gave information about their town's legal status, history, population, relative location to other towns, municipal government, resources, produce, religious practices, and famous sons. Noël Salomon was the first to systematically exploit the riches of this source, using the information to support the same arguments advanced by Carmelo Viñas y Mey twenty-five years earlier.[49] Salomon saw these places as relics of medieval feudal estates and interpreted the annuities that municipal councils paid to kings and lords as feudal dues. This interpretation has been sharply criticized as anachronistic by Salvador de Moxó and Miguel Artola, who pointed out that demesne farms and serfdom did not exist in the Castilian Middle Ages. Artola noted that Salomon cited nonexistent passages in medieval legal codifications. Moxó charged Salomon with mistaking early sixteenth-century municipal charters for medieval texts.[50]

In response to what he saw as Salomon's errors, Moxó carried out an exhaustive study of the medieval seignorial estates of the modern province of Toledo and a pioneering study of the sale of ecclesiastical jurisdictions in the sixteenth century.[51] These detailed legal-institutional histories, together with his earlier studies of the dissolution of the seignorial regime in the nineteenth century, might have produced the definitive study of the seignorial regime in New Castile. But Moxó did not take into account changes in the legal and administrative status of Castilian municipalities during the fourteenth and fifteenth centuries, much less during the Habsburg periods. The result was that his own studies, together with his devastating criticism of Salomon's chronology, leave the impression that the medieval institutions persisted until the nineteenth-century reforms and did not undergo drastic change in the intervening centuries.[52]

The nineteenth-century reforms also created an obstacle to understanding the economic basis of agrarian communities in premodern Castile. Whereas the eighteenth-century Bourbon monarchs failed in their attempt to take possession of seignorial jurisdictions by litigation, as Moxó has shown, the nineteenth-century Bourbons proceeded to do so by legislation.[53] The Bourbons' attempt at reform through litigation had failed because the lords were able to prove in the highest court of the monarch, the royal council itself, that their grants of seignorial jurisdiction had been given by kings acting within their powers as absolute monarchs. If the grants were valid, as the king's own courts had pronounced, then the only feasible means of abolishing seignorial jurisdiction was to purchase it from the owners. The question of compensation became a major political issue in the liberal government of 1820–23, but financial exigencies prevented a resolution until 1837, when the Cortes and monarch agreed to compensate lords for the loss of their seignorial jurisdiction by giving them land.[54] In each seignorial jurisdiction, the former lord received as private property the uncultivated commons (monte) of the municipality. The nobles ceased to be lords and became instead great landowners. The large, underdeveloped landed estate—the latifundium attacked by twentieth-century reformers and modern historians of Spain and Latin America—was the product of this 1837 expedient in the cause of modern state-building.

Although Moxó considered the 1837 legislation a travesty of Castilian law, he directed his indignation toward the Middle Ages rather than the Bourbon monarchy.[55] Neither he nor the more economically oriented historians of the last decade have been able to discard the rhetoric of the twentieth-century land reform movement; only recently has a prominent economic historian, Miguel Artola, perceived that the large landed estate is a modern creation.[56]

Ironically, these historians approach the Castilian countryside in an ahistorical manner. None of them studies the legal and administrative institutions of the agrarian economy as spatial relationships or pays heed to the vehemence of the antagonism expressed in litigation between villages and their ruling cities or towns. They treat the centuries between the medieval reconquest and the modern state as static, except for the inevitable injection of "the new monarchy" of Ferdinand and Isabella and an ill-defined "absolutism" under the Habsburgs. Dynamic institutional and administrative change at the local level does not figure in the models they apply to the political, social, and economic history of Castile. These social science models resemble nothing so much as the national super-highways. They conduct us to a desired destination quickly and efficiently by avoiding the small towns, the local roads, the complexities of daily life. The tourist on the superhighway and the historian with an economic or sociological model do not see the real Spain, the small towns and villages that are everywhere and were the source of Castile's power and reputation in the Habsburg centuries. They do not hear the voice of the farmers who, through their labor and ingenuity, produced Castile's wealth.

Chapter 1

The Constitution of Town and Land

Land and Council

On June 6, 1512, fifteen farmers appeared before the royal notary Juan de Luz in the town of Meco to complete the final steps in founding a new municipality, the village *(lugar)* of Miralcampo. They were the entire voting population of Miralcampo: thirteen male heads of household *(vecinos)* and two unmarried males representing their widowed mothers. The thirteen *vecinos* included all four of the municipal officers who formed the village council *(concejo)*: a judge *(alcalde)*, a sheriff *(alguacil)*, and two councilmen *(regidores)*. In the presence of the notary, the voting citizens of Miralcampo convened their town meeting to approve the agreement they had negotiated with their lord *(señor)* defining for all time their legal rights and duties. The contract redefined the terms of their tenancy on the land and affirmed their recognition of the lord's jurisdiction over them. Both the farmers and the lord were going through a process that for them was natural and one that they considered almost a duty—to place the possession and management of the land in the hands of a municipal council.

Such contracts were the first step in the development of municipalities throughout Castile. They functioned as constitutions, binding agreements between the governed and the governors. Whether they were unwritten oral agreements or written down and called *fueros, cartas pueblas, constituciones*, or, as in this case, *capítulos* (terms), these constitutions conceded possession of the land to the municipal council. This strategic possession of the land by municipal councils goes far to explain one of the peculiarities that plague the study of Spanish history: the land, its cultivators, and its lords do not seem to have anything to do with each other. The essential actors in the local economy, the taxpayers and the aristocracy, do not speak to each other. The lack of communication among individuals has led to a series of impressions that, at best, the records were lost or, at worst, the taxpayers were inarticulate and passive victims of absentee lords who did not care or know about their land and tenants. Ignorance and neglect, it is believed, damaged the productive capacity of the land and drove farmers into bankruptcy. Thus, the silence of the sources in itself

has contributed significantly to the interpretation that the Castilian economy was inefficient and oppressive.

Through the medium of the municipal constitution, however, lord and
farmer established an effective and mutually beneficial working relationship. Farmers did not speak individually but as citizens of a municipal
corporation, and kings and lords communicated with town councils rather
than with individual subjects or estate managers. In municipal constitutions, lord and farmer bound themselves to each other and to the land.
These constitutional constraints and privileges for both citizens and lords,
hitherto neglected by modern historians, shaped the words and actions of
the entire society during the Habsburg centuries.[1]

Some characteristics of these municipal constitutions were so pervasive
that they may be considered the fundamental principles of the relationship
between land and society. The town or city council exercised jurisdiction
over all the land in the municipal boundaries and managed the land for
the common good, designating which sections would be opened to clearing
and plowing by its citizens. A citizen who cleared land and cultivated it
with plow or spade for a specified number of years thereby converted it
into his own private property. If a farmer allowed his fields to go out of
production, they reverted to the council, which could allow another citizen
to cultivate and take possession of them.[2] If the council ceased to function,
the cultivated fields remained the private property of their owners, but
the uncultivated land (monte) would revert to the lord. Whether the lord
of the town or village was the king, a nobleman, a bishop, or master of
a military order, a constitution bound together the municipal council and
the land.

Towns sometimes established colonies within their municipal territory,
but most frequently a village formed simply by squatters' moving into a
section of the municipal territory and organizing a council. This population
movement was possible because Castilians were free people. Serfdom never
developed in Castile, probably because of the presence of the open
frontier.[3] Castilians were not subject to forced labor service, nor were they
bound to the land or any specific lord. Everywhere, a farmer who put new
land to the plow acquired the land as private property, to do with as he
wished, and each managed his own fields within the schedules for harvesting and grazing set by the municipal council.[4] This pattern of private
farms cultivated within a municipal rotation calendar and supplemented
by access to the municipal commons existed throughout Castile. The
farmers of Miralcampo negotiated these same conditions—the ordinary
and ubiquitous terms of tenancy that governed Castilian daily life. This
example of Miralcampo is rare only because its specific terms (capítulos)
were written down.[5]

The Miralcampo farmers had once lived in the town of Meco, where they were citizens. For years they had rented and worked the land of a farm called Moneder, which belonged to the count of Tendilla, lord of the town of Meco.[6] The farm occupied bottomland along the Henares River, and the farmers would have walked the five kilometers to the Moneder fields and five kilometers back to Meco every day. But after an epidemic swept through Meco in 1507, these fifteen farmers had moved their families out of Meco's residential center and built homes on the farm of Moneder. By electing a municipal council the renters had formed themselves into a village, which they called Miralcampo. In 1512 the count of Tendilla stopped in his town of Meco while traveling from Granada, where he was captain general, to Guadalajara, where he had family business to attend to—a distance of over five hundred kilometers. Since the rental contracts for the Moneder farm were due for renewal, he and his tenants took the opportunity of these negotiations to formally recognize their new relationship, he as lord and they as citizens of the village of Miralcampo. The citizens came before the notary to affirm their continued relationship with the lord as his subjects (*vasallos*) and to accept an agreement by which the count of Tendilla transferred possession of the farm of Moneder to the Miralcampo village council (see map 2).

The new contract permanently vested the use and usufruct of the Moneder farm in this council and formally recognized the transfer of the farmers' citizenship from the count's town of Meco to his village of Miralcampo, which lay within the Meco town boundaries. The notary drew up the agreement in the form of a petition in which the count graciously responded to a request from his subjects. The citizens began by defining the property over which they wanted to gain permanent tenancy: the farm of Moneder, which lay within the municipal boundaries of the towns of Meco and Guadalajara. They asked that the count of Tendilla grant to the council of Miralcampo in perpetual leasehold (*censo perpetuo enfitéusin*) everything the farmers had previously occupied as his renters: all the land, houses, plowed fields, and other improvements, as well as the groves, meadows, common pastures, and all the other resources belonging to the count. They also asked for any fishing rights that the count might own in the Henares River, which formed the eastern boundary of Meco.[7]

Instead of the short-term rental fees the individual farmers had previously paid the count for the fields they worked, the council of Miralcampo, on behalf of all its citizens, would in future pay an annuity (*censo*) fixed in perpetuity at one pair of chickens per household and six hundred fanegas of grain. The chickens were to be delivered live and healthy. The grain would be paid in the usual form for New Castile, half wheat and half barley, all clean, dry, free of spoilage, and ready for transport. The first

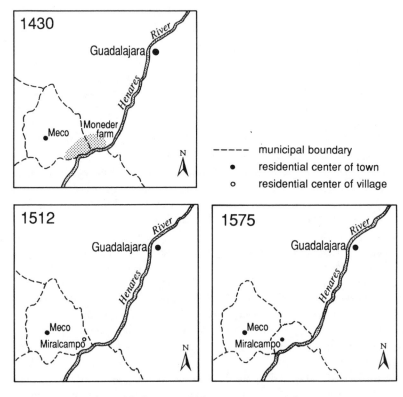

Map 2. Miralcampo and Meco, 1430, 1512, and 1575

payment would be due in August 1513, and the annuity would henceforth be payable every August on the feast day of the Virgin Mary.[8]

By transferring his land to the village council in perpetual leasehold, the count agreed that he and his successors would no longer manage or control the land in Miralcampo. Those functions now passed to the council and the citizens. The council gave to the individual farmers as heritable property the fields they already cultivated, and it could grant the same benefits to new citizens who cleared and plowed fields in Miralcampo. The citizens owned their house lots and cultivated fields as private property, which they henceforth could buy, sell, transfer, and bequeath within the terms of the law. The farmers would be free to sell their grain on the open market, and the lord and all future lords could not seize it for any price whatsoever.[9]

In exchange for the use and usufruct of the land, the citizens thus guaranteed the perpetual payment of the annuity. The count and his successors would be obligated to send a steward (mayordomo) to Miralcampo at harvest time to receive the annuity paid in grain and could not require a Miralcampo citizen to act as steward against his will.[10] If the steward did not appear, they were not obligated to transport the grain anywhere besides to the count's barns and silos within Miralcampo itself. If the steward should sell this grain, or grain brought in from any of the count's other estates, the sales in Miralcampo would be exempt from the sales tax.[11]

To ensure that Miralcampo would survive as a municipal corporation, the citizens promised to maintain a population of sixteen households, all in residence in Miralcampo. They agreed that if the number of households should decline because some family moved away or a house became vacant, they would bring in another household within four months.[12] As long as Miralcampo was populated and the council paid the annuity, the uncultivated land (monte) belonged to the municipal corporation. The council managed this uncultivated land, reserving some as commons open to the entire community and allowing other parts to be put to the plow and converted into private property as the population grew. If the population of Miralcampo should ever decline to the point that the council no longer functioned, the uncultivated land of Miralcampo would revert to the lord. The council agreed to reaffirm the contract every fifteen years in order to demonstrate that it still functioned as a municipal council.[13]

The men then affirmed the legal relationship between themselves as citizens and the count as lord of Miralcampo. They formally acknowledged the count's proprietary jurisdiction (señorío) over the village of Miralcampo and accepted his right to appoint or designate the judges and courts that would exercise his seignorial jurisdiction at the appellate level.[14] All present and future citizens of Miralcampo would be his subjects, exempt from the jurisdiction of any other government. They would be exempt from payment of the royal sales taxes, subsidies, and military obligations.[15] The count would guarantee their tax exemption by protecting them from royal or other officials who might attempt to collect taxes there. The citizens of Miralcampo would be free of all seignorial dues, payments, and obligations except the annuity in chickens and grain specified in the contract. They could not be required to cosign loans or provide collateral for the lord.[16] Labor services were not even mentioned: forced labor services to a lord were an anachronism in Castile by 1500.

They pledged themselves and their property to the fulfillment of these conditions and agreed to submit to the jurisdiction of courts and judges stipulated by the count in case of default. They asked the count to donate twenty thousand maravedís for repair and embellishment of their church and to issue the contract by signing and sealing it, giving his pledge of honor "as the person you are" to adhere to all its parts and conditions.[17]

The fifteen farmer-citizens of Miralcampo listened to the notary read the conditions aloud, approved them by acclamation, and asked him to make two copies of the contract, one for the count and one for their municipal council. Both documents were signed by the official witnesses to the proceedings—the count's appellate judge in Meco, the count's servant Juan de Valdepeñas, and four citizens of Meco. Then, because none of the citizens of Miralcampo knew how to write their name, they asked the same witnesses to sign the documents on their behalf.[18]

Immediately afterward, in the same house, the count of Tendilla himself agreed to all of the conditions that "you the judge, sheriff, councilmen, and solid citizens of my village of Miralcampo presented to me" and pledged to observe all the terms of the contract, which he signed and sealed with his signet.[19] The official witnesses signed the count's deposition, and Juan de Luz validated it, testifying that he was licensed as a royal notary, had been present at all the proceedings together with the council and citizens of Miralcampo, the official witnesses, and the count of Tendilla, and had faithfully composed the document according to the stated wishes of the signatories. He swore that he had allowed proxies to sign for the citizens of Miralcampo because they claimed they did not know how, that the count had signed his own name, that the count's seal was affixed below his signature and in the notarial register, and finally that he himself signed the documents in confirmation of the entire proceeding.

With this transfer of the use and management of the land to the council of Miralcampo, the farm of Moneder disappeared from the lord's accounting records. The name Moneder disappeared from written records because the farm itself disappeared as a single working and legal entity on the land.[20] The citizens of Miralcampo could farm their fields as private property and were free to work, buy, sell, and bequeath their farmland as private property without the lord's interference or knowledge. The council henceforth possessed and managed the uncultivated land as commons and collected and paid the annuity. The lord's accountant transported the chickens and six hundred fanegas of grain and recorded their receipt in his ledger as an annuity paid by the council of Miralcampo. In nearly every other town and village in Castile, this entry of the annuity payment (censo) in the ledgers is the only surviving written evidence of the council's possession of the municipal territory. The Miralcampo contract, because it captures the act of transfer from lord to council, reveals the relationship of lord, council, and land hidden behind the annual payment.

The individual house lots and plowfields appeared almost as rarely in written records, even after Miralcampo grew large enough to support a municipal clerk (escribano). This absence of written records for private farms was also typical of Castile. Farmers did not draw up written contracts for most of their business dealings. Within the village or town, they rented, exchanged, bought, and sold land and livestock by verbal agreement in the marketplace, witnessed by the judge or councilmen. When farmers died, their property was distributed equitably among all their legitimate children, as Castilian law required and the council ensured. The law permitted parents to donate up to 10 percent of their property to pious or charitable causes. This disposable portion of the property might appear in a written will, but the normal transfer of houses and farms from one generation to another was so strictly regulated by inheritance law that the testator could not legally dispose of it. Most of the private farmland in Miralcampo, therefore, never appeared in wills or other written records.

The continued payment of the annuity depended on the productivity and prosperity of Miralcampo's citizens, whose new municipality was limited in extent but contained most of the essentials for a farm village. The land was level and clear, the soil "hot," the air healthful and "with few diseases." There were no springs, so the people dug wells in their own household patios for their drinking water. They grew wheat, barley, rye, oats, and grapes and raised sheep, cattle, and horses. The village had no irrigated fields, but there were vineyards and willow groves on the riverbank, which supplied some fuel, as well as pasturage and small game. The Henares River provided eels and fish, and the farmers took their grain to the river to be milled. They bought salt for their livestock and for preserving their own food from the towns of Imón and El Olmeda and traveled to the markets of Alcalá and Guadalajara for their buying and selling.[21]

The village of Miralcampo, with its shortage of uncultivated land (monte), was far from the ideal that would supply its citizens with the means for their sustenance. That ideal, had it ever existed, would have appeared as a residential nucleus (caserío) of marketplace, houses, corrals, church, and vegetable gardens clustered around a year-round source of drinking water. Natural springs and artesian wells abound in Castile's mountainous topography and were the preferred source of the municipal water supply. On the alluvial plains, where the water table is close to the surface and the soil friable, wells were easily dug and maintained, as they were in Miralcampo. Streams and rivers generally were not suitable because they could dry up in the long summer drought and often flooded in the rainy season.

The layout of the residential nucleus depended on whether the place had been settled first by Muslims or by Christians. Spain's most prominent urban historian, Leopoldo Torres Balbas, observed that a "radical difference in urban concept" in the two societies resulted in distinctive layouts of public and private space. Muslim municipalities do not have open public spaces. The Muslim commercial district (suq, Spanish zoco) is a warren of streets just wide enough to accommodate loaded pack animals. Streets wind in no discernible pattern, sometimes come to a dead end, and are often so steep that the pavement is stepped. Official ceremonies of a

Muslim town or city take place indoors or within the walled courtyards of public buildings and residences.[22] The towns founded by Christians, however, are immediately identifiable by the open marketplace, or plaza, near the center of town. The plaza's shape influenced the layout of the surrounding streets and houses; if the town was originally founded as a planned community, the marketplace was laid out as a spacious rectangle, and the streets leading away from it formed a rectilinear grid. Most towns, however, began as squatter settlements on steep slopes, and their marketplaces followed the contours of the terrain, developing as irregular yet open spaces. Houses around the marketplace were faced with porticos that protected merchandise from rain, but the main business of buying and selling took place in the open plaza, where vendors put up temporary awnings (toldos) to shield themselves and their products from the sun. Streets were wide and straight enough to accommodate the wheeled carts in which farmers and merchants transported grain and produce.

Founding citizens in New Castile received the lots for their houses as private property. Each house had an attached corral for its domestic livestock or was built over a ground-floor barn. If the town had land suitable for irrigation (huerta), each citizen received the individual garden plot (huerto) that the family spaded and watered for vegetables and fruit. In large cities and in places such as Miralcampo, which had no irrigated land, householders grew their fruits and vegetables in the patio, where the plants could be watered by hand from the well.

Around this residential nucleus lay the arable, with its alternating planted and fallow fields, and the enclosed pastures for the plow animals. The largest portion of the arable was nonirrigated land (secano), which produced the staples of the Spanish diet—wheat, olives, and grapes. From the very founding of the town, the arable was divided into plowfields (hazas). Each farm (hacienda, from hazas) was made up of several plowfields located in different parts of the municipal territory. The founding citizens chose the best land for their plowfields, of course; newcomers had to make do with mediocre soils.

The potential for economic development, for expansion of production and improvement of living standards, did not, however, lie in the cultivated fields. David Vassberg has demonstrated that the standard of living and the possibility of improving that standard in this agrarian economy depended on possession of common land. In most towns, the commons was monte—land within the municipal boundaries that was too rocky, broken, or steep for plowing. The monte was covered with trees, brush, and grass that provided essential fuel, pasture, nuts, herbs, building materials, and game. Citizens could expand cultivation into the monte by terracing the slopes to plant perennials such as grapevines and olive trees. Ideally, the residential nucleus would have been situated in the center of its arable so that farmers could walk to and from their fields. Even if the surrounding soil had been endlessly fertile, the extent of the plowfields was limited by the length of time it took a farmer to walk out to his field, plow it, and walk back each workday. This distance limited the extent of a town's cultivated land and therefore, of course, the number of farms. When some farmers had to spend too much of their day traveling to their fields and back, the most common solution was the one chosen by the count of Tendilla's tenant farmers in Meco: the establishment of a new village within the municipal boundaries of a town or city.

Miralcampo was an ordinary farm village in sixteenth-century New Castile, and its development from a squatter settlement to a village had been unexceptional. By transferring the land to the new council, lord and subjects together took the first step in replicating the cell division that gave birth to most of the fifteen thousand municipalities in Castile. In New Castile, cities and towns were founded first.[23] Because cities and towns occupied all the land of Castile, new villages could develop only within already established city and town territories. Meco itself had been born through this fission process in the early fifteenth century, when it appeared as a village, subject to another municipality and without a municipal territory of its own. It lay within the municipal boundaries of the town of Guadalajara and was subject to the Guadalajara town council. In 1430 King Juan II (1406–54) exempted Meco and eleven other villages from the jurisdiction of Guadalajara and gave them some of Guadalajara's municipal territory in order to elevate them to the status of towns. The king then gave the jurisdictions of these new towns as heritable property to the count of Tendilla's grandfather, the marquis of Santillana. By 1512, when Meco gave birth to Miralcampo, it was one of the oldest seignorial towns in New Castile.

The ownership of the uncultivated land of Castile by town councils created a universal competition between the town and its own villages. The *fueros* and other municipal constitutions gave the city or town councils full authority to prevent settlement in their territory: "No settlements may be established within your boundaries unless the council agrees; otherwise, the council may demolish them without compensation."[24] Farmers who were citizens of the town and who controlled the town council used the commons as pasture and as a source of fuel to maintain their standard of living, or they put more land to the plow to increase their production. Farmers who were citizens of the villages wanted greater rights in the commons for their own sustenance and expansion. Most village councils eventually gained recognition from the town council and thus gained limited access to the town commons.

In the case of Miralcampo, the endemic tension between town and village flared into open conflict in the mid-sixteenth century. As long as

Miralcampo remained a village, its judges held limited juridical authority. Their jurisdiction extended only over the village's residential nucleus and citizens and was limited to petty cases. The citizens of Miralcampo had to go to the Meco judges for more serious cases and to settle disputes over the town's grazing land they shared. Typically, the villagers would attempt to restrict grazing on the stubble of their harvested fields to their own livestock, while the Meco town judges would order the stubble open to grazing for all citizens of Meco and Miralcampo. When disputes arose between citizens of the two municipalities, the Meco judges held juris- diction over the cases and, of course, ruled in a manner favorable to Meco's citizens. The villagers claimed that their founding charter gave them the right to take their litigation directly to the lord's appellate judge rather than be subject to the Meco town judge. The lord, the second marquis of Mondéjar, sided with the villagers, and the town of Meco brought suit against him. The dispute was finally settled in 1543, when the royal appellate court in Valladolid ruled that the marquis of Mondéjar must stop interfering with the selection of local judges in his town of Meco.[25]

In due course, some sixty years after the Miralcampo council acquired possession of the Moneder farm, lord and village took the final step of Miralcampo's legal development into a town (villa). The fifteen founding households had grown to forty-seven, the council was still paying the annuity of chickens and six hundred fanegas of grain fixed in perpetuity in the 1512 contract, and some of the descendants of the founding citizens were literate. By 1575 the citizens and lord considered the village stable and populous enough to exercise jurisdiction over a municipal territory of its own with full judicial authority in civil and criminal cases. Accordingly, the count of Tendilla's grandson, the third marquis of Mondéjar, drew a municipal boundary (término) between Meco and Miralcampo and granted a charter of township (villazgo) to the Miralcampo council, elevating the village to the status of town.

With this step, Miralcampo achieved the self-government that was the goal of every Castilian citizen—the status of town, free from the control of another municipality. Meco's farmers no longer had grazing rights on the Miralcampo stubble, and the Meco town judges no longer possessed jurisdiction over the land or citizens of Miralcampo. Meco and Miralcampo had become two separate and autonomous towns with the same seignorial lord. The two municipal judges elected annually in Miralcampo now exercised the lord's full civil and criminal judicial authority without having to remit cases to any other municipal court. Appeals from their decisions went directly to the lord's appellate judge in the town of Mondéjar and from there to the royal appellate court in Valladolid. They had the power to impose and execute the death penalty and styled themselves "the most magnificent lords judges of the town of Miralcampo."[26]

The municipal boundary (término) that Miralcampo received in 1575 completed the town's evolution as a Castilian municipality and gave it a new spatial configuration on the physical landscape. The boundary gave Miralcampo its own municipal territory and brought it closer to the Castilian notion of what an ideal municipality should look like.[27]

Citizenship and Municipal Government

The 1512 contract in Miralcampo defined the terms for a specific group of people on a given piece of land—price, payment schedule, provisions for default. It said nothing about the structure of the municipality's governance, nor did it define or bestow citizenship. Yet municipal government and citizenship were essential to the terms of the agreement and shaped its vocabulary. Noble lord, citizen-farmers, royal notary, and legal witnesses all shared a vision of their society as a landscape of municipalities peopled with citizens. Miralcampo's form of government and the citizenship of its residents were not negotiated because they were the organizing principles of Castilian society, unarticulated but implicit in documents, actions, and self-identity.

Municipal residence was the common heritage of laymen and laywomen in every region and occupation of Castile. The chances of finding Castilians living outside an urban nucleus were extremely remote: the isolated farmhouse out in the countryside was almost unknown in Castile. Most Castilians were farmers who lived in town and walked out to their fields to plow, hoe, and harvest.[28] Even their livestock lived in town, returning from pasture every evening to spend the night in the household barn or corral. A Castilian on the move transferred his household from one urban nucleus to another or established a new urban nucleus with other settlers.

By the end of the medieval reconquest in the thirteenth century nearly all the land of Castile was incorporated into municipalities. The few patches of unincorporated land that were exempted from municipal jurisdiction as game preserves (cotos) remained uninhabited, and the unincorporated lands that were enclosed, cortijos, were inhabited only seasonally by citizens of surrounding towns brought in as contract harvesters.[29]

Those few people who lived outside an urban nucleus were regarded as outside the norm, and both folklore and literature attributed to them every social perversity. The miller, who lived in the mill down on the river, became the symbol of lechery and greed. Shepherds and shepherdesses, in popular fantasy, participated in pastoral adulteries. Roadside inns that sheltered muleteers and merchants reeked of gambling and violence and, in the folkloric memory, conjured up all those imagined immoralities ascribed to the modern traveling salesman.[30] The great fictional hero of Spanish Golden Age literature, don Quixote de la Mancha, is already in a state of insanity when he leaves his hometown to wander from windmill to roadside inn, consorting with goatherds, muleteers, and transported criminals, and he is restored to sanity only when friends and family bring him back to town. Even in modern fiction, the Andalusian farmstead in the olive groves far from town—the *cortijo*—becomes the setting for romantic fantasies. Uninhabited most of the year, except by the steward and his family, then filled to capacity by contract laborers of both genders during the harvest and pressing season, the *cortijo* is the fictional setting of unbridled sexual promiscuity.

Municipal residence, in contrast, provided a secure and moral social world. The governance of municipalities, therefore, defined the daily lives of most Castilians in the Habsburg period. For the vast majority, including nobles and clergy, municipal governments were essential to the conduct of their everyday occupations and the security of their families. Municipalities were the source of public order, the providers of public services— and they were everywhere.

When disputes arose between cities, between towns, or between city and town, they were adjudicated before the royal council, which acted as an appellate court between jurisdictions of equal status. The royal appellate court applied legal principles that had been codified at various times through the centuries, each codification citing the earlier codes and incorporating previous royal rulings. These royal codifications, of which the most famous was Alfonso X's *Siete partidas,* guided the royal appellate judges in their decisions; they did not, nor were they intended to, supersede the law codes in the municipal charters. For the great majority of Castilians in the Habsburg period, civil status, legal rights, and political power derived from citizenship *(vecindad)* in a municipality. Each Castilian was by birthright a citizen of the municipality in which he or she was born. This universal experience of citizenship in municipalities shaped Castilians as an urban people.

Citizenship defined the civil status of lay persons who were not noble. The notarial registers remind us of this on every page. At the beginning of each document, the signatories are described first by name, then as citizens *(vecinos)* of a specific city, town, or village. A typical lease contract, for example, begins "María Carrillo, wife of doctor Ybarra, and Catalina Carrillo, widow of Manuel Gómez de Andrada, citizens [*vecinas*] of Alcalá de Henares"; or "Let all who see this lease contract know that I, Francisco Paredes, citizen of the noble town of Madrid"; or "Alonso de Garabaxales and Alonso de Garabaxales the younger, María de Garabaxales, and Beatriz de Garabaxales, children of the said Alonso Garabaxales, citizens of Mondéjar, consent." Noncitizenship was noted with equal care: "Juan Blela, Juan Nigo, Luis Laragaldia, dealers in cloth and other goods, residing in Estremera, of French nationality, acknowledge a loan made to them by Joseph Plugeant, also of French nationality and residing in Tembleque."[31]

Citizenship also bestowed economic benefits on its holders. Citizens gained legal title to arable land within the municipal territory by clearing and plowing it. Their livestock could graze on the commons and on the stubble (rastrojo) of unfenced private land in the municipal territory. Citizens had the right to bring goods for sale into the market without paying tolls. The municipal council paid their royal taxes and seignorial dues, developed the economic infrastructure of the municipal territory by building dams, bridges, roads, mills, and ovens, and safeguarded the citizens' access to the monte.

Of course, some Castilians did not need citizenship. Their civil status as clergymen, royal officers, or nobles gave them legal privileges and tax exemptions not available to the ordinary layman. Members of the clergy, living under the jurisdiction of prelates or abbots, were governed by canon law and subject to ecclesiastical judges. Their legal identity derived from their clerical position, which is the attribute they carry in notarial documents. For example: "In the town of Paracuellos, Antón Ruiz, curate of the town of Paracuellos, and Alonso Bartolomé Ruiz, citizen of the town of Vayona, his brother, agree to trade a certain estate."[32]

Royal officials, in taking their oath of office, made themselves vassals of the monarch and directly subject to the royal justice. If they lived at the royal court, their cases were tried before the judges of the royal household (alcaldes de casa y corte). Royal officials living in other parts of the kingdom took their cases to the judges of the royal appellate courts (chancillerías) in Valladolid and Granada. In legal documents, royal officials are identified by name and office alone. In 1555, Philip II, writing to Agustín de Zárate, the royal accountant and chronicler of the conquest of Perú, addressed him as "Agustín de Zárate, my employee," and later described him as "Agustín de Zárate, administrator of the Guadalcanal mines."[33]

Nobles, as vassals of the monarch (vasallos del rey), submitted directly to royal jurisdiction. Their name and noble title alone identified them in legal documents. Nevertheless, nobles were inextricably associated with municipalities; they could not be nobles without being lords of towns. Each noble title derived from the name of a town over which the nobleman possessed proprietary jurisdiction. The most powerful man in seventeenth-century Castile, Philip IV's favorite, Gaspar de Guzmán, inherited several towns near Seville, including the town of Olivares and the title count of Olivares, on his father's death in 1607. In 1623 he bought the town of San Lúcar la Mayor, and in 1625 Philip IV granted him the title duke of San Lúcar. Coveting the title of duke but not willing to give up the more venerable hereditary title, Gaspar styled himself count-duke of Olivares.[34]

A rare exception to the norm was the title of the duke of the Infantado, who was lord of a group of three towns (Alcocer, Salmerón, and Valdeolivas) that had been known collectively as the Infantado since the fourteenth century, when they belonged to the infante Juan Manuel.[35] Titled nobles rarely missed a chance to associate themselves with several of their seignorial towns, often listing one or more of them as part of their self-identity at the beginning of documents. In the 1512 contract with Miralcampo, for example, the count of Tendilla placed his jurisdiction over the towns of Tendilla, Mondéjar, and Valfermoso ahead of his royal offices: "I, Iñigo López de Mendoza, count of Tendilla, lord of the towns of Mondéjar and Valfermoso, captain general of the Kingdom of Granada, commander of the said city of Granada and its Alhambra and fortresses for the queen our lady. . . ." The citizens of his seignorial towns were not only his subjects (vasallos) but also subjects of the king, whereas citizens of towns in the royal domain were subjects (vasallos) of the king alone.

Until 1492 there were two groups of the king's subjects who were not citizens: Jews and Muslims had their own legal communities within the cities and towns where they lived. They chose their own judges, who exercised jurisdiction over members of the community according to the laws of their own faith or nation. These judges also negotiated and collected royal taxes within their communities, free from the interference of the city or town tax collectors. Civil and criminal cases that cut across two legal systems—between a Muslim and a Christian or between a Jew and a Muslim, for example—came before a royal appellate judge (alcalde mayor).[36] Individual Jews and Muslims who converted to Christianity became citizens of their place of residence. The advantages of citizenship may have been an inducement to conversion during the fifteenth century. Of course, the autonomy of minority communities became moot after Jews and Muslims were forced to convert or leave Castile after 1492 and 1501, respectively, and foreign merchants and bankers in Spain's great trading cities, with their separate corporate and judicial status, assumed the lending functions previously handled by Spain's non-Christian minorities. The Genoese in Seville managed their own judicial affairs with their own law court, housed in a former mosque. Their own judge enforced the laws of Genoa, although the Seville city council held appellate jurisdiction (i.e., between Genoese and Castilian) and enforced the rulings of the Genoese judge.[37] Castilian law provided for the naturalization of foreigners by royal decree, but such naturalized subjects of the king did not automatically become citizens of municipalities; they still had to fulfill municipal residency and property requirements and petition the city or town council in order to become citizens.[38]

Although this form of municipal government and citizenship remained constant over centuries, personal associations with specific towns changed with time and circumstances. Ordinary citizens moved to escape unhealthful or overcrowded towns or to find better land; lords bought, sold, and bequeathed towns. Monarchs granted township to villages in order to give the new towns to favorites or confiscate them from rebels. Kings and queens conquered cities and towns from neighboring Muslim countries and American natives.

Cities and towns trying to maintain or increase their population readily absorbed newcomers and granted them citizenship. Castilians who moved from one town to another with the intention of resettling were simply required to move their wives and households into permanent housing in their new towns—and they seem to have moved in massive numbers in the fifteenth century. More often, persons transferred their citizenship by marrying a citizen of another town and residing there. Castilians frequently attributed a decline in their town's population to its inability to retain newlywed couples in which only one spouse was a native.[39]

Most Castilians believed that a growing population benefited all residents of a town and freely offered citizenship to immigrants, but a few municipalities created obstacles to the granting of citizenship. During a locust invasion in 1448 the citizens of the village of Pezuela voted unanimously in town meeting to establish a confraternity devoted to the Assumption of the Virgin Mary and to San Benito, and the council passed a municipal ordinance requiring every citizen to join the confraternity or lose the status of citizen.[40] In cities and towns that enjoyed special tax exemptions, citizenship was more difficult to acquire and sometimes required a public act of petition followed by several years of residence. Each citizen of the city of Granada, for example, had the right to graze up to fifteen hundred head of stock on the municipal commons free. In 1498 the city council of Granada admitted Diego Hernández de Ulloa, citizen of Jaén, to citizenship in Granada with the stipulation that he reside in the city for ten years. If he left before that time, he would be subject to the municipal fees imposed on noncitizens who plowed or grazed the municipal territory.[41]

New citizens often took the name of their native town as a surname, with the result that in any growing town many persons carried the name of a neighboring town as their family name. In the village of Linares, halfway between the cities of Jaén and Baeza, for example, two of the principal actors in the struggle for township were Pedro de Baeza and Pedro de Jaén.[42] In Miralcampo, among the family names of ten of the founding citizens were the names of eight New Castilian towns and villages: Pioz, Viñuelas, Chiloeches, Pinilla (two), Galves, Corpa, and Yebes (two).[43]

Citizenship carried its duties, of which the primary one was paying taxes. All citizens were taxpayers (pecheros) subject to the royal head tax (pecho) voted irregularly by the Cortes as a subsidy (servicio) for the monarch's extraordinary expenses of war. This tax was assessed on each city and town according to population, and each city and town collected the pecho from its own subject villages. For tax and voting purposes, each married couple or widowed survivor of a marriage constituted a legal household, regardless of the number or relationships of people living in the house. Vecino or vecina designated the head of household in cadastral surveys. Households headed by widows counted as one-half in the assessment for the pecho. Most seignorial towns were shielded from royal taxes by the lord, who rendered military and government service to the monarchy and received the seignorial annuity. Here, too, women and men both bore the responsibility for paying the annuity, though not equally. As the Miralcampo and nearly every other contract specified, the annuity was paid to the lord in both chickens and grain, which effectively laid the burden of payment on both the men and the women of the village. Poultry were the domain of women's household management, grain was the product of men's plowing, and both were necessary to maintain the legal existence of the municipality. The unique role that women played in poultry raising was pointed out by Castile's favorite agricultural writer, Gabriel Alonso de Herrera, who included in his Agricultura general a chapter on raising chickens. He acknowledged that the ancient and medieval writers on agriculture had not discussed poultry because men did not raise chickens. Women were the chicken and egg experts, and they passed their knowledge on from mother to daughter over the centuries. But recently, Herrera continued, some men had tried to raise chickens, apparently with disastrous results, so Herrera compiled this chapter about poultry raising by observing and consulting many women.[44] The chickens included in the municipality's annuity payment to the lord were, therefore, necessary evidence that the town still contained family households and had not become depopulated.

All citizens, male and female, married and single, adult and child, attended town meeting (concejo abierto). They were summoned to the meeting by the town bell, which also gave the alarm to the farmers in the fields, called the citizens to church, announced the death of a citizen (one rhythm for deceased males, another for females), and convened the meetings of the town council. Each town had its traditional town meeting place—a portico on one side of the marketplace, the cemetery on the south side of the church, stone benches in the marketplace. In town meeting they were "la República," the body politic, or "la comunidad," the community of town and land, and although they usually convened only on the most solemn occasions—to hear royal letters and orders, confirm the town judge's judicial sentences, or debate a proposal from the town council—every citizen could join in the discussion.[45]

In contrast to citizenship and taxpaying, which were the birthright and duty of all native sons and daughters, voting and officeholding were priv-ileges restricted to married males. Women could participate in discussions but could not vote. When a town was trying to hide its intentions from the lord, women could be excluded from a closed town meeting (concejo secreto), held behind closed doors and convened without ringing the bells. The most famous town meeting in Castilian history, immortalized in Lope de Vega's play Fuenteovejuna, was a closed meeting in the town hall. The judge of the town of Fuenteovejuna tries to block entry to his daughter Laurencia, who is the latest rape victim of the town's lord and whose demands for justice precipitated the secret town meeting. Laurencia gains entry by arguing that she can enter the counsels of men because women, even if they cannot vote, can express their opinions.[46]

Each household had a vote in town meeting, but because women were not permitted to vote, widows asked male proxies, usually an unmarried son or the judge, to cast their vote. The men in the town meeting of Miralcampo in 1512, for example, described themselves as "citizens of Miralcampo for ourselves and, those of us who are not married, in the names of our mothers." The two proxies were "Alonso de Yebes, son of the widow of Bartolomé de Yebes, deceased, and Diego de Pinilla, son of the widow of Juan Sanz de Pinilla, deceased."[47]

Every married male was eligible to be elected to the council, to hold appointive public office, and to administer the municipality's legal juris-diction. Unmarried males, though they might vote as proxies for their widowed mothers, did not hold office, could not vote in their own right, and did not have active citizenship.

Women bestowed citizenship on husbands from other towns, and both women and unmarried males exercised the full range of passive citizenship: they paid municipal taxes, possessed the right of free access to the com-mons, marketed their produce and goods in the plaza without paying tolls, disposed of their own property, signed contracts, and deposed before no-taries and municipal clerks. The clerks and notaries, however, meticulously indicated their lack of full active citizenship by first describing the sig-natory's relationship to the male head of the household, whether alive or deceased. One of the earliest notarial registers from Madrid, for example, records a sales contract in which two of the three signatories, a married woman and an unmarried man, are described in terms of their relationship to their respective husband and father:

Let all who see this deed of sale and lease know that I, Juan de Villamayor, citizen of Madrid, and I, Catalina Alvarez, his wife . . . issue and acknowledge by this deed that we sell [a house] to you, the noble knight Diego de Luxán, son of the commander Juan de Luxán, citizen of this town of Madrid.[48]

Marriage was the rite of passage to full male adulthood and catapulted a man into the corporation of "solid citizens." Sanctified marriage to a woman exercised a normative force so powerful that it could bestow male legal status and active citizenship privileges on a person whose physiological gender was unclear. A unique case of ambiguous gender in the records of sixteenth-century Castilian towns found legal resolution through marriage to a woman. The citizens of the town of Valdaracete reported that a girl named Stephanie was born in the town in 1496, and that by the time she reached the age of twenty she had grown so agile, fast, and strong that no young man in town could win a competition with her in running, jumping, throwing a pole, or playing ball. "It was a marvelous sight," they recalled, "to watch her in these sports, running with her long, blond hair streaming behind." She traveled around performing notable feats, finally going to Granada, where the judges of the royal appellate court (chancillería) heard about her and ordered that she be examined by matrons and midwives to see whether she was actually a male masquerading in women's clothes. She was found to be a hermaphrodite, and the judges ruled that she had to choose whether she would live as a man or a woman and dress appropriately. She chose to live as a man and, now in male garb and called Stephen, married a woman. They lived as a married couple sanctified by the church. Stephen was licensed as a fencing master, with his own school and armor in Granada. Back in Valdaracete he was so skillful at his art that no man could win against him, as became evident when the king of France passed through the town as a prisoner of Emperor Charles V. The king had some of the brave and skillful men in his entourage fence against master Stephen, alias Stephanie, who disarmed, wounded, or drew first blood against all of them. Stephen lived as a married man ten years and held public office. But what the townspeople remembered as most remarkable about this woman/man was the burial. The mother and widow accompanied the body to the grave, the one crying "Ay, my daughter," and the other, "Ay, my husband."[49]

Stephanie/Stephen managed to enjoy the full range of citizenship by living as a married man. Despite the townspeople's understandable confusion about this person—the narrators switch from female pronouns to no pronouns at all after the judges declare Stephanie a hermaphrodite—the town council of Valdaracete recognized marriage to a woman as the legal requisite for male adulthood, making Stephen eligible for public office. Women could not be active citizens, but active citizenship was achieved by marriage to women.

From the Atlantic to the Mediterranean coasts of Castile, whether new towns began as authorized colonies or as squatter settlements, their founding settlers created the same municipal structure of government they had known as citizens of cities, towns, and villages. Throughout Castile, municipal government took the form of an elected council, whether the municipality was a city, town, or village and regardless of the size of its population. The sequence of events in Miralcampo was typical: the citizens settled their village, formed a council, and then appealed to the lord for official status.

The fundamental act in forming the municipal government was the first town meeting, in which the voting citizens elected their municipal judge (*alcalde ordinario*). In 1575 the village of Monachil, in the municipal territory of the city of Granada, for example, received royal permission to elect its own judges. Monachil was a newly settled village, though an old one: its previous Morisco inhabitants (converts from Islam) had been expelled after the Revolt of the Alpujarras (1568–70), and the new settlers were Christians who had immigrated from other parts. The Granada city council sent one of its notaries to supervise the first election, and he brought back the results so that the city council could make the final appointment:

I, Gaspar Gutierres, notary public of Granada and its jurisdiction by appointment by his majesty testify that on June 29 of this year in the village of Monachil, in the jurisdiction of this city, the citizens of the said village assembled in the church summoned by the bell and, in compliance with his majesty's provision to elect and name judges of the said village, they proceeded to vote, each one nominating two judges. Those who have the most votes appear to be Pedro de Arnedo, who has 23 votes, and Hernán Martín, 22, and Juan Ruiz de Palma, 8, and Diego López de Náxara 4. The said election was carried out in my presence and for its expense I submit this record. Dated in Granada July 5, 1575.[50]

Once the first judge and council were elected, most municipalities chose succeeding officers through sortition or cooption. The outgoing council nominated candidates from among the citizens, wrote the names of the nominees on broad beans or slips of paper which were drawn from a wine jar or basket, and then installed the new officers themselves or submitted the winning names to the lord for appointment. The lord sent an official to receive the oath from the new council and invest the new judges with the staff of office, which every judge and councilman carried while performing his duties.

The council comprised a minimum of five officers, as in Miralcampo. The outgoing council chose two municipal judges per term in order to ensure that one would be in residence at all times. The judges were to be over twenty-five years of age, "prosperous, and men of good conscience who fear God, and serve the lord king, and judge all equally before the law."[51] The presiding judge tried cases as they occurred, imposed fines and punishments, and presided over town meetings and sessions of the council. He was assisted by a sheriff, who was responsible for apprehending and arresting transgressors and had the authority to confiscate stray livestock and seize property as security for judicial fines. Two councilmen (regidores) administered the marketplace and corporate assets of the municipality, collected the municipal taxes and lease rents, and voted on all decisions affecting municipal policy, expenditures, and ordinances.

Castilians established this structure of judge, sheriff, and councilmen wherever they settled, without instruction from or the knowledge of royal authorities (see fig. 2). The village of Chamartín, within the municipal territory of Madrid, comprised only ten households in 1579. For thirteen or fourteen years they had been electing a judge and a sheriff every year on St. Michael's Day. The citizens recognized that this was not a full municipal government but explained that they elected no more officers because the population was small.[52] When a town's population declined, the number of officials tended to remain disproportionately high. A case in point is the village of Humanejos. It once had thirty households, but the place was unhealthy and by 1576 the population had declined to nine households, two of them headed by widows. Even so, the village had three municipal officials: a judge, a councilman, and a sheriff.[53]

Fig. 2. Municipal government in the Americas. A Spaniard in sixteenth-century Mexico confronts a town judge and councilman. Codex Osuna. Pintura del gobernador, alcaldes, y regidores de México. Códice en geroglíficos mexicanos y en lenguas castellana y azteca, existente en la biblioteca del . . . duque de Osuna (Madrid, 1878), p. 194.

With growing population, the number of municipal officials increased and more council seats were added. The village of Los Hueros had forty-seven households and was growing in the 1570s, when there were ten municipal officials in addition to the judges: two councilmen, a secretary, an attorney, a functionary, a judge of the commons, and four deputies to "accompany the councilmen in their council meetings."[54]

Towns that grew too populous to hold town meetings divided themselves along parish lines. Each parish elected one or more representatives (jurados) to the town council. In the fourteenth century the town of Guadalajara had grown too large for town meetings but still conducted its affairs in a democratic manner through a representative assembly. The town divided itself into four parishes whose representatives were called quatros or jurados. The council divided the villages in its municipal territory into six districts (sesmos), each represented by a sesmero. On October 28, 1406, Guadalajara held a town meeting in the church of Saint Gil, announced by the bell rung according to custom and usage. Those present were the four jurados: Diego Fernández, son of Benito García, quatro of the parish of Saint Gil; Gonzalo Fernández, servant; Sancho Sánchez, quatro of the parish of Saint Nicholas; and Pedro Fernández, lime maker, quatro of the parish of Saint Mary. The sesmeros present were Lucas Martínez, citizen of Taracena and sesmero of the sesmo of Albolleque; Juan Martínez del Exido; Christóval Fermoso, sesmero of the sesmo of Valdeavellano; Diego Fernández, son of Diego Fernández, citizen of Renera, sesmero of the sesmo of Taracena; and Diego Fernández de Sillas, citizen of Hontanar, sesmero of the sesmo of Málaga.[55] As the council's corporate assets grew and produced municipal income, the council hired salaried personnel for specialized offices. The first to be added were usually a municipal representative (procurador), clerk (escribano), treasurer (mayordomo), and inspectors of weights and measures.

In a large city the normal complement of councilmen was twenty-four (hence veinticuatro for councilman). In the sixteenth century Seville, whose transient population had grown rapidly after the discovery of the Americas, needed so many administrators that the monarchs permitted the council to increase the number of councilmen by about twenty and add more jurados from the parishes to participate in the deliberations and help administer the city.[56]

The elected council and its appointed officers administered the municipal assets and joined the judges in the day-to-day decisions shaping municipal legislation, appointments, and expenditures. The most solemn and important issues of municipal life, however, required a town meeting. These issues ranged from the decision to seek a new lord, the holding of a municipal election, adoption of a written legal code in place of the oral tradition, creation of a new confraternity in the face of a natural disaster such as a locust invasion, or the commitment of municipal resources to the construction of a mill or purchase of more commons. The Guadalajara town meeting in 1406 was convened to choose a new form of government, creating a town council to be composed of six councilmen (regidores) chosen by sortition from among the tax-exempt military citizens and two councilmen chosen by sortition from among the taxpayers.[57] In the town of Estremera the council tried to hold three town meetings per year for the sole purpose of familiarizing the citizens with their municipal ordinances and privileges.[58]

Given the ubiquity and importance of municipalities, it is not surprising that the holding of municipal office was an experience shared by all classes of the politically active men—and one not limited to any given stage of life. Members of municipal councils were drawn, as we might expect, from the upper levels of society, whether these were the most prosperous farmers in a small town or the sons of titled grandees residing in the large cities. A municipal judgeship was the highest civic office attainable in Castilian government, followed closely by the office of councilman. Sons of titled noblemen could serve as city councilman during some part of their early adult life and transfer their council seat to their son or client when they inherited the noble title. Monarchs gave council seats to retiring royal officials as a retirement pension or in lieu of salary arrears and sold municipal offices to others.[59] Royal officials resigned their position and rescinded their oath of royal vassalage to become salaried, lifelong councilmen in rich cities, as the royal notary Juan de Luz did: in 1516 he resigned his post as secretary to the captain general of the Kingdom of Granada to become a jurado of the city of Granada.[60]

In a farm town, the descendants of the founding families usually were the wealthiest citizens because their ancestors had chosen the best land for themselves when they settled the town. They dominated the municipal offices, particularly the office of judge. In 1562 the new lord of the town of Estremera prescribed new rules for the election of the town judge and council. He stipulated that men nominated for the offices of judge, councilman, and treasurer must possess real property worth one hundred thousand maravedís, could not be tonsured, and could not have been engaged in such occupations as innkeeper, weaver, carpenter, butcher, cobbler, tailor, tanner, or day laborer during the previous year.[61]

Participation in municipal government must have been much more broadly distributed than the most prestigious offices would indicate, however. The 1562 election guidelines in Estremera specifically stated that the property and occupational requirements for judges and councilmen did not apply to other elected offices, except for the prohibition against clergy.[62] In a pioneering study of the small towns of New Castile during the 1570s, Noël Salomon found that the population was distributed evenly between 83 municipalities of over 500 households each and 472 municipalities of under 500 households each.[63] Half of New Castile's active citizenry lived in small towns—about 71,000 heads of households, according to Salomon's data. It is likely that nearly all of these 71,000 men held some sort of municipal office. If we conservatively assume an average of five officials elected annually in each town and village and realize that the average number of households in these small communities was 150, then the likelihood of a married male holding municipal office during an adult lifetime of about thirty years was very high.

A lifetime of living and working in a small community in which municipal government supervised and legislated all aspects of life provided ample knowledge for the continuation of ritual and practice among the municipal officeholders, even when many of them were illiterate. In towns that attained some civic sophistication, the council took care to initiate new officials into the intricacies of municipal responsibility and prerogatives. The constitution of the town of Estremera required that outgoing councilmen give a report to their incoming counterparts on all the lawsuits in which the town was engaged within one week after the annual elections.[64] The Estremera council was equally careful to instruct the judges in their responsibilities as administrators of the spiritual well-being of the citizens: the council displayed in the town hall a chart showing all the pious donations and memorial masses of which the municipal judges were trustees and administrators.[65]

The council held full responsibility for the economic welfare of its citizens and territory. The daily supervision of the marketplace consumed much of the council's time and energy. Councilmen rotated weekly or monthly as administrators of the marketplace with responsibility for setting prices of goods and produce, witnessing verbal sales agreements, collecting sales taxes, imposing tolls on goods, produce, and livestock brought in for sale by noncitizens, and inspecting and auditing the municipal bakery and butcher and fish shops.

The council played the central role in the agrarian economy. All year long the sheriff patrolled the *monte* to arrest trespassers and seize stray stock. Every year as the crops ripened and harvest season approached, the council turned its attention to the cropland within the municipal territory. During the summer and fall the council hired extra deputies and field guards to keep animals and poachers out of the ripening grain, vegetable, and fruit crops.

Farmers received a wide range of economic benefits from their citizenship, including use of the *monte* and any commons that the town might own jointly with neighboring towns. There were two types of property in a municipal territory: private property, which was subject to the laws of inheritance, and corporate property, which was impartible and nonheritable. Most of the houses and arable were private property. Anyone could own private property in the town—the lord, clergy, citizens, citizens of other towns. Corporate property belonged to institutions such as the municipality itself, the military orders, the church, a monastery, or a confraternity. Members of the institution enjoyed the use and usufruct of these properties but could not own, inherit, or alienate the property itself. Corporate property tended to grow over time, since it was not easily partible and could not be alienated by private individuals.

Most of the corporate property in any town was commons or *monte*, belonging to the municipality. By making improvements on the *monte* or other municipal property and then collecting rent or user fees on the improvements, the council accumulated *propios*—income-producing corporate assets. Through the *propios*, the council provided its citizens with economic resources greater than any individual family could assemble and of far greater longevity than a family could command for future generations. The most lucrative *propios* in Castile were received as royal gifts by the councils of cities conquered from the Muslims. Of these, the most renowned—and justly so—are the city of Cuenca's pine forests, zealously managed and guarded by the council's own corps of forest rangers. To this day, every female citizen of the city proper receives as dowry a share of the annual lumber harvest from the *propios*. In most towns and cities, the *propios* and commons together provided the entire economic and social infrastructure of the community: grazing for draft and meat animals; *montes* for hunting, fishing, fuel, nuts, lumber, and wild plants; quarries for building stone, lime, and clay; wells, irrigation works, springs, mills, bridges and ferries, schools, hospitals, laundries, seed banks, butcher shops, taverns, and bakeries. The Castilian citizen was part of a tight corporate structure that provided security, resources, and expertise.

Hard pressed to explain the Castilian's sentimental attachment to even humble villages, the eighteenth-century Mercedarian priest fray Juan de Talamanco attributed the power of the municipality—which he called his "patria"—in part to its physical and material resources:

The Author of Creation bestowed on the patria a certain elusive and even occult quality which, with singular efficacy and power, calls us and sweeps us along unconscious, thus proving that it is the sweet loadstone of our hearts. Our fondness for it is a golden chain in which the will is pleased to feel itself captive without further protest. We are inclined to adore it as if it were a true deity, or as Herakles thought, another God; because the patria in a way gives us our existence and even the means of continuing it.[66]

Even the most independent and adventurous Castilians seemed unwilling to organize themselves into any form of government other than the traditional municipality. The Spanish conquerors of the Americas, widely regarded as the most rapacious and opportunistic of sixteenth-century adventurers, proudly described themselves as founders of new towns and cities and expected the monarchy to reward them for establishing municipal governments in new lands.[67] As Francisco Domínguez has observed, "It is evident that local institutions were established in America in a spontaneous manner and as a natural form of coping with the exigencies of life itself."[68] Non-Spaniards who lacked this municipal urge and tried to establish the Castilian royal authority in the Americas failed. Christopher Columbus and his brothers founded several settlements in the Caribbean that they administered as Portuguese factories, that is, as fortified trading stations with salaried employees. The Spanish settlers rebelled, and the Columbus brothers were arrested and brought to trial in Spain for their failure to properly administer the royal authority. Charles V granted the settlement of Venezuela to his German bankers, the Welsers, but the Spanish settlers of the Welser factory rebelled and established a town council and open marketplace.[69] As an American historian of Venezuela's settlement, John V. Lombardi, observes, "The Welsers' agents failed to get on with the primary business of conquest, the founding of permanent, organized towns."[70] The ideal royal administrator in the Americas was one who implanted the municipal organization of Castile. In the seventeenth century an admiring biographer looked back on the career of the marquis of Cañete in Peru: "In his tender years he exercised the profession of arms and governed the province of Chile, fighting and defeating brave and indomitable peoples, risking his person in serious dangers, and founding eight cities."[71]

When the conquistadores described their travels through dense jungles, over some of the most impressive mountain ranges known to man, and across some of the world's greatest rivers, they talked in terms of moving from one town or city to another. As Lombardi noted, "They cross mountains and discover great rivers, but their motion, their decisions, and their goals seem regulated more by the presence or absence of Indian towns, the distance to previously established Spanish towns, or the possibility of supporting a new Spanish center, than by the existence of geographic obstacles."[72] The conquistadores described the Indians in terms of their relationship to towns. Bernal Díaz del Castillo identified the Indian translator for the Cortés expedition, doña Marina, as a *cacica* "over towns and subjects since her childhood," and her parents as caciques of "the town of Paynala, which had other towns subject to it, about 24 miles from the town of Coatzacoalcos."[73] They described the Americas in the same terms as Castile, as a patchwork quilt of municipalities.

In 1518 Bernal Díaz del Castillo was in the city of Havana and heard that an expedition was forming in the city of Santiago de Cuba, on the other end of the island. The governor of Cuba, Diego Velázquez, had written to Spain asking for authority to send an exploratory and trading expedition to the mainland. Bernal Díaz was young, about twenty-one years old, and had recently arrived from Spain and become a citizen of the city of Santiago de Cuba. He wanted to make his fortune in the Americas and had already participated in two expeditions to the mainland in hopes of becoming a founding citizen of a new Spanish town, finding gold, even receiving land and a grant of Indian towns. On his second expedition to the mainland, led by Juan de Grijalva, Bernal had gone prepared to settle. One night when the expedition was camped on the beach near the Indian town of Tonalá, he and some other soldiers climbed up to an Indian temple to get away from the mosquitoes. There he planted some orange seeds that he had brought from Cuba because he believed the rumors that the Grijalva expedition would settle. After the Spaniards left, the Indian priests watered and tended the shoots, which they realized were different from the indigenous vegetation. Bernal claimed fifty years later that all the orange trees in that part of Mexico were descended from his orange seeds. While his orange trees flourished and Governor Velázquez made handsome profits in gold from the Grijalva expedition, Bernal and his fellow soldiers returned to Cuba with nothing but wounds and debts.[74]

The new expedition forming in Santiago de Cuba promised to be different, because it would be authorized to settle the land explored instead of just trading and coming back to Cuba.[75] Bernal overcame poverty and natural disasters to reach the city of Santiago and join the expedition. In describing his 1518 journey along the southern coast of the island of Cuba, Bernal imposed a Castilian perception of society on the world he was traveling through, a mental landscape of towns and municipal territories: his eyes were those of a citizen and town councilman.

Bernal could not afford passage on a regular sailing ship, so he and his friend offered their labor as canoers to another Spaniard, who had a load of Spanish shirts to sell in Santiago. The three Spaniards packed up their expeditionary gear—swords, trading goods, and padded cotton armor— and set out by canoe for the town of Trinidad, about 250 miles east of Havana. But as they came in sight of Trinidad after eleven days of rowing, a storm capsized their canoe, and they lost all their cargo and had to strip off their clothes and shoes in order to swim to safety.[76] The men managed to cross a reef to a sandy beach and then walked two days until they arrived at an Indian town called Yaguarama, which at that time belonged to fray Bartolomé de las Casas. The Indians gave them something to eat, and Bernal and his friends walked on to another Indian town, Chipiona, which belonged to a certain Alonso de Avila and another Spaniard. When they came to the town of Trinidad, a Spanish friend gave Bernal some clothes, so that he was decent when he arrived in the city of Santiago de Cuba. There he joined the governor's expedition led by Hernando Cortés, which Bernal himself would make famous with his *True History of the Conquest of New Spain* (see map 3).[77]

The modern reader of Bernal's book looks in vain for a glimpse of the flora and fauna, for some sense of confrontation with nature, for encounters with individual Indians. Days of canoeing on the open seas, tropical storm, coral reefs, desert beaches—all are incidental to Bernal's story. His Castilian eye focuses on a journey that begins in the town of Havana, passes through Indian pueblos and the town of Trinidad, and ends successfully in the city of Santiago de Cuba.

Restless seekers after greener fields and richer gold veins, those willing to move long distances from one part of Castile to another, or even from one hemisphere to another, identified themselves with their native towns long since left behind. Diego Gutiérrez de Salinas, for example, was a native of the town of Brihuega who spent over twenty years farming in towns around Madrid and Toledo. When he retired from farming, he returned to Brihuega and served at least one term as a councilman.[78] The conquistador Bernal Díaz del Castillo was a founding citizen of Veracruz and then of the city of Santiago de Guatemala, where he spent the last years of his adventurous life, but he begins his chronicle of the conquest of Mexico by identifying himself with his native town in Castile: "Bernal Díaz del Castillo, citizen and councilman of the most loyal city of Santiago de Guatemala, one of the first discoverers and conquerors of New Spain and its provinces . . . native of the most noble and distinguished town of Medina del Campo, and son of Francisco Díaz del Castillo, councilman of that town."[79]

Local pride shone through in jokes, proverbs, and names. The village of Getafe was a populous village of Madrid—comprising about a thousand households in 1577—that never achieved the status of town. In that year Getafe's loyal citizens repeated with relish a story that seemed as fresh to them as the day it happened fifty years earlier:

A rich gentleman named Villalpando lay dying. They were helping him make a good death by reminding him of God. But at the final moment he protested, "I believe everything you say, but Getafe is good, too."[80]

Fray Juan de Talamanco expressed these sentiments in the preface to his history of his native town Horche:

The force of this sentiment sharpened my pen to search out the history of Horche, my patria, which, though it may not equal others in grandeur, cuts a respectable figure in comparison with less glorious Republics; but even if it were less, one's own is foremost to each, because, as Seneca says, one's own is not esteemed for its greatness nor its smallness but for being one's own.[81]

Few towns boasted such a learned and eloquent native son as Horche's fray Juan de Talamanco. Castilians of all classes, no matter how far they

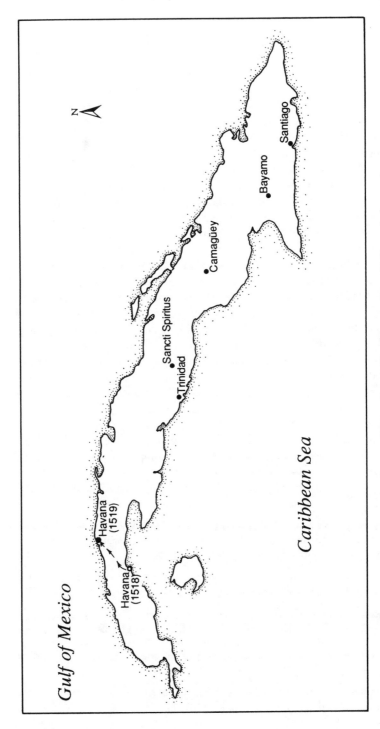

Map 3. Cuba: Cities and Towns Founded by Governor Diego Velázquez before 1518

Gulf of Mexico

Havana (1519)

Havana (1518)

Sancti Spiritus

Trinidad

Camagüey

Bayamo

Santiago

Caribbean Sea

N

roamed, felt strong sentimental attachment to their native towns and villages.

More enduringly than these local loyalties, Castilians shared a pervasive commitment to the democratic tradition of town government. Their hunger for justice and land could be satisfied only by municipal government, and Castilian citizens rose up in revolt against any foreigner who tried to deprive them of these essentials of daily life. The sentiments and practices of municipal government were entrenched in Castilian society not just because they seemed indispensable and natural but also because they were automatic. That which is most habitual most strongly resists change. It also escapes notice. The very depth at which municipal democratic habits were embedded in Castilian society makes them almost invisible.

Chapter 2

Lord of Land and Subjects

Building the Seignorial Regime

The motives that inspired the count of Tendilla to give his land to a village council are not apparent in the Miralcampo *capítulos*, nor do they appear in other written agreements between lords and councils. The motives and actions of the noble landowners should be abundantly clear from other types of documents, because the nobles of Castile were articulate, energetic, and passionate debaters of the great issues. They were successful entrepreneurs who accumulated lucrative offices, purchased vast estates, and maintained a level of indebtedness that is a testament to their creditworthiness. But lords were silent on the subject of estate management. In hundreds of thousands of dispatches, letters, and memoranda written by and to nobles, no discussion elucidates the estate management decisions and policies of the lords. For example, the duke of Alba, campaigning in Italy or Flanders, and the count-duke of Olivares, making war and peace from the royal palace in Madrid, do not give instructions about how to manage their agricultural property, do not speak of their estates as objects of concern, do not even receive reports from estate managers.[1] The one exception to this silence was the count of Tendilla. He alone of Castilian noble lords left a voluminous correspondence that describes the daily management of estates. A light of the Spanish Renaissance, well educated in a humanist tradition, cosmopolitan, and politically active, he was an eloquent reporter of a world in which thousands of witnesses remained silent. His letters cover every aspect of daily life in Castile; between 1504 and 1515 hardly a day went by that he did not write about his livestock, his crops, his subjects, and his towns and villages. The count of Tendilla's correspondence is our sole surviving record of seignorial estate management.

In this richly textured communication with his employees, town councils, lieutenants, relatives, and stewards, he states a clear set of goals: to provide for his family and make a profit. In order to achieve his goals, he acted within a legal structure that dictated his relationship with the citizens of his towns. The count of Tendilla lived in a perpetual process of expanding his fortune by acquiring more land, developing it into a village that would pay him an annuity, and then increasing the village's population until it could become a town. When the count gave Miralcampo its perpetual leasehold, he was implementing a process distinctive to the Trastamara period in Castilian history: the creation and development of seignorial towns. This development of municipalities was the foundation of the seignorial regime in Castile. It was a proven method of enrichment in his family: his ancestors had accumulated one of the richest fortunes in Castile by the time the count of Tendilla inherited his parents' estate in 1479, and he intended to do the same for his own children. He would have two disadvantages: Ferdinand and Isabella had little land to give away, and the count, as captain general of the Kingdom of Granada, was forced to be an absentee lord. In his efforts to overcome these two disadvantages, the count of Tendilla spent much of his energy and ingenuity in the last ten years of his life dealing with two of his estates, Almayater and Tendilla. In the spectrum of seignorial jurisdiction, these two were at opposite ends: Almayater was a new property whose administrative and economic existence was therefore precarious, while Tendilla was the ideal seignorial town, a venerable, hereditary possession that administered itself and had produced a bountiful income for its lords for more than a century. Almayater needed the count's attention almost daily; Tendilla flourished without him.

In 1509 the count was preoccupied with his newest estate, the deserted village (*despoblado*) of Almayater on the Granada coast. Almayater made inordinate demands on his time and skill because it was not yet organized as a municipality and he therefore had to manage the land himself. His plans to attract permanent settlers to Almayater and establish a village council brought him into conflict with the royal town of Vélez Málaga, in whose municipal territory Almayater lay. Yet he had to make the effort, because as long as there was no village council, the *despoblado* required more of his attention and energy than all his towns and villages combined.

Almayater was one of many Morisco villages on the Granada coast depopulated in early 1507 by order of King Ferdinand. The king had taken this uncharacteristic action as the result of a surge of piracy and kidnappings on the Granada coast in the aftermath of a Spanish military expedition against North Africa. In late 1505 Cardinal Cisneros, archbishop of Toledo, had financed and organized a military expedition that succeeded in capturing the fort of Marzelkebir in North Africa. Although the expedition was a military success, its repercussions in Granada damaged much of the silk industry and disrupted trade. In 1507 the Castilian captain general of the African coast, headquartered in Marzelkebir, was badly defeated in an expedition inland, and the commander of the Castilian galleys fighting against Muslim fleets in the western Mediterranean was captured and decapitated.[2] Pirates from North Africa raided the Granada coast, pillaging, stealing stock, and kidnapping. King Ferdinand, convinced that the local population must be cooperating with the raiders, ordered that no Moriscos could reside within two leagues of the coast. The few Old Christian farmers on the coast, all veterans of the siege of the city of Granada in 1492, were too few to maintain the defense and the municipal life of their suddenly depleted villages. The resulting depopulation made the coast even more susceptible to raids than before. In 1508 Ferdinand decided to repopulate the area with settlers from other parts of Castile and ordered a census and survey to determine how many new families could be accommodated in each depopulated village.[3] Almayater was appraised as suitable for sixty households. But the monarchy and the region were beset by so many pressing problems that the repopulation of the coast lagged. Realizing in 1508 that the coast was still depopulated and the danger from raiders was as serious as before, Ferdinand agreed to grant several of the villages to his noble creditors. To the count of Tendilla he granted Almayater as payment for the count's services as Castilian ambassador to the papacy twenty years earlier.[4]

In January 1509 the count of Tendilla, in his capacity as captain general of the Kingdom of Granada, decided to make an unannounced inspection tour of the royal military posts and personnel along the coast. He also wanted to get his first look at Almayater, "this gift that the king gave me and others would like to take away from me."[5] Accompanied by one groom and taking along his own bedding and tapestries so he could arrange lodging anywhere without advance notice, he intended to move quickly to assess the damage of the previous two years. After reaching the coast at Motril, he turned west through the ports of Salobreña and Almuñécar, past the small bay of La Herradura, where so many of his grandsons would die, through the towns of Nerja and Torrox, until he reached Vélez Málaga, the nerve center of the coast defenses. For several days he and his lieutenants inspected the inlets and moorings where North African pirates most often landed, and in Almayater he paid special attention to the condition of the houses and farms King Ferdinand had given him (see map 4).

The count of Tendilla returned to Granada shaken by what he had seen. The expulsion of the native population and an epidemic in 1507 had disrupted both production and defense: the kingdom could not meet its tax obligations. The garrisons were understaffed. Farmers were afraid to settle in undefended places such as Almayater. All this the count had known from dispatches and reports. The inspection tour showed him that the nature of the conflict against the Muslims had changed: the frontier had shifted from North Africa to the Granada coast. His company of one hundred cavalry headquartered in Vélez Málaga, even when it was at full strength, could not patrol the entire coast. He would have to devise a

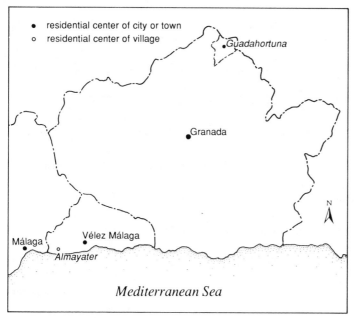

Map 4. Two New Villages in the Kingdom of Granada: Almayater and
Guadahortuna, 1570

new means of defense if Almayater and other coastal villages were to be
productive again.[6]

Tendilla had been a lord of subjects (*señor de vasallos*) ruling towns and
their citizens for thirty years, but he had never settled a *despoblado*. The
towns he inherited from his father were among the oldest and best established in Castile, and his villages in the Kingdom of Granada had been
well-populated Muslim communities when he received them in 1492. The
land of the one *despoblado* he bought in 1485, Anguix, he leased to the
town council of Alcocer when he left for his embassy in Rome early the
next year. Inexperienced in settling a new village, the count of Tendilla
thought that providing military defense for Almayater would be sufficient
to attract population from the town of Vélez Málaga. He quickly learned
that settling a seignorial village within the municipal territory of Vélez
Málaga, a town that did not belong to him, was not as easy as recognizing
a squatter village within his own seignorial jurisdiction, as he would do
in Miralcampo a few years later.

Almayater had already been depopulated and therefore unproductive
for a year when King Ferdinand promised it to Tendilla in October 1508.
The king, in order to narrow the discrepancy between what he owed

Tendilla and what he was giving him, made an exception, allowing Almayater to be settled by Moriscos as long as they were not the previous inhabitants of the village. Tendilla started trying to settle the *despoblado* in December, as soon as he heard that the royal secretaries had started the paperwork to give him full title.[7] He sent public criers to Málaga, Vélez Málaga, and Granada to announce his offer of land and a house to those who would move to Almayater and accept his lordship. He offered tax exemptions to the new settlers and offered to pay any taxes they might owe in the cities they were leaving. But when he visited Almayater in January, he found that his settlers were leaving as fast as they arrived: prohibited by royal decree from bearing arms, the Moriscos were defenseless against the raiders. The eight households of Christian veterans who had been settled in Almayater after the conquest could not occupy the village.[8] No wheat had been sown the previous fall, and now the perennials were being lost to uncontrolled grazing and neglect.[9]

Settlement was further obstructed by the council of Vélez Málaga, which reacted immediately to oppose him. The count of Tendilla had seriously miscalculated the reactions of the town to his repopulation efforts. Lords and their subjects had a common interest in establishing villages that would flourish and become towns; cities and towns were equally determined to prevent the uncultivated fields of their territories from falling into the possession of a noble, who invariably would try to develop them into villages and then would try to persuade the monarch to transform the villages into towns, in order to transfer them to the noble's jurisdiction. When the count advertised for settlers in Málaga, the town council objected to his luring away their taxpaying population.[10] When he wrote to ask the council of Vélez Málaga to help those who wanted to move their citizenship to Almayater, the council reminded him that he could not exercise jurisdiction in Almayater because it lay within the territory of the town of Vélez Málaga. Tendilla, as captain general, held jurisdiction over the military fortifications and personnel, but everything else in the municipal territory, including the villages, was under the jurisdiction of the town's council. Tendilla tried to dampen the dispute with soothing words, but the stage was set for a protracted struggle over jurisdiction.[11]

Tendilla's open recruitment of settlers had been premature: he wanted to settle Almayater before spring to ensure the timely pruning of the vineyards. By acting before the documents were drafted and countersigned by the royal bureaucrats, however, he alerted the council of Vélez Málaga in time for the council to send an agent to the court, where his own agent was proving ineffective. The town of Vélez Málaga proved to be a formidable opponent: the royal secretaries delayed the official signatures, and

Tendilla had to use all his skills and energies to prevent them from diminishing the size and quality of the concession.

The council of Vélez Málaga asserted its jurisdiction in Almayater by moving in some livestock for pasture and then complained to the king that Tendilla, by driving their livestock out of Almayater, was violating the town's jurisdiction over its own municipal territory. Tendilla responded that "the only thing I am preventing is the destruction of the farms by the animals. I am not keeping them from the grass, nor do I have any reason to."[12]

Tendilla then brought a serious charge against Vélez Málaga's management of the land, an argument that would become a familiar refrain in the next two centuries: councils that did not resettle *despoblados* destroyed the natural abundance of Spain and diminished the royal domain. He reminded the royal secretaries and councilors that while the farms of Almayater had belonged to the king the council of Vélez Málaga had allowed livestock to graze there as if it were open range. The grapevines had been eaten, the fruit and olive trees cut for fuel, and everything destroyed. It was because he refused to allow this to happen again that the people of Vélez Málaga were complaining.[13]

Draft wordings of the official documents were negotiated back and forth between Granada and the court for three months. The worst version for the count came in February, when the royal treasury secretaries Pedro de Madrid and Antón López refused to give him title to one-half of the property in Almayater on the grounds that the royal grant included only unoccupied land and houses. The count pointed out that it was he himself who had brought in the settlers during the months the secretaries were doing the paperwork.[14] His own inducements to immigration would be negated by treasury secretary Pedro de Madrid, who had "gone crazy" and wanted to send citizens of Málaga, veterans of the Marzelkebir campaign, to settle in Almayater. This would satisfy Málaga but not the count; the new veteran households would be tax-exempt hidalgos rather than subjects of the count of Tendilla. By March 1509 Tendilla and the secretaries agreed that his grant would include all the houses that had not been inhabited during the eighteen months since the expulsion order except for the eight occupied by veterans of the 1492 Granada campaign. The result was that "very few settlers are coming, and of those already there, so many have left that I'm afraid many of the farms will be ruined because the grapevines still have not been pruned. Last year the vineyards were not pruned, and if they aren't harvested this year the best income will be on the way to being lost forever, and if the silk isn't cultivated the place won't produce more than twenty thousand maravedís annually."[15]

Tendilla was still dissatisfied with the final version drawn up in March, because the secretaries wanted to exaggerate the value of what he was receiving by claiming that the eight houses occupied by veterans were worth 4 million maravedís and that his were of equal value. He had received this bit of information in a letter from the royal treasurer Francisco de Vargas, the most notorious peculator in the royal service.[16] Tendilla said he would have found this news incredible if it had been told him by an angel, let alone by the devil.[17]

He covered up his anger and wrote to thank all those at the royal court whose approval and intervention had been necessary to get the grant issued—King Ferdinand, Vargas, the marquis of Denia, the royal secretaries Lope de Conchillos, Miguel de Almazán, Suazola, and Francisco de los Cobos.[18] Tendilla could only respond ironically to a friend's congratulations: "What the king gave me were the houses and farms of Almayater except for eight houses that had already been given as grants to some veterans of the siege of Granada and others. They tell me it's a good thing. I couldn't say how much income it will produce, but I wish it were two-thirds of what they're claiming."[19]

All of his worst predictions would have come true if he had continued to lose time in negotiations, so Tendilla accepted the March draft of the grant and immediately gave license, in his capacity as captain general, for Moriscos to go to the coast to work in the vineyards and cultivate silk.[20] For the next few years he managed everything himself. He owned the houses and farmland in Almayater but not the jurisdiction. He could not turn the land over to the council on permanent leasehold, because the commons was not subject to his jurisdiction. He therefore rented the farmland of Almayater on short-term leases to individual farmers. He hired field guards in the spring to protect the vineyards from thieves who were taking his clusters of grapes, though this cost him much letter writing because his lieutenants sometimes arrested the Moriscos for carrying weapons.[21] His Morisco renters collected the mulberry leaves, fed the silkworms, and separated the cocoons into silk thread, though he found that no matter how good the harvest was, the Moriscos seemed to turn over to him the same amount of silk thread every year.[22]

All through the summer of 1509 the count of Tendilla searched for a way to solve the problems of Almayater and the rest of the Granada coast, while the raids, kidnappings, and pillages continued. His renters in Almayater were able to sow some wheatfields that fall, and the grapes were harvested without incident. He submitted a plan to the monarchy for changing the coastal defense system and increasing the population, but he knew that it would take months to persuade the royal councilors. He placed his oldest son, Luis, in charge of the coastal defense in the most critical periods, sent another son, Antonio, around to various posts to gather information and impressions, and himself stayed in the Alhambra corresponding with lieutenants, royal secretaries, councilors, noblemen, and the king himself.

In late 1509 he was catapulted out of Granada by a crisis in his town of Tendilla in New Castile. His old rival and cousin, the duke of Infantado, incited the city council of Guadalajara to violate the count's jurisdiction over the town of Tendilla, and the count's appellate judge in Tendilla mishandled the case. For months the count tried to rectify the situation through appeals to his powerful friends at court and through his attorney in Valladolid. In September he talked of sending Luis to court in order to handle the matter personally, but Luis was still young—about twenty-one—with a wife in the last weeks of her second pregnancy. In October the count finally became so frustrated and alarmed over the failure to resolve the problems in Tendilla that he decided to leave Luis in charge in Granada while he would accomplish the impossible—travel to the court to settle the Tendilla business, spend time in his towns to get at the truth and, if necessary, discipline his appellate judge, and use his friendship with King Ferdinand to gain seignorial jurisdiction over Almayater.

On October 4 the count of Tendilla set out from his headquarters in the Alhambra Palace. Traveling by mule, their baggage a few hours ahead, he and his entourage of secretary, servants, and grooms were off to visit his seignorial estates more than five hundred kilometers away in New Castile. He had been planning for weeks to make the trip, yet his responsibilities as captain general kept him so busy that the departure from Granada seemed hurried. The day before, he dictated more than twenty letters to military subordinates, city councils, and royal tax officers catching them up on unfinished business. When he reached the village of Albolote, just ten kilometers north of the city of Granada, his steward arrived with the news that the Mediterranean fleet had come into port at Málaga, and Tendilla stopped long enough to dictate a letter to the fleet captain instructing him to distribute his galleys among several ports along the Granada coast.[23] Letters with pressing official business continued to arrive, but he could not delay his departure any longer. He faced the typical dilemma of a noble lord, pulled in opposing directions as he tried to fulfill his diverse responsibilities. As chief commander of the royal military forces in Granada, he became an absentee manager of his seignorial estates in New Castile. As a leading member of Castile's most powerful and wealthy family, he could call upon family connections to expedite his affairs at the royal court, while hostile family members still living in the ancestral town of Guadalajara could easily interfere with his estate administrators and subject him to expensive and disruptive litigation. As the widowed father of a still-young family, he wanted to be with his children and grandchildren in Granada, yet the duty to arrange marriages and careers for his older children required his active presence at the royal court.

In the next two days, Tendilla crossed some of the highest mountains in Spain, where wolves still roamed and where just six years earlier the city council of Granada had founded the village of Guadahortuna to provide shelter for travelers between New Castile and Granada.[24] By the night of October 6 he reached the city of Huelma, where he ran into another traveling nobleman, Antonio de Cueva. They spent an enjoyable weekend together while Tendilla caught up on his correspondence. His thoughts were still at home in Granada, and his first letter was to Luis, whom he had left in charge of the family as well as the kingdom. He asked Luis to let everyone know that he and all his company were well and to give his love and kisses to Luis's wife and daughter, to the count's sister, and to his two youngest children, Diego and Isabel. He gave instructions and paternal advice to Luis—he was to sleep in the Alhambra rather than at home, no matter how much this upset his wife, for example. Luis was to send for his brother Antonio because the marquis of Denia, one of the most powerful members of the royal court, had written asking for him. One of the Alhambra guards, Lázaro de Peralta, must fetch Antonio and make sure he was properly clothed—he must dress in Castilian style—but he need not bother with bedding because the count had brought along enough for both.[25]

On Monday, the ninth, he arrived in Jódar and immediately wrote to thank Luis for the letter he found there. He reveled in the news that his little granddaughter was looking behind the tapestries trying to find him. He sent a letter to Peralta telling him to hurry Antonio and to use a piece of red cloth to make a skirt for the count's little daughter "Isabelica."[26] He thanked his notary Juan de Luz for the documents he had sent. He again gave Luis good advice about handling money, pacifying the coast, and managing Almayater.

Until this point his thoughts had all been of home, his letters full of family matters, and he had been traveling slowly, in short stages, in order not to become fatigued. Once over the highest mountain passes and eager to get on with the business ahead, he began sending letters written in his own hand because he was in too great a rush to wait for someone else to make a fair copy. He was rushing, he claimed, to stay ahead of the countess of Priego, who was going to see her husband. Tendilla did not want her to catch up with him because "I'm not going to see ladies, even though I'm healthy, thank God."[27]

He was rushing to Toledo in order to see the marquis of Denia, but now he received a letter from the marquis that indicated he had left the city. Tendilla reported to him that Luis's wife had given birth to a girl who died soon after, but he could not resist bragging that Luis and Catalina had a little girl who was "the prettiest I have ever seen. I don't know if everyone thinks his own grandchildren are so beautiful."[28]

Only matters of the most pressing urgency could uproot the count of Tendilla from his children and grandchildren. Usually he never corresponded with his towns in New Castile. Their experienced councils managed and governed themselves without his involvement. This was especially the case with Tendilla, the oldest and largest of the six towns he had inherited from his father. He could depend on his steward or appellate judge for the six towns to report any irregularity. But this time the appellate judge had mishandled a serious challenge to the lord's jurisdiction, and only the count himself had the prestige and authority to resolve the problem. While resolving these issues, he would try to achieve the first stage in his plan for Almayater, a grant of more land as his own private property so that he could attract enough permanent families to form a village council and transfer the land to it in perpetual leasehold. After that, he would begin the next phase of gaining control over the tax and tithe collection. Finally, he expected the population to grow enough to become a town, though this would require at least a generation to develop.

The count began lobbying as soon as he reached Toledo, even writing cordial letters to Cardinal Cisneros, whom he hated, singing the praises of the cardinal's new college in Alcalá de Henares: "At night, sir, I dream about the college and by day I talk about it. So help me and save me God, I never saw anything in these kingdoms nor out of them as notable or admirable. I don't see or imagine anything in it that could possibly be improved upon."[29] With the royal treasurer Vargas, lobbying took a more concrete form: the two men agreed that the count's son Antonio would marry Vargas's daughter Catalina.

Tendilla returned to Granada with more land in Almayater, and the population began to increase, though it was still unstable and seasonal. He still had to bring in contract laborers for the spring pruning of the vines, the summer harvest of fruit, and the making of raisins and dried figs. He built a fortified watchtower for the village, appointed a commander of the tower, and assigned a house and farmland as income to the post. The first commander of the tower, Iñigo Manrique, should have been on watch to give warning to the settlers in case of a raiding party from North Africa, but because of the labor shortage in the village, he spent much of his time plowing, planting, and harvesting the farm.

In 1512 Tendilla made another trip to the court, again to settle some litigation involving his towns in New Castile, and managed to persuade Vargas to give him a license to collect the royal taxes and tithes in Almayater. This privilege turned the trend of Almayater's settlement. In January 1513 the commander of the tower informed Tendilla that he had recruited several persons from Málaga who wanted to settle in Almayater, and this time Tendilla wrote to the corregidor in Málaga asking him to smooth the way for the colonists.[30] By May he thought Almayater was well established and began to anticipate collecting his first grain from the place. He wrote to the commander and reminded him that the king had given permission to store Tendilla's harvest from Almayater in the fortress and that if there was no space left in which to put the grain, he was to find some other place where it could be kept safe.[31]

In 1513 Tendilla was still trying to attract settlers from nearby towns and still struggling to make the terms of residence attractive. But again the royal secretaries placed obstacles in his drive to make the village of Almayater into a town. In 1514 he asked his agent at court to secure a decree reimbursing him fifteen thousand maravedís per annum from the royal taxes of Málaga, the equivalent of what his tenants in Almayater paid each year in royal sales taxes. The citizens of the other villages he owned in the Kingdom of Granada were free of royal taxes by virtue of the royal grant in 1492 giving him three villages in the municipal territory of the city of Alhama. Tendilla received annuities from the councils of the Alhama villages of Cacín, Fornes, and Algar, paid their royal tax assessment himself, and thus prevented royal tax collectors from operating in his villages. The king had promised to extend this privilege to Tendilla's subjects in Almayater, but the document that the royal secretaries sent incorrectly stated that the tax exemption was for only four years, while he understood the privilege to have been given in perpetuity, and the amount renegotiable every four years.[32] The next year he negotiated a tax agreement (encabezamiento) to collect the taxes of Almayater himself or, failing that, to have the council of the village collect them.[33] When this finally arrived, he found that the decree was written incorrectly to cover the years 1513–16 instead of 1512–15.[34] As long as the royal secretaries obstructed Tendilla's efforts to have the taxes collected by encabezamiento rather than by tax farmers, Almayater would "be lost and depopulated."

Having finally succeeded in gaining favorable tax terms for Almayater, he reached an agreement with the Almayater council. Although no document survives (or was never drawn up), the terms of the agreement were noted in later tithe audits.[35] He transferred the land and its management to the village council and agreed that he and his descendants would pay all the royal dues and taxes for Almayater. The council, in turn, paid the count one-half of the olives harvested in the village. Its citizens paid the church tithe on silk and other produce but no royal sales taxes, no royal share of the tithes, nor any other payments to the royal government.

In 1513 the count of Tendilla began to think of acquiring and developing another estate. He had toyed with the possibility of exchanging one of his Andalusian villages for a town belonging to a military order next to his New Castile estates.[36] When this exchange proved to be unattainable, he began negotiating to buy another village in Andalusia. He wrote to his son Luis, who was at the court that year, instructing him to make an offer on one of three villages near Málaga. Luis was to make an offer on a small village that could be developed by increasing its population, not on a large one that would be expensive to buy and would not provide an opportunity for profit through growth.[37] To make this purchase, the count proposed to borrow 750,000 maravedís from Gómez de Solís at a reasonable interest rate, secured by his Almayater income, which he claimed—falsely—was a minimum of one hundred thousand maravedís per annum. At the same time he tried to sell Almayater, advertising its annual income at two hundred thousand, but he had no success; it must have been obvious to prospective buyers that the village's future was precarious.[38]

By this time Tendilla's health was failing, and he decided in the last days of his life to bequeath Almayater to his younger sons. In his deathbed will, drawn up on July 18, 1515, he optimistically projected an annual income from Almayater at three hundred thousand maravedís; Antonio was to receive two hundred thousand, and his younger brother, Francisco, one hundred thousand, but Luis eventually acquired possession of it all. Antonio, appointed by Charles V as the first viceroy of New Spain, sold his share to Luis in 1535 on the eve of his departure for the Americas. Francisco died in Rome just after he was elected a cardinal, and Luis acquired his share of Almayater, too.[39] It was Luis, therefore, who benefited from the seignorial income that the count of Tendilla had developed in the village and negotiated with the royal court.

The terms proved advantageous to the lord and the citizens. In mid-century, Almayater prospered as a farm village with council and cultivated land. By 1561 it had a population of seventy-six households, including four headed by widows. While it produced its own wheat, barley, and other means of sustenance, the economic abundance of the lord and citizens came from the perennials—the olive trees and grapevines that the count of Tendilla had fought so hard to keep alive in 1508 and 1509. In 1560 the citizens paid in tithes thirty-seven pounds of silk thread, twenty *cargas* of bleached raisins, eighty *arrobas* of sun-dried raisins, fifteen fanegas of almonds, as well as wheat and barley and minor amounts of sheepskins, lambs, kids, cheeses and milk, grass, honey, wax, and chickens.[40]

Relations between the village of Almayater and the town of Vélez Málaga never ceased to be tense. The two councils were trapped in a legal anomaly because the count of Tendilla had not succeeded in getting Almayater exempted from the jurisdiction of Vélez Málaga. The village was therefore an island of seignorial jurisdiction within the royal jurisdiction of the Vélez town council. The Almayater council and citizens were subject to the count of Tendilla, but he paid their share of royal taxes assessed as part of the royal taxes paid by Vélez Málaga. Almayater continued to enjoy membership in the commons of Vélez Málaga, but the cultivated land of Almayater was not subject to the crop rotation or harvest schedule set by the Vélez town council. The count of Tendilla had hoped to be rid of these complications by having Almayater made a town, with a municipal territory of its own, if not in his own lifetime then through the efforts of his sons.

In 1560 Almayater, under the management of Luis, the second marquis of Mondéjar, seemed to have achieved a population stability and economic prosperity that would assure its survival as a town, and Luis made a serious attempt to achieve his father's goal. In 1564 he began buying up the farms and houses of the eight veteran settlers in Almayater, who owned most of the land but were citizens of Vélez rather than his subjects.[41] Apparently, by this means he hoped to acquire title to all the cultivated land not originally in his gift and then sell it to new settlers, who would be required to accept his lordship. But Almayater, because its population was made up of Moriscos, was fated to be "lost and depopulated" within ten years. The monarchy, despite strenuous objections from the marquis of Mondéjar, refused to allow the Moriscos to wear their customary clothes, use their traditional language, or follow their daily customs. After the Moriscos in the Alpujarras revolted and were crushed, the monarchy issued a decree expelling all Moriscos from the Kingdom of Granada, distributing them throughout Castile or forcing them to emigrate to north Africa. Almayater once again became a *despoblado*, this time definitively.

It should be noted that this depopulation of a seignorial village was imposed by a monarchy that ignored the vehement objections of the lord and citizens, whose economic interests they believed complemented each other. For three generations the lords of Almayater acted effectively to cultivate and protect the land and to develop its population. The lords' objective of economic profit could be achieved only through the customs and usages of Castile—by developing Almayater as a village with its municipal council to administer its own commons and juridical affairs and pay a fixed annuity to the lord.

Preserving the Seignorial Regime

While the count of Tendilla developed Miralcampo and Almayater as villages, he was launching them on a trajectory whose final goal of township had long since been achieved by his other seignorial estates. The oldest town in his jurisdiction was Tendilla, which his ancestors had long before developed into the ideal of the seignorial regime, a flourishing and self-administering town. The count of Tendilla's career took him far away from New Castile, making him an absentee lord of the town of Tendilla during the last thirty years of his life.[42] From the time of his appointment as captain general of the Kingdom of Granada in 1492 until his death in 1515 he made only two visits to New Castile—in 1508–9 and 1511–12— yet his towns there rarely received mention in his correspondence. When he did refer to Tendilla, it was with a nostalgia that contrasted with the difficulties he faced in managing the new estates he was acquiring through purchase, trade, and royal gift in the Kingdom of Granada.

The count turned the management of his revenues in New Castile over to a steward, who rented out any farmland that the count owned as private property, collected the lord's annuities, taxes, and other revenues from the municipal councils, and stored and transported the seignorial annuities paid in kind. After the count moved to Granada and no longer had access to the produce of his Castilian estates to provision his household, he sold all of it every year and depended on the steward to market it in Guadalajara, the major consumer of the charcoal and lumber from Anguix and the wine from the town of Tendilla. The count usually had only one steward for all his towns in New Castile, and often there were months after the death of a steward when he could not find anyone to take the job and thus could not be sure what was happening to his seignorial income. Even when the count had a steward actively engaged in this work, there were long periods when he could not find out what was happening. The steward's job was extremely complex because it required several tours of the count's towns and villages every year to collect money and in-kind payments after the harvests. In New Castile his stewards collected the sales taxes and other quarterly cash payments on January 1, because these did not change with the seasons. The steward also collected the royal tithe on "miscellaneous" crops (*menudos*) on January 1, because most of it was olive oil, which was harvested in late November and pressed in December. In March he col- lected the sales taxes from the annual fair in the town of Tendilla and the yearly lease rents on the lord's inns, ferries, and livestock transit fees. The day after the feast of St. Peter, on June 29, he collected the royal tithe on wool and lambs. The steward's work load eased in the summer until the fifteenth of August, when he collected the wheat paid in annuities and rents. On September 15 he collected the annuity for the woods and pasture in the *despoblado* of Anguix, on October 1 the wine for the royal tithe and rents, and on November 1 the wheat for the royal tithe and the land rents paid in cash. The count hired another steward for his estates in Granada, where the cash payments were collected on the same schedule as in Castile, but the produce collection followed a slightly accelerated seasonal pattern because the wheat and pastures ripened earlier.[43]

Juridical matters in Tendilla were equally remote from the count's man- agement. The town council governed and administered the judicial and

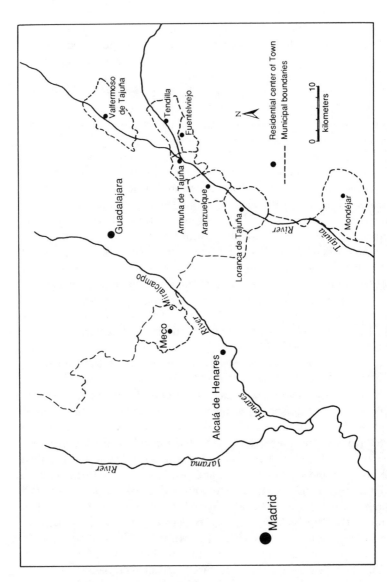

Map 5. Towns Acquired through Inheritance and Purchase by the Count of Tendilla, 1479–1512

political affairs of the citizens. Sometime after 1500 the count began appointing an appellate judge (*alcalde mayor*), who resided in Tendilla and held jurisdiction in cases appealed from the decisions of the municipal judge. The count's appellate judge also presided over any litigation between two or more of the six towns the count owned in the region. As surrogate for the lord, he could settle disputes throughout the count's seignorial estates; he could not adjudicate a dispute between the town of Tendilla and the city of Guadalajara, however, and just such a conflict over use of the Guadalajara commons brought the count of Tendilla north from Granada in 1509 and 1512.

For the count of Tendilla, this conflict seemed alarming because it involved his town of Tendilla, the jewel in his patrimonial estate. In 1479 he had inherited the estate and title of his parents, becoming for the first time in his thirty-seven years a seignorial lord (*señor de vasallos*). With these estates, the new count inherited the costs and benefits of admin-istering a seignorial jurisdiction. His inheritance was not a large one, but the six towns he inherited—Tendilla, Loranca, Aranzueque, Fuentelviejo, Monasterio, and Meco—were among the oldest of the seignorial juris-dictions in Castile (see map 5). He was driven by an acute awareness of his responsibilities as a link between ancestors and heirs—a chain of proprietary lordship that began at the end of the fourteenth century and would last until the Bourbon monarchy abolished seignorial jurisdiction in 1837. In his efforts to preserve the traditional rights and privileges of the town that gave his family the prestige of "old nobility," the count of Tendilla was not unusual.

For the citizens of Tendilla, the conflict with Guadalajara struck at their economic prosperity by challenging the privileges they enjoyed in the city's marketplace. The dispute reached back to the royal decree of 1395 in which King Enrique III exempted the village of Tendilla from the jurisdiction of Guadalajara, so that the village became an autonomous seignorial town but still enjoyed the privileges of the Guadalajara commons and marketplace.[44] The tension between old cities and newly autonomous seignorial towns kept noble lords dancing in a perpetual round of litigation and hostility, defending the rights and privileges of their seignorial towns against the claims of neighboring municipalities.

The earliest mention of the town of Tendilla appears in the document that linked the town to the count's family.[45] King Enrique III dismembered the village of Tendilla from Guadalajara and made it a town in order to give it to our count's great-grandfather, the admiral of Castile. The admiral and his heirs received in perpetuity the same proprietary jurisdiction and income in Tendilla that previously belonged to the king. What transpired before this grant was issued, however, was crucial to the later history of the town and lord of Tendilla. The king was so determined to give his admiral an estate of value that he required the council of Guadalajara to grant to the citizens of the town of Tendilla the same rights they had had as citizens of a Guadalajara village—the right to full use of the Guadalajara commons and the right to sell their wine in their own taverns in Guadalajara without being subject to the usual price controls of the council. The Guadalajara council conceded these rights to the citizens of Tendilla on October 5, 1395, and on November 20 the king issued the royal decree giving the royal town of Tendilla, its municipal territory, and jurisdiction to the admiral.[46]

In the space of two months in 1395 the people of Tendilla were transformed from citizens of a village within the municipal territory and under the jurisdiction of the royal town of Guadalajara into citizens of the royal town of Tendilla, with its own municipal territory and subject to no authority other than the king, and finally emerged as citizens of the seignorial town of Tendilla subject only to the lord. Tendilla's citizens would remain subjects of the admiral's heirs and successors until seignorial jurisdiction was abolished in 1837.

The admiral died soon after receiving Tendilla, but his son, the future marquis of Santillana, followed the characteristic policy of new seignorial lords in the fifteenth century.[47] He took advantage of the topography, which funneled travel onto the town's main street, to develop the commercial potential of the town of Tendilla. The municipal territory was in a strategic location, straddling the highway that linked central Castile to the Mediterranean port of Valencia.[48] Merchants on the move from Valencia toward Guadalajara traveled through Cuenca, across the Tajo River over the bridge at Sacedón, and then through the Alcarria, a rugged region of ridges and tablelands separated by small rivers. In order to traverse the Alcarria's steep heights and deep gullies they followed a highway down a narrow valley that ran all the way from the northeast to the southwest corner of Tendilla's municipal territory. The highway descended to the residential nucleus down an incline "so steep and deep that, when some people come down from the summits they get scared because, in fact, there is no place in Spain so proportionately deep."[49] The houses lined both banks of the stream at the bottom of the gorge, with the highway serving as the main street on one side.

The marquis instituted a month-long fair that began every year on the feast of St. Matthias, on February 24. For generations, the lords of Tendilla promoted this fair by setting a low sales tax of one-thirtieth on retail sales and exempting wholesale transactions from sales tax altogether. These favorable conditions and the fact that the Tendilla fair was the first of the spring season brought merchants from all over Spain and western Europe, making it one of the major international fairs of Spain. The sales tax from this fair was by far the greatest source of the lord's income from the town of Tendilla; at the height of its fame in the sixteenth century it produced an annual income of 1,200,000 maravedís in sales tax alone for the lord.[50]

Thanks to the foresight of the founding settlers, the houses along the main streets on either side of the stream were fronted with porticos that were supported by stone pillars, some of them carved from a single stone and all quarried from within the municipal territory of Tendilla itself. By staying under the porticos, "even when it rains one can walk the length of the town without getting muddy, a cleanliness usually not found in towns of this size." The houses were built of quarried stone, and most were two or three stories high. It was necessary to build this way because of the town's location in the lowest part of the valley, which often flooded. "One could almost say that it is built on the water like the city of Venice, and consequently people make their living quarters in the second story of the houses."[51]

The citizens who owned houses on the main street commanded handsome rents for fair stalls under the porticos that protected the merchant goods from water damage no matter how rainy the fair might be. The fair administrators arranged the business in an orderly manner, assigning stall space so that all the merchandise from Cuenca, Toledo, or Segovia could be found in one spot, for example. The citizens of Tendilla did a booming business in renting lodgings, serving food and drink, and providing feed and supplies. They also developed a commercial and industrial economy, including a number of cloth shops and artisan workshops—jewelers, embroiderers, silversmiths. They quarried the local limestone for construction materials which they sold to other regions, produced millstones for their own use and for sale, and were noted for their stone masonry and other construction specialties. There were carpenters, cabinetmakers, an organ maker, draftsmen, and architects who created many interesting pieces and took them to Madrid and other places for sale.

All of these activities were secondary, however, to the main economic activities of the town's permanent residents, the production of olive oil and wine. In the sixteenth century the knowledgeable citizen Juan Fernández, delegated by the council to respond to the *Relaciones* questionnaire, believed that "in all of Spain there is no town of comparable population with so many olive trees, because all its municipal territory is planted, so that it looks like mountains, slopes, and valleys of olive trees and vines." He found it awe-inspiring to see so many and such good olives in such rugged land, which he thought must seem like the fabled olive-producing Aljarafe region of Seville.

In the valleys, the citizens terraced and irrigated the banks of several streams to plant vegetables, fruit, hemp, sumac, and some walnut trees "so tall that it is a pleasure to see them." Citizens of Tendilla owned and plowed some grain land in the Guadalajara municipal territory, but not enough to supply the town's needs. By the mid-fifteenth century there was no *monte* left for grazing livestock, except on the Guadalajara commons. To provision the traders at the fair, the town bought wheat from the grain towns of Alcalá, Guadalajara, and La Mancha and meat animals from the mountain towns of Cuenca, Soria, Medinaceli, Segovia, and Estremadura. Some of the citizens of Tendilla were "intrepid dealers who traveled to many ports of the peninsula to buy fish and other merchandise."

The cash for these purchases came from the sale of Tendilla's produce, which the citizens processed and marketed themselves. Juan Fernández boasted that the town produced more olive oil and wine than any other in the region. In the sixteenth century the town had thirteen well-built olive presses, which, when the olive crop was good and the presses were operating at full capacity, "were thirteen money mints." The Tendilla wine caves were dug straight back into the slopes of the town "so long and straight and level that a pack animal can go all the way in to the end of them." And because Tendilla had "the best wine cellars in Spain," its wine was aged "longer than in any other town of the region and therefore it usually commands a much higher price." It was this access to the Guadalajara market without price controls that had been guaranteed in the Guadalajara concession of 1395.

The farmers profited from the by-products of their olive groves. In addition to processing their own olive oil and wine, the local people also washed and dyed cloth. Wherever there were olive presses, there were soap works that manufactured good bar soap, an olive oil by-product esteemed for washing wool. Several natural springs in the municipal territory supported these activities, and one, a hot spring, was particularly valuable because it could be used comfortably even in winter and had a bleaching effect that made it ideal for washing white cloth. The citizens used the olive and grape prunings and cuttings for firewood.[52]

The lords of Tendilla during most of the fifteenth century resided in the town of Guadalajara, about ten miles away, in the residential palaces that the admiral, an enthusiastic builder, had constructed there. The admiral built wine cellars in Guadalajara, known as "la bodega del almirante," to market his wine, which was also free of the Guadalajara price controls. The admiral's son, the marquis of Santillana, gained a much larger prize from King Juan II, who gave township to twelve more of Guadalajara's villages and gave them to the marquis in 1430. After Santillana's death in 1458, his sons partitioned their parental inheritance among themselves so that each one became the lord of enough of the twelve towns alienated from Guadalajara to give him three hundred subjects from the parental estate.[53] The son who inherited the town of Tendilla thus acquired a strategic military and economic position. As a result of this 1458 distribution, he became lord of the towns of Fuentelviejo, Ar-

muña de Tajuña, and Aranzueque, which formed a compact and contiguous bloc of territory around Tendilla. He also received in this distribution
the town of Meco and its farm of Moneder some distance away on the
other side of the Henares River.[54]

This lord of Tendilla received the title count of Tendilla from King
Enrique IV about 1467, and the new count and his countess placed the
bulk of their New Castilian towns in a perpetual trust (mayorazgo) for
their oldest son. The trust comprised their houses in the city of Guadalajara
and their towns of Tendilla, Fuentelviejo, Armuña de Tajuña, Aranzueque, Loranca de Tajuña, Monasterio, and Meco with its farm of Moneder.[55] The towns that had been informally associated by having a lord
in common were now legally bound together. Each town still was autonomous, with its own council, municipal territory, and corporate assets,
but the lord was prevented by the perpetual trust from selling or mortgaging
them and from partitioning them among his heirs. They would be inherited
as a group for the next three centuries.[56]

While the lord's fortunes were prospering, the town's population was
growing and extending the cultivated land. All the land within Tendilla's
municipal territory that could possibly be planted had been put into cultivation early in the fifteenth century. Desperately short of level land for
planting grain, the citizens cleared and plowed fields beyond their municipal boundaries in the Guadalajara commons, as they had a right to
do under the concession of 1395. But Juan II, by alienating twelve more
villages with surrounding territory from Guadalajara in 1430, left the city
with a diminished commons. Guadalajara fought back by imposing fees
and fines on the vineyards and grainfields in its commons that had been
cleared, planted, and owned by people who were not citizens of Guadalajara. Litigation sputtered for years until the count on behalf of his towns
appealed directly to the king in 1470.[57] This was at a time when Enrique
IV desperately needed the support of the count and his brothers, and the
king obligingly issued a mandate to the council of Guadalajara ordering
the city judges to cease demanding fees and taxes for this cultivated land
from the count's subjects.[58]

If Guadalajara could not win through litigation, it would attack through
other means. Competition for grainland and for wheat was so intense that
the town of Tendilla was no longer able to buy enough grain on the open
market to provision the large number of people who came to buy and sell
at the town's annual fair. Guadalajara refused to sell wheat from its municipal granary to the council of Tendilla. The count interceded with the
royal judges at court and sent a message to the council of Tendilla to
delegate persons who, by the authority of the council's writ, would buy
bread and wheat from Guadalajara for the provisioning of Tendilla.[59] Thus,
by the time the second count of Tendilla inherited his father's estate in

1479 and embarked on his career in Granada, the town of Tendilla already had been embroiled in litigation with the city of Guadalajara for over a decade. The new count kept on retainer a lawyer, Lic. Bernardino, who represented him before the royal appellate court in Valladolid, and Alonso de Barrionuevo, who acted as his agent at the royal court wherever it traveled. He needed these lawyers and pleaders to keep up with the litigation that usually hung over a noble town.

The most pressing lawsuit after the count of Tendilla moved to Granada was one brought by the council of Tendilla against the council of Guadalajara charging that Guadalajara had violated the 1395 concession by forcing the people of Tendilla to accept price controls on their wine. While the lawsuit was under consideration by the royal appellate court in Valladolid, the count of Tendilla in Granada depended on his lawyers and representatives to protect his interests. In March 1507 the royal appellate court in Valladolid issued a ruling in favor of Tendilla confirming the town's right to freely sell wine in the city of Guadalajara. After this, the conflict between city and town took a violent turn. Guadalajara's sheriffs patrolling the commons seized livestock belonging to Tendilla citizens, and the stock owners fought back with various means. The city sent one of its judges to the town of Tendilla to arrest the trespassers. It was this violation of his seignorial jurisdiction by the city judge that inspired the count's trip to the royal court in early 1509. According to a letter he wrote to the marquis of Villena, the situation was serious indeed. The count of Tendilla believed that the city's hostilities against his towns were subterfuges for a personal vendetta with his hated cousin, the duke of Infantado, who controlled the Guadalajara city government.

During this trip, the count played a very cool game against the duke. He stayed with the duke of Infantado in Guadalajara when the king was there, "more to show that we had no quarrel with one another than to get him to do something for me." From Guadalajara the count traveled with the king to Sigüenza, where the king issued the coveted tax privileges for Almayater. During this time the duke forced the councilmen and judges of Guadalajara to knife the Tendilla wineskins, spill the wine, and close the taverns that he himself had opened. The two enemies maintained a charade of amiability. When the count returned to Guadalajara, the duke visited him in his lodgings, and the count went to visit the duke in his. The next day the count left Guadalajara without saying anything to the duke about the matter. He believed that "the duke's intent had been to incite me to some act against a Guadalajara councilman or judge in order to be able to inform the king that I was doing scandalous things and such."[60] He began to lobby his influential friends at court, barraging them and the king with letters telling his own side of the story.[61] He claimed that if the duke had confined himself to inciting the city to write him insulting letters, there would have been only a war of letters, but "to make them send a Guadalajara judge carrying his staff of justice to my territory and right into Tendilla and then involve me again in litigation, which he did to screw me, has hurt me mortally. I intend to win and in spades."[62]

This dispute, the count believed, was a coverup for the duke of Infantado's true intention, which was to pressure the count into dropping a lawsuit over the town of Valfermoso. The duke was taking vengeance on the count's subjects in Tendilla, and the count fought back with still another lawsuit, which he vowed would be a good one: "I am about to serve him some more lawsuits even more serious than that one [over Tendilla], and I believe that with God's help I will bring him to his knees in many matters that affect him. When the emperor's peace is in effect, we all, big and small, have an equal chance for justice."[63] The dispute over Valfermoso went back over forty years, to the count's first marriage, to his cousin Marina de Mendoza (see fig. 3). Marina died in childbirth in 1477, less than a year after the wedding, and the count claimed her property—one-half of the towns of Valfermoso and Mondéjar. He based this claim on the fact that Marina had named him her universal heir in the will she made just before her death. But Marina's sister, Catalina Laso de la Vega, laid claim to the estate on the grounds that the will violated Castilian inheritance law, which stipulated that the inherited property of persons who died without legitimate children reverted to the natal family of the deceased. For ten years the count and Catalina sued each other for possession of the two towns, and in 1486 the royal appellate court ruled in Catalina's favor. Ferdinand and Isabella wanted to favor the count of Tendilla, who was at that time their ambassador in Rome, and so they bought the town of Mondéjar from Catalina and two weeks later sold it to the count. Nine years later, in 1496, Catalina's son, Pedro Laso de la Vega, acknowledged receipt of the full amount, the huge sum of twelve million maravedís, which the count had raised by selling his government annuities (juros) and the town of Monasterio.[64]

Catalina also won in the matter of Valfermoso and sold her share of it to the owner of the other half of the town's jurisdiction, her uncle the first duke of Infantado. He in turn left it to his son, Juan de Mendoza, lord of Beleña. The count of Tendilla brought suit against Juan de Mendoza, but the case became complicated when the third duke of Infantado claimed Valfermoso for himself, becoming a third party to the suit. While the count of Tendilla traveled with King Ferdinand in 1509 and 1510, he managed to settle the dispute over Valfermoso, though not the way he wanted. In 1511, after forty years of litigation, the appellate court ordered Juan de Mendoza to sell Valfermoso to the count. The count felt sick about it. He had to sell some of his best properties—irrigated farms on the outskirts of the city of Granada—in order to raise the money. King

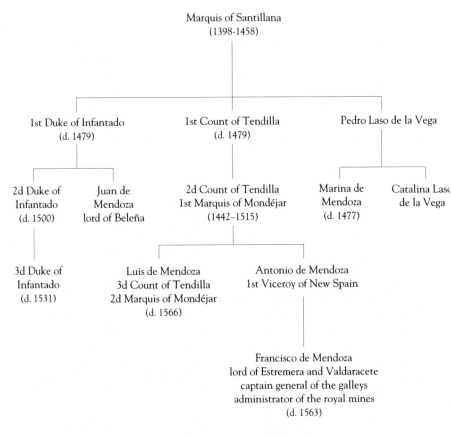

Fig. 3. Some members of the count of Tendilla's family

Ferdinand granted him the titles of marquis of Valfermoso and Mondéjar, but the count still felt chagrined and claimed he would have been happier if the king had granted him the gift he had asked for and left him with the title he had inherited from his father.[65] In fact, neither he nor his descendants used the title marquis of Valfermoso.

By purchasing Valfermoso from Juan de Mendoza, he intensified his conflict with the duke of Infantado, who claimed to be the heir of his brother Juan by denying the legitimacy of Juan's children.[66] The count of Tendilla's lawsuits against the duke dragged on for years. In 1513 he urged his new attorneys to hurry things up because the duke was powerful and he was old. The count thought of going to court himself to exercise his influence—"ready to cast my vote in my own land," he called it.[67] Instead, he sent Luis to court to manage the affair, and after counting votes in the royal appellate court in Valladolid, he thought the time was ripe to have the case brought to sentencing.[68]

Just when the count thought that he might regain for his citizens their right to sell wine in the city of Guadalajara, the duke and the city counterattacked in the Guadalajara commons again. The Guadalajara sheriffs tried to confiscate some Tendilla livestock grazing in the city's commons, but the Tendilla citizens attacked the sheriffs and got their stock back, claiming that the town of Tendilla had a right to graze in that part of the commons. The royal attorney, Lic. Zomeño, who was commissioned as the investigative judge (*pesquisidor*) in the case, entered the town limits of Tendilla and arrested the accused attackers.[69] The count's appellate judge, Juan Rodríguez de Arévalo, protested this intrusion into the seignorial jurisdiction but permitted Zomeño to impound the property of 120 citizens of Tendilla as a surety for the fine of two hundred thousand maravedís levied against the Tendilla town council. Against this violation of seignorial jurisdiction the count rose in full fury. He accused the royal investigative judge of violating the traditional municipal immunities of Castilian towns: "The Lic. Zomeño is destroying Tendilla as if it were a Muslim village,"[70] he declared, and he claimed that Guadalajara had no right to change the grazing rules without the consent of the other towns in the commons.[71]

Above all, the count of Tendilla appealed to King Ferdinand as his loyal commander of the Kingdom of Granada, whose subjects in New Castile were being destroyed by this obligatory absence of their lord. The appeal worked: in July 1513 Luis and the count's attorneys managed to have the litigation settled, piece by piece, through the king's intervention. King Ferdinand ordered the treasurer Vargas to release to Luis 150,000 maravedís of the amount that the royal judge Zomeño had confiscated from the citizens of Tendilla. With further urging from the count and continued lobbying by Luis, the royal appellate court affirmed the town of Tendilla's right to sell wine in Guadalajara.[72]

For the count of Tendilla, estate management was a battle to protect the citizens of his towns and villages against royal tax collectors and bureaucrats and a campaign of war against the competing jurisdiction of a neighboring city. Until he could develop the farms of Almayater into a self-sustaining and self-administering village, he had to involve himself in every aspect of the local agricultural economy. But this could never be a successful way to manage his estates; he could only be in one place at a time. Even when he was close to his properties, he had to depend on others to supervise them if they were not yet villages. The towns, in contrast, could administer their internal affairs without his intervention. Nevertheless, only the lord possessed the legal and political resources to preserve a town's economic privileges in another jurisdiction and defend a town's legal autonomy from other lords.

The count of Tendilla was not averse to handling money or the details of property management himself. On the contrary, he enjoyed the challenge of getting a better price or outwitting a competitor. In his enterprise as stockman, he corresponded with horse dealers all over Andalusia to find the right stud,[73] and he negotiated ruthlessly to get the best possible lease rent for his Sierra Nevada pastures.[74] No detail was too minute for his interest or his concern. On January 8, 1513, the count wrote to his lieutenant in the Alpujarras Mountains ordering him to investigate the disappearance of doors and other pieces of lumber from some houses that Tendilla owned in the *despoblado* of Meniar and retrieve them.[75] This attention to the details of his private property, the determination to retain control over every privilege and every resource that belonged to him, balanced other important aspects of the count of Tendilla's attitudes toward wealth and property. He would fight rising costs and losses to the penny, while investing vast sums in new estates and in preserving the estates he already owned. He believed in keeping a modest decorum in clothing and household, haggled over the price of stock in horsetrading, kept strict control over his accountants, yet lavished adornment on pious works and artistic monuments and bought and sold towns and villages worth a fortune.

Yet no fortune was ever enough for him or for any other lord. Apart from the property placed in perpetual trust, all of his accumulated towns and villages would be subject to the inheritance laws of Castile, which required an equitable distribution among all his children. The seignorial regime was constantly growing, always in development, repeatedly divided among the heirs, and perpetually embroiled in litigation with other jurisdictions.

Chapter 3

The Emergence of Absolute Monarchy and Town Liberty

From the point of view of kings and queens, Castile could never have too many towns. Like citizens and nobles, monarchs wanted to provide for their families, and this meant they had to retain and even increase the number of royal towns. At the same time, monarchies needed the support of powerful military and political leaders, and this required that the monarchs give away towns. They resolved the dilemma in the Middle Ages by conquering more territory from the Muslims, but this brought diminishing returns after Castile conquered the great Andalusian city-states of Seville, Cordoba, and Jaen in the thirteenth century. To reward faithful service, monarchs after 1300 had to give away a much more valuable commodity, namely, land already settled as towns in the royal domain. But these gifts depleted the resources of the new Trastamara dynasty (1369–1516), which ascended the throne through civil war and regicide. Beset by succession crises and civil wars, the Trastamara monarchs developed a third process, one that protected the royal domain from further shrinkage while still rewarding the dynasty's military supporters: they began giving away villages belonging to the cities. In order to justify this violation of the constitutions their ancestors had granted to the conquest cities, they adopted a theory of absolute royal power. The last Trastamara monarchs, Ferdinand and Isabella, bequeathed to their Habsburg grandson, Emperor Charles V, this heritage of using absolutism to justify liberating villages from their ruling cities.

The bond between kings and cities had been the distinguishing characteristic of Castile's growth in the Middle Ages. The Castilian monarchy had been built up in several stages by Christians moving south into territory claimed by the Muslims. After the Muslims conquered most of the Iberian peninsula and southern France in the early eighth century, Spain became a vast open frontier. The Christians withdrew to the Atlantic coast north of the Cantabrian Mountains, while the Muslims, with military outposts in the center of the peninsula but not enough population to fill it, collected in Andalusia. Christians during the next six centuries moved forward in four distinct stages: repeated thrusts into the Duero River basin in the ninth through eleventh centuries; a broad sweep through the Tajo River basin after capturing the city of Toledo in 1085, extending east to Cuenca and west to Lisbon; the lightning capture of the major cities of Andalusia— Murcia, Jaen, Cordoba, and Seville—between 1212 and 1252; and final conquest of the Kingdom of Granada between 1482 and 1492. The military aspects of the reconquest still capture the imagination and will continue to hold the spotlight visually, but permanent possession occurred only when the victorious kings fulfilled their duty to populate the realm by founding cities.[1]

In each region and phase of the medieval reconquest, kings created a distinct municipal tradition. In Old Castile north of the Duero River, they fought pitched battles against the Muslims and built fortified castles to defend the territory they captured. With permanent possession, the kings gave new settlers their own villages (aldeas) in the territory (alfoz) subject to the castle.[2] In the next phase, the kings followed a strategy in which royal forces besieged Muslim cities rather than fight pitched battles against armies. The defeated government agreed to abandon the city in exchange for favorable terms for those Muslims who wished to remain. The victorious Christian king installed his own military forces in the city walls and towers and placed the Muslim and Jewish populations under his direct jurisdiction as royal subjects. Then the monarch turned the city over to Christian settlers by granting a charter (fuero) to the new city council. With this charter, the victorious king gave the city as its municipal territory (término) all the land of the conquered Muslim state and ceded to the city council his royal jurisdiction over all the Christian population within the city and its término. The Castilian kings thus converted each conquered Muslim kingdom into a Christian city-state.[3]

The evolution of this close relationship between the victorious kings and their prize cities fills the pages of Castilian medieval history. Royal charters and privileges, boundary surveys and property allotments to founding citizens, municipal ordinances, copies of royal decrees, and litigation appealed to the royal court comprise the medieval treasures of city archives. These documents, in fact, have been a major source of information about the monarchy. No royal archive survives from the medieval period. Though historians have speculated about documents lost or destroyed, it is equally probable that no collection ever existed. The territory conquered in each phase of the reconquest was called a kingdom in royal documents— León, Castile, Toledo, Seville. The monarchy's correspondence with each medieval kingdom was supervised by a member of the royal court who served as the presiding notary (notario mayor) for that kingdom. The presiding notaries were not necessarily natives of the kingdoms whose correspondence they supervised, and the old kingdoms themselves had no territorial governments. Instead, the monarchs addressed the cities directly, and each city communicated directly with the royal court.⁴ Since the cities were the only territorial governments of the monarchy, the royal documents addressed to them and preserved in their archives accurately reflect the decentralized administrative organization of Castilian royal government.

After the king won and secured a great city, the battleground shifted to the countryside outside the city limits, where the most common military operation by both sides was the razzia, or raiding campaign. The purpose was profit—to seize livestock, harvests, and prisoners or to extort tribute. Here the monarchs founded another type of municipality, the town (villa), which would eventually displace the city as the principal administrative arm of the monarchy. The kings began by chartering royal and seignorial towns, each one a "community of town and territory" (comunidad de villa y tierra).⁵ The charter (fuero or carta puebla) gave the town council ownership and management of the land within the municipal boundaries and jurisdiction over both its land and its citizens. The charters served as constitutions— principles that guided the towns as they enacted municipal ordinances.⁶

The kings also gave large unpopulated territories in the Tajo River basin between Cuenca and Toledo to the church, especially the archbishop of Toledo and the military orders. These, too, became autonomous communities of town and land. Each grantee received jurisdiction (señorío) over the territory in exchange for creating a town and populating it. The king granted the land to the lord, and the lord in turn granted the land and his seignorial jurisdiction to the town council in exchange for an annuity. Bishops recruited settlers from other parts of Castile to populate their towns. Christian knights organized themselves into religious-military orders, pledging their lives to defend the disputed territory around the southern boundaries of Toledo, Cuenca, and the great cities of Andalusia. The king granted land to the masters of the orders, who built strings of fortified castles, gave land, citizenship, and town councils to their knights and soldiers, and grouped the towns into commanderies (encomiendas). The commander (comendador) established his headquarters in one of the fortified towns of his commandery and led the male citizens of the commandery towns into battle. But whether the lord was the king, a bishop, or master of a military order, the town charter gave ownership and jurisdiction over the land to the town council. Only if the council ceased to function did the municipal territory revert to the lord.

A council's ability to manage its land depended on the legal status of the municipality. The conquering Christian monarchs gave the greatest independence to cities, which had once been the capitals of Muslim kingdoms, making them resemble the imperial free cities in the Holy Roman Empire or the city-states in northern Italy. The royal charters guaranteed to the city councils full ownership of both the land and the government. The king agreed that royal judges could not enter city territory to investigate, arrest, or prosecute and allowed the city councils to prohibit appeals of their judicial sentences to the king.[7] The kings themselves entered a city and its territory only at the invitation of the city council, a courtesy acted out in rituals such as presentation of the keys to the city during royal entries.

The kings did not give such freedom from accountability to towns, because every town had a lord—a private individual, a bishop, a commander, or, in the case of towns that the kings kept for the royal domain, the king himself. Ecclesiastical, seignorial, and royal judges could enter the towns of their respective lords with inquests and summonses, and kings entered royal towns without the invitation of the town council and without ceremony.[8] Whether the new municipality was a royal, seignorial, or ecclesiastical town, the founding charter served as a constitution, setting down the relationship between the governed and the governor.

Lords advertised favorable terms to attract the first settlers, offering farmland as private property, grazing rights, self-governance, and, sometimes, plow teams and the first year's seed. In some cases, settlers formed a wagon train under the protection of the lord's cavalrymen in order to travel together to the site of the new town, which the lord's agents had already surveyed and divided into allotments. The first act of the new council usually was to distribute house lots, garden plots, and farm fields to the first citizens. Once a king or other lord had settled a town, he removed himself from its management. The town governed itself through its annually elected town council, and the lord limited himself to acting as appellate judge for all the towns in his domain. Sometimes the council sent out a colony to establish an official village (aldea) within the municipal territory. The colonists (aldeanos) and their descendants usually retained citizenship in the town, enjoying tax and legal benefits prejudicial to the aldea's later immigrants. Aldeas were usually located close to the town's residential nucleus and enjoyed full and free use of the town marketplace and commons.

The subjects of Castilian kings traditionally traveled extensively, to other towns to buy or sell, to shrines for pilgrimages, to the mountains for summer pasture, to newly conquered regions to start a new life, and to become citizens of new towns competing for population. The new towns, by offering good conditions to new settlers without requiring them to first participate in a war of conquest, invited ordinary farmers to move rather than just travel to other places and return home.

The resulting loss of population in the older regions in turn forced lords there to offer better terms to their farmers.[9] If medieval manorialism ever existed in Castile, it was in Galicia, the northwestern territory where most of the land was under the jurisdiction of monasteries and bishops. Through-out Europe, ecclesiastical lords were more reluctant than secular lords to grant municipal autonomy, and in Galicia they rented their land on short-term contracts to tenant farmers.[10] But with the population moving south, abbots and bishops in Galicia reorganized the administration and own-ership of their jurisdictions into the Castilian pattern of community of town and territory. Prelates in Galicia gave the towns charters (*foros*) delegating to the town council administration of justice and ownership of the municipal territory.[11] During the fifteenth century, direct exploitation of the land by the lord ended in Galicia, and with it disappeared the last remnant of manorialism in Castile. South of the Duero River basin, very few monasteries or convents received territory, and those that did orga-nized their settlers in the usual community of town and land. By the end of the fifteenth century only two monasteries in New Castile—Liébana and Monsalud—still farmed their land with renters, and by the end of the sixteenth century they, too, converted their territory into towns. The monarchs had incorporated all the reconquered land into cities and towns, and ecclesiastical lords in the north were also converting their territories into communities of town and land.

All of this began to change in the mid-fourteenth century. The recon-quest cities and towns degenerated under the pressures of natural disasters, epidemics, and war. New settlements began to appear in the form of squatter villages on the perimeter of the city or town territory. Beginning in the fourteenth century, monarchs acknowledged the villages by ad-dressing royal decrees not only to cities and towns but to "all the cities, towns, and villages of my kingdoms."[12] The face of modern Castile—its place-names, the location of towns, and the network of local trade roads—can be traced back to the growth of these villages within the municipal boundaries of Castilian cities and towns during the fifteenth century.

The coincidence of a new ruling dynasty, the Trastamaras, and a growing number of villages pushing for town autonomy changed the medieval relationship between the monarchy and the municipalities. In the Middle Ages, kings founded independent city-states with vast domains; in the fourteenth century, the Trastamara monarchs created a multitude of small towns owned by hereditary nobles and church institutions. The reconquest kings ruled a society organized for war, with cities protected by fortified walls and frontier towns defended by the military orders; the Trastamara rulers developed a society organized for peace, with autonomous towns engaged in farming and commerce. Kings and subjects drew legal distinc-tions between city, town, and village, and municipal councils lavished almost obsessive attention on preserving municipal boundaries and ac-quiring new prerogatives from the monarch. In this more complex society, kings acted more aggressively in the cities' jurisdiction and, in an un-

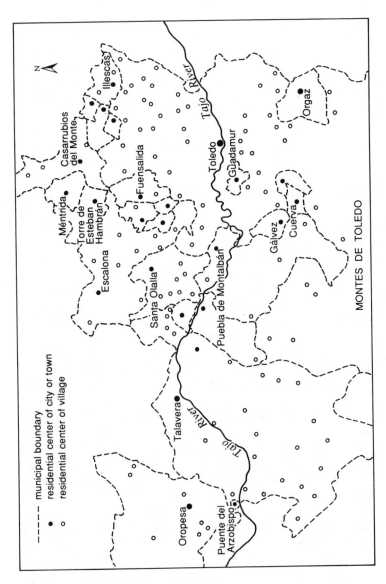

Map 6. Municipal Territories in the Western Tajo River Basin, c. 1500

precedented break with medieval tradition, violated the *fueros* by removing villages from city territory.

The founder of the Trastamara dynasty, Enrique II (1369–79), began his reign with the traditional and expensive process of granting royal towns to his supporters, but instead of making the donations for the lifetime of the recipient, he made them permanent. Enrique's grants—the infamous *mercedes enriqueñas*—permanently diminished both the territorial and the jurisdictional extent of the royal domain. Enrique gave the royal towns of Talavera and Oropesa, west of Toledo, to the political leaders who had brought the city of Toledo to his side during the civil war (see map 6). Castilian kings traditionally gave lifetime jurisdiction over the town of Talavera with its fifty-two villages to female members of the royal family. King Alfonso XI (1312–50) had given Talavera to his queen, María of Portugal, and because the town remained loyal to her and her son, King Pedro (1350–69), throughout the civil war between Pedro and Enrique, Talavera is still called Talavera de la Reina. The city of Toledo, in contrast, abandoned Pedro and switched over to Enrique's side during the civil war, largely through the machinations of the archbishop of Toledo, Gómez Manrique. Enrique II rewarded him on June 25, 1369, by granting the royal town of Talavera in perpetuity to the archbishops of Toledo.

Enrique's victory was also assisted by another important political figure in the city of Toledo, García Alvarez de Toledo. García had been appointed master of Santiago by King Pedro but joined the archbishop and several other leaders of the city in deserting Pedro and throwing their support to the usurper Enrique in 1366. At this point, Enrique gave him Valdecorneja, Piedrahita, and El Barco, between Segovia and Toledo. This grant was the kernel of what would grow to be the vast domains of García's heirs, the dukes of Alba. After the war, however, Enrique was caught between his earlier commitment to appoint one of his first supporters as master of Santiago and his obligations to García. García solved the king's dilemma by agreeing to resign the mastership in exchange for the royal town of Oropesa with its seventeen villages. The new lords, victorious in the civil war, immediately installed their military forces in Talavera and Oropesa. The king had given them more than enough self-interest to shield the city of Toledo from any invasion from Portugal by the relatives of Queen María.[13]

In these grants, the king gave all the royal jurisdiction over the land, the people, and the government to the new lord. In the royal document, Enrique first identified the recipient: "for you and for your heirs and successors who will come after you." The king then defined the geographical extent of the grant: "the town of Oropesa with all its villages and with its municipal territory both populated and to be populated, and with all the castles and fortresses in the town and its municipal territory."

Enrique specifically alienated—legally transferred—the king's lawgiving and law enforcing authority (*mero y mixto imperio*) from the royal domain to García Alvarez "with whatever belongs in any way to the jurisdiction of the said town and its municipal territory, and with the civil and criminal jurisdiction, and appeals, and lawgiving and law enforcing authority, and with high and low jurisdiction, and with the jurisdiction of the said town and its municipal territory." In the same document, the king described the natural resources of Oropesa that he was transferring: "*montes*, grasslands, pastures, meadows, running and still waters." The grant went on to describe the human resources being transferred to the new lord—"all the revenues, taxes, and dues of the said town and its municipal territory"—but reserved for the king any gold and silver mines there might be and the royal taxes, including the sales tax (*alcabala*) and the royal share of the tithe (*tercias*).

Enrique made explicit his intention that García should own the government of Oropesa; within the municipal territory, the king gave him the same authority and powers as the monarch had had when the town was in the royal domain. Within the municipal territory of his town the lord was subject to no higher authority: he had the power to give the laws—*mero imperio*—as well as the power to enforce them—*mixto imperio*. It is important here to note that the Trastamara monarchs transferred sovereignty in perpetuity as a hereditary, private possession to the lords. They did not simply delegate their authority.

Salvador de Moxó has analyzed the innovative language and character of the enabling clause in the donation of Oropesa: "We, the said King Enrique, full knowingly and by our full royal power make this gift to you García Alvarez and order that our heirs and successors never under any circumstances at any time shall dare to revoke or nullify this grant." Not since the reconquest had the monarch permanently alienated a major portion of the royal domain. Castilian kings had instead given the use and usufruct of portions of the royal domain as lifetime grants to members of the royal family, favorites, and loyal servitors. Enrique II, to make sure that his revolutionary intentions on this point were clear to his heirs, included a clause in his will forbidding the reversion of these towns to the royal domain. The disposition of the royal domain in the monarch's will was, of course, the law of the land, and Enrique's decrees and his final will became precedents cited by Castilian monarchs making further grants throughout the Trastamara period.[14]

The royal grants were large enough and lucrative enough to bind the new lords to the Trastamara monarchy. These towns could be immensely dangerous, however, if they ever came into the possession of someone who was not loyal to the new dynasty. Enrique II, the master usurper and regicide, was wary of the potential threat from a lord of Oropesa or Talavera not loyal to the Trastamara dynasty. He therefore made these grants in perpetuity and utilized an existing legal instrument, the perpetual trust (*mayorazgo*), to keep these former royal towns out of the hands of opponents of the Trastamara dynasty. Whoever received a royal town from Enrique II placed it in a perpetual trust of which the king was the sole trustee. The lord of a town in a perpetual trust could not partition, transfer, or mortgage it without the express permission and agreement of the king.

The unequivocal permanence of the early Trastamara grants shocked reformers in the eighteenth century and made Enrique's grants a notorious synonym for royal prodigality.[15] Salvador de Moxó's research tracing the fate of the property alienated from the royal domain lays out the full repercussions of these grants in modern Spain. His work draws a devastating picture of the depressive effect of these perpetual alienations on royal income as late as the nineteenth century. The effects on the citizens of these towns were equally significant and long-lived. Oropesa and its villages lived under the government of García Alvarez de Toledo's heirs until an eighteenth-century title holder was disqualified on the grounds of descent from an illegitimate birth. Nearly all the other *mercedes enriqueñas* persisted until king and Cortes abolished seignorial jurisdiction in 1837.[16]

Enrique's need to reward and empower military supporters did not seem as pressing in later reigns, which were less threatened by succession disputes. Later Trastamara rulers continued to make both lifetime and permanent grants but used a process less expensive to the monarchy. Juan I (1379–90) and Enrique III (1390–1406), rather than give away royal towns, alienated individual villages from the cities and towns. For the cities and towns, the most disturbing Trastamara innovation was the permanence of the monarchy's creation of hereditary seignorial towns out of villages that had previously been subject to the cities. The representatives (*procuradores*) that some cities and towns sent to the national representative assembly, the Cortes, had often demanded and sometimes achieved a reversion of territory and villages that the kings had given away. Trastamara rulers in the fifteenth century sought to stem this possibility by developing legal theories that guaranteed the permanence of their grants. In order to give a town as a grant, the monarchs developed a procedure of transfer and transformation that would become a commonplace in the Castilian countryside.

The new process, however, sowed a new type of conflict in Castile. It bound the citizens and lords of the new towns to the ruling dynasty but created a dynamic tension between the monarch and the older conquest cities. The Trastamara monarchs had to circumvent their own laws in order to continue creating more towns. To remove villages and farmland from older municipalities violated the medieval constitutions (*fueros*) that medieval kings had granted to their newly conquered city states. Equally serious to the Trastamara dynasty's precarious hold on the throne, their own royal grants often antagonized one set of military leaders while sat- isfying others. When Juan II (1406–54) confiscated villages from towns in order to enrich his favorite, Alvaro de Luna, the king's other, slighted supporters rose up in protest. The king himself recognized these grants as extralegal and sought a more elevated and universal principle. In this objective, Juan II and his successors were expertly served by royal attorneys and advisers, who provided them with a legal theory of absolute royal power. Later Trastamara and Habsburg monarchs developed the theory of absolute monarchy into a powerful and supple tool in their royal policy of abrogating the medieval charters in order to create new towns out of subject villages.

The king who severed a village from its previous jurisdiction, incor- porated it into the royal domain, and then granted it a town charter employed the usual description of what was being granted. One of Juan II's early grants to Alvaro de Luna, for example, stated: "I have granted as private property in perpetuity the towns of San Esteban de Gormaz, Ayllón, and Maderuelo and their appurtenant fortress and properties, with their jurisdictions and lawgiving and law enforcing authority." But this time the king employed a new formula asserting his absolute powers under the principles of Roman law to alienate portions of the royal domain: "by our own free will [propio motu], full knowledge [sciencia cierta], and absolute royal power [poderío real absoluto], which I wish to use and do use in this case as king and sovereign lord."

The royal secretariat, led by the redactor Dr. Fernán Díaz de Toledo, introduced in this grant the concept of absolute royal power that had been expounded by a Spaniard educated in Italy, Pedro de Belluga. Belluga studied at the University of Bologna and claimed to be a student of Imola. He returned to his native Valencia and produced a book that attempted to define imperium and jurisdictio.[17] In this work Belluga defined the mero imperio as supreme and absolute and attributed it to the prince as a sign of his universal dominion, superiority, and eminence. Belluga included absolute power in the mero imperio. His thesis simply put, as Luis Sánchez Agesta has explained, was that the king has, as an attribute of his preem- inence and superiority in the fulfillment of his royal functions, an ordinary power to define the law and an extraordinary power to break the law, applicable to specific cases and in exceptional circumstances. The king therefore had the power in exceptional cases to alienate the royal domain permanently despite the laws and agreements he and his predecessors had made to the contrary in the fueros and in spite of broader legal principles.[18]

Juan II used this justification to make enormous grants to many powerful leaders. The king alienated dozens of Castilian villages from their ruling

cities or towns, gave them municipal territory, and granted them to individuals. The king was more or less buying the aristocracy's acquiescence
in his great giveaway to Alvaro. In 1445 soon after granting San Esteban
to Alvaro de Luna, for example, Juan II alienated the village of Fuensalida
from the city of Toledo, granted it a town charter, and gave it to the
appellate judge of the city, Pedro López de Toledo. When the city council
objected, the king confirmed the grant with a document citing his "propio
motu, cierta ciencia, y potestad absoluta." In order to gain the allegiance
of a single individual, the king asserted his absolute power to diminish
the municipal territory that his royal ancestors had granted in the royal
charter to the city of Toledo.[19] As a result of the Trastamara policy of
extracting villages from the royal cities and towns in order to make them
seignorial towns, the conflict between monarchs and cities intensified, not
out of differences in theories of the state but out of competition for the
same villages.

Castilian monarchs had always shared their subjects' vision of the realm
as a society of municipalities (see fig. 4). Municipal governments were
indispensable to the exercise of royal authority in Castile, even the di-
minutive governments of villages becoming seignorial towns. During the
Trastamara period, monarchs dramatically increased the number of seignorial towns, but these were small and isolated compared with the vast
municipal territories typical of royal towns. Furthermore, the kings scattered their grants in order to avoid taking too much from any one city.
When Enrique IV continued his father's policy at an even faster rate, the
new lords began buying, selling, and trading towns to form compact,
contiguous blocs, creating an atmosphere of change at dazzling speed
during the fifteenth century.

But Enrique's half-sister Isabella reversed the family policy, though not
in ways that historians have assumed. King Ferdinand and Queen Isabella
(1474–1504) enjoy a reputation for having centralized Castilian administration and imposed royal authority throughout the realm. They did
make a number of changes in royal municipal policy, but the reforms for
which they are famous changed the administration of the royal household
and court without touching the direct links between monarchy and municipalities. The monarchs reorganized the royal court along functional
rather than territorial lines. In place of the old offices of presiding notaries
to communicate with the municipalities, they created royal councils to
handle such matters as war, finance, military orders, and foreign affairs
and the Council of Aragon and the Council of Castile to deal with their
respective hereditary kingdoms. Monarchs refined and expanded this con-
ciliar government at the royal court for centuries, yet neither the Catholic
Monarchs nor their Habsburg successors created territorial governments
to implement royal policy. The new royal councils, in the name of the

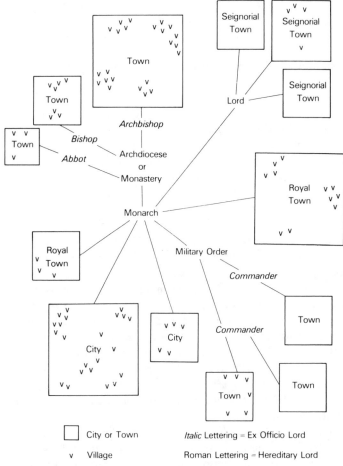

Fig. 4. Organization chart of Castilian administration

monarchs, addressed their documents to "all the cities, towns, and villages of our kingdoms."

Ferdinand and Isabella began their rule in Castile with the same policies as Enrique II and for the same reason: Isabella had to fight a civil war to assure her succession to the throne. In the tradition of her Trastamara ancestors, she had to grant towns to the military aristocracy, though she was less willing than her ancestors to reward any but the most loyal servitors who had supported her cause from the beginning. There were not enough villges and towns to satisfy the conflicting demands of cities, royal relatives, new lords, and unrewarded servitors. Strife among these competitors fueled the civil war (1474–82) that greeted Isabella's accession to the throne. Although the new monarchs won the war by using the old methods, the experience apparently inspired them to find new ways of increasing the number of towns.

Salvador de Moxó estimates that Ferdinand and Isabella gave only 13 towns as grants during her 30 years of rule, in contrast to the 160 granted by their Trastamara ancestors in the previous 105 years. All 13 were given to three of Isabella's most ardent partisans: Andrés Cabrera, his wife Beatriz de Bobadilla, and Gutierre de Cárdenas.[20] All of these grants were made up of villages alienated from the city of Segovia, the diocese of Segovia, and the royal town of Madrid. Each one was raised to the status of town before being transferred to the new lords.

This very small number of grants for a very large and important war is understandable only if we realize that the monarchs had won the war in part by calling upon a new resource, villages subject to towns owned by Isabella's opponents. The inspiration may have come from the example of some towns in the military orders. In 1476, soon after the war started, towns in the military orders whose commanders opposed Isabella defied their lords and allied themselves with Ferdinand and Isabella. The most famous case is the town of Fuenteovejuna, but Zorita de los Canes and several other towns also refused their commanders' orders to arm themselves against Ferdinand and Isabella.[21]

Cities and towns traditionally chose sides in civil wars, just as they did in this war, and throughout the centuries their territorial and demographic resources had given them decisive roles in civil conflict. Technically, villages did not possess the legal standing to act in politics independently of their ruling cities and towns. Nevertheless, the weakness of Isabella's resources during the succession war impelled her to invite villages to do just that. The opportunity arose in 1476, when the Cortes of Madrigal complained that ever since Isabella had begun to reign the kingdom had been unsafe for commerce and production. Isabella ordered the municipalities of Castile to appoint another set of judges and sheriffs to be responsible for patrolling the countryside. In addition to all the reasons historians have adduced for the creation of the hermandad, Isabella's efforts to subvert the jurisdiction of her opponents may also have played an important part in her decision.

The Cortes of Madrigal had requested an hermandad organized by the cities and towns themselves, but what is startling in the queen's instructions for organizing the hermandad is the provision for villages to have their own police powers outside the residential nucleus. The queen decreed that villages of thirty or fewer households were to elect one judge of the hermandad and those with more than thirty were to elect two. These judges were to to be appointed by the councils of the villages themselves and were to patrol the roads and the unpopulated areas around them.[22] Isabella defined any village with fewer than fifty households and no wall as a *despoblado,* and, presumably, it would be subject to the jurisdiction of these new judges of the *hermandad.*[23] This was not what the cities and towns of Cortes had asked for; their petition had specifically requested *hermandades* for the cities and towns to patrol all municipal territories.[24] The monarch appears to have been trying to wean villages away from opposition cities and towns.

Ferdinand and Isabella also tried to weaken the opposition by appealing to individual citizens. To this purpose, they employed still another process for creating new towns: they invited villages in seignorial towns to become royal towns. In 1480 the monarchs issued a proclamation that all persons living in pueblos subject to lords were free to change their lord and become subjects of the royal domain.[25] Most historians have seen this decree as an invitation for people to move from seignorial towns to royal towns, yet this would not have been anything new, because Castilians had always moved from one place to another. Isabella probably intended, rather, to deprive the opposition of income and resources by inviting whole villages to transfer their oath of loyalty and thereby receive charters as royal towns. This interpretation of the decree seems to explain the villages' response: they transferred their loyalty from the marquis of Villena, Juan Pacheco, to Isabella and, indeed, became autonomous royal towns.[26]

Juan Pacheco had been Enrique IV's favorite. He received a shower of grants from the king, including the group of royal towns known collectively as the *marquesado* of Villena, a vast portion of the royal domain that had often been granted to members of the royal family.[27] By the time Enrique gave the *marquesado* to Pacheco, the town of Villena had declined and the administrative center of the *marquesado* had shifted to the fortified town of Alarcón. During the succession war, Juan Pacheco led the party opposed to Isabella, and the battle for Alarcón developed into one of the most prolonged sieges of the war.

Ferdinand and Isabella were determined not to give away any more of the royal domain than was absolutely necessary, so during the siege of Alarcón they turned instead to the citizens of the *marquesado's* villages. There were at the time about thirty-five villages subject to the town of Alarcón. Ferdinand and Isabella offered these villages charters if they would abandon Pacheco and give their support to the monarchs. Between 1477 and 1480 virtually all of the villages did so, each one receiving its own municipal territory and becoming a royal town. The citizens of these new towns referred to themselves as having been "reducidos a la corona real" in the sense of having been returned to the crown.[28] Pacheco remained lord of the town of Alarcón, but Alarcón was left with only three villages after the war—Gil García, Casasimarro, and Madrigueras.[29] Juan Pacheco was still powerful, and Ferdinand and Isabella were able to end the war because they were willing to compromise with him. Once he surrendered Alarcón to them and they accepted his oath of vassalage (March 8, 1480), they began negotiations to agree on what compensation Pacheco would receive for the income he had lost in the *marquesado*. They gave him the royal town of Escalona, a much less lucrative estate than Villena but one to which Pacheco had an old claim.

The civil war proved so costly that Ferdinand and Isabella revived the medieval policy of conquering new territory. As soon as the succession war was ended, Ferdinand and Isabella embarked on the conquest of Granada. There was no other way to increase the number of towns without alienating more of the royal domain. Ferdinand and Isabella's conquest of the Muslim Kingdom of Granada, followed by the Castilian discovery and conquest of the Americas, vastly increased the number of towns in the royal domain. By the time Ferdinand died, in 1516, the royal domain had been more than restored to its medieval extent and wealth. Yet the royal domain of the early sixteenth century was fundamentally distinct not only because royal policy and power in the cities had changed but also because the new territory was inherently different from the vast empty spaces that had been characteristic of the medieval reconquest.

When the Kingdom of Granada was conquered between 1482 and 1492, both conquerors and vanquished came from societies and landscapes vastly changed since the thirteenth-century conquests. Christian Castile and Muslim Granada were thickly populated kingdoms of municipalities.[30] Instead of settling empty land, Castilians who immigrated to Granada were moving into cosmopolitan cities and towns provisioned from farms cultivated all year by sophisticated irrigation systems. Local Muslims who emigrated to North Africa were quickly replaced by immigrants from other parts of Castile.

Much of what the monarchs gained in Granada, they gave as private farmland to the soldiers who had fought in the conquest.[31] The largest cities and towns they kept for themselves, but about twenty commanders received towns, most of them small, many depopulated by epidemic and war. The count of Tendilla, for example, received two villages near Almería, Lixar and Cobdar, and the farmland and houses of two villages belonging to the city of Alhama, Cacín and Fornes, places that he must have known well in 1486, when he was commander of Alhama's fortress during a siege.[32]

In general, immigrants to Granada were not to live under a seignorial regime. Ferdinand and Isabella kept the jurisdiction over the conquered territory almost entirely in the royal domain or in the municipal jurisdictions of cities, which the monarchs attempted to control through corregidores. To modern historians, this policy has seemed a laudable centralization of power; to the settlers, the rule of city councils seemed an intolerable condemnation to an inferior legal and economic status. Immigrants seeking to be first settlers of a town of their own had to travel to the Americas, where Ferdinand and Isabella encouraged the establishment of royal towns and cities on the Caribbean islands. This pattern of conquest and settlement in royal towns became the standard for the Americas, where the monarchs granted hereditary seignorial jurisdiction over towns to only Christopher Columbus and Hernando Cortés.

Ferdinand and Isabella made an equally significant change in the management of the conquered territories. The increased royal participation in city governance that had developed since the fourteenth century made it impossible to follow the medieval policy of giving complete independence to conquered city-states. The monarchs now participated in the most minute decisions of city planning and even asserted control over the establishment of new villages.

A well-documented example of the new pattern of royal control over city territory occurred in the mountains north of the city of Granada. In 1502 the Granada city council proposed to Queen Isabella that the city should colonize a village on the site of the deserted Muslim town of Guadahortuna. A royal decree the previous year requiring Muslims to choose between conversion and expulsion by the beginning of 1502 had left many places in the Kingdom of Granada empty or seriously depopulated. The city's proposal for resettlement was forcefully argued by its representative to the royal court, who claimed that the monarch, by permitting the settlement and entrusting its colonization to the city council, would do much to restore and safeguard the kingdom's trade with New Castile. Although the queen was reluctant to give free rein to the city, she acknowledged that resettlement would help ensure safe highways (see map 4):

Doña Isabel by the grace of God queen of Castile . . . to you Alfonso Enriquez, my royal corregidor of the city of Granada, health and grace. You are informed that on behalf of the city of Granada and its citizens I have been given a petition saying that because Guadahortuna is on a mountain pass totally uninhabited and dangerous for travelers, and because it is where all the travelers from Castile cross on their way to the Kingdom of Granada, there is great need to populate it in order to make this region safe.[33]

The queen approved the venture but made it a royal project. She ordered the corregidor to go to the site with a surveyor, who would divide the land into allotments for up to fifty citizens. Each settler was to receive a lot near the marketplace for house and corral, irrigable land for garden, orchard, and vineyard, and about eleven acres of arable land for grain. She instructed the corregidor to distribute the land to the settlers by lottery and convey to the village council threshing grounds and pastures for draft and other work animals. The queen also ordered him to set aside building sites for the church and rectory, a single citizen's allotment of farm and garden land for the priest, and double that for the maintenance of the church building. The citizens themselves would build the church with funds that the royal governor was to give them.

The queen ordered that the new population of Guadahortuna was to be limited to persons of good character from outside the Kingdom of Granada. As a condition of their citizenship in the new village, the new inhabitants were to reside in their houses with wife and household for ten years before they received their land in fee simple. Once the ten years were over, they would be free to sell, give, donate, exchange, convey, and use it as their private property. Finally, she instructed the corregidor to send messengers to cities and towns throughout Andalusia to announce and publicize the new settlement.[34]

Monarch, corregidor, and citizens understood how the village would govern itself and what its relationship would be to the city. On these subjects no instructions were necessary and none were given. The queen's minute instructions concerning site selection, property distribution, and terms of ownership reveal her determination to guarantee the survival of Guadahortuna as a populated and productive farm village that could supply shelter and provisions to travelers on the royal highway. Guadahortuna's ability to survive would be put to the test by famine and pestilence within five years; thanks to the determined attentions of the city council of Granada and the growing population of Castile, it would succeed.

The monarch founded Guadahortuna, but the city council of Granada possessed the jurisdiction and protected the new settlement, which was located in a wild and dangerous pass of the Sierra Morena mountain range. The city's protective measures included offering a bounty for every wolf pelt brought to the Granada city hall. On February 18, 1513, for example, the city council paid "three reales to Miguel de Moya, citizen of Albolote, for a wolf that he brought to the city hall." The city council minutes for the next three months are punctuated by notations recording that the city paid fifty-four reales for eighteen wolf pelts brought in from the mountains.[35]

Although southern Castile and Andalusia suffered serious crop failures and epidemics in the next five years, Guadahortuna had a large enough population by 1512 to require its own flour mill. The council of Guadahortuna petitioned the Granada city council for permission to construct a mill nearby, in the city commons. The Granada councilmen agreed and chose one of their own parish representatives (jurados), Jorge Mósquera, to travel to Guadahortuna to approve the site selection and assert the city's supervisory powers over the project. They paid Mósquera 100 maravedís for the four days he spent traveling to Guadahortuna and carrying out their instructions.[36] With the city council's continued protection and favor, Guadahortuna became one of the most successful resettlements in the Kingdom of Granada. By 1557 its population had reached 351 households, and the village council attempted to achieve independence from the city of Granada by offering 2,457,000 maravedís to the monarchy for a charter as a town.[37]

The potential for a royal town was almost unlimited. The two royal towns that sent representatives to the Cortes, Valladolid and Madrid, grew from obscure, small settlements in the early fourteenth century to the most populous and powerful municipalities in the kingdom in the sixteenth century. It is estimated, for example, that the city of Toro had a population of about ten thousand taxpayer households in 1591 while the royal town of Valladolid had forty thousand in the same year.[38] Valladolid became a city after Philip II established his permanent capital in the royal town of Madrid. After Valladolid became a city, the Cortes referred to its constituent members as "the cities and town with vote in the Cortes." Madrid remains a town to this day.[39] With such glorious examples of success in the history of royal towns, it is small wonder that villages with the possibility of becoming a royal town were bathed in perennial optimism.

The least advantageous status was that of a village in the jurisdiction of a city or episcopal town; these villages had almost no hope of attaining the status of town, because the council of the ruling city or town competed directly with its own villages for the same land and resources. Cities acted harshly in their efforts to retain their commons for the benefit of their own citizens. Their early generosity in granting to colonists citizenship and the right to clear and plow the commons was withdrawn as the population grew. In the fifteenth century, cities did not need to offer inducements to colonists; squatter settlements popped up whether the city took the initiative or not. During most of the century villages in the jurisdictions of the cities enjoyed a period of benign neglect. The city of Seville throughout the fifteenth century collected royal taxes in its municipal territory according to an old division of tax districts. In the new tax census carried out between 1534 and 1540, officials identified eleven villages that had never paid taxes. The royal treasury did not even know of their existence, though one had grown to more than six hundred households, and another to more than four hundred.[40] But during the sixteenth century's fierce competition for resources, cities employed measures to discipline the villages and restrict their access to the commons. Cities and towns began vigilantly patrolling their municipal territories to display the symbols of city jurisdiction and prevent city prerogatives from lapsing by default. The reversal of attitude can be seen in the city of Toledo, whose council in 1284 had paid forty-five thousand gold *alfonsís* to King Fernando III to buy a large expanse of uncultivated land known thereafter as the Montes de Toledo. During the population decline of the next century some of the villages in the Montes de Toledo disappeared, and then new villages developed during the fifteenth-century population growth. The Toledo city council recognized the new villages but imposed on their inhabitants an oppressive regime that, by the sixteenth century, made them the most poverty-stricken and passively miserable villages in Castile.[41]

After the conquest of the Kingdom of Granada, the city of Granada and the monarchs worked together to reduce the privileges and rights of the villages in the city's municipal territory. In this as in other aspects of their municipal policy, Ferdinand and Isabella reversed some of the innovations developed by their Trastamara ancestors, while restoring older traditions of the medieval reconquest. Constrained by an exhausted treasury and wary of powerful municipalities in the hands of potentially traitorous subjects, the monarchs placed most Muslim towns in the Kingdom of Granada in the royal domain or under the jurisdiction of a few cities.[42] Only Granada, the one Muslim city that surrendered to the Catholic Monarchs without a fight, received an extensive municipal territory and the right to vote in the Cortes. After the Revolt of the Alpujarras in 1501, Ferdinand and Isabella reduced rebellious Muslim towns in the Kingdom of Granada to the status of villages and placed several other Andalusian towns under the jurisdiction of royal corregidores. By 1513, with the city of Granada's Christian population growing and replacing the population losses caused by conquest, revolt, and epidemic, the city council was determined to achieve fuller power over the villages in the municipal territory, at the expense of village citizens and to the profit of city councilmen.

In early 1513 the Granada city council received King Ferdinand's summons for the Cortes to meet in Valladolid. The council took advantage of this opportunity to pressure the king and court for greater city control over royal tax collection in the whole Kingdom of Granada. The council drew up a memorandum of all the concessions (*capítulos*) the representatives were to negotiate at court. Most of these were requests for more *propios* and for the privilege of having royal taxes in western Andalusia collected by the Granada city council rather than Seville or Cordoba. To gain these privileges, the city council was prepared to sacrifice the grazing and marketing rights of its own villages.[43]

The council elected two of its members, the commander Diego de Padilla and the *jurado* Domingo Pérez, as its representatives to the Cortes and, on April 7, ordered Padilla, another member of the council, and the royal corregidor to redraft the memorandum and add to it any other items brought to their attention. On April 26 the council formally gave its power of attorney to its representatives, and after several more weeks of preparation and travel, the representatives arrived in Valladolid in the last week of May. Ten days later, on June 6, they sent their first letter back to the city council reporting on their activities. In their letter the representatives quickly passed over the ceremonial highlight of a meeting of the Cortes, the formal opening in which the individual representatives pledged the oath of homage to the king. They well understood that the negotiations behind the scenes were the real business at hand. They reported that on their first day in Valladolid they rose early to be present at the king's morning prayers. Afterwards, they found that a great number of people were waiting to speak with the king because matters were already behind schedule. But the king waved everyone else aside and said: "Let those from Granada come forward."

After the king recognized them and they kissed his hands, Padilla acted as spokesman, telling the king that the city of Granada had sent them to visit him and express their thanks to the Lord for the king's restored health. They told the king that the city had been deeply pained by the illness and pain the king had suffered, which was only reasonable because the city of Granada was the king's own victory and creation. In addition, the city requested from his highness a few things that would be in his service and to the common good of the city itself. They asked his highness to order that the requests be examined and that they be amended and issued as might best benefit his service. The king responded, "I am gratified by your visit and I truly believe that you were distressed by my illness. But, thanks to God, I am well now." Padilla continued:

We were diligent in making this visit because we found out that other cities had done so, especially Seville and Cordoba from Andalusia, whose representatives we had run into. His highness appreciated it very much and in regard to the memorandum responded: "Explain everything to the Lic. [Francisco] Zapata and to Dr. [Lorenzo Galíndez de] Carvajal and to secretary [Lope] Conchillos." Since returning from visiting the king, we have had to visit them and explain all the terms and change everything. His highness and all these gentlemen have treated us with good will and a desire to expedite our affairs, and likewise we have given the city's letters to these gentlemen and to [royal secretary] Juan Velázquez, who also has treated us well. We believe that they will soon look at the terms and expedite them. We continue to exercise all the diligence and attention possible in everything.

After looking over the terms with the king, these gentlemen sent us on to the council, and in the session of last Friday they read the terms but postponed their response to us until today, Monday. We don't know how they will respond to us.

In the matters concerning Carvajal and Cobos we have negotiated a compromise which [Padilla] will explain in a letter he is writing to the marquis [of Mondéjar, count of Tendilla] because this seems a convenient way.

The hidden messages in this letter—the bribes of Carvajal and Cobos—became explicit in the Granada city council's discussion of the letter on June 21. Carvajal would receive tanneries on property belonging to the city. The councilmen were unanimous in their approval of this favor, and the city's appellate judge, conforming to the vote, wrote to instruct Padilla and Pérez to go ahead with the agreement with Carvajal.

The deal with Francisco de los Cobos turned out to be much more difficult for the councilmen to agree on. The count of Tendilla spoke first. He was one of the architects of the agreement negotiated by the representatives, and he defended it by saying that the citizens of Granada would not be harmed in any way if Cobos were given exclusive pasture rights in the Campo de Dalías. Juan de Gamboa argued that Cobos should have the privilege because he had served the city well and continued to do so. Juan Alvarez objected that the king had given the Campo de Dalías to the city as common lands of the *propios*, which should not be set aside for the use of just one person. If Cobos had served well, then the king should do him a favor elsewhere. The lawyer Dr. de la Torre reasoned that this would be a good deal if those who had arranged it believed there was no other way to get their terms approved by the king, but if they believed that the king would be fair to the city without this—and they should try to discover his intentions—then they should renegotiate. As the discussion continued, the *alcalde mayor* concluded that opinion was too divided for a resolution and that he and the chief constable would try to renegotiate the compromise.

Meanwhile, the city's royal corregidor, Gutierre Gómez de Fuensalida, wrote from Valladolid on June 22 urging the council to accept the compromise with Cobos. He argued that Cobos was in a position to do a great deal for the city and was willing to expedite its matters. But the compromise had to be accepted by the city, both because it had been negotiated by Granada's duly empowered representatives and because the right to decide the fate of the Campo de Dalías actually resided with the king, who might give it to Cobos, without any benefit accruing to the city.

The representatives to the Cortes, too, were alert to the trouble brewing over the Cobos privilege and wrote to the city council the same day, explaining that they had done some research into the history of the city's rights in the Campo de Dalías. They asserted that they had asked Fernando de Valor and other new Christians about customs during the period of the Muslim kings and found that in times of peace the officials in the Campo de Dalías had taken one out of every so many head of stock that had entered into the Campo, and in times of revolt they had taken a larger percentage. Thus, they argued, the Campo de Dalías had not been a free pasture historically. The representatives then reminded the council of what would happen if matters reached the point of litigation, especially when one of the parties was in a position to be of more value to the city in other ways than the privilege itself was worth. It was not worth the risk, and certainly not when, as it appeared, the king might give the Campo de Dalías to Cobos anyway. When the council discussed the latest round of letters on June 28, the disagreements were as deep as before and the arguments sharper. In the end, the royal appellate judge resolved the deadlock by instructing the representatives to proceed with the compromise, although two *jurados* insisted on lodging formal written protests against this whittling away of the city's common pasture.

Meanwhile, back at the royal court the representatives were proceeding with their negotiations. By July 7 the king had written a letter authorizing the disposition of the city's terms. When the representatives returned to Granada in late August, they formally presented to the council this letter of authorization and twenty-eight royal decrees in which the king ceded privileges, jurisdiction, and income to the city of Granada. Francisco de los Cobos received the Campo de Dalías pasture rights as a heritable property, and the rural residents of Granada's municipal territory lost the free pasturage that had been the one advantage of their citizenship in the city's villages.

Ferdinand and Isabella's royal ancestors had ruled over the first Castilian expansion into the Atlantic, granting municipal charters to cities and towns in the conquered Canary Islands.[44] The Catholic Monarchs continued this same pattern in the Americas, though their admiral Christopher Columbus still hoped to find the great cities of Asia with every new voyage. The monarchs' dependence on municipal governments for local administration, the Castilian urge to live in municipalities, and the implicit assumption of citizenship shaped both the daily lives of settlers and the grandiose actions of discoverers and conquistadores.

In June 1497 Christopher Columbus was in Seville preparing his third voyage to the Americas. He had already established settlements there, and now he petitioned the king and queen for authority to take the steps he considered necessary to ensure the success of his foundations. We do not know how many Europeans were living in the Indies at this time. Columbus founded the settlement of La Navidad on the island of Hispaniola at the end of his first voyage, but all thirty-eight or thirty-nine crewmen who stayed there perished before Columbus returned in 1493. More than twelve hundred people embarked on this second voyage, but they suffered a very high mortality rate (perhaps as high as 50 percent) owing to disease and warfare, and many ships deserted to return to Spain before the admiral. Columbus established a new settlement, La Isabella, on Hispaniola as a trading post, planted wheat, grapevines, vegetables, and sugar cane, and left his brother Bartholomew as his governor (*adelantado*), with jurisdiction over the entire island.

Back in Spain, Columbus submitted to the monarchs detailed lists of what would be needed to make La Isabella a successful factory (fortified trading station) and received authority to take back enough people to bring the population of La Isabella up to 330. These were to include 40 military officers, 100 enlisted men, 30 seamen, 30 ship's apprentices, 20 gold miners, 50 farmers and 10 vegetable gardeners, 20 masters of all trades, and 30 women. All of these emigrants, as well as the settlers already in La Isabella, were to be his salaried employees, buying their supplies and provisions from his factors.[45] He was to take wheat, barley, plows, spades, mining and construction implements, mill stones, and draft animals, as well as enough flour, biscuit, dried beans, and other provisions to last until the first crop came in and a flour mill could be built.[46] The disillusioned reports of the returnees from the second voyage burst the euphoria in which that voyage had been organized, however, and Columbus had so much trouble finding emigrants for the third voyage in 1497 that he asked and received permission to recruit convicts.

A month later, in July 1497, the monarchs—who were in frequent contact with Hispaniola—granted the petitions of the Spanish settlers themselves, whose view of what the new towns should be was purely Castilian:

On behalf of some persons who have become citizens on the island of Hispaniola and of others who want to establish citizenship there, we have been asked to order that they be given and allocated land on the said island on which they could sow grain and other seeds and plant vegetable gardens, cotton and flax fields, grapevines, trees, sugarcane, and other plants, and build and construct houses, flour mills and sugar mills, and other structures beneficial and necessary for their living.[47]

Ferdinand and Isabella ordered Columbus to survey the land and allot farms, house lots, and garden plots to those who had become citizens of Hispaniola and to those who wanted to emigrate to become citizens. The settlers had to clear, plow, and plant their land and would receive full title to it after four years of occupancy. The citizens could claim as private property only their enclosed fields; open range was to remain commons.

The royal decrees for the settlement of Hispaniola did not provide any guidelines for the governance of the colony. Monarchs and colonists took for granted that the new settlement would be a typical Castilian municipality. They did not realize until later that Columbus and his brothers had no experience with the organizing principle of Castilian society. The returnees' complaints attributed the Columbus brothers' incomprehension to their being foreigners.[48] Christopher Columbus lived in Castile for seven years while enlisting royal support for the first voyage, but he had little opportunity to observe the functioning of Castilian citizenship and municipal government. He spent most of that time and the years between the second and third voyages as a houseguest in Franciscan monasteries and in the rectory of Andrés Bernáldez (the chronicler of the epidemics around Seville), as a member of the Genoese business community, and as a supplicant in noble and royal courts.[49] When Columbus reached

Hispaniola on the third voyage, he found that La Isabella had been abandoned because it was insalubrious and inconvenient. Bartholomew had
established a new city, Santo Domingo (the present capital of the Do-
minican Republic), but most of the settlers had rebelled against the governor's rule and established a third settlement inland. Columbus recognized
the rebels' new settlement, but his efforts to quell the discontent were
unsuccessful, and he and his brothers were arrested and returned to Spain
on charges of exceeding their authority. Columbus eventually won ex-
oneration of these charges and regained his authority on the high seas
and in ports when he was reinvested with the title and income of Admiral
of the Ocean Sea, but the monarchs never restored him to the offices of
viceroy and captain general, which would have given him governing
authority on land.[50]

Only twenty-five years after Columbus's first voyage, the royal governor
Diego Velázquez had established seven Spanish cities and towns on the
island of Cuba; Bernal Díaz del Castillo, in his few days of travel along
the south coast of Cuba, passed through three of these Spanish towns.
And Cuba was not unusual. By the time Cortés and his five hundred men
embarked for Mexico, Spaniards had founded twenty-seven European
towns on the four major Caribbean islands.[51]

The degree to which municipal society and citizenship dominated the
mentality of even the most rebellious Castilian can be seen in the actions
of the Cortés expedition. Historians now recognize that the expedition's
decision to march on Mexico City, to confront the emperor Moctezuma,
was an act of rebellion against the royal governor in Cuba.[52] The rebels
rejected the governor's instructions for the expedition, set up their own
government—the town of Veracruz—and appealed directly to the Emperor
Charles V for recognition. They did not organize themselves into a county,
a kingdom, or an empire but created the same sort of municipal government
they knew as citizens of Castilian towns. They took it for granted that
the king would want his royal dominions on the American continent to
be organized into municipalities.

The conquistadores saw themselves as urban people, citizens and officers
of cities and towns. Bernal Díaz del Castillo was a veteran of nineteen
battles in the conquest of Mexico and Guatemala by the time he wrote
his *True History of the Conquest of New Spain*, and he began the history
by describing himself as a founding citizen and councilman of the city of
Santiago de Guatemala. The leader of the expedition, Hernando Cortés,
was a well-educated and experienced official. He had apprenticed with a
royal notary, so he knew the formularies of Castilian civic documents,
though he apparently left without taking the examination to be licensed.
In the Americas he first worked as secretary to the royal governor of Cuba.

Once in Cuba, he married a cousin of the governor and resigned his position as a royal official in order to accept the post of judge (*alcalde*) of the town of Santiago de Bayamo—the office he held when the governor appointed him to lead the expedition.

The municipal character of the Cortés expedition leaps out from the pages of chronicles, letters, and reports written by the conquistadores themselves. The Cortés expedition left Havana on February 10, 1519. In five months the men explored the coast of Yucatán, fought some battles with hostile Indian towns, and formed alliances with others. On the mainland Spaniards climbed their first volcano. Here, in a familiar landscape of nucleated farm towns with hereditary lords (caciques) and masonry buildings, they encountered for the first time in the Americas a society similar to their own: an emperor, Moctezuma, in the Aztec capital city of Tenochtitlán ruling over a vast empire of subject towns that rendered tribute. The Spaniards exchanged diplomatic messages with Moctezuma's representatives while persuading thirty towns already in rebellion against Moctezuma to transfer their allegiance from the Aztec emperor to the Holy Roman Emperor, Charles V.[53]

When Cortés began to entertain thoughts of traveling to the Aztec capital, controversy developed among the Spaniards. Those who were allies of the governor, Diego Velázquez, wanted to return to Cuba, arguing that they had accomplished the objectives of the expedition. They revealed that the governor had not requested authorization from Spain for the expedition to settle, as he had advertised in Cuba, and that his written instructions to Cortés authorized the expedition only to explore and trade.[54] Not only did the Spaniards lack the supplies and people to settle, they did not have the possibility of future support from Cuba. Cortés appeared to go along with this argument and gave the order to embark.

But secretly Cortés and his allies had decided to resist any move to abandon the mainland. During the night, several leaders came to solicit Bernal's vote, pointing out the futility and waste of expeditions that came to trade and explore without settling:

Do you think it is a good thing, sir, that Hernando Cortés has brought us here in this way, deceiving all of us by having advertised in Cuba that he was coming to settle, when now we find out that he carries no power to do so but only to trade, and they want us to go back to Santiago de Cuba with all the gold that has been acquired. We will all be left penniless, and Diego Velázquez will end up with the gold as before. Remember, sir, that you have come on three expeditions at your own expense with the hope of settling, going into debt, risking your life, and being wounded time and again. Tell us, sir, why should we go back to Cuba when there are enough of us to settle this land in the name of his majesty?[55]

But to settle in defiance of the governor's instructions would make them outlaws. The solution they proposed was to form a council and petition the king directly for recognition, bypassing the governor. If they, in a town meeting, elected Cortés as their military commander instead of accepting him as the governor's appointed officer, "Hernando Cortés could do it in the king's name and then send the news directly to the king our lord in Castile. And be sure, sir, to cast your vote, so that all of us elect him unanimously as captain, because it will be to the service of God and the king our lord."[56]

The next day, they demanded that Cortés found a town, complaining that it had been wrong to bring them under false pretenses, that in Cuba he had announced that he was going to settle and instead he had come to trade, and they demanded for the sake of God and the king that he should settle immediately and not do anything else.[57] They added other good arguments, pointing out that the natives would not let them land in peace again, that other soldiers would come from the islands to help them if the land were settled by Spaniards, and that Diego Velázquez had knowingly sent them on a fool's errand by advertising that he had authority from the king to settle, when the contrary was true. Finally, they said, "they wanted to settle, and whoever did not want to could go back to Cuba."[58]

Cortés agreed after a great show of "You beg me to do what I want," as the Spanish saying goes, and on the condition that they would elect him appellate judge and captain general and agree to give him one-fifth of all the gold they might get, after setting aside the royal fifth. As harsh as this last condition was, they agreed in order to get their town and drew up a formal contract before a royal notary named Diego de Godoy.[59]

In a letter to the king, they explained this rebellious act in the most loyal and traditional terms:

It seemed to all of us better that a town with a court of justice be founded and inhabited in your royal highnesses' name so that in this land also you might have sovereignty as you have in your other kingdoms and dominions. For once the land has been settled by Spaniards, in addition to increasing your royal highnesses' dominions and revenues, you may be so gracious as to grant favors to us and to the settlers who come in future.[60]

Cortés then proceeded to found a town. He appointed the usual municipal officials—two judges, a sheriff, a treasurer, an accountant, and councilmen—as well as military officers (because they were also a military expedition), erected the symbols of jurisdiction (a stake and a gallows), and named the town Veracruz because they had disembarked on Good Friday (April 22, 1519). The founding citizens began improvising homes while they explored the surrounding areas and formed alliances with some Indian towns.[61]

Having carried out an act of rebellion, they contrived to lend it legitimacy. The town council convened and demanded that Cortés show them the written instructions in which Governor Velázquez had authorized him to come to the mainland. The council found that the governor's appointment of Cortés "no longer had any authority, and as it had expired, he could no longer exercise the office of captain or appellate judge."[62] The council, now the only legitimate Spanish authority on the mainland, appointed Cortés as the town's captain and interim appellate judge and composed a letter to the emperor explaining what they had done:

It seemed to us, most excellent princes, that in order to preserve peace and concord amongst ourselves and to govern ourselves well, it was necessary to elect someone for your royal service who might preside in the aforementioned town in the name of your majesties as appellate judge and captain and leader . . . and seeing that no one could carry out such responsibility better than the same Hernando Cortés . . . we appointed him in the name of your royal highnesses as captain and interim appellate judge and received from him the customary oath in the service of your majesties, and we accepted him in our town meeting and council as interim appellate judge and captain in your royal name.[63]

The council entrusted this letter to the two municipal judges, Alonso Hernández Puertocarrero and Francisco de Montejo, who took ship on July 26, 1519, and (without reporting to the governor) arrived at the royal court in Valladolid in April 1520. Meanwhile, Cortés and the expedition removed all the equipment, fittings, and provisions from the rest of the ships and grounded them. They moved the site of the town to a more salubrious location on level ground half a league from the Indian town of Guiauitzlan and began building the residential nucleus:

Everyone from Cortés, who was the first to start digging out dirt and stones for laying the foundations, down to every captain and soldier set to it and worked to finish the town and fortress quickly, some working on the foundations, others on building walls, others bringing water, some working in the lime pits and in making bricks and tiles, others looking for food, or sawing lumber, the blacksmiths at their anvil, because we had two blacksmiths, and in this way we worked on it without stopping from the greatest to the least, along with the Indians who helped us until the church and houses were roofed and the palisade built.[64]

As soon as their home base of Veracruz was secure, they packed up their gear and, with their Indian allies, moved inland.

Thus did Hernando Cortés, captain general by authority of the town council, lead Bernal Díaz del Castillo and his fellow founding citizens of the town of Veracruz on the march to Mexico. In the next fifteen years Cortés, from his base in Mexico City, sent out conquering expeditions with instructions to establish fifteen Spanish cities and towns in central Mexico. By 1580 his followers and successors would establish and populate sixty more Spanish municipalities on the American mainland.[65]

Back in Spain, the Habsburg monarchy embarked on the now-celebrated reorganization of the central government and created viceroyalties, governorships, and appellate courts for the Americas. At the same time, the monarchy issued instructions ensuring that local government in Spanish America would replicate the municipalities of Castile. The royal instructions, issued in 1521 for exploration of Florida and elaborated throughout the sixteenth century, ordered that the first duty of all future explorers should be "to name all the cities, towns, and villages that may be found and that exist or may be established on the continent" and then to distribute house lots, set aside land for the marketplace, church, public services and buildings, elect town councilmen for one-year terms, and distribute land for plowfields.[66] In the Spanish expansion of the fifteenth and sixteenth centuries, rebel and monarch, Trastamara and Habsburg, extended the Castilian municipal government to new subjects and new lands. The Castilian monarchy became an empire by increasing the number of towns.

Chapter 4

The Habsburg Sale of Jurisdiction

The Process of Sale

Charles V inherited from Ferdinand and Isabella all the absolute powers necessary to convert the royal domain into a liquid asset. For Charles, however, the royal domain could not provide enough cash, in part because he became involved in foreign wars, which required sending money abroad in unprecedented amounts, and in part because, as a result of the Trastamara policies, much of the royal domain in New Castile had been transferred to other lords. Charles was determined not to reduce the royal domain further. In the several wills he attested, he instructed his son Philip to be diligent in conserving the royal domain and to follow the example that Charles and his grandparents, Ferdinand and Isabella, had set in not selling, alienating, or encumbering any of the cities, towns, subjects, jurisdictions, income, taxes, or perquisites of their kingdom.[1] Charles diminished instead the domain of the church.

The pope was the ultimate owner of church land and jurisdiction, which he delegated to the lords for life when he appointed them to their ecclesiastical offices. Charles's Trastamara ancestors, however, set a precedent for changing this situation. The monarchy had been receiving the masters' income from the military orders since the end of the fifteenth century, because Juan II and Enrique IV, with the consent of the pope, gradually incorporated the masterships of the orders into the royal family. The military and clerical character of the office apparently disqualified Isabella from holding it, so Ferdinand became master, and Charles inherited the masterships and their rich incomes after Ferdinand's death in 1516. Apart from the masters' income, the monarchy received only the royal sales tax and the royal share of the tithe from church territory. Towns and villages in the church domain paid their seignorial annuities to their ecclesiastical lords—commanders of the military orders, archbishops and bishops, and abbots of monasteries.

These ecclesiastical towns and villages became both a temptation and an irritant as Charles plunged into religious wars in Europe and North Africa. Why should the church not assist the monarch who was sacrificing so much to defend Christianity? Charles thought it should. He proposed that the pope give the Castilian monarchy title to church property in Spain, which Charles could then sell. The pope was understandably reluctant. Charles, by arguing that the sales were necessary in order to carry out the emperor's obligation to defend the faith, provided the papacy with a rationale for the property transfer. Still, tradition prohibited the alienation of property once it had entered the possession of the church, and Charles had to wring the concession from Pope Clement VII by applying pressure during a period of catastrophic conditions in Rome.

Charles's Spanish ambassadors to the papacy, Luis del Prado and Miguel Mayo, negotiated with Clement for months to extract a favorable agreement. Prado and Mayo had powerful leverage in their negotiations—the military force of Charles's armies, which were occupying Italy during the same months. Clement knew firsthand the consequences if Charles could not pay his bills, because in 1527 the pope had been a witness and near-victim of the sack of Rome by unpaid imperial troops. Though Clement opposed Charles's Italian policy, imperial military finance became urgent to the church in 1529 when the Turks laid siege to Vienna. As its contribution to the war effort, the church would transfer title to some of the assets of the military orders, with the understanding that the king would then sell these properties and use the proceeds to pay expenses of religious wars. On September 28 Pope Clement issued a bull permitting Charles to transfer from the military orders to the Castilian royal domain property yielding up to forty thousand ducados of annual income. A few days later, on October 12, Clement authorized Charles to transfer from the military orders property yielding an additional forty thousand ducados of annual income and to take an advance of five thousand ducados against future income from the masters' income in Andalusia.[2]

The pope entrusted supervision of the transfer in Castile to the archbishop of Santiago and the bishop of Calabria. During the negotiations leading up to the papal bull, these prelates developed procedures to identify and appraise the jurisdictions of the military orders. Charles, too, began preparations before the bull was issued. Beginning in 1528, royal officials fanned out with their notaries and, assisted by local officials, made a summary of data for each town and village. They sent the summaries to the royal court, where accountants checked and corrected the computations. Clement had given permission to transfer the tithes and first fruits paid to the military orders, and the bishops instructed appraisers to calculate this amount by taking an average of the previous five years' tithe. The accountants and secretaries continued to correct and touch up the summaries in order to bring this average up to date at the time of transfer. On March 5, 1529, just before departing Spain, Charles drew up a power of attorney in favor of his wife, Empress Isabella, so that she could sell places and subjects during his absence.[3]

Very soon Charles found it necessary to make use of the papal bull. He assigned his income as master to his German bankers as security for loans, hoping to profit from a campaign against the Muslims in North Africa, but his triumph at Tunis in 1535 was a Pyrrhic victory from which he recouped none of the expense. His rival, the king of France, invaded the Duchy of Savoy and entered Turin in April 1536. Charles wrote from Italy begging his wife to find some way to send him four hundred thousand ducados by selling places from the military orders if necessary. The empress proceeded to sell jurisdictions from the military orders to the full amount allowed by the papacy.

The sales process involved every level of Castilian administration from the king down to the village council. In contrast to the transfer of a royal town to a lord or of a seignorial town from one lord to another (which was done by a straightforward deed of sale), the transfer of an ecclesiastical town to a seignorial jurisdiction required extraordinary procedures and safeguards. Potential buyers needed legal documents, representative objects, and public rituals assuring the legality and correctness of the title deeds the monarch was selling. Each village or town first had to be transferred to the royal domain by the military order's procurator. The royal treasury appraised the town and negotiated the sale price with the buyer, then passed the papers to every relevant branch of the royal government at court, and finally to the king for his signature on the deed of sale. All of these documents were then taken to the affected town by a royal official commissioned as the royal judge for the purpose. The commissioned judge transferred the town to the royal domain in a ceremony witnessed and accepted by the citizens of the town itself. These ceremonies would become a familiar feature of small-town Castile during the Habsburg centuries, visible and tactile evidence of the monarchy's financial bankruptcies.

Among the first and largest transactions was the dismemberment of the towns of Almoguera and Fuentenovilla from the Order of Calatrava. The marquis of Mondéjar, Luis de Mendoza, offered to buy these jurisdictions in 1536. During the following year royal accountants appraised the size of the two towns, including Almoguera's five villages, at 884 3/4 households and the Order of Calatrava's annual income, which the councils paid in tithes, annuities, and judicial fines and fees, at 102,476 maravedís.[4] On January 18, 1538, the government agreed to sell the jurisdictions to the marquis for forty-seven thousand ducados. The bishop of Badajoz signed the warrant for dismemberment and transferred the towns to the royal commissioned judge Rodrigo Maldonado, who proceeded to Almoguera and Fuentenovilla and took possession in the name of the king.

On June 20 Charles, still in France, signed the royal deed of sale, in August the royal warrant for transfer was drawn up and signed in Valladolid, and on October 12, 1538, the marquis's agents took possession of Almoguera from Rodrigo Maldonado. In true Castilian fashion, the marquis's agents immediately proceeded to transfer ownership of the land to the municipal councils; the annuities and other sums the councils had traditionally paid to the Order of Calatrava were henceforth paid as seignorial annuities to the marquis of Mondéjar.[5]

    Almoguera adjoined the marquis's titular estate of Mondéjar, and the three towns of Mondéjar, Almoguera, and Fuentenovilla together could have formed one of the largest seignorial estates in Castile (see map 7). But a large estate under a single management—a *latifundium*—would have been out of character for Castile. During the next two years

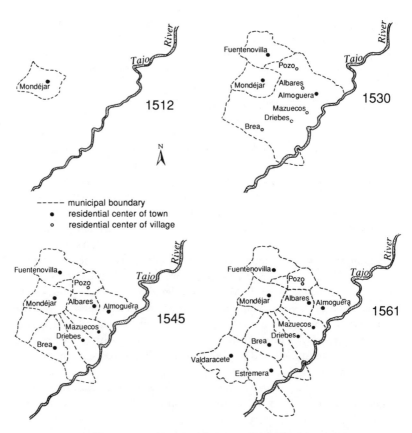

Map 7. The Evolution of Purchases by the Count of Tendilla, His Son (Marquis of Mondéjar), and His Grandson (Francisco de Mendoza), 1512, 1530, 1545, and 1561

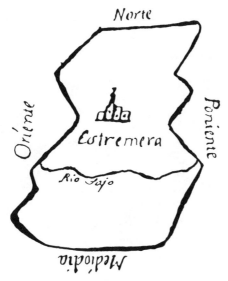

Fig. 5. Estremera, 1752. From the Catastro del
Marqués de la Ensenada, Archivo Histórico
Provincial, Toledo, lib. 264.

the marquis himself followed the tradition of Castilian lords and his own
ancestors by distributing that ownership and responsibility as widely as
possible: he granted township to Almoguera's villages—Albares, Mazuecos, El Pozo, and Drieves—and recognized the township claimed by Brea.
By 1542 the two towns and five villages had become seven towns, each
with its own municipal territory managed by its own town council (see
map 8). The marquis assigned appellate jurisdiction over his new towns
to his appellate judge in the town of Mondéjar, Juan Gutiérrez de Celada.
The appellate judge divided this judicial territory into two administrative
sections, because Mondéjar and Almoguera historically had operated under
different law codes. The new lord's income remained the same as that
previously received by the Order of Calatrava, and the seven towns continued to share each other's pastures and *monte* as commons.[6] This traditional Trastamara process of fission—the fragmentation of municipal
territory and prerogatives—would continue as an integral feature of the
Habsburg sale of jurisdictions.

Charles continued the sales throughout his reign, assigning the task to
his sister after the empress died and later to his son Prince Philip. Charles
admitted in his wills that he had accumulated enormous debts "because
of the great expenses and costs of the wars that we have not been able to
avoid" and suggested two ways Philip could clear the royal debts. First,

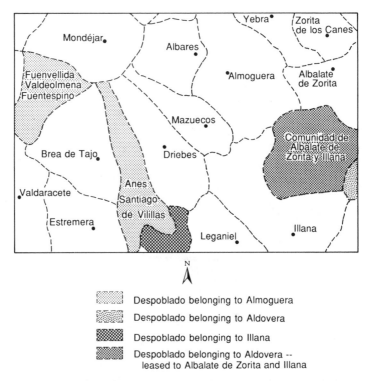

Despoblado belonging to Almoguera

Despoblado belonging to Aldovera

Despoblado belonging to Illana

Despoblado belonging to Aldovera --
leased to Albalate de Zorita and Illana

Map 8. Detail of the Mendoza Family Purchases and Their *Despoblados*

he ordered Philip to redeem the annuities the treasury was committed to
paying its creditors. The life annuities (*juros de por vida*) were to be paid
until the annuitant died, then not renewed. Philip was to redeem the
fixed annuities (*juros de alquitar*) by repaying the principal. Charles pointed
to a source of money for raising that principal: he reminded Philip that
Popes Leo X and Adrian VI had given him license to "incorporate into
our crown of Castile and León the three masterships of Santiago, Calatrava, and Alcántara, and accordingly they were incorporated in perpetuity." He then told Philip to use the income of the masterships (*mesas
maestrales*) for the next nine years to pay the back wages and other debts
that Charles owed. Finally, Charles acknowledged that some grandees and
caballeros had been allowed to collect royal taxes, tithes, and dues as
compensation for what the monarchy owed them. Charles claimed that
this was not a permanent transfer of royal domain or prerogative and
instructed Philip to reclaim those collections, but Philip's mounting war
expenses during the rest of the sixteenth century made this impossible.
Philip II continued the sales begun by his father and negotiated a further

concession of forty thousand ducados from Pius V, granted in a bull of March 14, 1569, which allowed the king to transfer more ecclesiastical properties. The pope also agreed that the Spanish monarch, rather than prelates, would administer these transfers. The royal treasury profited, at least in the short term, because the sales process itself was economical.[7] The sale expenses were largely bureaucratic—the salaries of the royal officials drawing up the legal documents, negotiating the sale terms, appraising the population and assets of the town to be transferred, and traveling to the town to perform the appropriate ceremonies of transfer and retransfer—but minor, and the monarchs usually managed to force the buyers to pay the salaries at the last minute.

For the citizens of the affected towns—places that were already towns and were now being sold to a lord—the royal sales of the military orders could change their legal jurisdiction in a matter of days, without any initiative from the townspeople or their council. Rich, famous, and powerful people came from the capital or from Seville to carry out their assigned tasks and depart, leaving the town as thoroughly immersed in its own affairs as before. Throughout the kingdom the ceremony of transfer followed the same pattern, and it became a practiced ritual in the last half of the sixteenth century. Though the annual number of sales throughout Castile was small—an average of half a dozen per year—the impact could be intense in a region to which the royal treasury turned its attention in any given sale campaign. In Andalusia the monarchy transferred five towns from the Order of Santiago in one year alone, 1573, in order to sell them to the city of Seville.[8] This may have been the inspiration for private buyers to submit bids for another two towns near Seville, Rianzuela and Carrión de los Ajos, in the following year, when the royal treasury faced bankruptcy.

During one week in November 1575 the citizens of Carrión de los Ajos witnessed rituals that transformed the town from an ecclesiastical to a royal and finally a seignorial town. They understood that King Philip II was selling Carrión to help pay his expenses in the religious wars of Europe. The citizens of Carrión de los Ajos did not initiate these procedures, nor did they participate in the preceding months of bureaucratic paperwork at the royal court in Madrid, but they had known for a year that these events would take place, and they were acquainted with the royal officials who now arrived to implement the royal policy. Royal notaries recorded every step of the transfer of Carrión de los Ajos from the military Order of Calatrava to an individual lord. Their records provide a detailed insight into the public rituals and legal procedures involved in the Habsburg sale of towns.

In 1574 Philip II accepted a bid for the town of Carrión de los Ajos in the Order of Calatrava's commandery near Seville.[9] The family of the purchaser, Gonzalo de Céspedes, had made a fortune in the Indies trade, his brother, Juan de Céspedes, was commander of the royal fortresses and shipyards of Seville, and Gonzalo himself was a citizen and councilman of the city of Seville.[10] Gonzalo's offer to buy Carrión de los Ajos served his family's interests, for the investment would supply him with a stable income and endow him with the hereditary jurisdictional powers of a lord. For the king, Gonzalo's bid came at one of the low points of his reign. Continuing revolt in the Netherlands, increasing attacks by Muslim pirates in the Mediterranean, and declining royal revenues from the Americas combined to make Philip's financial condition desperate. The king was selling his capital assets as master of the Order of Calatrava, including the town of Carrión de los Ajos (see map 9).

As unfavorable as Philip's position was, the procedures for selling a town guaranteed that the royal treasury would drive a hard bargain. Three factors determined the price of a town: size, real estate, and seignorial income. These three sums were calculated by applying the treasury's conversion rates (reglas de factoría) to the data estimated by the buyer and verified by a royal appraiser.[11] The size (vasallaje) of a town could be measured by population or geographical extent. The Madrid agent of Gonzalo de Céspedes bid fourteen thousand maravedís per household if there were at least one hundred households. If there were fewer, he offered four thousand ducados [15 million maravedís] per square league of municipal territory. The value of the Order of Calatrava's real property in the town would be set by a committee of two, composed of the royal appraiser and a person appointed by Céspedes. If these two could not agree, then the town council would appoint a third appraiser, and Céspedes would pay whatever price two of the three agreed on. Céspedes offered 37.5 times the annual seignorial income of Carrión.

The Order of Calatrava's procurator in Madrid nominated an experienced implementor of royal expedients, the royal accountant Agustín de Zárate, to verify the appraisal of Carrión de los Ajos.[12] Zárate spent several days during November 1574 appraising Carrión de los Ajos. Following the treasury's methods spelled out in his commission, he set the number of households at 77.5. All heads of households, except mendicant poor who had no income other than begging from door to door, were included, even if they shared a house. Each male head of household counted as a full household, each widow as one-half. All the unmarried children under age twenty-five still living in their parents' house counted as one household, with the exception that an only child who was female counted as half a household. All orphans in the custody of a single guardian counted as one household. Hidalgo and clerical heads of households counted as one-half, and hidalgo orphans counted the same as orphans in the custody of a widow. Grandchildren and salaried employees of the household were not

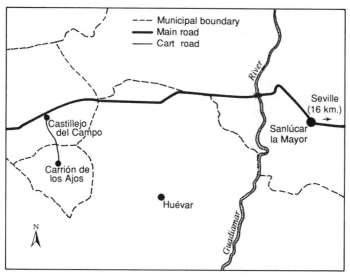

Map 9. Carrión de los Ajos, 1575

counted. At the rate of 14,000 maravedís per household, Zárate appraised the population of Carrión at 1,085,000 maravedís. Zárate measured the area of Carrión's municipal territory at less than half a square league, using the treasury's legal league of five thousand *varas*. At the rate of four thousand ducados per square league, this method of calculating size yielded a lower appraisal than did the method based on population.[13]

Real property usually did not constitute a significant portion of the seignorial property in a jurisdiction, and this proved to be the case in Carrión de los Ajos. Zárate appraised the order's real estate—buildings, a brick and tile kiln, the bakery, and some fields, excluding the olive oil presses and soap works—at 133,773 maravedís.

To appraise the Order of Calatrava's annual seignorial income from Carrión, Zárate followed the treasury rule of taking an average of the previous five years' income (1569–73) in cash and kind. The major portion of the seignorial income was paid in cash and derived from legal fees, fines, sale of offices and unclaimed property, and the commander's monopoly on the sale of soap. These payments Zárate calculated from the relevant account books. The order's principal income in produce came from two sources: its one-fifth share of the olive oil produced in Carrión and two-thirds of the tithe (the remaining one-third belonged to the cathedral and archbishop of Seville). The sale agreement between Céspedes and the king excluded the olive oil, olive presses, and soap works, which the order and the king would retain, so Zárate did not include these in his calculations. Following the guidelines of the treasury and the terms of the sale agreement, Zárate valued the average annual grain tithe by averaging the government fixed price of wheat in the previous five years at 220 maravedís per fanega and other grains at 110 maravedís per fanega. He valued other types of produce by averaging their market price at harvest with their market price one month later. Zárate appraised the commander's average annual seignorial income at 51,992 maravedís.

Zárate sent his total appraisal of 2,740,473 maravedís to Madrid, where the treasury officials made adjustments. They had instructed him to find out whether the master's treasury of the Order of Calatrava—and therefore the king—had a firm obligation to pay the salaries of the priest and sacristan and, if so, for what reason. Zárate found that the master's treasury paid the clergy's salaries, which amounted to 8,000 maravedís annually. The treasury discounted this from the annual income because Céspedes had agreed to assume this payment in exchange for the right of nominating the priest. To the remaining 43,992 maravedís of the commander's annual income from Carrión the treasury added 5,499 maravedís per annum— the commander's pro-rata share of the 5,000 ducados of income the king had earlier taken from the military orders in the Kingdom of Granada by virtue of the papal bull of 1529. This left a total annual income appraised at 49,499 maravedís. The treasury chose to accept the *vasallaje* appraisal based on population rather than on area. The treasury calculated the total sale price—the sum of the *vasallaje*, real property value, and 37.5 times the adjusted annual seignorial income—at 2,740,473 maravedís.

Treasury officials checked, signed, and sealed these calculations, and the secretary, Pedro de Escobedo, drew up a final draft of the deed of sale on July 23, 1575. The deed was then signed and countersigned by the *mayordomo*, Francisco de Garnica, the notary, Hernando Ochoa, the chancellor and chief notary of the Kingdom of Granada, Juan de Ribera, the chancellor for *relaciones* and *mercedes*, Francisco de Valmaseda, and the clerk for *mercedes*, Francisco Deza. The documents then went to the Order of Calatrava's procurator general, who acknowledged that the property belonged to the king as master and perpetual administrator of the order. On September 18, 1575, the king signed the sale agreement and commissioned Zárate to take possession in his name as king and transfer the town of Carrión de los Ajos from the Order of Calatrava to the royal domain in order to sell the order's *vasallaje*, income, and real property in Carrión de los Ajos to Gonzalo de Céspedes.

On Monday, November 21, 1575, Zárate, with his staff, royal notary Juan de Llamo, and other officials set out from the city of Seville on the road to the town of Carrión de los Ajos. They crossed the Guadalquivir River and traveled due west for fifteen kilometers through Sanlúcar, across the Guadiamar River, then southwest on a cart road to Carrión de los Ajos. There Zárate and his staff performed legal acts and public ceremonies similar to those that farmers all over the realm witnessed in their own town halls, marketplaces, and fields. The purchaser, Gonzalo de Céspedes, had deposited one-quarter of the sale price at the time of his bid. Now, a year after Zárate's visit to appraise Carrión, the final price had been established and all the paperwork was completed in Madrid; Céspedes in Seville was now prepared to pay the balance. Zárate carried the completed documents with him, and the notary carried a supply of blank paper to record their actions during the next few days. The description of the ceremonies they would perform in Carrión, notarized in Seville a few days later, covered both sides of twenty-four folio sheets of paper.[14]

On Tuesday, November 22, in the marketplace of Carrión de los Ajos, the town crier read to the council and a crowd of local people Zárate's commission to act in the name of the king. Zárate instructed the council to convene a town meeting the next day. On Wednesday morning, thirty-four men, including the members of the council, met in the town hall, declared themselves a quorum of the healthy citizens, and convened the town meeting. After Zárate's commission was read and explained to them, the citizens agreed to obey and comply with the royal provision. Zárate then demanded that the council relinquish its jurisdiction, turn over to him the staffs of justice (*varas de la justicia*) and all that the staffs represented—"all the legal jurisdiction, civil and criminal, first and second instance, law making and enforcing, corporal, civil and natural," and the town itself with its jurisdiction, population, income, tithes, produce, presentation and nomination of priests, judges, officials, and ministers spiritual and temporal. He was informed that one of the two field guards had moved from the town, and Zárate promptly appointed a new guard, exercising his powers of appointment as royal corregidor of Carrión de los Ajos.

As a symbol of the judicial powers they were transferring to him, the council members and the citizens in town meeting conducted Zárate around the marketplace with its column of justice (*rollo*) and into the town hall, where he stripped the elected officials of their offices. They relinquished the town hall to him and, without protest, allowed Zárate to expel them from the building and lock them out. Zárate then brought them back in to witness him presiding over a judicial appeal brought by a citizen who asked for the return of some property that the council had impounded as surety for a fine he claimed was unjustified. Zárate took the matter under advisement.

Having thus asserted his jurisdiction over the council's membership, chambers, and judicial powers, he proceeded to do the same for each property included in the sale. In each case he was conducted to the site by the council, accompanied by citizens and visitors, assumed possession in the name of the king, expelled the responsible official, took possession of the key or other representative object, and then reappointed the just-deposed officials. Zárate thus transferred to the royal domain the municipal seed bank (*pósito*), expelled its administrator, then reappointed him, with instructions to measure the grain in his care and render an account. Zárate took possession of the accounts, minutes, and other documents in the council's archive (the usual chest with several locks), removing from office and then reappointing the council's clerk and enjoining him to make an inventory of all the documents. In the town square he took possession of the market, where a man brought him a load of fresh sardines to price. Zárate inspected the fish and set prices for large and small ones, and without protest from the council, the man began selling. (This must have been a prearranged performance to demonstrate that Zárate had assumed juris-diction over the market and that he regulated the price of goods brought into the municipal territory by noncitizens, since Carrión's municipal territory contained no salt water that would have produced sardines.)

Zárate and the crowd then moved around the town, taking possession of the property that belonged to the commandery: the jail, the house where the jailer lived, the corral, the seignorial dues in cash, straw, and chickens. At this point Zárate took action to provide for the public safety. He noted several open wells and silos in which "people might fall acci-dentally" and ordered the council to see that the owners covered them. Then he continued, taking possession of the municipal butcher shop, the bakery, the shrine of Our Lady outside the "walls" of the town, the parish church (keys to the church door and sacristy, a missal, communion bell, wine and water cruets, censor), and the church's seed bank. From half a fanega of unplowed land representing the commandery's residual ownership of uncultivated land he picked up a handful of soil and scattered it.

During this tour of the town Zárate removed from office the town's appointed officials and reappointed them—sheriff, clerk, priest, and sacristan. He deposed and reappointed the field guard, whose job included impounding unbranded strays as well as protecting crops from human and animal predators. The guard pointed out that the corral under his juris-diction was in a ruinous state, and Zárate ordered the council to repair it.

Zárate then transferred ownership of the municipal territory to the council, reconstituted as a royal town council. "Seeing the many burdens and cares he had in carrying out his possession and commission and that he could not take care of every aspect of the governance, republic, and administration of justice himself, and that business was stalled, and both individuals and the republic were being hurt by the delay, for the relief of all," he appointed the members of the council to their previous elected offices to serve at the king's pleasure. Zárate then asserted the king's retention of supreme jurisdiction in Carrión by adjudicating a property dispute between two citizens, rendering a decision of Solomonic equity.

The next day, November 24, Zárate defined the limits of the municipal territory belonging to the royal town of Carrión. A subcommittee headed by Zárate's *subdelegado,* the Sevillian *jurado* Melchior de Vaena, went out to survey, inspect, and repair the old municipal boundary markers. Vaena's party included the royal notary, citizens of Carrión, and officials from the adjoining towns of Castilleja and Huévar. This subcommittee also took possession of the commandery's brick and tile kiln in the municipal territory. The site of this kiln and the *cortijo* where the olive presses and soap works were located were the only plots of land in the municipal territory that belonged to the order and would henceforth belong to the king; the town had no *monte,* and all the cultivated land was private property belonging to citizens of Carrión and other towns.

Meanwhile, back at the marketplace Zárate named the prior of San Pedro in Seville as judge of first instance for the priest and the parish property. He took possession of the sweet-water well in the meadow on the road to Castilleja del Campo and of the soap works that had been a commandery monopoly. Finally, he claimed all the legal fees, fines, and penalties. At the end the only possessions retained by the commandery were the olive presses and one-fifth of the olive oil production.

The official party took care that all the proceedings were public, recorded in detail, and verified by witnesses. The entire procedure in the town was witnessed by the citizens, and the notary's description of each step was read to the audience and formally attested to by one or two citizens, some of whom made "personal marks" because they did not know how to sign their names.

But all of this was temporary. On November 23, while Zárate was in Carrión taking possession of the town in the name of the king, notaries in Seville were preparing to transfer the town to its new lord, Gonzalo de Céspedes. Céspedes presented to the notaries the agreement of sale signed by the king in Madrid two months before on September 18. Philip II prefaced the agreement of sale by explaining his decision to sell Carrión in the context of global events. Notwithstanding his desire to have and retain for himself the town of Carrión, the king explained, he could not keep it in the royal domain because of the great expenses of unavoidable wars against the enemies of Christendom—which he listed in detail, ending with his recent naval victory at Lepanto. Now his royal domain and reputation and estate were so encumbered and endangered by these obligatory expenses that he had agreed to sell the town and jurisdiction of Carrión as private property to Gonzalo de Céspedes, city councilman of Seville. He then ordered Agustín de Zárate "at the moment our royal corregidor in the town of Carrión," who had dismembered the town from the Order of Calatrava and incorporated it into the royal domain, to transfer it to Céspedes. And he ordered the people of Carrión to accept Céspedes as their lord, always remembering that the king reserved for himself the supreme jurisdiction, to which they could appeal through the royal appellate court in Granada.

After presenting this royal letter to the Seville notaries, Gonzalo de Céspedes delegated his brother Juan de Céspedes to receive the town in his behalf from Zárate. In the House of Trade (Casa de Contratación) Gonzalo paid the balance of the sale price to the royal accountants, 2,740,753 maravedís in cash, as well as the 21,000 maravedís that the king owed Zárate as salary for the appraisal the previous year. On Saturday, November 26, Juan de Céspedes presented his credentials to Zárate in Carrión. The two delegations from Seville and the people of Carrión then reenacted the entire procedure, this time transferring possession of the town to Juan de Céspedes, who received all that had been in Zárate's powers for two days as corregidor—the staffs of justice, the property, and buildings. On behalf of all the citizens, the members of the council, kneeling before Céspedes and kissing his hand, gave him their oath to accept him as their lord. Juan de Céspedes, touring the town as Zárate had earlier in the week, took formal possession of all his brother had bought from the king (which did not include the soap works) and reappointed all the officials to their posts. After they submitted their accounts to him—or promised to do so—he returned their staffs, keys, and documents. By royal permission, he changed the name of the town to Carrión de los Céspedes.

The paperwork involved was massive, as each document required authorizations and countersignatures from several officials. In order to minimize copying errors and ensure that exact legal terms were used consistently and accurately, the treasury printed the documentation for the alienation and sale. A printed version of the documentation for Carrión— ninety-four pages of text—circulated among the royal officials for their signature as they entered the transaction in their registers. In the Escorial Palace on January 14, 1576, the royal secretaries and accountants acknowledged receipt of the money. In Madrid the transaction was recorded in the ledgers of the royal treasury on April 24, 1576, in the sales ledgers on July 1, 1579, and in the *Relaciones* ledgers on September 9, 1579. All signed and dated the printed version as it passed through their hands. In addition to the original documents or their notarized copies, Céspedes received this signed and notarized printed version, beginning with the papal bull of October 12, 1529, which gave Charles V permission to sell ecclesiastical property in the military orders, and ending with the final signatures of September 9, 1579.

As further assurance to Céspedes, the Order of Calatrava was instructed to transfer to him all the documents in its archives concerning Carrión, including the records of any audits the order had carried out. Carrión de los Ajos all but disappeared from the order's archives, and Céspedes now possessed the record of its past, as well as controlled its future as Carrión de los Céspedes.[15] In 1579 Gonzalo de Céspedes had every reason to feel assured that his deed of sale was irrevocable, and he may even have felt considerable pleasure in becoming a *señor de vasallos*. No celebration was recorded in Carrión, however. Carrión de los Ajos had been a town in the Order of Calatrava; Carrión de los Céspedes was a seignorial town. The citizens had been transferred from the jurisdiction of one lord to another without expense to them but without gaining any autonomy.

The orderly and peaceful events in Carrión appear to have been typical of the transfer and sale of towns in the military orders. Although large numbers of people and wide expanses of territory were transferred, the financial obligations, commons rights, and jurisdictional prerogatives of the town remained the same. There were few villages in the military orders to gain township and thus acquire portions of the municipal territory of towns. Private property—virtually all the cultivated land and residential lots—remained unchanged. Municipal citizenship and government continued with the same calendar and customs, with the exception that the new lord now had the right, previously exercised by the commander, of selecting the annually elected officials from a list submitted by the council. The calm with which the transfer was received can be attributed in large part to the fact that the kings had been effective masters and lords of the military orders since the reign of Ferdinand and Isabella. This may also have helped the royal administrators proceed knowledgeably. The monarchy compensated commanders for their lost income by promising them portions of the royal silk tax. The few commanders who resisted were allowed to die in office, which was not heritable, and the monarchy took advantage of the resulting vacancy to dismember the commandery.

As these sales came to a close in the 1550s, Philip II embarked on a new program of appropriation and sale. By virtue of a papal bull issued by Julius III on February 1, 1551, Philip claimed the right to alienate permanently five hundred thousand ducados' worth of jurisdiction, households, and income belonging to the monastic orders in his kingdoms without the consent of their abbots, priors, or other officials.[16] Throughout the 1550s the royal treasury annually sold township to five or six villages, exempting them from the jurisdictions of the Benedictine, Jeronimite, Bernardine, and Augustinian orders. Philip negotiated a broader concession from Pope Pius V in 1569 which allowed the king to alienate ecclesiastical properties belonging to bishops and cathedrals, in addition to the

property of military orders and monasteries. In 1574 Clement VIII conceded an additional forty thousand ducados' worth of ecclesiastical jurisdiction from the archdiocese of Toledo.[17] The royal and papal documents
repeated the earlier justifications—the holy and expensive work of fighting
heresy.

John H. Elliott has noted that much of the enormous income of the
archdiocese of Toledo was appropriated by the king during the seventeen
years that the Inquisition, at the instigation of the king, imprisoned and
tried Archbishop Bartolomé de Carranza.[18] The political conflict between
king and archbishop and then between king and pope injected conflict
into the sale process itself, which added distrust to a series of sales that
were both less systematic and more complex than the sales of the military
orders had been. The royal government had no systematic knowledge of
this ecclesiastical property, which had not belonged to the monarchy and,
in most cases, would be incorporated into the royal domain for only a few
days during the sale process. The royal officials needed to distinguish
between royal prerogatives that the monarchy would retain—such as royal
taxes, mining rights, and supreme appellate jurisdiction—and the church's
seignorial property. Seignorial prerogatives varied from diocese to diocese,
from order to order, and even from village to village and might include
any or all of a long list of possessions: the civil and criminal jurisdiction,
municipal properties developed or built by the ecclesiastical lord, fields,
income, tithes, taxes, fees, lease rents, fishing rights, fines, and livestock
that might, for historical reasons, belong to the lord rather than the
municipality.

In order to gain a detailed knowledge of what would be involved in the
property transfers, Philip ordered a survey, the *Relaciones topográficas*, of
all the cities, towns, and villages in the archdiocese of Toledo.[19] The
Relaciones provide a unique view into the daily lives of over five hundred
municipalities during the years 1575 to 1580. The town and village people
speak to us in their own pungent words, revealing their hopes, fears,
discontents, and local pride. Designed by and for the accountants and
commissioners who would verify the appraisals and carry out the transfers,
the *Relaciones* reveal how royal administrators valued each aspect of municipal life. Several royal secretaries contributed questions for the survey,
and in 1575 the government printed questionnaires and sent them out to
the royal corregidores in New Castile. The royal council's covering letter
instructed that "the governors, corregidores, and other officials and persons
to whom his majesty is addressing this immediately shall make a list of
the municipalities within their jurisdiction and another list of those that
have already been exempted [*eximidos*] from their jurisdiction and made
into towns, explaining which is which, and shall send them to his majesty."[20]

The corregidores were to send their deputies with the questionnaire to all the villages in their jurisdictions and order them to make a *relación* (response) to the questionnaire. Towns already exempted were to be approached more diplomatically: the corregidor wrote politely to the town council to request a response. The corregidores collected the *relaciones* and sent them back to the royal secretary Juan Vázquez de Salazar. After studying the first *relaciones*, the council reduced the number of questions from fifty-seven to forty-six and then sent the revised questionnaire to corregidores in 1578.[21] By 1583 more than seven hundred *relaciones* had been returned to the court, some of them multiple responses from individual towns. Another royal secretary, Juan López de Velasco, was delighted with the results, and he urged the king to survey all of his kingdoms by this method, though as royal cosmographer he was interested in the information more for scientific reasons than for the monarch's financial needs:

Seeing that in these kingdoms there is a need for a good description, such as those that exist in other kingdoms less powerful and notable, and that it would be very slow and costly to have it done by the hand of a single person visiting and appraising all the municipalities, it was decided to send printed instructions drawn up for this purpose so that all the councils would respond to them at the same time and send them back to the corregidores who distributed them. By this means were collected without any inconvenience, expense, or delay the *relaciones* of the municipalities in the archdiocese of Toledo, which your majesty was pleased to do first in order to see how it would turn out, and *relaciones* have been brought from many municipalities in the Indies that otherwise, even with great expense, would not have been possible in many years.[22]

The *relaciones* remained at the royal court, where the treasury officials and representatives of prospective buyers could refer to them. By reviewing the *relación* of any town or village, the treasury could evaluate its size and annual income when a buyer bid on it. If the bid seemed realistic, and the bidder financially sound, the treasury accepted a down payment of one-quarter or one-third and thus set in motion the procedures for exemption and sale. Immediately upon accepting a down payment, the royal treasury notified the procurator of the affected military order or diocese. The procurator nominated a royal official to verify the jurisdiction's appraisal. Verification (*averiguación*) invariably yielded higher appraisals than the estimates based on the *relaciones*. The treasury's examination of a *relación* targeted ambiguities that an experienced appraiser could resolve to the king's financial advantage.

The former lords of the exempted towns—the military orders and the archbishop of Toledo—were to receive annuities (*juros*) drawn on the Granada silk tax as compensation for the annual incomes they lost from the towns. Yet although they received the proper legal documents confirming their rights in the silk tax, they rarely received full payment of the annuities. The Habsburg period was not a prosperous one for Granada or its silk industry. Production diminished and then nearly ceased as royal policy first restricted travel by the Moriscos, next uprooted them from Granada in order to relocate them throughout Castile, and then expelled them from Spain altogether in 1609. Even had the industry flourished, the holders of annuities could not have received full payment, because the silk tax was already fully encumbered before Charles began alienating property from the military orders.

The specter of Castile's civil wars and royal confiscations in the previous two centuries hung over the Habsburg sales, driving both Charles and Philip to invoke the Roman law precept of absolute royal power that their Trastamara ancestors had incorporated in official documents to justify disposing of the royal domain. Once the church property was incorporated into the royal domain, Charles V invoked his "propio motu y cierta ciencia y poderío real absoluto." By invoking these powers, Charles placed himself squarely in the tradition of his Trastamara ancestors and could truthfully claim that he was following the example of his grandparents, Ferdinand and Isabella. Throughout the sixteenth century Charles and Philip II utilized this legal theory and language developed by the Trastamara monarchy, with the additional step of first alienating towns from the military orders and church before incorporating them into the royal domain for sale.

Even with these safeguards, however, confusion plagued the sales of monastic and episcopal jurisdictions, much of it created by the monarch's reversal of his own earlier decisions. The monasteries accepted annuities paid from government revenues in compensation for their lost income, but the female orders asked for relief from this erosion of their seignorial powers. Philip, in consultation with the Council of the Treasury, considered the bids submitted for these places and decided which would be alienated and which not. By 1586 the towns that "someone had wanted to buy but their alienations had been overturned" numbered more than thirty-six. The Committee of Council Presidents decided to draw up a list of all those ecclesiastical towns that had been made immune to alienation by the king and sent the list to the royal accountants "so that if some bidder should ask about them, the accountants will know what has been decided and provided for these places."[23]

If the royal treasurers at the highest level of administration needed a list to keep track of towns whose status had been reversed, one can imagine the confusion among commissioners in the field. In addition to coping with ecclesiastical lords and ladies angry over the potential loss of their jurisdictions and their own lack of prior knowledge about the territories in question, the commissioners had much more complex responsibilities in the episcopal territories. Bishops and archbishops traditionally preferred to keep their jurisdictions organized as a large number of villages ruled by a few towns, in contrast to the military orders and lay lords, who preferred self-governing towns and granted township to any village that gave evidence of being able to survive autonomously.

The major portion of the archbishop of Toledo's seignorial jurisdiction in 1550, for example, comprised five major towns—Talavera de la Reina, Alcalá de Henares, Talamanca, Brihuega, and Uceda—whose municipal territories included more than 150 villages. Here a more complicated process was necessary. The royal treasury transferred the villages into the royal jurisdiction, elevated them into township, and sold them individually or in clusters to private buyers or to the new towns themselves. The towns that bought their own jurisdiction remained in the royal domain and thereby became royal towns, no matter how small they were.

Alcalá de Henares remained in the jurisdiction of the archbishop, but twenty-two of its twenty-five villages were exempted from Alcalá's jurisdiction, given part of Alcalá's municipal territory as their own, and granted township (see map 10). Some of these towns bought their own jurisdiction and remained royal towns; others were bought by private purchasers and became seignorial towns. All remained members of the Alcalá commons with full rights and prerogatives.[24] The town of Talamanca in 1568 and the towns of Brihuega and Uceda in 1579, with their thirty-two villages, were all exempted from the archbishop's jurisdiction and transferred to the royal jurisdiction.[25] Most of these villages became towns and were bought by private purchasers. In Andalusia the archdiocese of Seville lost all its towns, keeping only one village and a few *despoblados*.[26] The complexity of the transfers is revealed by the royal treasury's accounts receivable ledgers for these transactions, which indicate that many prospective buyers, whether individuals or town councils, failed to complete their payments or traded properties with other buyers in mid-transaction.[27] Although complex, they were nonetheless popular and reasonably honest.

In a more remote area of the Kingdom of Castile the sale of ecclesiastical jurisdictions fell into the hands of a swindler of the first order. While the town of Carrión de los Ajos could feel honored that the royal commissioned judge who carried out their transfer was the famous and trusted Agustín de Zárate, villages and towns belonging to the bishop of Oviedo in Asturias fell victim to the infamous Alonso de Camino. The story of this confidence man has been unraveled by Alfonso Menéndez in his investigations of the sale of ecclesiastical jurisdictions in Asturias. Camino was a citizen and councilman of Valladolid, one of its representatives in the Cortes, and false banker to King Philip's governor in Flanders, don Luis de Requeséns.[28] Claiming that he had lost three hundred thousand ducados in the royal bankruptcy of 1575, Camino got himself included in the schedule of royal creditors who were to be assigned proceeds from the sale of ecclesiastical

Map 10. Evolution of the Villages in the Town of Alcalá de Henares,
1500–1752

jurisdictions in Asturias. The royal treasury evaluated households in Galicia and Asturias at a lower rate than in Castile—twelve thousand maravedís as opposed to sixteen thousand—because the land was less fertile,
but Camino apparently bribed the accountants to falsify the amounts and
then undertook the sales himself so that he could falsify the appraisals.
He and several relatives persuaded twenty councils exempted from monasteries and the bishopric of Oviedo to purchase their own township,

mortgaging their property in order to avoid being bought by (fictitious) hidalgos. In the end, the relevant accounts and documents were so intricately falsified and selectively destroyed that the royal treasury's investigators were not able to bring Camino to judgment. The royal council recognized the duped villages as towns, although the royal treasury had not received the full sale price. The royal government's deliberations in the case have not been found, but the consequence of their decisions was to guarantee the sales, assuring purchasers that their charters of township were valid even if the royal treasury had been defrauded by a third party.

The Extent of the Sales

Geographically, the sales extended from Asturias on the north Atlantic coast to Murcia on the Mediterranean, from Extremadura in the west to Albacete in the east. They began with the Habsburg financial crisis of 1536, yet they did not end with the Habsburg period, for sales continued through the War of the Spanish Succession (1700–1715), when both Habsburg and Bourbon pretenders granted township to win supporters, and began again in the late eighteenth century, during the Bourbon monarchy's financial involvement in the American and French revolutions. Within these broad parameters of space and time, variations and emphases produced long-term differences within the monarchy. The Habsburg sale of township drastically altered the map of Castile. The large medieval municipal territories belonging to a few hundred cities and towns were carved up into hundreds of smaller territories belonging to new towns that had been villages. The 1752 census revealed that Spain was composed of over 28,000 cities, towns, villages, and *despoblados*.[29] In the area of New Castile surveyed by Philip II from 1575 through 1580, the proportion of towns to villages reversed as a result of the royal sale of township. Of the 528 cities, towns, and villages in the survey—the *Relaciones topográficas*— a majority (60 percent) were villages before the Habsburg period; by 1752, when the Bourbons made their first survey, the Catastro del marqués de la Ensenada, a majority (77 percent) were towns (see fig. 6).[30] The boundaries and prerogatives of these new towns were established in the sixteenth and seventeenth centuries in a steady stream of five or six sales per year by the Habsburg kings. Yet each ruler adopted his own style, his own self-justification, and explanation for the sales. Each king chose to focus on a different bloc of towns for exemption and sale. By the end of the sixteenth century towns and villages had been sold from the military orders, monasteries, and bishops. In the seventeenth century most of the sales were directed against the cities.

Philip III (1598–1621), because of his own religious scruples, agreed not to alienate ecclesiastical lands. Pious historians have praised him for

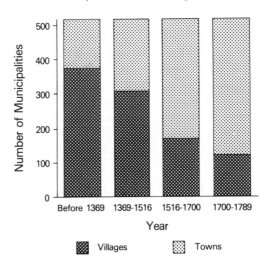

Fig. 6. Changing proportions of towns and villages in
New Castile

this abstinence, though it seems the only virtue in an otherwise vapid
and extravagant reign. King Philip and his principal minister, the duke
of Lerma, resorted to other expedients to raise money.[31] Philip III sold
offices on an unprecedented scale.[32] He employed the old Trastamara
principles and language to return (*reducir*) municipal offices to the royal
domain in order to sell them to the highest bidder. Modern historians
have interpreted the monarchy's *reducción* of city council seats as a failed
attempt to reduce the size of city governments, but the policy in fact had
the opposite intention and effect. The number of council seats increased
because the monarchy was creating new seats for sale. In the royal towns,
the government of Philip III created royal offices that had never existed
before—auditors of tax and municipal accounts, real estate brokers—and
thus coerced the towns into buying the offices themselves. The town
council records reveal that these new offices were "returned" to the monarchy, were bought by the town council, and disappeared all in the space
of a few months.

Philip III, like his father, also raised capital from old towns by selling
to them land they thought they already owned. The sixteenth-century
land sales, described by David Vassberg,[33] were carried out by traveling
royal commissioners who claimed as royal property any land for which the
council could produce no legal title or which was not being used for the
purposes stipulated in the legal title. After taking possession of these lands,
the commissioner sold them back to the municipal council. In order to

recoup this cash expenditure, the council sold some of the commons to private citizens or, for a few years, charged rental and pasturage fees for the use of commons. The extent of these land sales and their impact on the farming economy may never be fully known but, as Vassberg points out, must have imposed a significant hardship on the poorest people, who could not afford to lose free access to previously public sources of fuel, pasturage, and new plowlands.[34]

Even with the sale of offices and land, Philip's finances were such that he agreed to sell some of the royal domain in Old Castile.[35] For the first time, the Castilian kings sold royal towns (behetrías) that had formed part of the royal domain for centuries. Despite the differences distinguishing these towns in Old Castile from the ecclesiastical villages that were transformed into royal towns for the purpose of sale in New Castile, the processes were the same. In 1608 Philip transferred eleven towns in Old Castile to his favorite, the duke of Lerma, whose family had an old claim to the jurisdictions. Though the local vocabulary differed from that of New Castile and Andalusia, the ceremony transmitting ownership in the north reveals the same municipal structure as that in the Andalusian town of Carrión de los Ajos.[36] The king transmitted to the duke all the royal jurisdiction in the towns and their territories, "from the highest leaf of the mountains to the rocks in the river," as the traditional phrase described it.

One of the middle-sized of the eleven towns was Palacios de Meneses, appraised at 236 households in 1608.[37] Because Palacios de Meneses was a larger town than Carrión de los Ajos, it had many more municipal services and corporate assets. The duke sent his representative, Jorge de Tovar, who, in a town meeting on August 28, 1608, received in the name of the duke the staffs of justice, and with them possession of "the town and its offices, with its jurisdiction, lordship, and subjects." Tovar then took possession of the town jail in the house of the sheriff, who turned over to Tovar the shackles, chains, and stocks. Tovar locked and unlocked the jail door and asked to interrogate the prisoners, but the sheriff replied that there were none. Tovar took possession of two municipal shops—a fish market and a fruit and dry goods shop. He took possession of two municipal inns, where he ordered the price lists that were posted on boards to be taken down; until further notice straw and barley were to be sold at the price set by the royal justice. He then took possession of the butcher shops in the town hall on the plaza, expelling from them all who were within; then walking through them and not finding anyone of whom he could ask the price at which meat was sold, he asked that it be recorded. The town clerk resigned his office in favor of the duke, and Tovar accepted it and noted in the official documents that he had not repaid the clerk the 3,920 reales paid for the office that year. In this calm and pacific manner, Palacios de Meneses was transformed from a royal into a seignorial town.

In two other towns, however, the seignorial yoke did not slip on so easily. In Santa María del Campo the townspeople were reportedly so distressed that they tore down the duke's coat of arms from the town gate and remounted the royal arms. In Torquemada the townspeople dirtied the duke's coat of arms. A judge was sent to find out who the guilty ones were, and another judge was sent to the town of Tudela to investigate the appearance of some pasquinades assailing the duke. The fact that all these protests, mild as they were, occurred within days of the duke of Lerma's taking possession indicates that the objections of the townspeople were not against some specific act or acts of injustice by the duke but against having lost the prestige of being a royal town. They may also give some idea of the repute in which the duke was held in these towns so close to Valladolid, where the royal court was rumored to pass its days and nights in a haze of scandal and foolishness.

In the Americas the imperial government of Philip III used the granting of township for more elevated purposes. The royal government in Mexico City granted township to a rebel community in order to rid the viceroyalty of a serious threat to the capital's supply lines. In the early seventeenth century the transport route between Mexico City and its port at Veracruz was under attack from a bandit community of escaped African slaves called the Yanguicos, who were based near Mount Orizaba. The Yanguicos successfully raided a wagon train in 1609 and the viceroy in Mexico City sent a military expedition to capture them. The commander, with more than three hundred soldiers, marched into bandit territory, engaged in several skirmishes with the Yanguicos, but was not able to defeat them. Finally he arrived at an agreement with the leader, reportedly an Angolan prince named Yanga, who had escaped from his owners thirty years earlier. Yanga and the commander agreed that the bandits would stop harassing the Spaniards, and the viceroy promised to grant the escaped slave community a charter of township. Yanga and his descendants would rule the town as its "governors," and the viceroy would appoint a Spaniard as interim appellate judge (justicia mayor). The monarchy would pay for the materials to build and furnish a church, and Yanga would permit Franciscans to live in the town. Viceroy and governor agreed on San Lorenzo de los Negros for the name of the town, which still survived at the end of the seventeenth century.[38]

During the seventeenth century the finances of Philip IV became so strained that his government resorted to the extreme measure of selling the tax bases of the cities and their subject villages. The pressures of renewed revolt in the Netherlands, naval disasters on the Atlantic, and military support of the Austrian Habsburgs in the Thirty Years' War

brought the monarchy to request authorization from the Cortes for alienating and selling city jurisdictions. Philip III died in March 1621, just a
month before the truce with the Netherlands expired, and the young King
Philip IV and his principal ministers, led by the count of Olivares, began
a long reign of financial expedients in the name of military necessity.
After three years of extraordinary exertions and lobbying by Olivares and
the king, on May 1, 1625, the Cortes and the cities agreed to a higher
level of taxation. A few days later a memorandum from the council of
the treasury advised Philip that even this would not be enough to meet
the terms of the contract then being negotiated with the bankers: it would
be necessary to ask the Cortes for consent to sell villages from the cities
in order to provide collateral for the loan. On May 6, 1625, the treasury
signed a loan contract (*asiento*) with two consortia of Italian bankers,
secured by the sale of 17 million maravedís' worth of royal income. On
September 18 the Cortes voted to approve the sale of twenty thousand
households (*vasallos*) from city jurisdictions.[39]

Cities that already felt aggrieved by the monarchy's diminution of their
municipal territories during the sixteenth century resisted. The representative from Granada, Mateo Lisón de Biedma, who had led the three-year
resistance to the subsidy, argued that the sale violated a condition of the
millones subsidy negotiated with Philip II in 1590, a law to this same effect
published in 1621, and Philip IV's oath upon his accession to the throne
to preserve the rights of cities, towns, and villages. Lisón de Biedma
demanded that the Cortes submit these issues for adjudication, but he
failed to stop the measure. Throughout the fall months, the Cortes received
and recorded cities' formal agreements to the sales.[40]

What argument in 1625 could have induced the Cortes cities to agree
to dismember their own jurisdictions? The answer did not lie in a sack of
Rome, nor in the trial and imprisonment of the archbishop of Toledo,
nor in the physical force and imprisonment corregidores employed to
coerce city councils to agree to what their representatives in the Cortes
had voted. The cities' sovereign lawmaking power—the *mero imperio*—
over the municipal territory and its citizens was at stake. A city that agreed
to the alienation of its jurisdiction thereby demonstrated its absolute power
over its territory and villages as clearly as a city that refused. If, by refusing,
city councils and the Cortes goaded the king into claiming supreme jurisdiction over the cities, they would be plunged into a legal quagmire.
Throughout Europe in the sixteenth century jurists had debated whether
justice and political power emanated from the king or whether he exercised
it on behalf of the community, and increasingly by the beginning of the
seventeenth century monarchists were deciding in favor of absolutism. In
Castile an open confrontation on the legal issues would quickly lead the
disputants to the charters (*fueros*) through which medieval kings had given

the cities and lords the municipal territories over which they held juris-diction.[41] The force of legal argument was on the king's side, and the cities had the example of their own history during the sixteenth century to remind them how much it would cost to resist a combined assault by king and villages.

When the Habsburg kings claimed the right to alienate city jurisdictions in the sixteenth century, they did so in response to the refusal of the Cortes cities to raise taxes or relinquish their control over tax collection. Charles V and Philip II alienated villages from city jurisdictions during the monarchy's worst years of crisis in military financing—1537 and 1588—and during the two or three years before the royal bankruptcies of 1557, 1575, and 1596. The Cortes objected forcefully to these sales during the sixteenth century, but achieving nothing this way and fearing the consequences of a confrontation on the issues, it resorted to expedients of its own, persuading cities to pay higher taxes rather than bring the issue into open conflict. The Cortes sent representatives to the cities themselves to help the councils negotiate adjustments (*composiciones*) with the king: the council paid an indemnity to the king in exchange for guarantees that he would not change or alienate the city's jurisdiction. In 1537 the city of Seville reached a compromise with Charles V for thirty-seven thousand ducados, and the city of Baeza gave him fourteen thousand ducados for his promise not to alienate Linares or Vilches.[42] In 1559 the cities of Avila, Arévalo, Olmedo, Málaga, and Granada paid *composiciones* to Philip II; cities that could not or would not find municipal funds to pay for these guarantees were forced to sell some of their municipal assets in order to pay their taxes. Guadalajara, after losing much of its municipal territory in the 1530s and 1540s when a dozen of its villages bought *villazgo* from the monarchy and became towns, now agreed to give the king eight thousand ducados by selling more of its own municipal territory to the new towns.[43] Guadalajara lost so many villages that the royal corregidor there in 1588 could suggest no way for the city to raise the special subsidy levied after the destruction of the Armada, and the committee sent by the Cortes could find no way to avoid excising more villages from the municipal territory of Guadalajara.[44] In 1592 and 1593 the Cortes again assisted in negotiating *composiciones* to help Guadalajara, Cuenca, Baeza, Ubeda, and Huete avoid further alienations from their jurisdictions.

In contrast to the justifications offered in the sales of ecclesiastical jurisdictions, the seventeenth-century arguments do not dwell on money or the monarch's financial distress. An argument based on financial need would not have reassured prospective buyers of villages alienated from cities. A century earlier the kings successfully sold jurisdictions of the military orders and bishops because they had the permission of the pope

to transfer ecclesiastical property to the royal domain. The popes themselves used an argument based on religion to justify the alienations: they
were giving away church property in order to defend the church against
the enemies of Christianity—the same reason medieval popes had licensed
the military orders as ecclesiastical institutions in the first place. If the
king, as the fount of all justice, had given jurisdiction to the cities, then
the achievement of a more perfect justice was the only legitimate reason
for him to alienate that jurisdiction from the cities.

The argument required a delicate touch. To suggest that kings had
delegated authority to unworthy or unjust courts would be self-defeating.
Instead, the documents consistently begin by explaining that geographical
distance or difficult terrain, by making travel to the ruling city or town
difficult, deprived the villagers of the full benefits of the king's justice.
The variations on this argument appear infinite and leave a vivid impression of physical impediments to justice—rocky roads, steep ridges, and
flooded rivers. The Cortes, as well as villagers and the king, knew how
to make this argument. Justice was not discussed, however, in the debates
preceding the Cortes vote of September 18, 1625. Money, political prerogatives, and the damaging consequences for their tax bases preoccupied
the representatives during the formal lodging of their votes. Yet once the
vote was given, as if to assert that the Cortes held the jurisdiction that
was being sold, the representatives entertained and granted a petition from
the village of Villamanta, which asked to be liberated from the jurisdiction
of the town of Casarrubios del Monte. The petitioner's attorney presented
a brief that served as a model of the monarchy's justice argument; the
Cortes accepted and recorded the petition in order to assert its own authority over the process.[45] If the monarchy was going to sell city jurisdiction, then the Cortes would limit the extent and define the conditions
for the sales just as it had defined and limited the millones tax since 1590.

By mid-January 1626 the secretary Pedro de Lezama had drawn up and
published the twenty-three conditions of sale.[46] Most of the conditions
were similar to those of the previous century. The villages sold must be
"eximidos" from their former cities and given municipal territories of their
own, carved out of the city's boundaries. Any fortresses and castles within
the municipal boundaries would be included in the sale. The rate of
payment for vasallaje was fixed at seventeen thousand maravedís per household north of the Tajo River and eighteen thousand per household south
(these amounts were later adjusted to fifteen thousand and sixteen thousand maravedís, respectively). The price of vasallaje based on extent of
territory was fixed at fifty-six hundred ducados per square league north of
the Tajo and sixty-four hundred ducados per square league south. Veri-
fications of vasallaje were to be made according to the treasury's conversion

rates, and the king retained the prerogative of deciding whether to cal-culate *vasallaje* on the basis of population or area in villages with fewer than one hundred households.

Certain features of the conditions of sale negotiated by the bankers in 1625 were highly favorable to purchasers and prejudicial to the cities. The conditions the Cortes accepted in 1626 provided royal legal support and generous financial terms to buyers. Legal prohibitions against buyers mort-gaging or selling their heritable and inalienable property (*mayorazgo*) were suspended for the purposes of these purchases. The monarchy promised to act as codefendant with the buyer in any lawsuit challenging transfers of jurisdiction financed through such sales of inalienable property. The king abrogated Charles V's 1537 guarantees that city territories would never be alienated yet assured the new towns that they would retain their old rights in the city commons. A city that lost a lawsuit it brought to prevent the alienation of its villages would pay the costs of the lawsuit. The buyer purchasing a village of fewer than six hundred households could pay an additional sum to acquire the royal prerogative to appoint a lawyer as appellate judge over all his towns. By making a larger down payment of one-third, buyers could take possession at the time their bids were accepted instead of having to wait until they had paid the full price. They could pay the balance in negotiated installments within two years at an interest of 8 percent, compared with the 14 percent interest the monarchy charged on unpaid balances in the sixteenth century. Payment had to be in silver, but the laws prohibiting exchanges of copper-based coinage for silver were suspended for these purchases.

The Cortes could set conditions and limits, but it could not administer the sales; these were in the hands of the Genoese creditors. The king's principal credit broker, Bartolomé Spínola, was named factor general to supervise the sale of city jurisdictions. Sales proceeded quickly at first. On January 15, 1626, a royal decree authorized Octavio Centurión, Carlos Strata, and Vicencio Squarzafigo to sell towns with 17,500 households to repay the 1,580,750 ducados and escudos they had advanced in payment of the monarchy's expenses. On March 31, 1626, Antonio Balvi received a license to sell towns with 1,666 households, and on August 20, 1626, Pablo and Agustín Justiniano received license to sell towns with 834 households. By the end of the first year of the new policy, the king's Italian bankers had been authorized to sell jurisdictions with 20,000 house-holds to repay total loans of 1,640,995 ducados and escudos. In December 1628 the Cortes complained that towns with more than 20,000 households had been alienated, and yet the sales continued. The treasury secretary, Antonio Alvarez de Bohórquez, reported that according to the population estimates submitted by bidders, 14,229 households had been sold. Re-cognizing that bidders underestimated population in order to keep their down payments low, however, he calculated the number already sold at 16,899 and advised the treasury to authorize the factor general to sell another 3,000 households before declaring this subsidy from the Cortes exhausted. The treasury was receiving even more money from this sale of jurisdiction than the sales amounts would indicate, because some cities agreed to pay *composiciones* in order to prevent their jurisdictions from being sold. Badajoz paid the treasury 12,000 ducados, Cáceres paid 20,000, and Trujillo paid 30,000, rather than lose villages from their municipal territories.[47]

A second sales round of another 20,000 households began in 1630. The monarchy issued a decree in May 1630 for the factor general Spínola to sell 12,000 households in payment of the 666,000 escudos negotiated with him. The monarchy would also attempt to sell an extra seat on the city council in each city, town, or village of the kingdom. These sales proceeded much more slowly than those in the 1620s, and it was not until 1639 that the first 12,000 were sold and the monarchy issued another decree for the sale of 8,000 households for partial payment of 600,000 escudos owed to the bankers. The economic historian of Philip IV's reign, Antonio Domínguez Ortiz, speculated that these final sales were slow and difficult owing to domestic disturbances and the general economic crisis plaguing the kingdom from 1630 to the end of the century.[48] In the Cortes meeting of 1670 representatives objected to the continued sale of jurisdictions, claiming that more than the authorized number had already been sold. The queen regent, in order to win the Cortes's consent for a new tax, agreed that the excess collected from the continuing sale of jurisdictions would be credited to the amount voted in the new tax. Still, there were few sales after 1670.

How much of Castile experienced these changes is a question that still requires many, many hours of research, and we may never be able to definitively measure the proportion of the population transformed from one status to another. The 528 cities, towns, and villages in the *Relaciones* were not all the municipalities of New Castile, which itself was only a fraction of the Kingdom of Castile (see tables 4.1 and 4.2). We can get some idea of the scale of the operation in the seventeenth century, since in that period the treasury measured the volume of sales by population. In 1628 the Cortes agreed to allow Philip IV to sell towns with a total population of 40,000 households, but years later it realized that the sales were exceeding this limit. Audits of the treasury's sale accounts revealed that in the forty years after 1628 the factor general sold 270 towns in all parts of the kingdom, with a total population of 52,306 households. This was a rate of about 6.7 towns and 1,300 households per year.[49]

For the sixteenth-century sale of ecclesiastical towns and villages, however, such comprehensive figures do not exist. The volume of sales in that

TABLE 4.1

Grants of Township to Towns and Villages Responding to the
Relaciones Questionnaire

Ruling Dynasty	Number of Charters Granted	Towns as Percentage of All Municipalities
Towns before 1369	133	25
Trastamara, 1369–1516	77	40
Habsburg, 1516–1700	146	67
Bourbon, 1700–1789	48	77
Total town charters	404	
Villages remaining in 1789	124	
Total towns and villages	528	

TABLE 4.2

Town Charters per year in Towns Responding to the
Relaciones Questionnaire

Years	New Townships	
	Total	Annual average
Before 1369	133	—
1369–1454	38	0.45
1454–74	8	0.40
1474–1516	31	0.74
1516–55	24	0.62
1556–98	50	1.19
1598–1621	5	0.22
1621–65	57	1.30
1665–1700	10	0.29
1700–1789	48	0.54
Total	404	

period was negotiated between the monarchy and the papacy in terms of appraised value in ducados, not in population. But even when we know how many households were in these towns, we still will not know what proportion of the population lived in towns that were sold. That would require population information for the entire kingdom in every year of the century and a half when the sales were in progress.

Legally, the power of the citizens was enhanced by township. Their new independence did not diminish the authority of the monarchy, since the new towns were directly responsible to monarch or lord. In practice, however, by multiplying the number of autonomous municipalities, the Habsburg monarchs fragmented royal administration of their Castilian subjects. The Habsburgs did not create an administrative structure to replace the internal organization of the church, military orders, and cities. Instead of working through a limited number of cities and towns that, in turn, administered thousands of villages, royal officials had to communicate with thousands of towns individually. It is some measure of the Spanish Habsburg monarchy's desperate military and financial straits that in 1623 the count-duke of Olivares sought to raise the money for an army of thirty thousand men by eliminating the indirect taxes on consumer goods and instead levying a direct tax on each town and village in Castile, a measure that the count-duke estimated would require the royal officials to deal directly with more than fifteen thousand Castilian municipal councils.[50] Even Olivares, usually absorbed in setting policy and driving it through the highest levels of the royal government, knew that Castile's self-administering towns supplied the monarchy's taxes, fighting men, and administrative services. The Habsburgs failed to prevent the spread of Protestantism or contain Muslim expansion, but they achieved one of Charles V's goals: they carried out their foreign ventures without diminishing the Castilian royal domain. In fact, the Habsburgs, by freeing church and city villages to buy charters as royal towns, may have enlarged the royal domain.

Chapter 5

In Pursuit of Justice
and Jurisdiction

On June 24, 1566, the Andalusian mining village of Linares celebrated the reception of a charter transforming the village into a royal town. The council met in the town hall, and as soon as the clerk had recorded its official receipt of the royal charter, its members left the council chambers. Accompanied by two trumpeters and the public crier, they climbed up to the balconies of the town hall. The trumpets sounded several times, and after a great crowd of people had assembled in the plaza, the public crier, standing on the balcony that faced on the plaza, read out in a loud and intelligible voice the royal "charter and exemption of this town."[1]

The council had earlier appointed some of its own members as a committee to organize a fiesta. Throughout the afternoon and evening the trumpets sounded again and again, musicians played from the town hall balconies, and in the plaza there were riding contests, a bullfight with six bulls, cane fights, and other competitive sports. The next morning the trumpeters and musicians again played, and there was a procession from the church to the Monastery of St. John the Baptist, with dancing along the way.[2] The trumpets sounded from the balconies again, and the council's clerk, Gómez de Frías, "gave true and faithful witness" that the royal charter had been received, announced, and accepted with full legal and public ceremony.[3]

For the citizens of Linares, the royal charter granting them township culminated centuries of struggle to gain independence from the city of Baeza. Land was not the main issue: the villagers wanted control over their own laws and law courts. Linares, like any village, was characterized by its lack of municipal territory and autonomous jurisdiction. The village existed physically within the territory and jurisdiction of another municipality—the city of Baeza—and was subject to its council and laws. Villagers lived under the ordinances of the ruling city, and village judges had jurisdiction only in petty cases involving their own citizens in cases arising within their own residential nucleus and private property. More serious cases had to be tried by the city judges. No matter how close any village might lie geographically to its governing city or town, villagers felt ill-used by the city or town judges and council. City and town ordinances prescribed unequal fines and penalties for villagers and townspeople. Heath Dillard has pointed out that in the municipal code of Plasencia, for example, the fine for raping an unmarried woman from one of the city's villages was only a quarter of the fine imposed when the victim was a citizen of Plasencia itself.[4]

Villages could petition, but because they did not have full legal standing, they did not litigate and possessed *propios* and commons only at the sufferance of the ruling council. The city or town council invariably put the interests of the villagers last when setting the schedule by which sectors of the municipal land would be harvested and planted. Most city and town ordinances allowed their own citizens to sell wine in the marketplace for a month before villagers were permitted to bring wine in for sale. Since most villages began as squatter settlements, their very existence inspired suspicion, and their pleas for greater autonomy met harsh rejection from the ruling council. By petitioning the monarchs, the village of Linares had acquired some municipal territory in the early sixteenth century, but the village's desire for juridical independence continued to fuel conflicts with the judicial officers of Baeza. The conflict between Linares and Baeza demonstrates how the tensions between an ambitious village pursuing independence and its determinedly possessive ruling city could lead to generations of legal maneuvers, from which the monarchs did not hesitate to extract financial gain.

Baeza was conquered from the Muslims on November 30, 1227, by King Ferdinand III, and on that same day the Christians captured several Muslim castles in the city's jurisdiction, including Linares. From the beginning, the relationship between Baeza and Linares was adversarial. The first mention of the village of Linares occurs in a royal decree issued by King Alfonso X in 1259, which begins: "In the dispute between the council of Baeza and the pueblo of Linares, its *aldea*, over the properties in the place called Cazlona, which the people of Linares claim were given to them by my father King Ferdinand as their private property and the people of Baeza claim as theirs." The king sent "his man" Sancho Márquez to investigate; he then ruled that the property belonged to Linares, established boundary markers, and ordered Baeza not to contest the decision under penalty of fine.[5]

Linares and Baeza took opposing sides in the fifteenth century during Juan II's war against the infantes of Aragon; the commander of the Linares castle refused to submit to the orders of the commander in Baeza. This defiant act was followed by skirmishes, confiscation of livestock, and even the killing of Alonso de Valenzuela in 1441 by the defenders of Linares because he tried to turn the castle over to Baeza. Linares achieved some release from Baeza's control in 1483, when Ferdinand and Isabella deprived

Baeza of the privilege of appointing the commander of the Linares fortress and gave the post as a hereditary possession to their own supporter, Carlos de Biedma.

In 1500 the judge and councilmen of Linares petitioned Ferdinand and Isabella for greater authority in their own judicial affairs. The monarchs granted them a decree raising the jurisdiction of the municipal judges to include civil cases involving fines and penalties of up to 150 maravedís rather than the previous limit of 60 maravedís. As soon as Linares received the decree, the council sent Juan Gómez de Gil Gómez and the council's clerk to Baeza to inform the city council. Two days later sheriffs from Baeza arrived in Linares to arrest the Linares judges. Linares quickly sent messengers to Seville, where the monarchs issued a letter to the council of Baeza stating that it was the royal will that Linares have the added measure of jurisdiction.[6]

In the next few years Linares several times tried to enclose some land and achieve more independence from Baeza. In 1520 Charles V gave Linares a large municipal territory. Local historians later claimed that this was a grant of township, but the documents themselves seem to indicate that the king wanted to define rather narrowly the area in which he authorized some Linares citizens to exploit at their own expense silver and lead mines north of Linares, with the right to apprehend any "evildoers." Charles also granted, perhaps to provision the mines, the council's petition to "enclose and allocate uncultivated royal land for planting, preventing entry to livestock from any other pueblo [i.e., Baeza]."[7] Baeza protested this threat to its jurisdiction for several years and finally resorted to the argument Charles could never refuse: in 1537 the king accepted fourteen thousand ducados from Baeza in exchange for a royal guarantee that neither then nor in the future would he allow any change in Baeza's jurisdiction over the villages of Vilches and Linares.[8]

Linares remained a village in the jurisdiction of Baeza throughout Charles's reign. Members of its elected council, including the two judges, were subject to annual audits and inspections by Baeza judges. The Linares judges could hear civil and criminal cases involving fines up to 150 maravedís. For more serious cases, litigants and prisoners had to travel to Baeza, where the city judges tried their cases and rendered judgment. The Linares council managed the new land received from the king in 1520, enclosing some to be rented and cultivated. The *monte*, the part that remained uncultivated because it was too steep for plowing or too rocky to be terraced, was now reserved exclusively for the use of Linares citizens for its firewood, pasture, and wild crops and game. Linares officials patrolled the *monte* with the power to apprehend and fine illegal woodcutters, grazers, and hunters. The municipal treasury grew with fines and rents, and the population increased from 624 households in 1528 to 988 in 1561.[9]

The more Linares grew and prospered, the more oppressively Baeza's jurisdiction weighed on the dignity and initiative of the Linares judges. By 1564 the economic resources of Linares were sufficient to justify the village's decisive step toward independence from Baeza. Of course, growth and prosperity were not what the council argued in its petition to Philip II asking for township. Charles V had promised Baeza in 1537 that the status of Linares would never be changed, and the council of Linares needed to give King Philip a rationale for breaking his father's promise. The village had to make the classic argument: it was deprived of justice, and the king was losing subjects and resources. The Linares council complained that Baeza officials harassed and mistreated the people of Linares, preventing the population from growing and even causing the village to decline.[10] The petition claimed that Linares suffered injustices arising from the 1537 decision, because the city of Baeza had not clearly explained to the emperor that Linares would be cut off from the king's justice in Baeza by distance, topography, and the need to travel through an intervening jurisdiction. These circumstances made Baeza's jurisdiction oppressive, because it violated the spirit of the 1537 guarantee. As a result, private property and the citizens' income were being destroyed in endless litigation and appeals, with damage to the royal domain. Therefore, the king's duty was to revoke his father's promise.

Baeza sent an attorney to the royal court with copies of its 1537 guarantee from Charles V, but after much negotiation between the Linares council and the royal treasury, Philip II agreed in 1564 to grant township to Linares.[11] He explained this reversal in terms of the highest aspirations of Castilian political life, noting that the 1537 agreement with Baeza had been "noxious and prejudicial" to the citizens of Linares, depriving them of "the hope they had maintained of liberating and separating themselves from the said city." The price of liberty: 20,000 ducados.[12]

Linares transmitted 13,000 ducados immediately to Nicolás de Grimaldo and Lorenzo Spínola in partial payment of a loan the Genoese financiers had made to the king earlier. The balance was advanced by the royal treasurer, Diego de Orvea, and was to be financed out of the Linares municipal assets. Several citizens of Linares mortgaged their real property to the royal treasurer as security for this debt. The council had offered the standard rate of 7,500 maravedís per household in its bid, and a royal appraiser established a rather inflated count of 1,136 households, which translated into a final price of 22,720 ducados.[13] The difference between the village's bid and the final price created a tangle of difficulties.

The prominent Linares citizen Pedro de Baeza, who traveled to Madrid,

Barcelona, and Segovia with the royal court for a year to negotiate these terms, signed a contract in Madrid committing the council and citizens of Linares to pay the full sum to the royal treasurer by the end of 1564. The council, the treasurer, and the king all expected the final payment to be made without trouble, even though the final price was 10 percent higher than the council's bid. But as is typical in these transactions, both buyer and seller overestimated the profitability of the *propios*, and by mid-1565 the administrative expenses and 2,720 ducados of the balance were still outstanding. Philip now authorized the council to raise the balance by an assessment (*repartimiento*) levied on the citizens "with all rectitude and equality."[14]

But at this point a concerned citizen, Pedro de Jaén, began a campaign against the council's payment plan, which fell heaviest on the poor, first by depriving them of free access to the commons and then by charging them a levy through the assessment. Pedro de Jaén appeared before the council asking, among other things, that the assessment be graduated according to the value of each citizen's real property. He had done some research himself by traveling to other Andalusian towns that had bought township, and he demanded that Linares follow their method of raising the funds. He presented notarized testimony that the towns of Campillo de Arenas, Torredonjimeno, and Pegalajar had collected assessments "from each according to the value of his property, and for those citizens who owned no property but were wage earners, adjustments were made so they paid only small amounts." Other citizens of Linares supported Pedro de Jaén's charge that the assessment was unfair, that the poor were assessed at high rates and the rich at low rates, and "what is worse, they collect and harass and seize from the poor" but not the rich. The complainants carried their case to the royal appellate court in Granada, which ruled in their favor on August 31, 1565, and ordered the council of Linares to pay the sums contracted or forfeit both township and the 20,000 ducados.[15]

Pedro de Jaén was not satisfied and demanded that the council draw up a new assessment. The council stated that because some of the population was very poor and hard-pressed, it had no intention of collecting the assessments and would continue to pay off the debt from the income of the *propios*. The appellate court of Granada again ruled in Pedro de Jaén's favor, ordering the council to carry out a new and more equitable assessment, which the council did in January 1566. Although some of the assessments were still in arrears as late as 1569, Linares transmitted its final installment to the late treasurer's heirs in mid-1566. By paying off its corporate debt, Linares cleared the way for publication of the royal charter, and the council scheduled the great event and its celebration to coincide with the feast day of the town's patron saint.

The municipal judges now embodied the king's justice. When the judges and the councilmen published the royal privilege on June 24, they styled themselves appropriately as "the lords Linares."[16] The judges and councilmen had no difficulty assuming increased juridical powers when Linares was transformed from a village to a town, because the practices and symbols of justice were essentially the same in cities, towns, and villages throughout Castile. All municipal judges were *alcaldes ordinarios*, but not all were equal. The judge of a village had jurisdiction over only petty cases involving very small fines in civil cases and minor penalties in criminal cases. No matter how large the population of his village, he could not exceed the authority of a village judge. Once the village became a town, however, the judge exercised the full range of judicial power, including the death sentence, over a legally recognized municipal territory. Towns did not enjoy judicial independence theoretically, yet the lord, by delegating his jurisdiction to the town council in the founding charter, agreed that "neither he nor any of his men would lay a hand on any citizen of the town."[17] City and town judges sent their sheriffs to investigate crimes committed within the municipal territory and arrest or indemnify the accused. The judge rendered summary justice on the spot, without writs or other written proceedings.[18] The judge's ruling and sentence could be appealed to an ad hoc subcommittee of the town council or to the full council itself. In towns small enough for town meetings, the town meeting confirmed the most serious penalties.[19] Once the council or town meeting confirmed the judge's sentence, the case could be appealed directly to a royal appellate court. After the Linares judge received these increased powers, he continued to carry the same staff of office (*vara*), to administer the same legal code and ordinances, and to live among the same neighbors and fellow citizens.

As instruments and symbols of its new power Philip ordered that the town of Linares should have a gallows, stake, execution block, jail, stocks, chains, "and all the other insignia of jurisdiction that the cities and towns in our kingdoms that are free and exempt from all other jurisdictions have and use for and over themselves" (see figs. 7 and 8). Linares thus joined the company of even the oldest towns of the kingdom, who described themselves simply as "an ancient town with gallows and stake" or as "having the gallows and stake of a town from time immemorial."

Soon after Linares celebrated its royal charter of township, the Linares council erected the usual symbol of township, a stone column (*rollo*) of justice, at the entrance to the town where the highway came from Baeza.[20] The type of column that Linares erected as a symbol of its independent jurisdiction could be found throughout Castile in both royal and seignorial towns. Symbolically it represented a stake—a wooden post with a pointed top, where the severed head of the executed was impaled—and therefore the column was widely known as a *picota*. Most columns had short arms

Fig. 7. Instruments of judicial punishment. A Spanish royal appellate judge in Mexico abuses Indian municipal judges by putting them in the stocks. *Codex Osuna*, p. 204.

Fig. 8. Instruments of judicial punishment. A Spaniard is restrained by a shackle and leg chain. *Codex Osuna*, p. 191.

just below the peak, reminders of the hanging tree and gallows (see fig. 9). The column of jurisdiction symbolized the judge's power of capital punishment and, therefore, the town's independence from any other municipality.

Many towns probably began by erecting a wooden stake, as the founders of Veracruz in New Spain did, until they could commission a stone column mounted on a stepped stone platform. The column's platform and steps were used as a seating space and were popularly disparaged as places of bragging (*mentideros*).[21] The stone column itself was often a highly decorated work of the stonecarver's art, with classical allusions linking the "republic" of the town to the justice of ancient Rome.[22] Some columns were fluted, some, like the ancient columns that commemorated military victories, were embellished with spiral carvings, others were surmounted by little temples of justice, with their classical pediments and columns (see fig. 10).

The Linares column stood on a platform with four steps, as did the column in Morata, which was described in the eighteenth century as follows: "In the marketplace the column of local stone, with four steps at the base, measures ten *varas* in height." In Pastrana the jurisdictional column was mounted on three steps and surmounted by the cross of the Order of Calatrava (see fig. 11). In Garovillas the council commissioned a multipurpose structure in the center of the marketplace, combining the municipal fountain with a stone platform and steps supporting a Doric column of jurisdiction embellished with a cross. A more humble—and utilitarian—symbol of jurisdiction was the iron ring (*argolla*) in Serranillos del Valle, a town in the jurisdiction of the count of Chinchón that never attained a population of more than about sixty households.[23]

Such highly decorated columns and their homey platforms clearly were not used as instruments of the death penalty, which, in any case, was rarely imposed. Municipal charters and ordinances prescribed fines as judicial penalties for most crimes and civil sentences, and the municipal archives of the towns contain no judicial records other than total annual fines and penalties collected by the judges. The harshest penalty actually carried out with any frequency was exile from the town for ten or more years. If a guilty party were condemned to death, there would not necessarily be any written record of the execution: the judge of a town had the power to impose and execute the death penalty but was not required to keep records of cases and sentences. Capital crimes appear to have been extremely rare in the sixteenth century. Townspeople could remember only the occasional spousal murder, and in every case the murderer who was a citizen of the town fled the jurisdiction (presumably with the complicity of the officials) and disappeared.

The few instances of capital punishment for which we have descriptions

Fig. 9. The column of justice and the fountain in the Hueva marketplace. The column's steps are a favorite meeting place. Photo by Jeffrey A. Wolin.

did not occur until the eighteenth century and were reported as worthy of note long after the fact. The priest of the town of Navalagamella in 1782 recounted an execution carried out in 1744. The judge Francisco Miguel, in the Plaza de Abajo of the town, condemned to death Roque Belázquez, native and citizen of Adamuz, thirty-three years of age and married to María Ana, for killing and robbing Juan Bermejo, native of San Bartolomé de Pinares, while the latter was escorting five loads of money to Madrid. After the condemned man was executed by hanging, his body was quartered, the four parts were impaled at the entrances to the town, and the head at the scene of the crime.[24]

The most fearful symbol of judicial authority was also the most fragile—the staff of justice (*vara de justicia*). The presiding officials carried the staff as a sign of office everywhere within the municipal territory. They carried the staff as a symbol of jurisdiction when they walked the municipal boundaries to establish and inspect the limits of the municipal territory. In 1476 Ferdinand and Isabella ordered the judges of the *hermandades* to carry a green-colored staff in order to distinguish themselves from the municipal judges.[25] The staff of the municipal judges was the same as the

Fig. 10. The column of justice in the Fuentenovilla marketplace, in front of the town hall. Below the peak a miniature classical temple is mounted on the backs of four caryatids atop a fluted column. Photo by Jeffrey A. Wolin.

staff carried by the royal judges and by ad hoc judges appointed for specific situations. Military commanders on campaign carried the stubby baton of command, but as commanders of frontiers, royal forts, and city walls they appointed *varas* with jurisdiction over all the military personnel and their dependents.[26] The staff alone was considered sufficient to instill respect in potentially dangerous situations. The royal official who took possession of the newly discovered silver mines in Guadalcanal in 1555 appointed a citizen of Llerena to guard the mine at night with his staff of office and two sheriffs.[27]

If the person of the judge or the sanctity of his staff were violated in any way, the full weight of royal justice fell on the offender. In the village of Manzaneque at the beginning of the sixteenth century the council planned a bullfight for the feast of St. John. The night before, some young men from the neighboring towns of Orgaz and Mora got together, went to Manzaneque, and hamstrung the bull as it was coming out of the corral. The judges of the village ordered the sheriff, Juan Gil Domingo, to arrest the young men, but they drew swords, cut the staff he was carrying, and

Fig. 11. The column of justice in Pastrana, topped by the cross of the Order of Calatrava. In the background is the palace built in the 1530s by the princess of Mélito, Ana de la Cerda. Photo by Jeffrey A. Wolin.

severed a finger from his right hand. The young men fled from the plaza to the parish church, which the villagers surrounded and guarded while they sent for a judge from their ruling city of Toledo. The next evening many people came from the town of Orgaz with weapons and took the young men out of the church by breaking down the church doors. When this happened, certain citizens of Manzaneque went to the king to protest about the incident and its perpetrators. The king appointed a commissioned judge with salary, per diem, sheriff, and clerk, who stayed in the village a few days and took many prisoners from the towns of Orgaz and Mora and held them in the old castle of the village. He imposed serious penalties on those found guilty and ordered that the house in Orgaz where the assault had been planned should be torn down, and its land sown with salt.[28]

In the Americas the staffs of justice continue to hold great prestige in Indian communities. In Peru the boundary judge is known as the *varayok* (staff bearer) and carries a black staff surmounted by a richly worked silver head. In the United States the Pueblo Indian towns of New Mexico still possess and use staffs of office, which are called canes. The canes are carried by the elected mayor or municipal governor and other members of the town council. Several pueblos own three staffs: the Spanish cane, presented by the colonial viceroy after the Pueblo revolt was crushed in 1692; the Mexican cane of the early nineteenth century; and the Lincoln cane, presented by President Abraham Lincoln at the request of a delegation sent by the Pueblos in 1862.[29]

Despite the council's joy at becoming a town, the powers granted to the Linares judges were not as full as those enjoyed by judges of most royal towns. Philip could not entirely rescind the emperor's 1537 promises, for which the city of Baeza had paid in good faith. The council of the treasury, in consultation with the king, decided that the charter of 1537 should be "clarified and modified." Linares would receive its own full civil and criminal jurisdiction, yet it would remain in the *corregimiento* of Baeza in specific instances. This last condition of being subject to the corregidor of another municipality was incompatible with the status of town, and for that reason the royal document granting township in this case listed in great detail what powers the Linares judges would exercise in full and what limitations they would have to accept. The Linares charter spells out the powers of township that Linares would not receive and thereby makes explicit those judicial powers of a town that usually remained unstated in documents.

First, the king specified the geographical extent of Linares's jurisdiction. This is more straightforward than in most cases, because in 1520 Charles had given Linares its own municipal boundaries.[30] The surveyor Lorenzo de los Ríos laid out the boundaries, designated topographical features, and, where necessary, erected stone boundary markers to encompass the residential nucleus of Linares, the lead and silver mines, the water and fuel necessary for the mining operations, and the usual cultivated land and *monte*.

In the 1566 privilege, Philip gave Linares full jurisdiction over everything within the municipal territory, excluding Baeza's officials from the territory altogether and transferring to Linares all the powers Baeza had once exercised. The king confirmed and accepted the boundary survey drawn up by Lorenzo de los Ríos and excised and separated Linares, as thus defined geographically, from the jurisdiction of the city and royal corregidor of Baeza:

I make you a town so that in your boundaries, as they are recognized, surveyed, and marked apart from those of the city of Baeza and other adjacent municipalities, you may use and exercise our civil and criminal jurisdiction.

Linares was to use the same law code (*fuero*) as Baeza and would have the same powers over its own citizens, residents, lodgers, and inhabitants.

The king enjoined royal and local officials, particularly officials from Baeza, from interfering in Linares:

We order our corregidor or judge-auditor from the city of Baeza and any other judges and the council, judges, councilmen, knights, squires, officers and good people of the city of Baeza and its villages, and all other cities, towns, and villages of our kingdoms now and at all times not to intervene in or disturb the said jurisdiction that we thus give and concede to you.

With this grant of Baeza's *fuero*, the Linares town council became one more of the many autonomous judicial bodies in Castile, administering one of many law codes. To hear appeals from the sentences of municipal judges and adjudicate cases between equal jurisdictions (such as litigation between the city of Baeza and the new town of Linares) the monarchs traditionally appointed a royal appellate judge for each of the medieval kingdoms or regions of the monarchy. These royal appellate judges were given different titles, depending on when the region became part of the Castilian monarchy—*merino mayor* in the region now known as Old Castile, *prestamero mayor* in the Basque region, *adelantado mayor* in New Castile and in Andalusia. By the fifteenth century these royal judges were superseded by the royal appellate court, the *audiencia*, which Ferdinand and Isabella later divided into two *chancillerías* permanently based in Valladolid and Granada. This reorganization of the royal appellate courts did not affect the autonomy and independence of the municipal judges, whose powers and jurisdictions remained unchanged. Appeals from the decisions of the municipal judges and disputes between equal jurisdictions now went to the *chancillerías* and, on appeal, from there to the supreme court of the monarchy, the royal council. The royal justice continued to be equally as dependent upon municipal government as the political administration of the monarchy.

For the city of Baeza, recognition of Linares's autonomy was to be eight months retroactive—the city's judges were ordered to remit to Linares all the pending cases and their files, both criminal and civil, initiated during the previous eight months in matters that would have come within the purview of the Linares judge for final disposition and sentencing. Baeza's judges and other officers also were forbidden to enter the town of Linares or its municipal territory for purposes of investigation, arrest, confiscation, or any other act of jurisdiction. Nor could the Baeza judges or officials summon the people of Linares to appear in Baeza for any reason. They were to treat Linares in the same way as other towns, under pain of the fines and penalties incurred by those entering an alien jurisdiction.

Linares, in turn, could not interfere with Baeza and its villages, and particularly the people of Linares could not claim any new rights or changes in matters concerning the pastures, meadows, watering holes, clearings, cuttings, plowing, or any other benefits in the jurisdiction of Baeza and neighboring towns. The king limited changes to the specific jurisdiction he gave Linares, and he reserved for himself the privilege of appointing the clerk of the Linares council, a post that previously had been filled by Baeza.

Philip ordered that Baeza and Linares work as equals to maintain their commons, each council appointing experienced persons to meet and draw up appropriate ordinances, with the provision that these ordinances could not be put into effect until they had first been reviewed by the royal council and confirmed by the king. Once the ordinances were approved, the citizens of both Baeza and Linares would be required to observe them until such time as others might again be drafted in the same way.

In order to implement this jurisdiction, the king gave Linares the right to elect and appoint its own town council and officers, which included two municipal judges, two more for the commons, a sheriff, councilmen, a treasurer, an attorney, market inspectors, field guards, and all other officers usually and customarily elected and appointed in the towns of the kingdom that had jurisdiction for and over themselves. The king delegated his own royal authority to these elected officials: "To the said judges and sheriffs we give the power and competence to carry in our name the staffs of our justice." Before this the Linares judges had presided in the name of Baeza; henceforth they would preside in the king's name and without reference to Baeza in all lawsuits and civil and criminal trials of whatever type and magnitude that might occur, originate, or develop in the municipal territory of Linares. The Linares judges were instructed to preside and act in the same manner as the judges of the other autonomous towns in the kingdom and as the royal corregidor and the city judges of Baeza, who had previously exercised the royal authority in Linares. The judges in Linares were to execute all the laws and try all law cases, reserving to the king only supreme sovereignty and to the royal chancery court appellate jurisdiction.

The traditional hostilities continued between Linares and Baeza throughout the seventeenth century. The two rivals would appear unequal if measured by extent of territory or population: Baeza, with 5,172 households, was five times the size of Linares in 1591. Yet, by this time the Linares council had grown to include ten councilmen, as well as the two judges and the high sheriff. The council was assisted by a large paid staff: a field guard and a "sheriff of the mines," a commander (appointed by the council), two lawyers and three procurators, a council clerk, a depositor general, a schoolmaster, a public crier, a porter, a steward, and inspectors of the butcher shops, weights and measures, and marketplace.[31]

The royal decree granting township to Linares did not intimidate Baeza for long. In a meeting on May 29, 1599, the Baeza city council voted to prevent Linares from operating the town's latest addition to its *propios*, a ferry service across the Guadalimar River, which formed the boundary between the city and the town. Baeza commissioned its high sheriff, Juan de Torres, to carry out its decision. He arrived at the river on June 19 and arrested the startled ferryman, Francisco Molina, citizen of Linares. After taking Molina's "confession," the sheriff released him with a warning not to ferry again, under penalty of two hundred lashes. The sheriff then moored the ferryboat to the left bank of the river and returned to Baeza. Linares brought suit against Baeza before the royal appellate court in Granada and received a favorable ruling on March 29, 1600. The court ordered the council and officers of Baeza to restore the ferryboat to the Linares council and threatened the city with a fine of one thousand ducados for any future interference with the ferry service.[32] As a town Linares now enjoyed equal legal standing with the city and used its independence not only to prevent Baeza's aggressions but even to grow at the expense of Baeza. Linares bought more municipal territory from the monarchy, always contested by Baeza, and won favorable rulings in 1645, 1667, 1677, and 1697.[33]

Most royal towns that bought charters from the Habsburgs were not subject to the royal corregidor of another municipality. But the king had a moral obligation to cities such as Baeza, which had paid for royal guarantees of its jurisdiction in 1537. Philip therefore exempted Linares from the jurisdiction of the Baeza city council but kept it under the supervision of the royal judge in Baeza, the corregidor. Philip imposed the same limitations on several other new towns liberated from cities that had paid large sums to Charles V, such as the town of García, exempted from the jurisdiction of Trujillo, and Usanos, exempted from the jurisdiction of Guadalajara.[34] These few towns, such as Linares, whose full autonomy was compromised by Charles's early guarantees to cities were an anomaly in the Castilian judicial system (see fig. 12). When a lord was present in person in his town, his jurisdiction superseded that of the town council; at all other times the council exercised the lord's judicial powers. The major exception to this direct link between municipal judge and royal court developed in cities and royal towns in the fourteenth century in the person of the corregidor. To settle internal conflicts that the city governments failed to resolve, monarchs began to appoint royal judges (corregidores) to preside over the city councils as proxies when the monarch was not present in person.[35] The corregidor's area of jurisdiction (his corregimiento) was exactly the same as the city council's—extending to the city boundaries and no more. Within his corregimiento, the corregidor co-administered the city's fuero and municipal ordinances—not Las siete partidas or some other royal law code—along with the municipal judges and city councilmen. Although the appointment of the corregidor represented the monarchy's attempt to inject a more direct royal authority

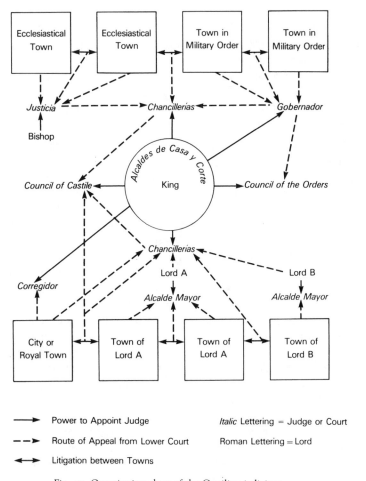

⟶ Power to Appoint Judge	*Italic* Lettering = Judge or Court
⤍ Route of Appeal from Lower Court	Roman Lettering = Lord
⟷ Litigation between Towns	

Fig. 12. Organization chart of the Castilian judiciary

into the municipal governance of Castile's turbulent cities, the monarchs did not extend the *corregimiento* beyond the geographical bounds of the municipal territory, nor did they create new laws or law courts superseding the *fueros*.

The limitations placed on the town of Linares gave the corregidor of Baeza the right to hear appeals from Linares and to audit the Linares jurisdiction. The corregidor could not remove a prisoner from the town of Linares for any offense, even though Linares remained within his *corregimiento* and even though the case might come before him at the appellate level. In civil cases tried by the Linares judges involving fines of ten thousand maravedís and more, and in criminal cases involving major penalties of death, whipping, mutilation of a limb, loss of one-half or more of one's goods, and condemnation to the galleys or exile for five or more years, the condemned could choose to appeal to the corregidor rather than to the royal appellate court in Granada. But once the corregidor passed sentence in such an appeals case, he could not execute the sentence or delegate one of his subordinates to execute it. Instead, the corregidor had to remit the execution of appeals cases to the Linares judges or dismiss the case once sentence was rendered.

The corregidor of Baeza, furthermore, could not even travel to the new town in an official capacity, except for an annual audit, which the charter of township limited in both duration and authority. If the corregidor of Baeza wished to audit the judiciary of Linares, he might reside in the town once a year for no more than eight days. Only during this annual audit could the corregidor try cases of the first instance in Linares. Even during this period, however, a strict separation was to prevail between him and the local judges. He could not intervene in cases pending before the municipal courts. During his audit, the corregidor was to employ the Linares clerks and sheriffs; under no circumstances could he employ Baeza clerks, sheriffs, or other officers. On leaving Linares, he was to release the files of all pending cases initiated before him to the Linares judges, who were to pronounce sentence definitively. Sentences involving penalties of less than ten thousand maravedís imposed by the town's judges or by the corregidor acting as auditor in cases of first instance could be appealed only to the full council of the town sitting as an appellate court, not to the royal appellate court in Granada. The sentences in these appeals were to be carried out by the Linares town council. In such a case, the council would transcend the local *fuero* to enforce the relevant royal laws, Cortes agreements, and ordinances of the kingdom relevant to the case, just as the corregidor and royal appellate court in Granada would in appellate cases of more than ten thousand maravedís. Despite the limitations and conditions that prevented Linares from enjoying the total jurisdiction of a town council, Linares received by this privilege "full authority to call and entitle and describe yourselves as a town free and exempt from the said city of Baeza," with all the same honors, favors, concessions, privileges, liberties, exemptions, preeminences, prerogatives, and immunities "as the other royal towns of our kingdoms have."

The complexities and limitations in the judicial authority gained by Linares were the direct result of the king's piecemeal attempts to rationalize the judiciary, which his own financial expedients were plunging into organizational chaos. The traditional jurisdictions of cities, military orders, and prelates dissolved into hundreds of smaller units at irregular rates and without respect to geographical location. Some towns were left isolated in a sea of alien jurisdiction, towns from historically disparate jurisdictions were joined under a single lord and his appellate judge, and towns that bought royal privileges that contradicted earlier ones were compelled to endure the interference of royal corregidores.

The monarchy, by attempting to maintain the appearance of standing by the 1537 guarantees to the cities while giving effective full jurisdiction to the new towns and new lords, created a complex web of jurisdictional authority. The city councils lost both territory and jurisdiction. The royal corregidores posted to the cities appeared to retain authority but in fact were severely restricted in the reach and power of their office.[36] The territorial jurisdiction—*corregimiento*—of the corregidor had always been limited to the municipal territory of the royal city or town to which he was posted, without extending to neighboring seignorial or ecclesiastical towns. Historically, the corregidor had exercised the king's full power to act within the *corregimiento*. Philip II's sale of jurisdiction to Linares and other new towns placed the corregidores in the difficult position of having to maintain two different standards of authority and behavior, one in the new towns exempted from the city and another in the city and its remaining villages. This deliberate dismantling and complication of the corregidor's authority in cities and royal towns was matched, if not exceeded, by the accelerating transformation of villages from ecclesiastical jurisdictions into royal towns.

The effects of this multiplication of royal jurisdictions quickly became apparent to the royal court: the sixty to sixty-five royal corregidores who had been able to coordinate the implementation of royal policy to the cities and royal towns at the beginning of the sixteenth century could not handle the increased number of royal towns (and villages in the process of becoming towns). In the first two decades of the seventeenth century the number of *corregimientos* still had not surpassed seventy.[37] Towns that had shared a single appellate court in the archdiocese of Toledo separated into their seignorial or royal jurisdictions for civil and criminal cases. The case of Alcalá de Henares is an extreme example of this dismantling of the power of corregidores, because the town of Alcalá itself was completely dismembered during the sixteenth-century sale of the archbishop of Toledo's property. Most of the twenty-five villages in the jurisdiction of the town of Alcalá de Henares bought their own township and thus became royal towns. They were exempt from the municipal judges of the town of Alcalá, but for appeals they could choose to go before the corregidor in Alcalá, appointed by the archbishop of Toledo. Alternately, they could take their appeals before the royal "corregidor of the town of Pezuela and the other new towns" or to the royal appellate court in Valladolid.[38] As if this situation were not complex enough, all twenty-five new towns retained their rights in the Alcalá commons and took their grazing and boundary disputes to the judges of the commons, headquartered in Alcalá.

The old juridical structure of the military orders became a shambles as some towns were alienated and others remained in the military order. In the medieval structure, appeals from the elected judges of the towns in a commandery had been taken before the commander, and appeals from the commander's rulings had been ruled on by the master of the order and his council. By the mid-1560s the commanderies had disintegrated as a result of the sale of towns from the military orders. On December 5, 1565, Philip II issued a royal decree intended to reorganize the juridical structure of the military orders. The old commanderies were eliminated in all but name. The towns remaining in the military orders were grouped into judicial and administrative districts called provinces, which defied all geographical and historical logic. Each district was administered by a governor (*gobernador*), who was, in effect, a lifetime lord. Each governor appointed an appellate judge (*alcalde mayor*), whose jurisdiction superseded that of the elected municipal judges in the towns, even in cases of first instance. Three months later, in February 1566, Philip issued a second decree, sweeping away even the old terminology of commandery and commanders: all the towns of the military orders were to be subject to the governors and organized into appellate jurisdictions (*alcaldías mayores*).

Philip's attorneys, of course, defended his attack on the traditional local system of justice in the military orders as a reform of abuses. The royal decree alleged that municipal judges (*alcaldes ordinarios*) could not adequately administer the king's justice, because they were not trained lawyers and their vested interests in the town led them to abuse the judicial powers of their elected office to enrich their own families. But the intended benefits of the reorganization either did not materialize or were not valued by the towns themselves. The towns of the military orders were among the oldest in Castile, and those that remained in the orders after the early sixteenth-century sales deeply resented the reorganization. In the Order of Santiago, the town of Villarrubia, which "had possessed its own civil and criminal jurisdiction since its foundation, the charter for which could be found in the archive of Uclés," could not conceal its frustration with the 1566 reorganization, which "had restricted its jurisdiction along with that of the other towns in its district, so that the *gobernador* in Ocaña could preside over any criminal case at will."[39]

Twenty years after reorganizing the judiciary of the military orders, Philip II reconsidered and opened the way for the towns remaining in the military orders to regain their traditional autonomy. In a decree of March 23, 1587, he explained that the old system seemed, in retrospect, to have been more convenient, because even though the municipal judges were not lawyers, they sentenced with the advice of legal counselors, and any injustice could still be appealed to the governor. Furthermore, the king noted, it had been more convenient when the judges were natives and citizens of their jurisdictions, because it reduced costs and trouble for the litigants. For all these reasons, the king appointed Fernando del Pulgar to negotiate with the councils of the towns in the military orders about the sum of money they would offer in order to have their jurisdiction reinstated to what it had been before.[40]

Almodóvar, a town of eight hundred households in the Order of Calatrava, was visited for this purpose in 1592 by Dr. Sánchez Méndez, commissioner of the royal treasury. For three days Dr. Sánchez and his notary stationed themselves in the portal of the parish church to record the votes of the citizens. In the final tally, six hundred citizens voted in favor of repurchasing the old jurisdiction, and thirteen against. The council agreed to pay thirty thousand ducados in three years, to pay the wages of the sheriffs and other judicial expenses, and to contribute two hundred escudos per year to the treasury in the future. As collateral for the financial obligation, the council mortgaged its *propios*, and a number of citizens mortgaged private property. The monarchy accepted this bid and issued a royal license to the town in 1594 that removed the appellate judge then presiding in the town and transferred jurisdiction in cases of the first instance to the town itself, to be exercised by the usual elected town judges. When the council was not able to pay the full sum within three years, it received permission from the treasury to take out further mortgages on the municipal income but finally managed to pay off the full sum in 1602. In that year the council of Almodóvar received from the royal court in Valladolid its "privilegio de jurisdicción en primera instancia."

During the Trastamara period the city corregidores emerged as the most powerful judges in Castile, because their jurisdictions were the cities, the most extensive and powerful territories in the kingdom. Most cities and royal towns lost significant portions of their municipal territory and jurisdiction in the sixteenth and seventeenth centuries. Of the cities, Guadalajara was the biggest loser, shorn of all its villages by the end of the seventeenth century, whereas Toledo appears to have resisted dismemberment most successfully, losing eight of the twenty-two villages in the Montes de Toledo, all bought by members of the Toledo city council, and a handful more villages and *aldeas* from the municipal territory proper.[41] Most cities were diminished in territorial extent by the Habsburg sales of the sixteenth and seventeenth centuries, and with the shrinking of the cities, the corregidores lost much of their status and power.

At the same time, the territorial jurisdiction of noble lords was expanding, because many lords were buying towns alienated from ecclesiastical jurisdictions.[42] This process of increasing the extent of seignorial jurisdiction by purchasing former ecclesiastical villages that had already been converted into towns intensified one of the traditional characteristics of seignorial jurisdictions: the proportion of towns to villages was very high compared with the proportion in ecclesiastical jurisdictions. This became even more pronounced after Philip II found a way to profit from even the seignorial jurisdictions: taking advantage of the desire of every village to become a town, the royal government in the second half of the sixteenth century sold township to seignorial villages. The lord's consent was required and apparently freely given, but the money went directly into the royal treasury. These new towns did not become royal jurisdictions: they remained within the jurisdiction of their hereditary lords and took their appeals cases to the lord's appellate judge.

The steps leading to this opportunity resemble the development of royal claims for the ecclesiastical properties. Charles and Philip laid claim to the absolute possession of jurisdiction in seignorial territories and therefore the authority to dispose of that jurisdiction. One of the earliest tests of this absolute royal authority over seignorial jurisdiction developed in territory belonging to the duke of Infantado, and it may have been considered a test case for the monarchy. In March 1549 the royal chancery court in Valladolid issued a ruling in favor of the duke of Infantado and his town of Saldaña, who together had opposed the claims of the twenty-two villages in Saldaña's jurisdiction. The villages had brought suit against the town of Saldaña, claiming that the town did not have the right to audit their judicial and financial records. The chancery ruled in favor of Saldaña but imposed limitations: the Saldaña judge could audit the villages of the jurisdiction once a year but must do so in person, not delegate the task to any other person, not even the lord's appellate judge; and the town judge was to make the audit as if he were applying the king's justice to the royal subjects, without collecting from the villages any expenses or other impositions. With this ruling two principles were firmly established: the royal government exercised the ultimate disposition of justice even in seignorial jurisdictions, and villages were subject to their ruling town even if the lord had appointed an appellate judge for his jurisdictions.[43]

The combination of these two principles provided the incentive and the opportunity for another round of sales to the benefit of both seignorial villages and the royal treasury. Villages desperate to achieve freedom from their ruling town were willing to pay as much as villages buying freedom from a ruling city. In the 1560s most of the villages belonging to the dukes of Infantado bought exemption from their ruling town. In 1566, for example, with the consent of the duke, the village of Las Chozas offered the king 7,500 maravedís per household for exemption from the duke's town of Manzanares. The royal appraisers counted 136 householders, and the council of Las Chozas paid the 1,200,000 maravedís in full on September 22, 1568. The king issued the privilege of exemption on December 31, 1568, and Las Chozas became a seignorial town with full criminal and civil jurisdiction over its own municipal territory. Appeals from the judges of Las Chozas now went directly to the duke's appellate judge rather than to the judges of the town of Manzanares, and Manzanares judges could no longer audit the judicial and financial records of Las Chozas.[44]

Lords often ended up with dozens of autonomous judges operating under municipal ordinances that varied only slightly from one town to another. But because lords also bought towns and their villages from ecclesiastical jurisdictions in the sixteenth century and from city jurisdictions in the seventeenth, no single set of laws or ordinances prevailed within the lord's jurisdiction. Appeals from the municipal judges were heard by an appellate judge (*alcalde mayor*) appointed by the lord. He wielded the lord's jurisdiction in all his towns and villages, just as the corregidor wielded the royal jurisdiction in cities and royal towns. The appellate judge's decisions and sentences could be appealed only to the royal appellate court. But as the lord's towns multiplied, the appellate judge's job became more complicated. In order to establish some kind of order in the shifting and expanding world of seignorial towns, the monarchy required lords with more than one town to appoint an appellate judge to supervise and rationalize the proceedings of the annually elected municipal judges. The lord's appellate judge adjudicated disputes between the councils of the lord's towns, as well as between his subjects from different towns. If these towns had originally come into the lord's possession from different jurisdictions, the appellate judge arbitrated between the differing law codes and ordinances.

The function of the appellate judge in the cities before 1492, when Christians, Jews, and Muslims lived in the same city under their different laws, was to find an equitable settlement of conflicting claims brought from two legal systems.[45] The historian Prudencio de Sandoval recounted that one of his ancestors, Fernán Gutiérrez de Sandoval, city councilman of Seville, was appointed Juan II's appellate judge "between the Muslims and the Christians."[46] The Muslims of the city of Granada negotiated favorable terms in the peace treaty with Ferdinand and Isabella in 1492, which allowed them to retain their religion, language, customs, laws, and judicial system. The Muslim and Christian legal systems coexisted in the city, and the monarchs appointed Andrés Calderón as the appellate judge for cases involving subjects from both laws. After 1501, when the Muslims were forced to convert to Christianity or leave Spain, the city was ruled by a single municipal council, with its two elected judges and a corregidor. But the appellate judge continued to preside over the Granada city council meetings during any absence of the corregidor.

In the sixteenth and seventeenth centuries corregidores were usually the appellate judges in royal jurisdictions, and *alcaldes mayores* were the appellate judges in seignorial jurisdictions. One anomaly developed in the estates of the duke of Infantado, who was reputed to own jurisdiction over eight hundred towns and villages. In 1503 he was living in the city of Guadalajara, where he literally owned most of the royal income from the city and the right to appoint the city council. He set up his own judicial court in Guadalajara with two judges to hear appeals from his towns. The court grew to five judges by 1537, but the duke lost control of the city government in the 1540s and was required by the king to accept a corregidor for his seignorial jurisdiction. The duke's corregidor resided in his town of Real de Manzanares,[47] although the largest town in the corregidor's jurisdiction was Colmenar Viejo, which had become a town in 1506. Although its jurisdiction extended only over its cultivated land (*dezmería*), by 1579 the population had reached one thousand households and was still growing. Colmenar Viejo described its courts as "attached" to the *corregimiento* of Real de Manzanares. The two town judges were equal to the corregidor in jurisdiction, and when the corregidor was not in the town itself, he could not issue any official orders or remove cases from the judges to hear them himself.[48]

During the sixteenth century the lord's judicial activity was restricted to appointing the judges over his towns. For the municipal judges, the lord chose one of two slates of candidates submitted by the outgoing judges. The lord appointed and dismissed the appellate judges at will, but any interference with the nomination of the municipal judges or in their jurisdiction would bring down the wrath of the royal justice, particularly if the lord was out of political favor. In 1543, as we have seen, the royal appellate court in Valladolid agreed to hear the complaints of the town of Meco against its lord, the marquis of Mondéjar. In that year the marquis was in disfavor because as captain general of the Kingdom of Granada he was resisting the royal court's determination to rid the Moriscos of their non-Christian practices (if necessary, by ridding Castile of the Moriscos). The royal appellate judges ruled in Meco's favor, ordering the marquis to stop interfering with the municipal judges.[49]

Lords found municipal constitutions and ordinances an attractive solution to the problems their appellate judges faced in reconciling the conflicts and contradictions of the different *fueros* in their towns. Litigants who were citizens of villages had to travel to the ruling town to prosecute their cases. But the citizen of a town had the right to the lord's justice without traveling to another town. The *alcalde mayor* often had to travel from one to another of the lord's towns, moving from one law code to another and adjudicating between conflicting ordinances. Lords had granted municipal ordinances to their newly acquired towns for at least two centuries, but in the 1560s, after the monarchy required lords to appoint *alcaldes mayores* over all their seignorial jurisdictions, the need to rationalize the local codes became urgent. Some towns appear to have accepted the changes in their ordinances supinely. The ever-vigilant coun-cil of the town of Estremera, in contrast, was determined to retain as much autonomy and advantage as possible and submitted numerous draft constitutions to its new lord over a period of ten years.[50]

These ad hoc expedients and experiments raised concerns about judicial excess and corruption. Learned jurists such as Jerónimo Castillo de Bob-adilla gamely wrote handbooks to lead corregidores and appellate judges through the maze of local law codes and imperfectly joined royal and seignorial practice.[51] But these judicial guidelines did not provide the monarchy with a systematic or hierarchical structure of local administra-tion. In the resulting benign neglect, power shifted by default to the small farm towns of Castile. To many lawyers and royal officials, the situation seemed ripe for abuse. The *alcalde ordinario* of a town, without being learned in the law, had the power to impose and enforce the death penalty. What was to prevent him from exceeding his jurisdiction? History had shown that a town that carried out a just but illegal death sentence would win the support of the king.

Some excesses of the past became stage hits of the royal court. In Lope de Vega's *Fuenteovejuna*, probably written and produced in 1613 or 1614, Laurencia demands justice from the town meeting, even though the town has no jurisdiction over the accused, who is their lord. Her father, Esteban, the *alcalde ordinario* that year, admits that he has no authority to correct the abuse of the lord and deprecates his *vara*: "Why do I carry this useless stick?"[52] But Laurencia argues that to do nothing would make them bar-barians rather than Spaniards. The men of the town take the law into their own hands, kill the lord, and refuse to reveal who struck the mortal blow. When royal judges come to investigate, the men insist even under torture that the town as a corporation did it: "¡Fuenteovejuna lo hizo!" Faced with this conflict between justice and jurisdiction, King Ferdinand sides with the town.

In 1641 Pedro Calderón de la Barca's drama *El alcalde de Zalamea* ad-dressed the growing conflicts between equal jurisdictions. The farmer Juan Crespo is elected judge of Zalamea by the council just after his daughter is raped by a captain of the royal army marching to Portugal. Crespo arrests the captain, who points out that the municipal judge has no jurisdiction over a military officer: the Council of War will hear his case. Crespo finds the captain guilty and sentences him to death. The captain's commander claims jurisdiction because the judge of a town does not have the authority to execute a military officer by garroting, but Crespo sets him straight: the commander must not underestimate the authority an *alcalde ordinario* has within his own jurisdiction. Crespo executes the captain himself, and finally, when King Philip II arrives, reminds the king that the royal justice is a single body with many hands; it does not matter whether justice is meted out by one or the other. The king agrees that Crespo was correct on the major issue though wrong in detail.[53] The moral lessons acted out on the stage by Lope de Vega's *Fuenteovejuna* and Pedro Calderón de la Barca's *El alcalde de Zalamea* lingered on to disturb the sleep of any lord or royal official who might dare to violate the justice of a town or its *alcalde ordinario* or to underestimate the bonds of mutual interest between towns and an impoverished monarch eager to sell the charms of township.

The general perception was that being a seignorial town was preferable to being a village of a city but worse than being a royal town. This ranking was based on the valid assumption that the best government was the most distant one and on the dreaded possibility that the lord might decide to reside in the town itself. Such cases were rare and could hardly have been a reality for most seignorial towns. The wealthiest nobles with the oldest titles owned so many towns that they could not possibly visit all of them in a year, much less keep informed of their day-to-day operations, even if they had wanted to. Lords granted township to their subjects much more readily than did the monarchy or the church, since this did not diminish their authority. In fact, it was more prestigious to be lord over many towns than to be lord of a town and many villages. Township was also attractive to the lord because it made each town as self-sufficient and therefore as efficiently administered as possible. A town newly exempted from the jurisdiction of another town belonging to the same lord received a municipal territory and judicial autonomy equal to that of Linares; the citizens of that town too could put up a stake or column to emphasize their new status as an autonomous jurisdiction.

The judges and councilmen in seignorial towns were chosen in much the same way as in other jurisdictions. Most were nominated annually by the outgoing council or judges, who submitted the names or two lists of names to the lord for his appointment. The outgoing officials transferred their duties and staffs of office directly to the incoming council, without the intervention of the lord or any seignorial representative. Ideally, the lord audited the council's administration of his jurisdiction once every three years; in practice, most audits occurred when a new lord inherited the jurisdiction after an inheritance battle or if the lord was led by a drop in his seignorial income or complaints from his subjects to suspect misfeasance. The judges in seignorial towns carried the same staffs and the same authority as judges in other towns. When lords carried out their periodic audits of administration in their towns, they asked the local citizens if the judges had wielded the staff "in the name of the lord" and not in their own right nor in the name of any other authority.

The Habsburg kings and their ministers at the royal court were more concerned about the opposite problem: the proliferation of towns under the jurisdiction of absentee lords. The royal corregidor Jerónimo Castillo de Bobadilla believed that subjects of the king were better off judicially than subjects of lords, because "to be subjects of the single, supreme lord is the supreme liberty."[54] Castillo de Bobadilla wrote from the point of view of royal judges, who were required to reside in the city to which they were assigned for one or two years, and he believed that judicial ills in seignorial towns stemmed from nonresidence by the lords. He leveled his criticism against the appellate judge, whom he dismissed as "some private employee." The lord's absenteeism, he charged, left the citizens with no recourse from the harm done by the appellate judge who, to gain perquisites from the public treasury, as well as gifts and presents from individuals, conducted affairs in a crooked way.[55] Modern historians unfamiliar with the judicial structure of the premodern Castilian countryside have misunderstood the thrust of Castillo de Bobadilla's argument. Historians who believe that the seignorial regime must have been inherently unjust, when they cannot find examples of injustice by lords, overlook Castillo de Bobadilla's accusations against the appellate judge and assume that the absence of the lord led to injustice by "local elites."[56] Castilians in the small country towns had just the opposite opinion: if they could not be free of the lord's jurisdiction, they at least preferred to be free of the lord's presence.

The administrative competence of new lords who had never owned jurisdiction before was of special concern to citizens. Only one instance of seignorial abuse was enough to haunt the imaginations of citizens confronted with transfer to a seignorial jurisdiction, and a disastrous case in the sixteenth century fulfilled the stereotype of the resident lord so perfectly as to be comedic. The town of Peñalver had belonged to the Order of the Hospitallers of St. John since the early thirteenth century, and its fortified castle was the headquarters of the commandery of Peñalver and Alhóndiga. The town survived epidemics in the fourteenth century but hardly appears in written records after that time, and its only claim to fame was a native son, Cristóbal de Vega, who became a professor of medicine at the University of Alcalá and published books on medical subjects that went through several editions in Spain and France.

In 1552 the bishop of Lugo, Juan Juárez de Carvajal, bought Peñalver and Alhóndiga from the king for his son, Garci Juárez.[57] Conflict between lord and citizens erupted almost as soon as the bishop took possession of the town. In 1555 he attempted to assume control over the civil and criminal jurisdiction by appointing the municipal officials himself. The people of Peñalver revolted "en comunidad" against the bishop, assaulted his appellate judge, who had to barricade himself in the church, announced that they would do the same to the bishop if he should appear in the town, and committed other acts of open rebellion. The king sent a judge from the royal court to investigate the incident and punish this violation of the royal justice.

To the frustration of the citizens, the bishop's son, Garci Juárez, came to live in Peñalver, built a residential palace in the town because the castle was no longer habitable, and began interfering with the town government. Within ten years the council of the town brought suit against the bishop and his son. The council's attorney presented a bill of grievances before the royal appellate court in Valladolid, representing that his clients previously had governed themselves and the town very well under the terms of their 1532 agreement with the Order of St. John. The 1532 agreement had followed years of conflict between the commander of Peñalver, Alberto de Lago, and the town. The council had accused the commander of "extortions," and finally lord and town had agreed that Peñalver would conduct its lawsuits and appeals, which were the specific topic of discord, according to the procedural norms of the *fuero* of Guadalajara.

But, the council charged, the new lord and his son had ignored the agreement, which they were obliged to observe by the terms of the sale. The council's attorney made the classic Castilian argument of impending depopulation: the new lords repeatedly violated the rights of the citizens and oppressed the town to the point of nearly destroying it; some citizens had already moved from Peñalver to escape the oppression, the lawyer argued, and others were threatening to do the same if they did not receive some relief.[58] Whether Garci Juárez moved to Peñalver for personal reasons or in response to the rebellion we do not know, but his presence and actions led directly to the council's lawsuit against the bishop. The council's bill of particulars against Garci Juárez has the detail and specificity of truth. The most serious accusations were that he violated the council's sphere of administration. Garci Juárez denied the right of the people from time immemorial to nominate their own officials, forbidding them to present him with a list of candidates before he made the appointments; he required the citizens to send a gift of six thousand maravedís to the bishop of Lugo; he inspected the jail; he released prisoners; he made demands on the tavern keepers, hostelers, and shop owners; he inspected the boundary markers; he refused to allow audits of the judges, who were his own "creatures"; he took game for his own consumption; he brought before himself appeals from the municipal courts of first instance; he ordered that the accounts of the *propios* be kept in the fortress or in his own house.

Equally serious were the council's charges that Garci Juárez plundered the *propios* for himself. At times he seized the wheat in the municipal silo, cut down hundreds of the oak trees in the commons called El Rebollar, seized the hospital and ten fanegas of enclosed land called El Castillo Viejo; tore down some houses belonging to the council in order to create a plaza in front of his own house; took for himself the best acorns from the *monte*. Furthermore, he perpetrated injustices. He repeatedly imprisoned whomever he was displeased with without any legal cause whatever, simply out of anger and without respect to age or gender; in addition, he physically mistreated the citizens and required them to address the castle with their caps removed, and so on.

A municipal council jealous of its hard-won victory against the commander now fell subject to an inexperienced lord who imprudently resided in the town itself and intruded on the daily lives of his subjects. For the citizens of Peñalver, transfer to a seignorial jurisdiction exacerbated conflicts of jurisdictional procedure and prerogative that had flared in less colorful forms years before.

Castilian justice is usually described as essentially the application of royal law, codified in Alfonso X's *Las siete partidas* and other medieval compilations, by royal judges and corregidores.[59] The evidence from the local judiciary, however, reveals just the opposite in both theory and practice. There was no law code common to all Castilian municipalities. The founding charters of cities and towns prescribed the law code to be enforced by the municipal judges. No two municipal charters were exactly alike to begin with, and most evolved over time to suit local conditions and added ordinances as circumstances required. This multiplicity of jurisdictions and variety of law codes seemed as normal and effective to Castilians in the Habsburg centuries as the concept of states' rights does to Americans in the twentieth century. To the eighteenth-century Bourbons it seemed the embodiment of all the irritating obstacles to royal control of the local administration. The Bourbons promulgated a new royal codification in 1805, the *Novísima recopilación*, and finally succeeded in suppressing the local *fueros* entirely in a series of new national law codes promulgated in the 1880s.

Chapter 6

The Economic Pleasures and Perils of Liberty

New towns achieved their coveted judicial autonomy the moment they received the royal charter of township; economic prosperity took longer to achieve and depended, above all, on timing. Town councils in the sixteenth century grappled with an array of new problems. In the first half of the century, the councils were using credit to buy municipal autonomy and then investing municipal funds in the communal infrastructure, which raised productivity during the mid-sixteenth-century period of stable climate and unprecedented population increase. After 1575 they were confronted by a sustained worsening of the weather, which destroyed capital investments, and by population decline, which cut production. Councils that achieved township early enough to take advantage of favorable conditions survived the crop failures, epidemics, and declining population that afflicted Castile during the last quarter of the sixteenth century. Towns that had managed to get one set of debts paid before the other set arose did reasonably well; their councils mobilized the towns' *propios* to avert the worst economic consequences. Those that sought to do both at once went bankrupt. The places most likely to fail were those that bought township between 1575 and 1600; they did not have a chance to pay off their loans and develop their *propios* in time to cope with the stressful conditions of the last quarter of the century.

One of the new towns that successfully developed its economic resources in time to take advantage of the sixteenth-century expansion was Horche, which first appeared in a document of 1399 as a squatter settlement within the municipal territory of Guadalajara.[1] The first settlers were sheep grazers who built their homes around a spring gushing out of the side of a mesa. The village overlooked the site of a *despoblado* down in the little valley of the Ungría River. The Horchanos cultivated the fields of the *despoblado* for grain and grazed their sheep on the commons of Guadalajara. In 1399 Guadalajara officials asserted jurisdiction over the squatter settlement, granting Horche the legal status of *aldea*—an official colony with rights to pasture in the commons of Guadalajara and with title to the fields already under cultivation.[2] As a village, Horche had no control over its judicial or administrative affairs, which were entirely in the hands of the

city council of Guadalajara. Guadalajara exercised veto power over elections of the local council, limited the powers of the municipal judges, and
collected for its own city treasury the fines and fees paid by the Horchanos.

During the fifteenth century the Horchanos diversified their fiber production by terracing and irrigating the mesa's lower slopes to plant and
process hemp. Horche became an important producer of fibers (hemp,
flax, and esparto grass, as well as wool) and manufacturer of utility textiles
(straps, sacks, tarps, ropes). Farmers from Horche cleared, plowed, and
tried to enclose more land, which led to violent confrontations and legal
disputes between Horche and Guadalajara.[3] Horche's population and need
for arable land were growing just when King Juan II was lopping off
Guadalajara's municipal territory to the southeast of Horche and granting
it to the ancestors of the count of Tendilla as seignorial towns (see map
5). Every effort Horche made to gain more equitable treatment at the
hands of the city's judges was frustrated by Guadalajara's determination
to preserve its remaining municipal territory to the advantage of its citizens
only. Trapped between the towns of the count of Tendilla and Guadalajara's obduracy, Horche appealed to the monarch, and in 1488, 1491,
and 1533 the Castilian monarchs ordered Guadalajara to cede more commons land for cultivation to accommodate the growing population of
Horche. Thanks to this royal intervention, the Horchanos were free to
clear and plow land for cultivating wheat and to terrace the steep slope
on the opposite side of the Ungría for olive trees and grape vines.[4]

By 1533 Horche's population had grown to 304 householders, who felt
they had suffered enough at the hands of the city. The council of Horche
wrote to Charles V complaining that its judges were allowed to hear cases
involving fines up to only sixty maravedís. For more serious cases the
Horchanos had to appear before the courts in Guadalajara, whose officials
were not always fair or moderate. The Horchanos claimed that the trip
to Guadalajara to appear in law cases caused many inconveniences, expenses, and absences from their farming activities. Further, they alleged
that Guadalajara's judges were needlessly harsh in petty cases and that
the city's officials made excessive demands in their annual audits of
Horche's municipal accounts. The Horchanos borrowed five thousand
ducados from wool dealers in the town of Medina del Campo by mortgaging
the income from their herds of sheep for the next seven years and they
offered this sum in cash to the king in exchange for making Horche a
town with the right to elect its own town council empowered with full
civil and criminal jurisdiction and with its own municipal territory. On
December 20, 1537, Charles V accepted their offer, and Horche became
a town.[5]

On the day Horche received the royal charter of township, the town
celebrated its independence with a fiesta and ceremonies marking each

power gained. First, the senior member of the town council officially accepted the royal charter by kissing it and placing it over his forehead. The town crier then read the charter aloud to the townspeople, who had been summoned by the ringing of the church bell. The citizens in town meeting elected new municipal officers, who swore to fulfill their duties and then, accompanied by the crowd, carried out the first symbolic acts of their new powers. They established a jail and erected a column of justice (rollo) in the plaza and a gallows on a nearby hill. The municipal judge heard and passed sentence in some civil and criminal cases. The council renewed the leases on the municipal tavern and butcher shop, inspected the weights and measures used in the marketplace, surveyed the new municipal boundaries, and approved town ordinances.[6] Nature provided the opportunity for the town to live up to its new status as "Horche, her own mistress," when lightning blasted an old elm in the town plaza. From its lumber the town made desks for the schoolchildren and a collapsible stage for the annual Corpus Christi play.[7]

What was equally important, the Horchanos now had a municipal territory of their own and the authority to expend its income. Although neither the king nor the townspeople themselves mentioned the local economy or finances as incentives for judicial autonomy, the citizens could hardly have overlooked the financial benefits that would accrue to their community if court fees and fines remained in their own municipal treasury instead of being paid to a ruling city. This would have been particularly apparent in places such as Horche, whose vigorous and expanding population competed with citizens of the city itself for the resources of Guadalajara's municipal territory. Once the first euphoria of township had faded and its initial cost had been paid, the council used its corporate income to invest in capital improvements. Horche embarked on a half-century of development, financed from the new municipal revenues.

After Horche became a town, it set about improving its propios. In 1545 the council purchased from private owners several bleaching ponds and a fulling mill and then built a flour mill. The council completed construction of ditches to irrigate the bleaching ponds in 1552 and in 1556 built a new race for the two flour mills. In 1561 the council purchased more municipal territory from the city of Guadalajara to encompass all the private property owned by Horchanos.[8] Agriculture began to surpass the manufacture of utility textiles as the major occupation, while the population grew to five hundred households in the last quarter of the sixteenth century. The council invested in a new well for the draft animals (1570), a seed bank (1578), and a perpetual leasehold on plowland belonging to a church in Alcalá.[9] Finally, the municipal territory included a grass meadow, a section of foothill covered with rosemary, kermes oak, and gall oak, all used as commons by the citizens of Horche, and a pasture reserved for the municipal butcher.

By 1578 the council of Horche owned as *propios* two flour mills, which produced an income of two hundred fanegas of wheat every other year; a fulling mill for hemp, which yielded twenty ducados annually; and a perpetual leasehold on land belonging to the Magdalen Chapel of the Church of St. Justo in the town of Alcalá de Henares, for which it paid an annuity of forty-eight hundred maravedís. The municipal revenues from these corporate assets swelled: they yielded five hundred ducados in cash and two hundred fanegas of wheat per year.

By 1596 Horche had grown to six hundred households, but three years later half the town's population died in a plague epidemic. The councilmen assumed that the population would increase again, for they soon made a series of further investments to ensure control over their own town. Their possession of the town government should have been secure as a consequence of the charter of township given to Horche in 1537 by Charles V. But in the early seventeenth century the Spanish monarchy could no longer afford to allow towns such as Horche to develop their own resources without contributing more to the royal treasury. Though Philip III (1598–1621) ruled over much of Europe and the Americas, he needed money from the small towns of Castile. Unable to raise taxes in the face of resistance from the Cortes and unwilling to continue his father's policy of selling ecclesiastical jurisdictions, Philip III resorted to a policy of claiming for the monarchy municipal offices that had never existed in most towns.[10] Town councils were forced to decide whether to buy these new offices themselves—in effect, paying a one-time tax—or run the risk that private investors would buy the new offices and gain influence in the town government. In 1603 Horche bought from the monarchy the right to carry out its own audit rather than have it done by a royal judge. In 1613 and 1617 Horche bought from the king the municipal offices of broker, inspector of weights and measures, and clerk. There is no evidence that royal judges had ever audited Horche's municipal government, and the town had functioned throughout its existence without a broker.

Philip III's financial difficulties and expedients paled in comparison with those of his son. During the reign of Philip IV (1621–65) Spain's silver fleet for the first time lost ships on the high seas to Dutch and French attacks, its armies suffered unprecedented losses in battle, and the monarch finally agreed in 1648 to withdraw from the European conflict. Within Spain, the monarchy needed the support of the nobles, the professional military class, more than ever; tax revolts had erupted in the Basque country and Catalonia, and Portugal was fighting for its independence from Castile. Unable to compensate the nobles in cash for their years of military and diplomatic service, Philip IV gave them portions of the royal domain in payment of arrears, converting more royal towns into seignorial towns. Though the acquisition of towns did not satisfy the nobles' need for cash, it shifted their demands from the royal treasury to the towns themselves.

In 1652 Horche lost its status as a royal town. Philip IV removed Horche and several other nearby towns from the royal domain and gave them to the heirs of the duke of Pastrana in payment for the duke's services as royal ambassador thirty years earlier. Overnight, Horche became a seigno- rial town, still independent of any other municipality but now subject to the jurisdiction of its lord. In contrast to the benign neglect Horche had enjoyed as a royal town, it was now threatened with the close supervision of the lord's appellate judge (*alcalde mayor*). Horche reacted vigorously to preserve its judicial independence.

Like every seignorial town that was not in a perpetual trust (*mayorazgo*), Horche had the option of transferring its jurisdiction from one lord to another. In theory, this privilege derived from the autonomous medieval towns known as *behetrías,* which had the right to choose their own lord. In the fourteenth century Enrique de Trastámara and his supporters used the theory of the *behetrías* to encourage towns to transfer their support from the legitimate king, Pedro, to the usurper, Enrique. In the succession war of the 1470s Ferdinand and Isabella used the theory of the *behetrías* to encourage seignorial towns to transfer their jurisdiction into the royal domain and out of the jurisdiction of lords who were fighting Isabella's claims to the Castilian throne. The Habsburgs turned this tradition to profit through the process of *tanteo:* the royal treasury allowed a town to transfer its jurisdiction from a lord to the royal domain by matching the price the lord himself had paid for the jurisdiction; by negotiating a sale price with the royal treasury and the lord, the town could buy its way out of the seignorial jurisdiction. Horche reached an agreement in 1658, paying the new duke a sum of money in exchange for its release. So Horche, which had begun its history as a royal town by making investments that increased its productivity in the mid-sixteenth century, was prosperous enough even during the agricultural depression of the mid-seventeenth century to buy its way back into the royal domain.

Horche suffered the same epidemics and harvest failures as the rest of Castile during the last quarter of the sixteenth century, but by the time the natural disasters began, Horche's municipal debt for township had long since been paid off, and the council had been able to invest the municipal income in developing the town's economic infrastructure. In the seventeenth century the citizens complained of a high tax assessment, which was not reduced by the royal treasury when the population collapsed, but they were able to pay the taxes from the *propios*. Using the irrigation systems, bleaching ponds, and fulling mills of their town, the Horchanos were still able to manufacture and sell textiles for enough cash to pay their fixed obligations. The town owed its success in surviving as a royal town largely to good timing. Horche bought its township after the worst natural disasters of the early sixteenth century had already passed. Throughout the next sixty years weather and crops were unusually and consistently good. At the same time, the population grew rapidly: between 1530 and 1590 the population of Castile doubled, and in the Tajo River basin the population grew even faster. Even though there were no national or long-term food shortages, grain prices stayed high, and even the government-fixed price tripled.

Horche and other places that were already towns were able to profit from this mid-century economic expansion. Spanish farmers understood perfectly the relationships between prices, demand, and production. As the chronicler Bernáldez pointed out in describing the price drop of 1508, "The greatest cause of the price drop was that, because half the population of Castile had died in the epidemics of the year 1507, there was no one left to eat the good harvest of 1508." With their eyes keen for profits, and with food prices rising steadily throughout the century, farmers tried to meet the demand by increasing production. But the most suitable land had been put to the plow long before, and in the last half of the sixteenth century farmers in the Tajo River basin resorted to terracing and irrigating areas that could not withstand heavy rainfall. When erratic weather in the last quarter of the century inflicted serious environmental damage, many towns that had invested in large-scale capital improvements failed to pay their municipal debts and had to place themselves once more under a seignorial jurisdiction.

The fastest way to increase production was to acquire more land. This strategy was successful in the short run, but every scrap of land was quickly cleared and plowed. Old towns abandoned in the depopulation of the fourteenth century, areas previously considered too far from town or too unhealthy for human habitation, and lands never before cleared now became farmland. Grazing land was so scarce that livestock moved to the extremely poor pasturage of the scrublands. By 1575 the ecological balance of the *monte* had been destroyed. Towns responding to the *Relaciones* questionnaire lamented that they lacked fuel because the *monte* had been deforested and that large game had disappeared because so much of the land was being plowed.

Farmers knew that by plowing and grazing marginal lands they were reducing long-term productivity, but they were determined to take advantage of the rising demand for grain and were willing, for a while at least, to pay the price. Grazing lands became so scarce and so desirable that during the sixteenth century most pastures in Castile were the subject of litigation between towns. Towns accused each other of moving or destroying the markers, of invading each other's pastures, of forging written documents, and of misidentifying the pastures for which they claimed to have leaseholds. Some of these lawsuits lasted generations, because each time a court handed down a decision, the losing town would appeal to a higher court. To handle these lawsuits, councils hired attorneys on retainer to plead their cases before the royal courts. In most towns the attorney's fees were the single greatest annual expense of the council, and in cases where the litigation dragged on for years, the attorney's total fee exceeded the value of the land in litigation. The heavy legal expenses councils were willing to undertake attest to the tenacity with which towns pursued a policy of increasing productivity.

The council of the town of Belinchón exhausted its financial resources in litigation against its lord, the archbishop of Toledo, and its neighbor to the north, the town of Estremera. By 1580 the Belinchón council perceived that its population had once been much larger—it was said that there had been days when forty or more maidens went to the springs for water—and that Belinchón's prosperity could be improved by the council's gaining control over all the land in its municipal territory. But during the period of depopulation, Belinchón had lost the usufruct of some of its territory to its neighbor Estremera. In the fifteenth century the Estremera council negotiated a perpetual leasehold with the archbishop on a portion of Belinchón's arable land. In the sixteenth century Estremera claimed the right to enclose the land its citizens farmed in Belinchón, preventing the Belinchón livestock from pasturing on the stubble. Both towns lacked *monte* because they lay on the alluvial plain of the Tajo River, where almost all the land was cultivated. The Belinchón council owned only one pasture for draft animals and one for the municipal butcher shop, while the Estremera council owned as *propios* four pastures that together produced annual revenues of one hundred thousand maravedís in rents and pasture fees. Belinchón faced a formidable enemy in Estremera, whose aggressive council had been buying and leasing land in neighboring towns throughout the fifteenth century.

For the citizens, the municipal council was both their municipal court of law and their advocate against the claims of neighboring towns and cities. Alert and ambitious councils such as Estremera's bought grazing rights, leased farmland, rented logging and woodcutting rights on neigh-boring *despoblados* during the fifteenth century, and emerged in the six-teenth as the most powerful municipal governments and most prosperous farm towns in their regions. Less aggressive towns were left with the least desirable parts of the commons and often without access to the stubble within their own municipal territory. The economic significance of the council's legal activities was expressed in the draft constitution that the town of Estremera drew up in 1568:

Item: Since this town is very short of municipal territory and has privileges within the territory of neighboring towns that continually try to deprive this town of its privileges, and since, if the officials of the municipality do not understand what is happening in this matter and do not try to conserve its benefits, this town could easily lose the said privileges and would not be able to support itself and the consequence would be that his most illustrious lordship [the lord] would receive a disservice and the citizens of this town would receive notable harm and loss, and since this conservation is best understood and achieved by those who are natives of this town or persons who have lived in it many years, therefore, it is ordered and decreed that no person may be elected judge or councilman of this town unless he is a native of it or has lived in it for twenty full years continuously. [11]

Towns also considered it imperative to increase their productivity by improving the land and resources they already owned. In the long run, the most effective means of increasing productivity was to plow deep, frequently, and with plenty of fertilizer. This was a practice of Spanish farmers throughout their history, part of the common agricultural lore and reinforced by the advice of many books on farm improvement. The abundant labor supply of the period made it possible to plow deep and often, but the benefits diminished over time because of the "manure barrier," a common problem throughout Europe. The large-scale plowing of grazing lands reduced both the quality of pasturage and the size of herds and therefore reduced the amount of manure available.

As demand and prices continued to rise, councils tried to increase productivity by making capital improvements on the property they already owned. Horche's frantic effort to invest every financial resource in capital improvements in order to increase production was typical of the period: throughout Spain in the mid-sixteenth century, small farm towns built bridges, roads, mills, reservoirs, wells, and irrigation works. While the monarchy continued to favor consumers by imposing price controls, farmers expanded production by investing municipal profits in capital improvements.

But even with all of these improvements and the expansion of arable land, Spanish agriculture was still dependent on good weather; and 1570 marked the beginning of a twenty-year period of erratic weather and crop failures. The disasters began with unseasonal rains. The soil could not absorb the increased rainfall, and the runoff caused floods, landslides, and soil erosion. Newly cut roads were buried under landslides, new and old bridges were washed out by unprecedented floods, and livestock and crops drowned as rivers crested over their banks for the first time in the century.

The extension of cultivation to unsuitable slopes during mid-century had changed the environmental consequences of such heavy rains. The greatest physical damage to the region around Horche and its market area occurred on January 20, 1545, for example, without causing municipal bankruptcies. That year, the Tajo River rose all the way to the level of the church in Zorita de los Canes and washed out the Zorita bridge that had stood for 350 years.[12] The destructive force of this winter flood was as much a tribute to the size of the debris thrown up against the bridge as it was to the volume of snow and rainfall that produced the flood. Huge tree trunks and rolling boulders broke loose from scoured slopes whose ground cover had been destroyed by terracing. The terraced land also made earthquakes more destructive. Whereas quakes normally only damaged man-made structures, now they shook loose river banks and hillsides.

More damage to this region of unstable new plantings occurred two decades later, just when many towns were depending on the newly planted terraces to pay off the indebtedness they had undertaken to buy township. The town of Romanones, perched one ridge over from Tendilla, was shaken by an earthquake on May 10, 1566, which was followed by a rockslide that "left us ruined." The same earthquake brought the side of a hill crashing down into the irrigated land of the town of Pezuela, clogging the stream, so that the water ran backward. In the same town, a landslide in 1570 buried some olive trees.

The decade of the 1570s brought not only unseasonal rain but freezing temperatures as well. After fifteen minutes of hail and rain in the winter of 1572 a wall of water swept away the dikes and ditches of the irrigated land of Santorcaz. It poured down a street in the middle of the town, flooded houses and a wine cellar at the bottom of the hill, sweeping carts, timbers, and stones weighing as much as ten tons out through the lower gate of the town to destroy more irrigation channels, and finally broke down the doors of the shrine of Ocalles, sweeping its statues out into the fields.[13] The olive trees in the Alcarria region suffered serious damage in the cold that settled down in the valleys. In the town of Tendilla forty thousand olive trees were killed by a hard freeze on January 9, 1571. That same day, Almonacid de Zorita had snow and a hard freeze, followed that same year by a serious famine, which "led to many illnesses and deaths."[14] The shortage was so severe that the town consumed the entire seed reserve, and on August 15 the council authorized Francisco Salido to seek a loan of two thousand ducados to provision the town with wheat.[15]

In the late 1570s heavy rainfall during the growing season significantly reduced crop yields of Spain's drought-resistant wheat. As the village of Leganés reported, its grain tithe usually amounted to 150 *cahizes* of wheat and barley, "except in very rainy years, which reduces it seriously." Three "very rainy years" of heavy rains brought serious hardship. The population of Miralcampo declined from about forty-five to about thirty-seven households "because of the sterility of the years 1577, '78, and '79, when we had no wheat harvest." Torralba claimed that it had once been a richer town but had become impoverished by the conditions of recent years.[16] In 1579 the duchess of Pastrana's revenue collector described how bad weather had ruined him:

Your grace knows how much I have done in increasing this income and the misfortunes I suffered with it. Last year a hailstorm destroyed most of the crop, almost all of it, and the year before there was a freeze that did the same, so that the income from the vineyards of Estremera, which used to yield a thousand reales or forty thousand maravedís, that first year could not produce more than eleven hundred maravedís, and as a result of this misfortune others followed, and it has been a great and devastating loss for me.[17]

Despite the severity of crop losses in the 1570s, councils took a long time to realize that these were not just isolated incidents. They continued for several years after 1570 to make capital improvements as if the mid-century weather were still the norm.

The town of Almonacid de Zorita paid a high price for its poor timing. It made an overoptimistic investment in economic expansion during the last quarter of the century, when the erratic weather and a previous municipal debt would combine to prevent the town from flourishing. One day in May 1542 the citizens of Almonacid de Zorita were alarmed to observe that their distinguished visitor, Ana de la Cerda, lady (señora) of the neighboring town of Pastrana, was so taken with the charms of their town that she wanted to buy its jurisdiction. She expressed interest in buying the hemp fields near the large spring that provided most of the town's irrigation water. Her engineers began marking out the site in order to build a large residence for her. The next day, the citizens surreptitiously convened a town meeting and considered various ways to prevent being dismembered from the Order of Calatrava. They appointed two citizens, Juan Escudero and Alonso Lozano, to be in charge of this project and stipulated that one of them should travel to Valladolid and negotiate secretly with the emperor and the royal council. By the luck of the draw (they drew straws), Lozano made the trip, which he faithfully carried out in the greatest secrecy.[18]

When he arrived in Valladolid, he went immediately to "Dr. Bonifacio, a great theologian," who was a native of Almonacid de Zorita and a member of the household of the archbishop of Toledo. The two sons of Almonacid de Zorita began working immediately, though with great difficulty because such a matter had never been negotiated before. The royal council demanded that Almonacid de Zorita pay 12,000 ducados to the emperor for a confirmation of its status as a town—a search of the municipal archives had not produced a charter of township—and a royal privilege guaranteeing that it would never be alienated by the monarchy. After much negotiation, the parties agreed on the price of 2 million maravedís (5,333 ducados), which the town would be allowed to raise by mortgaging or selling part of its *propios*.

Lozano immediately notified the council of Almonacid de Zorita of these terms. The townspeople spontaneously celebrated the successful negotiations, releasing the bells to ring freely with the wind, setting off fireworks, playing music and dancing in the streets, and holding a magnificent procession the next day. Ana de la Cerda was astonished to hear of such rejoicing, because she too had sent negotiators to Valladolid. Ana de la Cerda had offered the emperor more money than had Almonacid de Zorita, but her offer had arrived too late, and the royal council had rejected it.

The council of Almonacid de Zorita authorized Alonso Lozano to negotiate a loan, using the *propios* as security, and he borrowed the 2 million maravedís from the treasurer of the Order of Calatrava at an interest rate of 6.67 percent. On June 9, 1542, having received the cash, Charles V issued a royal privilege guaranteeing everything Almonacid de Zorita had requested. The town of Almonacid de Zorita paid off the loan within three years, and Philip II confirmed the royal privilege in 1560.

The citizens of Almonacid de Zorita had good reason to retain their status as a town in the Order of Calatrava, and Ana de la Cerda had good reason to admire and want to live there. As early as the fourteenth century the citizens of Almonacid de Zorita behaved in an assertive and self-confident manner that brought them growth while neighbor communities declined. Almonacid de Zorita had been a Muslim farm town, captured by the Christians in their advance on the city of Cuenca and given to count Ponce de Cabrera by Alfonso VII in October 1152. The count had sold it to a noble lady, Sancha Martínez, who had donated it to the Order of Calatrava in 1174. Within the order, Almonacid de Zorita was an *aldea* of the town of Zorita de los Canes. In the fourteenth century, when Zorita de los Canes declined and the commander moved his headquarters to Pastrana, Almonacid de Zorita began calling itself a town and took the lead in managing the commons of Zorita. The commanders in Pastrana retained their military responsibilities and the income of the commandery but had little influence on the day-to-day affairs of Almonacid de Zorita.

All of this ended in 1539, when Charles V alienated from the Order of Calatrava the town of Pastrana and its villages of Escopete and Sayatón and sold them to the widowed princess of Mélito, Ana de la Cerda, for eighty thousand ducados. In 1540 she arrived to take possession of Pastrana, where she built a grand residential palace, reputed (in Almonacid de Zorita) to have cost more than forty thousand ducados (see fig. 11). The commander, Alonso Carrillo Margarit, moved his residence from Pastrana to Almonacid de Zorita. In Philip II's 1566 reorganization of the towns remaining in the military orders Almonacid de Zorita became the administrative center of the Order of Calatrava's newly created Province of Zorita. From this time on, both town and governors worked to maintain Almonacid de Zorita as a strong and prosperous town.

In 1569 the newly appointed governor of the Province of Zorita, Fr. Francisco Ortiz, proposed building a dam on the Guadiela River for the purpose of irrigating the previously uncultivated land on the slopes between the Guadiela and Tajo rivers.[19] He asked the town to contribute labor for the project. Carried away by dreams of profit and abundance, the council agreed. Once Ortiz had built the dam, the citizens of Almonacid de Zorita would dig the canals and ditches to lead the water to the slopes they were going to terrace. They also agreed to pay Ortiz an annuity of one-tenth of the produce of the newly irrigated land, in addition to paying the church tithes. In the next twelve years Ortiz invested thousands of ducados, and the townspeople, thousands of hours of physical labor. Their investment was all in vain, however, for what they did not realize was that the weather pattern had once again shifted; the very rocks, earth, and tree trunks they used as construction materials were converted by unprecedented floods into battering rams that destroyed all their labors.

By the winter of 1570 Ortiz had built the dam to its completed height of forty-five feet, but an early summer flood carried half of it away. He rebuilt this half, but the melting snow from the storm on January 9, 1571, washed away the entire dam. Ortiz consulted some Venetian engineers, who contracted with him to use explosives to blow up the side of the gorge and fill it with rubble. Ortiz purchased forty-five quintals of powder, which the Venetians used to set off two explosions in April 1571, displacing tons of rocks but failing to stop the flow of the river. The next year, Ortiz contracted with a Spaniard named Pedro Lucas, who promised to build the dam— of dry masonry this time—for fifteen hundred ducados. This dam was almost completed when it was washed out by a flood at the end of October 1572. In the remaining months of 1572 he again almost completed the dam, but in the spring of 1573 between March 3 and May 13 there were only six days with no rain, and on April 11 it snowed for three hours and then froze hard—a sequence that had never occurred before in the sixteenth century. When the snow and ice melted, the rivers rose, there were terrible floods, and again the dam was destroyed.

By now Ortiz had come to appreciate the force of the current at flood season, and he started over, bringing large timbers from the Sierra de Cuenca to strengthen the foundation. In the floods of August 1577 water reached the lower levels of the dam, and it continued to rise during the winter and spring of 1578. The dam held firm and appeared to be trustworthy. The citizens terraced the slopes where they would plant their new crops and started digging the canals and ditches that would distribute the river water to the terraced fields, while Ortiz finished off the dam until it was forty-five feet high and fifty-five feet wide. On September 21, 1578, a severe hailstorm was followed by heavy rain and then by floods and landslides. The dam held firm, but three days later, on September 24, there was more hail and rain. The river flooded, uprooting every tree along the riverbanks and destroying the dam and all the ditches.

In 1579 Ortiz began building again, this time a 130-foot-long wet masonry dam at another site. In the three years it was under construction the dam held firm while it was built up with a network of timbers and boulders and then plated with pine boards. The finished dam became a sightseeing attraction and was admired by the local residents: "The dam was so smooth with this wooden plating that it appeared as if the entire dam had been made of a single piece of wood. It was very agreeable and beautiful to the eyes of men and quite a sight to behold." But on September 26, 1581, this dam was leveled by a flood, leaving neither timber nor stone, to the distress and discouragement of Ortiz and the town: "The river rushed through as if there had never been any structure there. It was a sad thing for this town and for the Commander because the ditch had already been dug to bring the water to irrigate the fields in order to profit from the fruits of the river's irrigation water."[20] Ortiz and the town did not try again.

Every means of increasing productivity seemed to be blocked by the weather, and even normal levels of production could not be achieved in these worsening conditions. In fact, the 1570s and 1580s were punctuated by years of hard freezes, excessive rain, and floods. Faced with this desperate situation, even prosperous and aggressive towns had to abandon efforts to make capital improvements and instead concentrated on simply maintaining enough seed reserve to get through a bad crop year. Partly in response to the urgings of royal decrees, towns all over Castile built and stocked seed banks (*pósitos*), whose grain was available for seed to any needy farmer on the condition that he return as much as he had borrowed once the harvest was in the following year. Horche built a municipal seed bank in 1578, Almonacid de Zorita built one in 1585, and about three-quarters of the farm towns in Castile had a seed bank by the end of the century. By the summer of 1584 the shortage of grain was so serious, and the threat of famine so frightening, that the king ordered his administrators to take the grain from the royal tithe barns and distribute it for seed. Thanks to the planting made possible by this intervention, 1585 was a good harvest year—the only one in the 1580s.

With people wandering all over the countryside during these hard times in search of work and food, the varieties of infection, and opportunities for their spread, multiplied; and as the country people poured into the cities to buy or beg grain, sanitation broke down. Epidemics spread throughout the peninsula. Bubonic plague inflicted heavy losses in La

Bureba and other farm regions around the city of Burgos in 1565–66 and appeared again in 1576 and 1589. The population of the small towns in this region fled to the threshing grounds, field cabins, and dovecotes outside the towns.[21] In the Tajo River basin no epidemic after 1507 had been serious enough to drive the people from their houses until 1576, when plague once again swept through Europe. Madridejos reported that it was not an unhealthy place except in that year, when "contagious diseases were going around," and Sacedón reported that many of its residents died in that year.[22]

The population did not recover as it had after the terrible epidemic of 1507, in part because Spain in 1580 suffered the influenza epidemic that pervaded Europe, and an unusually high proportion of its victims were young adults. The few towns that responded to the *Relaciones* questionnaire in November 1580 reported an exceptionally high mortality during the late summer and early fall of that year. The town of Talamanca voted to establish a devotion to the Elevation of the Cross "because of the many deaths this town suffered from the flu."[23] New Castile lost nearly half its population in outbreaks of bubonic plague in 1598, 1599, 1600, and 1601. The Jesuit historian Juan de Mariana believed that this plague epidemic hit small towns harder than large cities.[24] The Alcarria town of Berninches recalled that more than five hundred of its citizens died in less than three months and that four hundred houses were left empty, with the result that many fields were left to revert to *monte* and brambles.[25] Because of epidemics during the period 1590 through 1605, the town of Serracines moved from its old site and relocated one-quarter league away on higher ground within the municipal territory, but its population continued to decline.[26]

In Horche the tempo of investment in capital development slowed as the population diminished—the number of households did not rise above three hundred until the mid-eighteenth century. But the pace of Horche's investments in spiritual benefits quickened. During the period of Horche's greatest economic expansion, the council had done no more than begin to construct a bell tower (1511), commission a retable (1530) for the parish church, and embellish a shrine (1561). The end of the sixteenth century, with its epidemics and economic stagnation, however, was a period of aggressive investment in spiritual and lifestyle improvements. In response to the 1580 epidemic, the council rebuilt the ruins of another shrine (1581). In 1587 it constructed a portico on the front of the parish church. In the next decade the town leveled and paved the streets, built a splendid municipal laundry, and added more fountains to the municipal water system. In 1605 the town offered a subsidy to some Franciscans to settle in the town and paid for the construction of their monastery chapel, which was under construction until 1655. The parish church was further embellished when the tower was finally finished in 1621 and when an inlaid wood ceiling was installed in the nave in 1622. A citizen of Horche built a chapel in the church in 1670, and in 1692 the apse, whose foundation had been laid almost a century earlier, was completed. In the same year, the town added a sacristy to one of the shrines it had built in the sixteenth century.

These seventeenth-century construction projects added little, if anything, to Horche's productivity. With the diminished demand for food and the subsequent drop in agricultural prices throughout Castile in the early seventeenth century, farmers abandoned marginal lands. Fiber and textile production once again became the major occupation of the Horchanos.

Horche and Almonacid de Zorita suffered in the economic constriction of the seventeenth century, but they survived as towns and managed to escape the clutches of lords. Towns that mortgaged their corporate assets after 1580, in order either to purchase township or to transfer from seignorial to royal jurisdiction through *tanteo*, had much more difficulty surviving the natural disasters of the late sixteenth century. Several of these late bloomers failed financially and had to ask a lord to buy their jurisdiction by assuming their mortgage. Typically, the council borrowed the cash for these changes in legal status from big moneylenders—royal secretaries, wool brokers, or Italian financiers—and assigned the revenues from their corporate assets to the lenders for from two to seven years. The citizens, including the members of the council, mortgaged their private property as security for the loans. Only a handful of towns defaulted on these loans, and most of these failed towns evidenced population decline in the crucial years. The records so far have not revealed whether residents moved away to avoid the heavy financial burdens of these municipal loan payments or whether epidemics reduced the population, leaving too few producers to pay off the loans. Most of the towns that failed undertook relatively large mortgages in the decade 1580–90, indicating that the negotiated price was unrealistically high for a period of crop failure and population decline. The economic fate of towns that Philip II alienated from the archbishop of Toledo is particularly well documented, because ecclesiastical property was the special object of the great cadastral survey carried out in 1752 by the Bourbon monarchy, the Catastro del marqués de la Ensenada. In the eighteenth century, councils of towns that had been liberated in the sixteenth century from the archbishop of Toledo took the precaution of commissioning notarized copies of their receipts and charters of township and attaching these to the town's response to the Catastro.

In 1564, for example, Philip II sold township to the village of Romancos for eight thousand ducados, liberating it from the jurisdiction of the town of Brihuega but leaving it in the jurisdiction of the archbishop of Toledo.

In 1579 Philip transferred its jurisdiction to his secretary, Juan Fernández de Herrera, in payment for a debt of eight thousand ducados. The secretary promptly sold Romancos to Diego de Ansúrez, a citizen of Brihuega. In 1585 the citizens of Romancos petitioned the king for their *tanteo* by matching the price of twelve thousand ducados paid by Ansúrez. On payment of that amount to the royal treasury for transmission to Ansúrez, the town of Romancos for the first time became a royal town, independent of all its former owners—the cathedral chapter and town of Brihuega, the archbishop, and the two lords. But the town was not able to repay the loan it had undertaken. By 1606 Philip III had transferred its jurisdiction to the marquis of Salinas del Río de Pisuerga. In 1618 the citizens again tried to exercise the *tanteo,* offering to pay the royal treasury the same sum that the marquis Luis de Velasco had paid. In the eighteenth century the council was still refusing to recognize the seignorial rights of the marquis, who, from his residence in Mexico, sued for payment of his seignorial annuity: a dozen chickens, twelve *orzas* of honey, and seventy-seven reales in cash. The council did not pay, and the town clearly was in difficulty. By 1785 it still belonged to the marquis, and its population had declined to 140 households from the 400 households of 1580 and 1606.[27]

Philip II alienated the town of Fuentes, with its villages of Castilmimbre, Gajanejos, Pajares, San Andrés, and Valdesaz, from the diocese of Toledo and, in 1581, gave San Andrés township and sold it to Lic. García Barrionuevo de Peralta for four thousand ducados. San Andrés almost immediately began negotiations to exercise the *tanteo,* pointedly changing its name to San Andrés del Rey when the king accepted the town's offer of four thousand ducados in 1584. The price was exceptionally high: the royal treasury had required Barrionuevo to pay the *vasallaje* by extent of territory, because the town had only forty-five households in 1580, while its municipal territory, at more than a square league, was large for its population. The four thousand ducados that the council offered the king was the equivalent of eighty-seven ducados per household at a time when most towns were paying less than twenty ducados per household. During the years 1584–92, San Andrés described itself as a royal town in official documents, but by 1591 it had defaulted on its loan, and ownership of the jurisdiction passed back to Lic. García Barrionuevo de Peralta, who had never received full payment from the royal treasury.[28]

Such sums were not readily available to villages that had never before possessed municipal property or to towns that had just finished paying off the loans they had contracted in order to buy township. To lose the status of royal town after making these financial sacrifices must have been humiliating and frightening, and citizens fought with every financial and legal weapon to avoid such failure. One of the most spectacular failures was that of Uceda. In 1579 Philip alienated the town and its nineteen villages from the archdiocese of Toledo. He granted Uceda to Diego Mesía de Avila y Ovando, apparently in payment of a debt, and bestowed on him the title count of Uceda. But the citizens of Uceda, in a town meeting on April 21 and April 22, 1582, voted to challenge the transfer to the new lord by exercising the *tanteo*. The council gave power of attorney to Captain Juan de Bolea to negotiate the *tanteo* with the royal treasury. In Madrid one week later Philip initiated the process of *tanteo*, but Uceda had to struggle against the opposition of the count for years before finally becoming free of his jurisdiction in 1593.

Having achieved its independence, the town of Uceda then proceeded during the next few years to claim authority over its former villages, which were still members of the commons of Uceda. The judge of Uceda demanded that the former villages contribute to repairing the bridge of the commons of Uceda and summoned their judges to a meeting to deal with the affairs of the commons. The judges of El Cubillo and Pueblo de Valles refused to pay for the repairs and ignored the summons. Uceda's attorney brought suit against the two defiant judges to force them to obey the authority of Uceda. All the former villages of Uceda thereupon united with El Cubillo and Pueblo de Valles, claiming that they were exempt from Uceda's authority by virtue of the royal alienations of 1579 and that therefore the old commons of the "tierra de Uceda" no longer existed. The former villages won the court case in 1621, thus gaining clear legal recognition of their claim to exemption from Uceda's jurisdiction.

The indebtedness Uceda had undertaken to buy its township, the loss of judicial income from its former villages, the heavy expenses of years of litigation, and the ultimate failure of its court case brought the town to a state of bankruptcy. Within three years of losing the case against its former villages, Uceda was forced to sell some of its remaining municipal territory, including the village of Galapaguillos, and accept the jurisdiction of the duke of Lerma's son, Cristóbal de Sandoval y Rojas, who became duke of Uceda.

Cristóbal's impressive title signified little. By this time the town of Uceda was sadly diminished. The commons of Uceda no longer functioned. Its capital improvements—the bridge and dams—were falling into disrepair because the old members of the commons were now a dozen towns interested more in their own prosperity than in Uceda's. Neither the judge nor the duke of Uceda held administrative authority over the new towns. Whereas the king had once sent royal directives to Uceda to be broadcast to all the villages of the commons, the monarchy now sent a dozen copies to be debated, negotiated, and, perhaps, obeyed in each new town of the old commons. Nominally under royal jurisdiction, these towns effectively managed themselves under no jurisdiction at all, because the Habsburgs created no new bureaucratic apparatus for governing the new royal towns. The citizens of the commons of Uceda had bought their political independence and were free to use their autonomy for their own economic good rather than for that of Uceda.

Another type of town that failed to profit from the Habsburg sales was the town belonging to a military order, such as Carrión de los Ajos, that was bought by a private investor. Already a town before the sale, it gained no autonomy by being dismembered from the military order. Rather, such a town now faced the expense of outbidding its new lord to becomes a royal town. Carrión, as we know, remained a seignorial town; it did not even attempt to make use of the *tanteo*, if the absence of a bid from Carrión in the royal treasury records is indicative. Because the retrospective records of these towns were transferred from the archives of the military orders to those of the new lords, whose private archives were dissipated after the suppression of seignorial jurisdiction in 1837, we have few materials for assessing the economic condition of these towns before their sale. One of them, however, gave an evocative report to the *Relaciones* questionnaire describing the difficulties it had survived before dismemberment. These difficulties in the medieval centuries hindered the town of Valenzuela from any possibility of using the *tanteo* in the Habsburg centuries.

The town of Valenzuela enjoyed the advantages of membership in a grazing commons in the Order of Calatrava, yet it struggled for centuries to retain enough municipal territory to survive as an autonomous municipality. Before the law, Valenzuela held equal status with its intransigent enemy, the neighboring town of Almagro. In the Order of Calatrava they were both members of the same commons; but in economic resources, Almagro was a giant amoeba gradually surrounding Valenzuela's territory and leaving it politically and economically weaker with every loss. Valenzuela's early promise as a town settled by the Order of Calatrava in the thirteenth century derived from its location in a fertile and well-watered region of La Mancha (see map 11). Valenzuela's population collapse in the fourteenth century led the council to make changes in the town's legal status that, despite the town's revival in the fifteenth century, left Valenzuela in a dangerously weak legal and economic position in the sixteenth century.

In 1575 two knowledgeable citizens of Valenzuela, Juan de Palacios and Juan Gómez, responded on behalf of the town council to the *Relaciones* questionnaire.[29] In answering the questions, Palacios and Gómez gave a brief history of their town, chronicling Valenzuela's struggle against the neighboring town of Almagro. They declared that Valenzuela's status as a town was so venerable that it had been listed in the catalogue of towns belonging to the Order of Calatrava long before Almagro even had a name. The catalogue, in case the royal officers should care to inspect it,

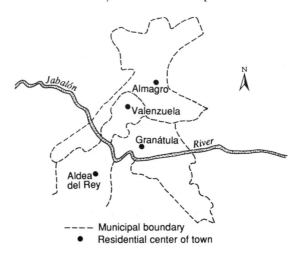

Map 11. Valenzuela and Almagro, c. 1600

was kept in the archives of the monastery headquarters of Calatrava. Fourteenth-century documents from the military order and legal rulings demonstrated that Valenzuela had been a town with jurisdiction for and over itself since its foundation, without being subject to any other government. Valenzuela's legal preeminence in that period was also evident from the petitions sent by judges in Almagro to the judges of the town of Valenzuela asking for justice.[30]

But, Palacios and Gómez continued, after the plague years (presumably of the fourteenth century) so few people were left in the town of Valenzuela that they could not maintain the offices and taxes of the municipality. Following the advice of others, the Valenzuela council joined their township to that of Almagro, giving up their separate jurisdiction on the condition that they would keep their own pastures and other prerogatives. The joint township lasted only a short time because the people of Almagro did not fulfill the conditions and agreements they had made. The council of Valenzuela therefore disaggregated itself from the town of Almagro, once again asserted its own township, and exercised jurisdiction over its own municipal territory and citizens.[31]

The council continued exercising its own jurisdiction for many years, until in the year 1507 the town of Almagro initiated a lawsuit against Valenzuela, citing the terms of the old agreement and claiming that Valenzuela was not a town but Almagro's *aldea*, a village within Almagro's municipal territory, whose residents enjoyed the benefits of Almagro citizenship. The Valenzuela council, eager to defend its autonomy, sent one of its own to file a countersuit at the royal appellate court in Granada. It was said, the two men related, that he took the town privileges and charters with him in order to argue Valenzuela's case but lost them on the way. The most popular theory in Valenzuela was that some crafty people from Almagro got him drunk. Whether or not that was the case, Valenzuela's agent arrived in Granada, initiated the countersuit without the documents, and returned. The council did not pursue the case legally, because by the end of 1507 no more than thirteen households remained in Valenzuela as a result of the great pestilence and famine of that year, and those few that survived were left so poor that they could not pursue the lawsuit. Consequently, Valenzuela was sentenced to be an *aldea* of Almagro.[32]

And so it remained until the year 1538, when the citizens of Valenzuela paid two thousand ducados to Charles V for their liberty. The king gave them a charter of township on November 10 of that year, "since which time it enjoys its own former jurisdiction, both lawgiving and law enforcing, in cases of first and second instance."[33] Valenzuela was now independent from and equal to Almagro—each still a town within the order of Calatrava but recognizing only the master of Calatrava, the king himself, as lord. In the town, Valenzuela's coat of arms, mounted high on the town hall, sported the two winged eagles and cross of Calatrava and the same castle and fleece used by Almagro.

Valenzuela should have shared in Castile's mid-sixteenth-century prosperity. Its population was growing, and its land was productive. Valenzuela lies on the alluvial plain of the Jabalón River, where the topsoil is deep and level and the water table is close to the surface. All the land within the municipal territory was private property suitable for plowing—there was no *monte*—and every year it produced wheat, including the candeal variety prized for white bread, barley, and garbanzos. Thanks to the high water table, the Valenzuelans used well water raised by norias to irrigate their numerous vegetable gardens, in which they grew all sorts of beans, turnips, eggplants, melons, cucumbers, radishes, lettuce, cabbage, and hay, and more than thirty orchards, producing almonds, pomegranates, olives, and figs.[34] In those seasons when the Jabalón River flowed fully the townspeople fished and caught eels.

Valenzuela claimed to raise exceptionally fine domestic livestock, especially plow oxen "better than those bred in other places," mules, milk goats, and sheep.[35] But the municipal corporation owned very little pasture for the domestic animals. The council held clear legal title to two meadows outside the municipal territory, and east of the New Meadow between Valenzuela and the village of Granátula lay the Monte Meadow, which the two towns owned in unequal partnership. Sometime in the past, the council of Valenzuela had bought a small, enclosed pasture called Los Parrales next to the town for the use of the municipal butcher, whose function was to sell fresh meat to those too poor or infirm to maintain their own animals. Valenzuela's transhumant sheep could feed and water on the commons shared by the Calatrava towns of Almagro, Argamasilla, Ballesteros, and El Pozuelo.

Despite its promise, Valenzuela never had a chance to grow or prosper during the sixteenth century. After Almagro lost jurisdiction over Valenzuela, it tried to take part of Valenzuela's municipal territory. Almagro instituted a lawsuit in 1539 charging that the Valenzuela judges were exceeding their jurisdiction by patrolling land in Almagro's municipal territory. The territory at issue involved cultivated fields belonging as private property to citizens of both Almagro and Valenzuela. Redrawing the municipal boundary would not affect ownership of the land itself, but it would determine in which municipality the fields lay and, therefore, whether the domestic livestock of Almagro or Valenzuela could pasture on the stubble (rastrojo) of the harvested fields. For Valenzuela, with its high ratio of arable to pasture, the issue was critical, because the stubble became available just when the grass pastures dried up in the summer drought. The case dragged on for thirty-five years. Three times the Granada appellate court ruled that the boundary divided the fields equally between the two towns, and three times Almagro appealed the ruling.[36] Despite the expense and frustration of this litigation, the town of Valenzuela prospered, and by 1553 its population had grown to comprise 180 households.

But Philip II alienated Valenzuela from the Order of Calatrava in 1554, transferring it temporarily to the royal domain in order to sell it to a citizen of Almagro, Diego Alfonso de Madrid.[37] Valenzuela thus became a seignorial town, still free of any other city or town but subject now to its lord rather than to the military order or the king. The elected council, instead of holding supreme judicial and executive power in Valenzuela, was now supervised by a corregidor appointed every two years by the lord.

Most seignorial towns could expect to benefit from the influence of a powerful lord, but Diego Alfonso could not or would not rescue Valenzuela from its greatest danger, the claims of the town of Almagro. In 1574 Almagro appeared to triumph over Valenzuela. The Granada chancery commissioned a boundary survey that removed more than half of the disputed fields and their pasture rights from the jurisdiction of Valenzuela. The council of Valenzuela appealed the decision, which it regarded as extremely prejudicial to its economy and prerogatives.[38] By the end of 1575, when Palacios and Gómez responded to the royal questionnaire on behalf of the town's council, the future of Valenzuela seemed uncertain. The town hall, with its coat of arms, had been torn down because it was too old, and a new one was under construction, without the townspeople knowing what the lord would display in place of the old coat of arms.[39]

The population had declined to 120 families, because, as Palacios and Gómez explained, "many have left the town, and others have died, and others do not want to get married in this town because it is seignorial."[40] Valenzuela could not exercise its option (*tanteo*) to purchase its own jurisdiction from Diego Alfonso. The interminable lawsuit against Almagro consumed the municipal funds, yet the cause could not be dropped, because the town's economic survival depended on winning clear title to the stubble. Without any *monte*, the municipal corporation owned no capital assets that could secure a loan with which to buy its jurisdiction from the lord.

The people of Valenzuela perceived their world as one of turbulent change that required vigilant protection of their municipal independence and privileges. They knew with certainty that the prosperity of any town depended on exercising legal jurisdiction over its own municipal territory with its gifts of water, fuel, and pasture; fighting off the encroachments of neighboring towns; and resisting the interference of lords. This perception was grounded in one of the historic realities that shaped Castilian society in the sixteenth century: there was not enough arable land to meet the demands of a population that was pushing the limits of Castile's productive capacity. Valenzuela's understanding of the dilemma did not suffice, however, to save it from becoming a seignorial town.

The *tanteo* that was legally but not economically available to Valenzuela was denied to two types of towns, those in perpetual trusts (*mayorazgos*) and, in the late sixteenth century, those villages within a five-league radius of the town of Madrid. Villages in seignorial jurisdictions that were in perpetual trusts could become towns—and often did so with the encouragement of the lord—but once they were towns, they could not exercise the *tanteo* to become independent of the lord's jurisdiction. Villages within five leagues of the royal court in Madrid did not even have the option of becoming towns. This handicap was owing in part to the repressive policies of any ruling town or city fearful of losing some municipal territory. The town of Madrid became particularly vigilant of its southern municipal territory after Queen Isabella gave some villages there to her favorite courtiers.[41] Determined to prevent any violation of its jurisdictional authority within the town boundaries, the council frequently patrolled the municipal territory. In the mid-sixteenth century, a dozen citizens of Getafe settled a village called Perales and began clearing the land for plowing. When the government of Madrid discovered what they were doing, it sent out some councilmen accompanied by armed and mounted sheriffs to forcibly remove the squatters. The settlers appealed to the only alternative authority, the royal courts, but lost the lawsuit. By 1578 Perales was considered a *despoblado*, and the remaining seven households, prevented from farming, converted the place into an overnight stop for teamsters traveling to Madrid.[42]

Madrid became an unusually harsh governor of its municipal territory after Philip II made it the capital in the 1560s. The judges of the royal household and court (*alcaldes de casa y corte*) held full and exclusive jurisdiction over all civil and criminal cases within a radius of five leagues of the monarch. They were the only judges who applied royal law in cases of first instance, and wherever the monarch traveled, this bubble of royal law moved, too, taking precedence over all local judges and jurisdictions within its five-league radius. When the court moved on, the local municipal judges resumed their traditional powers to try cases according to their municipal law codes, and the municipal councils resumed their customary functions as the sole administrators of royal authority and government at the local level. In addition, the judges of the royal household and court had the authority and responsibility of controlling the sale of products necessary for the provisioning of the royal court. Villages within the five-league radius were obliged to provide food and supplies to the court at fixed prices, without being able to sell and trade them on the free market. The provisions included barley, hay, and straw for the royal stables, as well as fuel, food, and drink for the royal family and staff.[43]

The supreme jurisdiction exercised by the judges of the royal household and court required much diplomatic negotiation and adjustment when the king visited a city or a seignorial jurisdiction. The suspension of the city's sovereignty and the temporary nature of the suspension must have played an important part in the advance preparations for a royal visit and in the symbolism of the presentation of the key to the city and the festivities of the royal entrance. As long as the monarchs kept moving, as they did throughout the Trastamara period and during the reign of Charles V, no one city felt the full impact of the five-league restrictions for very long. After Philip established permanent residency in Madrid, however, the judicial powers of the towns within five leagues of the capital and the king's favorite palaces in El Pardo and El Escorial were severely limited. These towns and villages were also victims of the continuous struggles between the Madrid town council and the judges of the royal court and household.

At first the villages around Madrid did not realize that their condition of being within the five leagues would become nearly constant. The villagers of Aldea del Campo paid the king seven thousand ducados in 1555 to buy exemption from the town of Alcalá—"This town ransomed itself and entered the royal domain," they said—and changed the name to Villa del Campo. The town received jurisdiction for and over itself, with no court other than that of the town judges, who were elected annually by the outgoing judges. Appeals for cases involving more than ten thousand maravedís went to the royal appellate court in Valladolid, while appeals involving less than that were heard by the town's council. The population grew to more than five hundred households by 1580, but by that time the king had sold the town again, this time for seventeen thousand ducados to the Genoese Baltasar Catano, who changed its name to Campo Real. Despite its name, it had become a seignorial town, but it was still proud of its autonomous jurisdiction and deluded itself into thinking that its subjection to the judges of the royal household and court was just temporary: "At present we are under the jurisdiction of the court because we are five short leagues from Madrid."[44]

The village of San Sebastián de los Reyes faced the reality of its subjugation to the royal court much sooner and found a way to profit from it. San Sebastián took advantage of its name and its proximity to the royal court to develop itself into a site of religious pilgrimage. In Castile, religious and civil life were intimately intertwined. For most Castilians, local devotion was not distinguished from Christianity itself, and participation in local religious events was one more aspect of identity as a town citizen. The parish church, the confraternities, and the religious life of the town were all the responsibility of the town council. In San Sebastián de los Reyes, where the council was barred by proximity to the royal court from developing the village's agricultural infrastructure, the church became the major economic asset of the village.

The village of San Sebastián de los Reyes had a tradition of looking out for itself and perceived its own history as a saga of communal cohesion triumphing over oppression and disloyalty. This perception suffuses its response to the *Relaciones* questionnaire, where the citizens gave two slightly different yet mutually reinforcing versions of the village's origins. According to their response, the village had been founded by refugees from the neighboring town of Alcobendas. During the reign of King Ferdinand and Queen Isabella the lord of the town of Alcobendas, Juan Arias de Avila, required the Alcobendas town council to act as his co-signers on a loan that he contracted with certain merchants in order to purchase a supply of wool and silk cloths. When the loan came due, and Juan Arias did not pay, the merchants demanded payment from the town council.[45] Although Alcobendas was a town, its municipal territory was so small that the council had for years been paying a seignorial annuity (*martiniega*) to the council of Madrid for the privilege of pasturing Alcobendas livestock on the Madrid commons. The merchants took their claims to the appellate justice in the town of Madrid, who ruled that the citizens of Alcobendas, by paying the seignorial due, acknowledged Madrid's jurisdiction over them. Madrid asserted jurisdiction over the Alcobendas livestock and ordered that some of it be seized and held pending payment of the merchants' debt. The owners of the confiscated animals, seeing no other way to retrieve their livestock without paying, decided to transfer their citizenship to the town of Madrid. In the year 1492 they moved out of the jurisdiction and dominion of Juan Arias de Avila,[46] settling near a shrine dedicated to Saint Sebastian just across the municipal boundary between Madrid and Alcobendas. They formed a village within the municipal territory of Madrid, acknowledged Madrid's jurisdiction, reclaimed their livestock as persons no longer subjects of Juan Arias de Avila, and were permitted by Madrid to put back into cultivation the farmland of three *despoblados* in Madrid's municipal territory that had been abandoned after the epidemics of the previous century. They lived in cabins made of broom and holm oak while they began building their permanent homes, using the local adobe to construct the walls and buying timbers in the Madrid market for the roofs.[47]

Juan Arias de Avila, seeing that his subjects were deserting his town, resorted to violence. One night he and his men raided and set fire to the village of San Sebastián, burning down all the cabins and the eight houses that had already been built. He arrested some of the settlers and took them prisoner to Alcobendas. Those who escaped met and, hearing that King Ferdinand was on his way from Alcalá de Henares to Madrid, went to meet him at the bridge of Viveros on the Jarama River. There the citizens gave the king a report on everything that had happened—how they had formed this village within the jurisdiction of the town of Madrid, how their companions had been arrested, while they had escaped, and how Juan Arias de Avila had burned their cabins and homes. The king acknowledged the justice of their case and ordered Juan Arias to release the prisoners and allow them to proceed freely in building and founding their village without interference. The king decreed that the village was henceforth to be named San Sebastián de los Reyes in honor of the shrine and the royal protection, which he and the queen extended in a royal warrant instructing the town of Madrid to favor and help them in every way possible. In compliance with this warrant, the Madrid council gave and assigned to the council of San Sebastián de los Reyes two meadows as the village's *propios*, and this grant was later confirmed by Emperor Charles V.

The council of San Sebastián managed the municipality's assets with a sober regard for improving the village's economic resources. The new village grew quickly, although the citizens judged the cultivated and pasture land to be of mediocre quality. They were better off than in Alcobendas, however, because in addition to the farms individual citizens owned as private property once they had cleared and plowed the land, and the municipal meadows for their domestic animals, they also had the right of free pasture on the Madrid commons. By 1576 the council's corporate assets provided substantial municipal revenues: a tract of irrigated land rented out for 16,000 maravedís annually; part of one of the municipal meadows rented for cultivation earned 630 fanegas of wheat in rent annually; and lease rents on irrigated plots and corrals produced 612 maravedís annually. In 1567 the council planted willows on the bank of the Jarama River to provide a supply of wood for the town, which could barely supply its own fuel, much less its lumber requirements for equipment and construction.[48]

By the mid-sixteenth century the population comprised about 255 households, all of them farmers and day laborers. Alcobendas, with about 300 households and still paying seignorial dues to Madrid, claimed in 1580 that its population had not increased by more than ten households since about 1520.[49] The economic growth of San Sebastián de los Reyes in this century of population growth made the council eager to gain control over its own jurisdiction and territory, but it was subject to the limitations of the five leagues. The San Sebastián farmers could not enclose more land, because their village lay within the boundaries of the royal town of Madrid, whose council was determined to keep an open range to the benefit of its own citizens and of the town's lord, the king. Another serious economic handicap San Sebastián de los Reyes struggled with during its first century of existence was its status as a village next to the grounds of the royal palace of El Pardo. As San Sebastián grew and tried to expand production, its citizens complained that they could never overcome their poverty nor develop any trade or industry other than being farmers and day laborers because the deer and game from the royal forest at El Pardo impoverished them by eating much of their grain and grape crops.[50]

The church remained a dependency of the parish in Alcobendas, yet like the village itself, which never became independent of the jurisdiction of Madrid, it flourished and became the focus of the village's image of itself as a place of healthy and curative resources. In the absence of anything else of note in the village, the council boasted of the salubrious air and sweet springs of drinking water. To this healthy environment it attributed the longevity of the first person to be baptized in the new village, Sebastián Perdiguero the elder, who was still alive in December 1579. The council described this citizen as "a tall man, erect of body and face, who had never been delicate, lived all his life in the country, and had never been ill before he suffered a quartan fever in the late summer of 1579, when he was more than seventy-six years old."[51] For those less fortunate than Sebastián Perdiguero the elder, the council maintained the usual small hospital, a simple house where the sick or transient poor were brought. A local citizen, Maria Marcos, wife of Martin Garcia, had endowed the hospital with grain fields that produced an average of ten fanegas a year, half wheat and half barley. Apart from this endowment, the hospital had no income or resources except some donated bedding for the poor.[52]

The village developed its church as a pilgrimage shrine late in the sixteenth century, when the citizens retrospectively placed great emphasis on this shrine and its pilgrimage as a test of town loyalty. Local pride and economic advantage depended on a strict separation between San Sebastián and Alcobendas, enforced by the local devotion to the town's patron saint. Local religious devotion and municipal religious customs reinforced pride in one's birthplace and loyalty to the town that provided one's civic identity. In a recent study of local religion in early modern Castile, William A. Christian, Jr., demonstrated the great variety of religious devotions and cults that marked one town from another. The priest often supplied the knowledge or enthusiasm about a particular saint, but it was the local government—the municipal council—that committed the community to observing the holiday, imposed public conformity, and disbursed municipal funds to embellish and dignify the local cult. Rivalries with neighboring towns were intensified by competing devotions, and a citizen's observance of the rituals of a rival town seemed like a betrayal of one's own civic identity.[53]

Frustrated in its desire for economic development and juridical autonomy, the village developed its economy and identity in a grand building project. With a shrewd sense of what their village had to offer to the courtiers in Madrid, the people took advantage of their church's patronage by Saint Sebastian, protector of those afflicted with bubonic plague, just when Madrid and the rest of New Castile began suffering new waves of epidemic. On April 6, 1576, the village council began construction work on the old shrine of San Sebastián, rebuilding and expanding it to provide appropriate housing for a growing collection of holy relics. In two years the council collected eight thousand ducados in voluntary donations, most of it from pilgrims from the royal court. The council used the funds to construct a church ninety feet long and sixty feet wide, with a nave and two aisles supported by granite pillars, brick ribbing for the vaulted ceiling, and roofing timbers from the forests of Cuenca. Within this impressive space the council installed a cross hung with a silk drape, candlesticks, and a canopy.[54] In the sagrario, where the consecrated things were deposited, were kept the precious relics donated by generous patrons: two of Saint Sebastian's bones, one a hand bone and one a finger bone, donated by the princess of Portugal; and eleven bones from Saints Calixto, Ursula, Venaranda, and others, which had been brought from Rome in a reliquary by the curate.

By the end of the sixteenth century the shrine of San Sebastián de los Reyes was a favorite object of royal and noble pilgrims and patrons, to whom villagers sold food and lodging. The local citizens' devotion to San Sebastián became an important source of income and the distinguishing characteristic of their civic identity. Both self-interest and civic pride guided them in interpreting the sudden death years earlier of a citizen who had mocked and defied the religious customs of his own village while participating in those of San Sebastián's rival, the town of Alcobendas. In San Sebastián devotion to the town's namesake, civic identity, and antagonism toward Alcobendas were intricately bound together by the origins of the village itself. San Sebastián de los Reyes and Alcobendas retained amicable relations, brought together by family ties, custom, and proximity, yet the two towns quickly developed different rituals and loyalties. In San Sebastián the story was told of a local citizen named Portazguero, who suffered a terrible fate after defying and mocking the pious customs of his own village. Every year people from Alcobendas walked in procession to the shrine of San Sebastián, arriving before high mass on the morning of the saint's feast day, January 20. As their act of devotion the citizens of San Sebastián de los Reyes abstained from eating meat and animal products on the eve of the saint's day. But on January 19 about the year 1520 Portazguero walked to Alcobendas solely for the purpose of eating meat there. After dining, he walked home that night with the Alcobendas pilgrims, sat down in his chair, and, learning that his wife, children, and servants had devotedly supped on turnips, began to mock them and the custom, ridiculing them for having eaten their turnips while he had just come from eating his fill of meat. At that moment he fell dead in his chair without uttering another word.[55]

In contrast to Valenzuela's citizens, with their dismal pessimism, the people of San Sebastián de los Reyes knew how to turn their subjection under the town of Madrid into an advantage. Their success bolstered their self-esteem to a degree that seems exaggerated, considering the paucity of resources at their disposal. Yet their spirited enterprise had been apparent from the earliest days of their history, when they moved as a community from the jurisdiction of an oppressive lord, formed a village council, and sought the king's help in wresting favorable treatment from the town council of Madrid. In San Sebastián, devotion to the village's namesake, civic identity, and economic interest were intricately bound together by the origins, location, and legal status of the village itself.

Chapter 7

War and Taxes

At the beginning of the Habsburg rule in 1516 Spain had been the paragon of empires, the model of how to acquire world power through royal marriage and inheritance. By 1700 Spain had become an object lesson of the costs of world power. Years of warfare in defense of religion and empire had exhausted the monarchy's usual financial resources and driven the royal treasury to raise cash from villages thirsting to be free from the jurisdiction of a ruling town or city. In this absolute monarchy, villagers, noble lord, royal treasurers, and king cooperated in extracting from villages large, one-time tax payments in the form of town charter purchases. Meanwhile the regular taxes continued and, at the end of the sixteenth century, began increasing. The weight of these taxes fell un-evenly on individual noble lords, cities, towns, and villages, depending on how each chose to fulfill its obligations and on resources and timing. New lords whose seignorial incomes were still encumbered could lose everything in a single military disaster, while older noble estates could weather years of unremunerated military expenses. Towns skilled in ne-gotiating with the royal treasury could manipulate tax collection reforms to their own advantage, while other towns and cities that had exhausted their capital to retain villages in the sixteenth century could not meet their tax obligations in the seventeenth and eighteenth centuries.

For the nobles, the requirement of service to the monarchy imposed a fatal burden of financial expenditure and physical danger. The new captain general of the Mediterranean galley fleet appointed in 1564, García de Toledo, compiled a long and bitter list of reasons for not accepting a naval command from Philip II. García noted that by merely staying put and doing nothing, one's fortune would increase by the pound, whereas taking a command would diminish it by the ton. Worse, naval commands de-stroyed one's health, leading to death and the loss of all the income that went with the office. "The example of this you have right in front of you," he warned, "if you remember what Francisco de Mendoza lost by his death and the harm that his death has done to his estates."[1] García was partic-ularly bitter about Mendoza's fate because Francisco had preceded him as commander of the Mediterranean fleet and the disastrous consequences of Francisco's career could not help but sound a fearful warning to those

who were called to serve the king. Francisco had been well on his way to
building a personal fortune and estate through service as a royal administrator and purchase of towns alienated from the military orders when he
made the mistake of committing his personal estate to the royal military
service.

While still a young man, Francisco went to the Americas in 1535 with
his father, Antonio de Mendoza, the first viceroy of New Spain and later
viceroy of Peru, and assisted the viceroy unofficially while engaging in
trade and investment on his own account.[2] When father and son arrived
in Peru in 1550, the viceroy was already terminally ill, and he sent Francisco on an inspection tour to assess what measures would best serve the
royal government. Francisco, according to some historians, submitted a
report on the state of Peru from Lima to Charcas, with maps, diagrams,
and sketches of the principal cities and especially of the mines of the
remarkable silver mountain at Potosí and the mineral resources in its
immediate region.[3]

After Antonio's death in 1552, Francisco returned to Castile and won
the confidence of his father's eldest brother, the marquis of Mondéjar,
president of the Council of the Indies and councilor of Castile.[4] Francisco
quickly received a royal commission to inspect all the mines in Castile,
with instructions to assess their potential and evaluate which ones should
be developed by the monarchy, and was appointed general administrator
of the Guadalcanal silver mines, north of Seville. In the words of his
commissions, these were positions "of great importance requiring a person
of character, honesty, and experience."[5] At Guadalcanal Francisco assumed responsibility for a major source of the monarchy's income. The
interim administrator, Agustín de Zárate, had organized the accounting,
employment, and security procedures from late 1555, just a few weeks
after the silver strike in Guadalcanal, until the questions of mining technology became more complicated in early 1556. Francisco strengthened
security measures for transport of the refined silver and sent it under armed
guard to the royal accountant in Seville, Pedro Luis de Torregrosa, who
consigned it to the royal mint to be coined and then forwarded the money
to the royal paymasters. During Francisco's tenure as administrator the
Guadalcanal mines produced about 340,000 ducados a year, most of which
was destined for military purposes. In 1556, for example, a sum of 60,000
ducados from Guadalcanal was shipped to pay the garrison at La Goleta,
the Spanish fortress that controlled the harbor of Tunis.[6]

By this time problems of mining technology had become an obstacle
to Guadalcanal's production. The mine shafts had been sunk deep enough
to encounter flooding, and the traditional methods of extracting silver
from the ores already brought to the surface were inefficient. Mendoza
was skeptical of a bid from German mining specialists to employ the new

patio process for extracting silver with mercury and became entangled in disputes at the royal court among supporters and opponents of the process. From this moment on, Francisco's life would pass in a blur of travel between Guadalcanal and the royal court. He persistently lobbied the royal ministers to authorize new procedures in the mines and then would rush back to cope with a shortage of employees or refining difficulties at the mine site. Leaving Zárate as administrator, Mendoza joined the royal court in Flanders as the king prepared for war and stopped payment to his bankers. Francisco returned to Valladolid in February 1557 to shepherd the mine's paperwork through the bureaucracy, but within a few days the princess regent ordered him to return to Guadalcanal because she had received a report that the amount of silver being extracted from the ore had declined. Francisco was back in Guadalcanal in March; he put things in order and established an agreement between the German contractors and a new lieutenant administrator. No sooner had he arrived in Guadalcanal than he received a letter from the royal secretary Francisco de Eraso dated February 16 that sent him back to Valladolid. He went grudgingly: "Please God that it will not be necessary for me to return to Flanders, but I will do it if the royal despatches come written in a way that does not accord with his majesty's service."[7] Francisco found his uncle the marquis seriously ill with malaria, so he began reporting to the king by way of his own brother, Iñigo, who was with the army in Flanders. In July Francisco was appointed administrator and director of all the mines in Spain, but in October 1557 he complained to the king that the council still had not summoned him to discuss the mines. In February 1558 he was in Guadalcanal negotiating with the town's judge, who claimed that the town's *monte* was reserved for the citizens and thus its timber could not be used by the royal officials for mine construction or for fuel in the smelting furnaces. Mendoza then returned to Valladolid, where he negotiated new contracts and regulations for the mines.

While he carried on these official negotiations, Francisco's personal affairs became more complicated. His brother Iñigo died, and Francisco received Iñigo's commandery of Socuéllamos in the Order of Santiago. Francisco was at the peak of his fortunes—recently returned from twenty years in New Spain and Peru, a trusted administrator of the monarchy's most productive silver mine in Spain, nephew of the president of the Council of the Indies, and cousin of several of Philip's highest military officers. At the age of about forty-five, he was ready to settle down, to invest his profits and salary in seignorial jurisdiction. Francisco entered a bid for the towns of Estremera and Valdaracete in late 1559, the king accepted the offer, and royal administrators carried out the appraisals and legal procedures during the following months.[8] The final transfer of title and jurisdiction took place in the first months of 1562, and Francisco then married a young cousin, Catalina de Mendoza.

To finance these changes in his lifestyle, Francisco apparently intended to use the profits from his business investments, which he had brought from Peru in the form of silver bullion and which the House of Trade had impounded as soon as he disembarked in Seville. In 1560 Francisco's bullion still had not been released to him, so he used his credit at the House of Trade to buy the towns of Estremera and Valdaracete from Philip II for 2,800,000 maravedís (7,450 ducados). The auditors of the House of Trade in Seville credited his account with the silver bullion he had brought with him from Peru, but the royal treasury, desperate for cash, would not authorize him to withdraw the money required for purchase of a jurisdiction. Francisco launched a complicated series of loans, borrowing 2,400 ducados in Seville from Leonor de Toledo, wife of Perafán de Ribera, to make the required down payment for the towns in 1560.[9] He refinanced this loan in August 1561, after the royal appraisal of the towns confirmed his bid. The full payment to the king was made by the priests of the chapel of the parish of San Andrés in Madrid, where, in September 1561, Francisco's aunt, María de Vargas, widow of Antonio de Monrroy, signed a note for 2,800,000 maravedís in her nephew's name at an annual interest of 7.14 percent. Francisco pledged the seignorial income of the towns of Estremera and Valdaracete as security for this loan but had already taken a new loan of 18,000 ducados from Captain Miguel de Oquendo in Seville in August, at 8.33 percent interest.[10] In January 1562 Francisco received the royal deed of sale and gave the town of Estremera new rules for electing the town's officials.[11]

But all his plans for the future sank in the whirlpool of Spain's Mediterranean naval campaigns, pulling the towns of Estremera and Valdaracete into the monarchy's wars for the first time in two centuries. The death of Francisco's brother was the first in a series of tragedies that pulled him away from the intended course of his career in the royal administration to invest his career and fortune—including the seignorial income of Estremera and Valdaracete—in war. Soon after the Spanish victory at St. Quentin in August 1557 the king appointed one of Francisco's cousins, Juan de Mendoza, as captain general of the Spanish galleys, the oarpowered fleet that protected Spanish shipping and coasts from the attacks of the resurgent Muslims in the western Mediterranean.[12] Philip returned to Spain from Flanders in the fall of 1559, and plans for a major counteroffensive to retake Tripoli were debated. In early 1560 a joint Spanish and Italian fleet under the command of the duke of Medinaceli was caught by surprise at the island of Djerba; half the king's galleys were lost and ten thousand Spanish troops were stranded, only to be captured by the

Turks. This disaster opened the way for the North African Muslims to step up their harassment of Spanish shipping and threaten the coast of Spain and Spanish garrisons in North Africa.[13]

Juan de Mendoza rebuilt the galley fleet through extraordinary financial exertions in the next few months, and it was to this cousin's project that Francisco fatally committed his own fortune and career: from early November 1561 through January 1562 Francisco borrowed thirty thousand ducados against his future income from Estremera and Valdaracete.[14] In late 1561 and most of 1562 Juan de Mendoza cruised Spain's coasts from Valencia to Oran. In October Juan brought his squadron of twenty-eight galleys with thirty-five hundred infantry into the port of Málaga to load supplies and ammunition in preparation for an assault on North Africa. During a violent storm on October 18 Juan received a report that a levanter of hurricane force was approaching the city. Intending to save the squadron, Juan took on board many of the soldiers' wives and children and moved the entire fleet forty miles east to the small bay of La Herradura. Juan was imitating his own father, Bernardino de Mendoza, his predecessor as captain general of the galleys, who had twice saved the fleet by moving it to La Herradura during levanters that devastated the city and port of Málaga.[15] But this time the storm veered away from Málaga and hit La Herradura. All but a handful were lost: the commander's galley capsized, taking all on board except the pilot, nine sailors, and thirteen galley slaves, who had been released from their irons when the storm came up. The survivors reported that Juan de Mendoza began swimming to save the two small sons of the commander of Oran but was knocked unconscious by flying debris and drowned. Juan's son and a son of the marquis of Mondéjar also drowned at La Herradura.

In mid-November, one month after his cousins died in the bay of La Herradura, Francisco appointed an interim administrator of the Guadalcanal mines while he went to the court, and in early 1563 he became captain general of the Spanish galleys. In Málaga on March 9 he drew up his will, and throughout April and May he reconstituted the fleet, collecting ships, arms, men, and supplies. On the last day of May he sailed from Málaga at the head of a fleet of thirty-four galleys manned by more than four thousand infantry and volunteer cavalry. The fleet arrived in Oran on June 16, just in time to save the Christian defenders of Marzalquibir. Francisco returned to Málaga a hero, but he was suffering from malaria. The fleet sailed under a different commander to attack the island of Peñón de Vélez de Gómera, returning on August 2 to learn that Francisco had died the night of July 26.[16] Those who returned alive from Peñón de Vélez received rewards from the king; Francisco's heirs received nothing.[17]

Much of the damage to Francisco's estate fell on his widow, who was left to pay off these huge debts and, at the same time, comply with the terms of Francisco's will. Francisco and Catalina, because they had been married just a few months, had no community property that would have accrued from the usufruct of the property each brought to the marriage. Francisco nevertheless ordered in his will that Catalina should receive an income of five hundred ducados per year from his estate, in addition to retaining her *arras* and dowry. He ordered that his estate should be placed in a perpetual trust (*mayorazgo*), of which the beneficiary should be his closest male heir. If he and Catalina should have a son, he ordered that the boy be named Antonio de Mendoza; if not, then any son of his sister, the countess of Ayamonte, should be the beneficiary of the *mayorazgo*, on the condition that the heir change his name to Antonio de Mendoza. Finally, Francisco ordered his executors to pay his debts in the Americas, selling Estremera and Valdaracete if necessary.

As it happened, Catalina was not pregnant when Francisco died, and there was no son to inherit the perpetual trust. She and Francisco's executor, Pedro Luis de Torregrosa, made a serious effort to pay the American creditors from the revenues of Estremera and Valdaracete. They repaid 10,000 ducados' worth of loans to three creditors by 1565, collecting the seignorial revenues of 800 ducados per year from Estremera and an equal amount from Valdaracete. In 1565 Francisco's creditors brought bankruptcy proceedings against Catalina and Torregrosa, who were required to offer the towns for sale to the highest bidder. In public auction the king's favorite, Ruy Gómez de Silva, prince of Eboli, and his guarantor, the Genoese banker Nicolás de Grimaldo, offered the high bid of 160,300 ducados for both towns. Catalina and Torregrosa agreed to this, on the condition that in addition to the down payment, Ruy Gómez would invest the 160,300 ducados in annuities (*juros*) on government revenues in the city of Seville, payable to Torregrosa. From these Seville annuities, Torregrosa gradually paid off 32,000 ducados of principal and interest to four more creditors by the end of 1573. This left another four creditors still receiving about 1 million maravedís annually in interest. Meanwhile, Ruy Gómez sold Estremera and Valdaracete to the royal treasurer general Melchor de Herrera, but this sale fell through in 1572, and Ruy Gómez's chamberlain repossessed the towns in the prince's name just before Ruy Gómez's death that same year.

Ruy Gómez's widow, the duchess of Pastrana, Ana de Mendoza, was exiled from court in 1579. She established residence in Pastrana and actively administered the towns on behalf of her young son, the duke of Pastrana. But on June 4, 1585, Francisco de Mendoza's nephew Diego de Córdoba, alias Antonio de Mendoza, brought a lawsuit in which he demanded an inventory of Francisco's estate at the time of his death, claimed the revenues of the towns of Estremera and Valdaracete under the terms of Francisco's will, and attempted to sell the annuity of fifteen hundred ducados per year drawn on the Seville revenues. The death of the duchess of Pastrana in 1591 and that of Torregrosa in 1592 delayed the case even further. The duke of Pastrana sued Torregrosa's executor, Fabioneli de Espinosa, and in 1601 finally won a favorable ruling from the courts, which ordered Fabioneli to use Torregrosa's property to pay off the last four creditors of Francisco de Mendoza. By this time Francisco's notes had been sold and resold, brokered, discounted, and inherited by two or three generations of investors in Spain and the Americas. While gold and silver flowed from the mines of Mexico and Peru to Spain, the seignorial dues from Estremera and Valdaracete made their way to the accounts of investors in Panama and Guatemala.

The financial costs of war to individuals such as Francisco and Catalina replicated in miniature the costs to the royal treasury. The old give-and-take negotiations between the monarchy and the Cortes cities were adequate for the small-scale wars typical of the fifteenth century, but as the Habsburg monarchs plunged into warfare on a European scale and the expenses of war soared, the monarchy sought to change the tax system. For nearly a century the Habsburg kings in Spain tried to wrest the power of taxation out of the hands of the Cortes; not until the mid-seventeenth century did they finally succeed in creating a royal tax collection procedure only nominally supervised by the Cortes. Carla Phillips has demonstrated that during most of the sixteenth century the effect of rising taxes on the taxpayer was negligible: with prices increasing, population growing, and massive infusions of revenue from America, average nominal and real taxes actually declined until about 1575. King and Cortes agreed on a 13 percent increase in the subsidy between 1516 and 1541. For the next thirty-five years (1541–75) both sides refused to make concessions, and no new tax agreements were concluded; the subsidy remained at the 1541 level. Meanwhile, the cost of wars in Italy, France, Germany, and the Netherlands outstripped even the royal revenues, which, thanks to silver imports from America, increased more than ninefold between 1494 and 1590. These fiscal demands of war pushed the monarchy into several bankruptcies and then a long and bitter struggle with the Cortes to impose new taxes.[18]

In theory, the Cortes negotiated a subsidy with the monarchy and then supervised the collection and delivery of the tax, but a great disparity developed between the ideal and the reality of royal tax collection procedures. In theory, the Cortes negotiated the total sum of the subsidy on behalf of all the taxpayers of the kingdom. The cities and town in the

Cortes believed their tax function was fundamental to the functioning of the royal government, but their powers of tax collection were limited by the municipal structure of the realm. Each Cortes city and town collected the taxes from its own municipal territory, including its villages. Some cities enjoyed tax exemptions for their own citizens; others found ways to avoid collecting taxes directly from their own citizens by pushing the great burden of taxation onto the villages within their municipal territory. Most cities organized their villages into districts (*partidos*) and required the villages of each district to meet in a designated village (*cabeza de partido*) to distribute the tax assessment. In the cities that lost territory, these *partidos* ceased to function, and the villages had to send representatives to the city itself to be assessed.[19] Given their subservient status, the villages could do little to find relief from their disproportionate tax burden other than buy township from the Habsburgs.

The towns' view of tax collection was just the opposite. Beyond their own hometown, Castilian citizens of towns were indifferent toward or ignorant of the political power that cities wielded in the monarchy. While royal officials and large cities thought the whole world centered on the court and its relationships with the Cortes, people in the towns saw the world as centered on their own town and its direct links to the monarch. They were so accustomed to administering themselves, litigating in the highest courts of the realm, negotiating with lords, monarchs, merchants, and other municipalities, that the affairs of the royal court and large cities were irrelevant except as sources of juicy gossip—on which they were remarkably up-to-date. Their attitude toward court and city was not antiurban: they were either indifferent toward irrelevant institutions or hostile toward threats to their own municipal jurisdiction. In the late sixteenth century, people in many small towns might not even know in which of the medieval realms they lived. The citizens of Iniesta, for example, were divided on how to answer this question in the *Relaciones* questionnaire. Some thought they lived in the Kingdom of Aragon because their region was commonly called La Mancha de Aragón, while others believed the town was in the Kingdom of Toledo.[20]

Townspeople were equally unsure of their links to the Cortes, and a large number did not know which city represented them. The town of Albaladejo simply did not know which city spoke for it in the Cortes. The town of Tarancón reported that it was not certain whether it was represented in the Cortes by the city of Toledo or the city of Cuenca. There was confusion in Valdeloso, which reported that it lay in the district of both Cuenca and Huete and that whichever of these cities had a vote in the Cortes must represent it. The town of Arenas deduced that the city of Toledo represented it in the Cortes, because that was where Arenas delivered its royal tax payments. The town of Illescas stated that it had no vote in the Cortes and that it did not send representatives anywhere else to vote, much less negotiate its affairs; it arranged its own tax assessment without meeting with any other council.[21]

Towns in the jurisdiction of the military orders were particularly fuzzy on this point. A large proportion of the towns in the military orders acted autonomously in tax matters; they debated their own tax bid within the town meeting, sent a representative to the Council of the Military Orders to submit and negotiate the bid, collected taxes from the income of their corporate assets (*propios*), and delivered their tax payments directly to the royal court. Villaescusa de Haro handled all these matters right at home, as many towns in the military orders asserted they did. Villarrubio believed that Toledo must represent it in the Cortes, since the town lay within its kingdom, but the citizens met in their own town hall to arrange their tax assessment. El Toboso was confused by the question, reporting that it had no vote in the Cortes and did not know whether it was supposed to go to Toledo or to Cuenca to deliver royal taxes.[22]

Perhaps the citizens of El Toboso deserved the reputation of being country rubes, immortalized in *Don Quixote,* for they had misunderstood the question. Towns in the military orders and royal towns did not deliver their taxes to a Cortes city, nor did they negotiate their assessment through the Cortes: they delivered their royal taxes directly to the court or to the chancellery in Granada or Valladolid, whichever was closest. Almodóvar del Campo reported more accurately that the city of Toledo proposed and negotiated for it in the Cortes and that in matters related to assessments for royal taxes the town went to the royal treasury to negotiate the sales tax and to the town of Almagro to arrange the assessment for its share of the subsidy voted by the Cortes.[23]

The most profitable of the royal taxes was the sales tax (*alcabala*), of about 3 percent. This was paid in cash, could be collected all year long in the town marketplace, and was readily transported directly to the royal tax offices. The ease and cost-efficiency of collecting the sales tax contrasted with the difficulty of collecting the royal third (*tercia*) of the church tithe. Tithe collection was a risky enterprise, susceptible to the vagaries of crop production and easily manipulated by tax evaders. Most tithes were paid in kind and therefore had to be collected seasonally and were awkward and expensive to transport and convert into cash. The procedure itself did little to mitigate these risks and abuses. Bidders estimated the tithe by visual inspection of the crop before harvest. The winning bidder paid the full sum in advance to the royal treasury in exchange for the privilege of collecting and retaining the tithe. If the harvest was damaged by weather, the tithe contractor was still liable for the full bid.

In both royal and seignorial towns, the town council could choose to take no role in collecting royal taxes, leaving the way open for individual bidders to win the tax farming contract for the town from the royal treasury. This process of tax farming (*arrendamiento*) relieved the town council of responsibility but could backfire on the town's economy. In order to compete successfully for the *arrendamiento*, the tax farmer had to offer an inflated bid, and to this was added an additional sum to provide a profit to the winner. The tax farmer was required to pay the full tax collection and profit in advance to the royal treasury in cash, whereupon he received full power to collect from the town by whatever means during the following year. If the municipal revenues proved inadequate, the tax farmer could imprison councilmen or individual citizens and impound their property to extract more money from the town. Tax collection by *arrendamiento* necessarily resulted in high tax rates, and if a harvest failed or the municipal revenues were already strained by other obligations, it sometimes led to humiliating scenes and serious tensions in towns and villages. These disadvantages induced towns to exercise one of the economically most advantageous privileges of township, the option of collecting the tax communally through the procedure known as *encabezamiento*. *Encabezamiento* had been the prerogative of a few privileged cities until 1537, when the Cortes conceded a subsidy of 22 million ducados to Charles V in exchange for his extending the option of *encabezamiento* to all cities and towns.[24] Through *encabezamiento*, the council itself submitted a bid to administer and collect the royal taxes, pledging the income from the town's *propios* to meet the town's tax obligation if necessary. Because taxes collected through *encabezamiento* were due at the end of the fiscal year, the royal treasury deemed the town in arrears until payment was made; therefore, the citizens were required to post surety bonds in the amount of the total tax obligation contracted. Through the procedure of *encabezamiento* the council avoided tax collection by *arrendamiento*.

Lords traditionally considered royal tax collection a prerogative inherent in the jurisdiction. The prerogative could bring considerable profit, since the lord could use the negotiations to limit the amount of tax collected from his subjects and at the same time assure his own share of the collection. One of a lord's principal activities was to negotiate with the royal government the level of royal taxes, including the royal portion of the tithe, in his towns. But in the early sixteenth century royal lawyers argued that in the absence of explicit, written grants for any specific town, collection belonged to the monarchy.[25] A large number of lords were able to produce documented grants of the privilege of collecting the tithes in their towns. To achieve this, however, required the good will of the royal officials and the strenuous lobbying of the lord's own agents at the royal court choreographed by the lord himself. Others were forced to enter competitive bids for collecting royal taxes in their own jurisdictions or in some other person's jurisdiction.[26] The growing population of sixteenth-century towns provided opportunities for increasing profits, and lords who could not gain a royal grant to collect the royal taxes resorted to contracting an *encabezamiento* themselves. A lord who collected the royal taxes in his own jurisdiction through an *encabezamiento* retained a portion of the collection. The lord could subcontract the job to a tax farmer through competitive bidding, but towns found the latter method so repugnant, because tax farmers had to make a quick profit above and beyond the advance they had paid to the royal treasury, that the town councils often subcontracted with the lord to pay the taxes by *encabezamiento*.

In 1505 the count of Tendilla received from King Ferdinand the prerogative of collecting the royal taxes from the count's towns of Azañón and Viana and from his *despoblado* of Anguix.[27] The contract fixed the royal taxes at 36,500 maravedís per year—of which the count retained 6,500 maravedís. For four years the count collected the taxes through a tax farmer, and then in 1509 he accepted a proposal from the town councils of Azañón and Viana. The councils agreed to collect the taxes in their towns by *encabezamiento* and to collect the tithes from the *despoblado* of Anguix. The count informed his agent at the royal court, Alonso de Barrionuevo, who was to draw up the agreement with the royal treasury, that the taxes of Azañón and Viana would amount to 35,000 maravedís per annum. He had negotiated this with King Ferdinand, with the understanding that 30,000 maravedís would go to the royal treasury and 5,000 would go to the count himself. In addition, the councils of Azañón and Viana had agreed to collect 1,500 maravedís in royal tithes from Anguix each year, all of which was to go to the count. Barrionuevo was to approach the marquis of Denia, at that moment the most powerful figure at court, to argue that the count of Tendilla was asking for the same arrangement that Denia himself enjoyed in some places he had bought, which did not have to submit to a tax farmer. He cautioned Barrionuevo to watch the time, because the agreement to collect by *encabezamiento* was valid until April 15, and if he had not succeeded by then, the tax would be collected by royal tax farmers, who would mercilessly squeeze the tax payers of Anguix, Azañón, and Viana. In 1522 Charles V conceded another 2,500 maravedís per annum from these towns to the count's son Luis, second marquis of Mondéjar. By that time the total tax collection was fixed at 39,000 maravedís, yet the king still received the 30,000 set in 1505. Just five years later, in 1526, the annual tax collection had risen to 45,000 maravedís, and Charles granted the increase of 6,000 maravedís to Luis, while the royal share remained at 30,000. Tax collection could be a profitable enterprise, one that no lord wanted to let slip through his fingers. It was especially important to protect the lord's subjects from the higher tax rates that necessarily were collected when the taxes were let by bid to tax farmers. The count of Tendilla had to apply unrelenting pressure at the royal treasury, year after year, to profit from royal tax collection in his estates and to keep these tax advantages for his subjects.

During most of the sixteenth century, from about 1535 to 1590, royal tax levels remained fairly stable, with the exception of the tripling of the royal sales tax for the year 1576, and lords and councils cooperated to keep them that way. In 1530 the count of Benavente's steward drew up an accounting of all the income the count received annually from his estates in Extremadura. In Extremadura, the count was lord of two towns, Arroyo del Puerco and Talaván, and two villages, Serrejón and El Bodón, near Cáceres and Ciudad Rodrigo, with a total population of about eleven hundred households; he also owned several farms and pastures in these and other Extremadura towns. The lease rents from the count's farms and pastures provided him with 419,023 maravedís annually, while the four towns paid him annual dues, fines, and rents of 1,451,839 maravedís.

The count's subjects in these four towns paid him an average of 1,320 maravedís per household, but the burden of these seignorial taxes and rents was not distributed evenly. The citizens of Talaván paid the highest rate, 3,282 maravedís annually per household, whereas the citizens of Arroyo del Puerco, Serrejón, and El Bodón paid 1,619, 1,100, and 920 maravedís per household, respectively.[28] The steward tactfully criticized the count for not exacting more from Arroyo del Puerco, pointing out that the town's council was renting the Almedias pasture from him for 180,120 maravedís when the pasture could be bringing in 250,000. The largest single source of the lord's income in Arroyo del Puerco was the sales tax, which, according to the steward, should have yielded 465,000 maravedís but amounted to only 400,000 that year "because of the seizures."

In 1540 the council of Arroyo del Puerco authorized its representative, Francisco Sánchez Talavera, to negotiate an agreement with the lord. Just as they had in the recent past, the citizens of Arroyo del Puerco would pay him 400,000 maravedís annually for the next four years in sales tax and seignorial annuity. Instead of paying the sales tax in advance, as the tax farmers did when they won a contract for the tax collection, the council would pay by *encabezamiento:* the members of the council and other citizens mortgaged a portion of their private property as collateral for the 1,600,000 maravedís they owed the lord. The count agreed to these terms, and the council itself collected the sales tax in the municipal market, paying 200,000 to the count semiannually, on Christmas and St. John's Day.[29]

On January 2, 1553, in a town meeting the citizens of Arroyo del Puerco debated the advantages and disadvantages of bidding on the tax collection for the next four years. The citizens voted unanimously that the council should buy out the contract, for the tax collection had been won by certain citizens to the "obvious prejudice of the general welfare of the town."[30] In 1579 the sales tax was collected by tax farmers and yielded 515,452 maravedís (in addition to 555 maravedís from the ten Morisco households that had been relocated in the town from the Kingdom of Granada).[31] The next year the council again negotiated an *encabezamiento* of 400,000 maravedís per annum for the sales tax. All through this long period of amicable relations, the council was able to negotiate a lower tax rate by assuming the costs of tax collection and providing the lord with a guaranteed income for the duration of the contract. The council negotiated the contract with the steward, who recommended at the end of every contract period that the tax be raised.

During most of the sixteenth century the counts of Benavente preferred to take the lower income in cooperation with their subjects. The same policy may account for a similar flatness of tax levels in the count of Benavente's estates in the Tierra de Campos region in Old Castile. Bartolomé Yun, in his economic history of this region, calculated that the greatest increase in the sales tax collected by the counts took place between 1493 and 1536, when it increased from 8.3 million maravedís to 16.1 million. The same tax collection in 1572 produced about 18.5 million maravedís. When Yun deflated these sums by taking into account the price rise, the results were similar to those noted by Carla Phillips in Ciudad Real, in southern New Castile: real taxes declined in the Tierra de Campos from 41.5 million in 1536 to 9.3 million in 1572.[32]

All of this changed in the catastrophic economic conditions of the 1580s and 1590s. In 1575 the Cortes agreed to raise both the subsidy and the royal sales tax.[33] The subsidy was increased by 137 percent and remained at that level until the end of the century. The most lucrative royal tax, the sales tax, had been set at 3.5 percent during most of the century. For the tax year 1576 it was tripled, and then for the remainder of the century it stayed at about 150 percent of its pre-1576 level. In 1588 the council of Arroyo del Puerco was forced to offer a contract of 660,000 maravedís annually in order to outbid the tax farmers. At the end of that contract the steward recommended that the lord demand 700,000 if the council agreed to collect the tax and guarantee it by *encabezamiento;* he recommended that it be increased even more if the count decided to give the contract to a tax farmer. The steward insisted that the *encabezamiento* be written for a short term, in order to negotiate a higher sum when it expired, and that he inventory all possessions in the town in order to keep track accurately of all sales and acquisitions.[34] By this time the monarchy had become alarmed at the number of farmers whose incomes were committed to payment of interest on the mortgages they had signed in order to guarantee previous *encabezamientos.* Many of these *encabezamientos* had failed when the monarchy's sudden tripling of the sales tax in 1576 was followed by the crop failures of 1576–79. A new royal decree forbidding the mortgaging of farmland now forced the count of Benavente's steward to suggest that the council of Arroyo del Puerco mortgage its *propios* as collateral for the tax collection.

But this solution assumed that the crop failures and epidemics of the last quarter of the sixteenth century were passing phenomena and that prosperity would return soon to make the *propios* as profitable as they had been. The lords and the council acted on this expectation of restored productivity and profit just when Castile was falling to the low point of population and productivity in the Habsburg period. The results became evident by mid-century: in 1657 the council of Arroyo del Puerco signed a note acknowledging its debt of 2,680,000 maravedís to the count of Benavente and assigning to him the income of the *propios*.[35]

The mechanism of Arroyo del Puerco's transformation from a prosperous, growing farm town into a mortgage-ridden debtor can be seen in the parallel story of the town of Mondéjar, in the Alcarria region of New Castile. In 1575 the council of Mondéjar negotiated an *encabezamiento* with its lord, the marquis of Mondéjar, for the payment of the sales tax in 1575 and 1576—the latter a disastrous year in the Alcarria.[36] The council agreed to deliver to the marquis in Madrid five hundred thousand maravedís and two hundred hens "en pluma" per year. In exchange, the council would act as the lord's revenue collector in his towns of Mondéjar, Fuentenovilla, and Anguix.

The council agreed to collect and deliver to the marquis all the customary seignorial annuities from these towns: wheat, olive oil, chickens, and other payments in kind due to the lord from the towns of Mondéjar and Fuentenovilla and the cash revenues from these towns and Anguix, including short-term and perpetual annuities, as well as sales taxes and lease rents on ovens, tanneries, mills, and fields. In addition to these revenues collected from the citizens and municipal treasuries, the marquises over the years had developed the annual fair of San Andrés into a major, international fair, particularly for hides and other leathers, and the sales tax on merchandise sold during the fair provided a significant portion of their income.[37] The marquis agreed that the citizens of Mondéjar would be exempt from the San Andrés sales tax on wheat, barley, wine, olive oil, and other produce that they sold from their own harvest and on the sale of livestock they had possessed for at least one year prior to the fair.

In 1575 the council agreed that the sales tax collected in Mondéjar during the San Andrés fair would be turned over to the lord directly, without being counted in the five hundred thousand maravedís of the contract. The council agreed that a 10 percent sales tax paid on all the meat and fish sold at retail during the fair, whether by the concessionaires who held the leases on the municipal butcher and fish shops or by any

other citizens of the town, would be outside the purview of the council
and its *encabezamiento*. The marquis would appoint someone to collect
this tax, which would go to him directly, without being discounted from
the sum agreed on in the *encabezamiento*.

The council also agreed to the marquis's condition that the *encabezamiento* should not adversely affect the size of the population in the town
of Mondéjar. The council could not collect sales taxes, royal taxes, or
any other type of levy from new settlers who wanted to become citizens
of Mondéjar for as long as they had such a concession from the marquis.
Furthermore, the council could not require the new settlers to serve as
sheriff or field guard against their will. If any revenues were collected from
these new settlers by the marquis's agents, these sums would not be discounted from the amount agreed on in the *encabezamiento*.

The *encabezamiento* reassured a lord because it guaranteed that the
responsibility of revenue collection would be spread out among a large
number of people. The council's representative (*procurador*) negotiated
the terms of the agreement, and then the members of the council and
about thirty other citizens, on behalf of all the citizens of the town, signed
the contract. Those who signed also listed the private property they offered
as collateral for delivery of the total sum to the marquis. When the value
of the property put up as collateral by the cosigners reached the amount
of the contracted revenue collection, no further signatures were required,
although it was acknowledged that the cosigners were acting on behalf of
all the citizens of the town. Communally and individually the citizens
were responsible for the collection as liable, listed in the tax roll, and
cosigners—"obligados, encabezados y juradores."

The disadvantages for the community became manifest when harvest
failure or some other disaster deprived the citizens of their usual income
during the term of the *encabezamiento*. In 1575 the town of Mondéjar
collected the full amount without difficulty, just as it had throughout the
sixteenth century. But in December 1576 the council's payment to the
marquis fell short by 707,108 maravedís. In 1584 the widowed marquise
of Mondéjar demanded payment of the balance from the council, the two
citizens who administered the *encabezamiento* that year, and all the other
citizens of the town of Mondéjar. Those citizens still in arrears were
required to sign notes to the marquise, putting up real property as collateral.
The council negotiated other *encabezamientos* with the lord in the next
few years and succeeded in fulfilling them until 1598 and 1599, when the
Alcarria region and much of Castile were depopulated by plague epidemics.
The unpaid balances from this contract were still yielding interest to the
marquis of Mondéjar's heirs and creditors in 1608.[38]

Finally, in 1590 the king and the Cortes agreed on a new, value added
tax, the *millones*, designed to bring in 1 million ducados a year in royal

revenues. In the 1590s, according to the calculations of Carla Phillips, the average annual payment of *millones* per household was about 450 maravedís, the average subsidy 145 maravedís—the equivalent of one to two fanegas of wheat during most of the years the tax was collected from consumers.[39] The *millones* did not satisfy the monarchy's ever-growing need for revenues, and it aroused great hostility in the cities, which had lost some of their tax collection jurisdiction.

Claiming to be acting in response to legitimate complaints of consumers, the monarchy lobbied to substitute its own tax collectors for the private tax contractors who had traditionally collected the sales taxes and tithes, to their own profit. In 1626 the Cortes of Castile agreed that all the villages of Castile should receive the privilege of collecting the royal sales tax and share of the tithes in their own municipal territories. The representatives of the kingdom presented the classic argument: the citizens of villages were at a financial disadvantage, suffering vexations and irritations that drove population, trade, and commerce from the villages to towns, which had the right to collect their own taxes. The Cortes urged that all municipalities in the kingdom, even villages of towns that did not have *encabezamientos*, be given the right to negotiate a tax agreement— an *encabezamiento*—with the royal treasury so that the monarchy could save the expense of salaries, commissions, and expenses usually taken by the tax farmers and officials. In order to maintain a reasonable level of tax revenue, the Cortes representatives suggested that each town and village desiring to collect its taxes by *encabezamiento* be given the contract at the average of the previous five years' tax, before expenses.[40] Still, the revenues were inadequate, and the monarchy declared bankruptcy in 1627 and in 1647. Furthermore, the monarchy had now decentralized tax collection further, so that villages, as well as towns and cities, were permitted to negotiate their own tax and postpone payment until the end of the tax season by mortgaging public and private property as security. Finally, in the 1650s the king managed to achieve two changes in taxation that should have worked to the monarchy's benefit: the burden of payment of the *millones* was shifted from the consumers to the producers, and royal rather than city officials collected it.

The results the monarchy had hoped for did not materialize. The new tax system became snarled in innumerable difficulties. The old *millones* agreements had been negotiated individually between the monarch and the eighteen cities and towns of the Cortes; the new *millones* agreements had to be negotiated with the producers—the thousands of towns that made up the realm. The monarchy did not have the personnel to carry on such large-scale negotiations. Yet Philip IV's principal minister, the count-duke of Olivares, believed that direct collection by royal officials, no matter how expensive, would produce more revenue for the royal treasury than the old system of collection by the Cortes. The monarchy entrusted the assessments and collection to traveling commissioners or written correspondence, two unproven methods that, in the end, prolonged the assessment process until the government finally settled for less than half of its original demand. Once agreement was reached, there were further delays because the monarchy did not have enough tax collectors to send to the towns annually or even every two years.

The consequence at the local level was prolongation of the negotiations about the amount and terms of the assessment. Because delay worked to the advantage of the taxpayers, and because the town councils no longer felt responsible for taking the initiative, as they had under the traditional system, councils simply bided their time until the monarchy was so desperate for cash that the royal tax collectors agreed to the old levels of assessment. In Estremera, tax negotiations with the monarchy dragged on for months. In February 1643 Estremera's clerk recorded receipt of a royal decree issued in late 1642 ordering Estremera to pay a total of 1,033,600,000 maravedís in sales taxes and tithes for the nine years 1642 through 1651. The town was ordered to make the payments semiannually, in cash. The sales taxes for 1642 were to be paid on January 1, 1642, and the tithes for 1642 on August 15, 1643. The town council responded that it would agree to pay at the rate Estremera had paid in 1641—a nine-year total of 3,644,820 maravedís—and to collect the tax themselves by a special levy rather than from the sales taxes and tithes. Furthermore, the council agreed to this amount only on condition that the tax would be collected in nine payments of 404,980 maravedís, without adjustment for monetary fluctuations. The first tax collection, which was not carried out until 1647, was a compromise between these two positions. The royal and municipal tax officials collected the tithe and sales taxes, sold the produce, and retained for the monarchy 404,980 maravedís in cash for each year.

The council had agreed to a tax that seems high by sixteenth-century standards—1,258 maravedís per annum for each household—yet the increase did not lead to tax defaults. In the ten tithe rolls that survive from 1647 to 1703, a total of seventeen citizens were in arrears, while five had been in arrears in the 1579 tithe roll alone. The whole community enjoyed a windfall from the new system. The royal tax collectors were years late in making their rounds. They came to Estremera in 1650 to collect tithes, sales taxes, and millones for 1647, 1648, 1649, and 1650; in 1673 to collect for 1671 and 1672; and in 1703 to collect for 1701, 1702, and 1703.

Most observers have concluded that because of the combination of depressed prices, lower global production, and rising taxes, the agrarian population must have suffered food shortages and financial distress. The evidence above from the Alcarria, however, indicates that even in the depths of the seventeenth-century depression, farm families maintained a level of consumption at least comparable to what they had enjoyed in the palmier days of the sixteenth century. Rural towns had enough expendable municipal revenue to indulge in adorning and increasing their spiritual establishments. The overwhelming majority of citizens were able to meet their tax obligations in cash and kind on time. While the monarchy sank to the nadir of its fortunes in the seventeenth century, the Alcarria farmers found and maintained a stable balance of population, production, and expenditures.

Some towns did not fare so well in the seventeenth century. Old towns that had successfully fought dismemberment by outbidding their villages could not pay their tax assessments under the new tax regime. Their frustrated and oppressed villages took advantage of the town's tax arrears to buy the coveted charters of town liberty. The relationship between the town of Peñaranda de Duero and its village of San Juan del Monte followed this course. In 1654 the village council and citizens of San Juan del Monte offered to pay the royal treasury one thousand ducados in cash if King Philip IV would make the village into a town separate and free from the town of Peñaranda de Duero. The villagers had every reason to believe that their offer would be accepted, for they had taken advantage of the 1626 tax reform and were collecting their own royal tax assessment. Through *encabezamiento* they paid their royal taxes separately from Peñaranda de Duero. They also had the full support of their lord, the duke of Peñaranda, who gave his consent to the separation and agreed that the new town should receive possession of up to one-fourth of Peñaranda de Duero's municipal territory. The duke, lord of several towns in addition to Peñaranda, regarded the liberation of San Juan del Monte as "a good thing that would not prejudice my interests." Furthermore, the duke certified, San Juan del Monte's fifty families already possessed the normal municipal government: every New Year's Day they elected a village council of two judges, two councilmen, a representative, a treasurer of the municipal granary and assets, and a sheriff.[41] Years of experience in self-government made it clear that the San Juan village council was competent to administer justice, collect royal taxes and seignorial dues, and manage the municipality's corporate assets for the public good.

The king was equally ready to grant township. Though he ruled a worldwide empire, Philip IV needed money. The village's petition began by addressing the king's natural concerns of justice and equity. San Juan alleged that the half-league of distance between town and village hindered the administration of justice by making it costly for the Peñaranda magistrates to travel to the village in order to carry out property inventories, auctions, and partitions after someone died in the village, "to the harm and prejudice of minors and pious works."[42] From this and other failures of justice, the petition pointed to the logical conclusion that the king—fount of all justice, protector of widows and orphans, defender of the faith—ought to draw: "The only remedy for all this is to separate and divide the village from the civil and criminal jurisdiction of Peñaranda . . . to be made a town by and over itself."[43]

Only the town of Peñaranda objected; its town council acted swiftly to prevent this loss of territory and subjects. As soon as the king authorized the liberation of San Juan but before the decree was dispatched, the town council of Peñaranda de Duero made a counteroffer of three thousand ducados in cash if the king would promise never to free San Juan del Monte from the jurisdiction of Peñaranda. Invoking his absolute royal powers once again, Philip IV revoked the charter of township. San Juan del Monte, fearing the "fatal results that this new enslavement would produce,"[44] offered to match the amount paid by Peñaranda, but the bid was refused.

The royal treasury's refusal to accept San Juan's bid aroused the disgust of the duke of Peñaranda and the alarm of the villagers. The duke accused the treasury of rejecting the bid solely because Peñaranda had offered more money than the village.[45] The villagers' fear of retaliation from Peñaranda proved realistic: during the following years the town recouped its three thousand ducados by oppressing the villagers with fines, imprisonment, seizure of livestock, and high tax assessments.[46]

The abuses alleged by the villagers in the next century catalogued the ways in which a village economy suffered because its municipal corporation did not have the full political and judicial standing of a town. No sooner had the final verdict been issued than the town of Peñaranda began to treat the village "with a certain air of tyranny," redrawing the boundary markers of San Juan's grazing land so severely that there was not enough for the village to feed even half of its livestock. Further litigation between the village and its ruling town brought some relief for San Juan in 1671, when the town of Peñaranda was ordered by the highest court of the sheep grazer's union, the Council of the Mesta, to restore the old boundary markers.

But the antagonisms continued to cause resentment and competition, and the village took advantage of the change in royal dynasty at the beginning of the eighteenth century to exact some advantages from the new Bourbon monarchs. In 1718 some citizens of the village of San Juan harvested their grapes without first obtaining permission from the town council of Peñaranda. They were arrested and subjected to such heavy fines and punishments that they appealed the case all the way to the royal appellate court, which finally ruled in 1722 against the town of Peñaranda. Peñaranda's judge and town councilmen were ordered to pay the plaintiffs' court costs and return the fines. Henceforth, the villagers were free to harvest their grapes whenever they ripened, without having to coordinate their schedule with that of the town.

In 1744 conflict again erupted between the town of Peñaranda and its subject village. Some citizens of San Juan del Monte had tried to sell their cattle in Peñaranda'a annual livestock fair, but the Peñaranda judge and town council impounded the animals, arrested the owners, and treated them so harshly that the prisoners carried their appeal all the way to the royal appellate court. The court ordered that the plaintiffs be freed, condemned the Peñaranda judges to pay the court costs, and ordered Peñaranda not to seize the villagers' heifers without paying a fair market price for them.

Further abuses of the villagers were alleged when Peñaranda assessed the village one-third of the annual royal taxes due from Peñaranda's jurisdiction, instead of the one-fifth to which the village was obligated, and leased part of the village's uncultivated land to a private person in order to raise the money, thus depriving the villagers of free access to their own pasture. The royal chancery ruled in favor of the village of San Juan del Monte in these and other tax disputes in 1755. In another case between town and village, the royal judges noted that San Juan was oppressed by the necessity of traveling to Peñaranda for registering property transfers and divisions; in 1766 they granted the village the right to maintain its own property inventories and audit its own accounts in order to protect itself against the continuing assaults of its ruling town. Although the royal chancery acknowledged that these events "demonstrated the despotism of the town," the judges were reluctant to grant the village's repeated petitions for township until the duke and the village council demonstrated that San Juan del Monte had been negotiating and paying its own royal taxes through *encabezamiento* for over a century and that the two municipal councils did not even deliver their taxes to the same royal tax collection center. Furthermore, Peñaranda de Duero was hopelessly in arrears on its royal tax payments. The San Juan council agreed that its payment for township would be credited to Peñaranda's tax arrears, and this compromise convinced the royal courts. Finally in 1790 a Bourbon king, Charles IV, uttered the words that San Juan del Monte had coveted for so long:

In consideration of 3,500 ducados with which you have served my royal treasury, and by virtue of my royal absolute power as king and natural lord, I exempt, remove, and liberate you, the village of San Juan del Monte, from the jurisdiction of the town of Peñaranda, and I make you a town by and over yourself.[47]

In these tax negotiations and manipulations by town and village councils, sometimes in collusion with their lords, municipal governments safeguarded the political autonomy of Castilian taxpayers and cushioned their local economies from the worst effects of the monarchy's financial distress. These safeguards were unavailable to noncitizens. The church lost vast amounts of territory and jurisdiction in the sixteenth century as a direct consequence of the monarchy's wars to defend the faith. The nobles could gain wealth and influence through military service, but the unlucky ones paid personally for their tax-exempt status with their lives and their estates. But the towns, bound to the monarchy by mutual dependence, were able to use their corporate assets and negotiating skills to survive the centuries of war and royal bankruptcy with remarkably little financial or political damage.

Conclusion

Municipalities were the basic administrative units of the Castilian monarchy and the seignorial regime, the cells that made up the body politic of Castile from the medieval conquest through the nineteenth century. A cell is a complex system of parts and events, all interconnected, but if we study the municipal cell in the traditional method of going through a sequence of topics, the interrelationship does not emerge. Through the process followed here, of exploring the connections between parts and events, the municipality emerges as a dynamic system of interrelationships. For success in their activities, citizens, lords, and monarchs depended on a detailed and usually unexpressed knowledge of the internal parts of the municipality and its natural course of development, the complexities of royal and seignorial jurisdictions, the internal workings and political sophistication of town councils, and the legal constraints on municipalities, noble lords, and monarchs. The most powerful absolute monarchy in early modern Europe governed itself through thousands of direct connections to minute municipal corporations. In order to assess the efficacy of royal policy, therefore, we must understand the connection between the royal court and the monarchy's smallest units, the cities, towns, and villages.

Castilian monarchs acted as if the proliferation of autonomous towns contributed to the strengthening of royal government, because town liberty and royal absolute power were necessary for each other: a royal grant of town liberty was the ultimate exercise in royal absolute power. In order to excise a village from the jurisdiction of its ruling city or town, the king had to violate the founding charter in which his ancestors had granted all the land within the municipal territory to the city. Because there was no royal law at the local level other than the municipal charters, this arbitrary abrogation of the municipal charter required an extraordinary appeal to principles of Roman law. The architects of this appeal argued that the king possessed extralegal powers that it was his duty to invoke when extraordinary circumstances threatened the well-being of the republic.

The lawyers and municipal councils of villages seeking a town charter knew exactly how to describe those circumstances that threatened the public well-being. In hundreds of petitions for town liberty, village councils painted a picture of failure of justice, declining population, and the abandonment of cultivated land. The king's very reason for being—his functions as fount of justice, populator of the realm, and defender of the land—was in danger. These allegations of disaster—impending or already in progress—which have played a significant role in the historical interpretation of the decline of Spain, were in fact evidence of a vigorous people exercising their political expertise to secure for themselves control over the local justice and economy.

Citizens knew how to express their desires in terms that would serve the monarchy, and the monarchs satisfied those wishes in order to replenish the royal treasury. By creating more self-administering towns, monarchs and lords increased the number of entities responsible for justice, the public good, and tax collection. The cumulative effect of increasing the number of independent municipal jurisdictions during six centuries resulted in a perpetual decentralization. The wealth and consistency of the Habsburg documentation demonstrate that there was such a trend. Decentralization as well as centralization could serve the needs of government. Several layers of bureaucracy that a more centralized government would have needed, such as provinces, duchies, or counties, were unnecessary. Town judges generally dispensed justice acceptably to local communities, town councils managed the public land to such profit that Castile was a major source of Habsburg wealth and resources, and town officials collected royal taxes in a volume that was the envy of other European states.

The long-term economic consequences became manifest in the seventeenth-century efforts to reform tax collection, when the royal government found itself virtually incapable of collecting taxes at a crucial moment in its attempt to salvage its international situation. The earthy concerns of small farm towns and villages had not been of much interest to the royal government in Madrid, swept up in the race for imperial power. The kings and their ministers in Madrid performed miracles of financing and diplomacy. The army and navy sacrificed lives, limbs, and health to turn disasters into victory. In the Americas, Indian laborers and African slaves forced the earth to give up its mineral and vegetable treasures for provisioning and arming the great war effort in Europe. At home, cities represented in the Cortes voted subsidies to finance the monarchy's war against Atlantic pirates and Dutch rebels. Yet imperial grandeur in the Habsburg centuries proved elusive, and the sturdy loyalty of farm towns and the financial sacrifices of the farmers—more than 80 percent of the Spanish population— again and again saved the monarchy from the financial consequences of its own misjudgments.

The rapid and massive increases in taxation that the crown imposed on Castile elicited creative and energetic responses from towns. Rather than the often portrayed mythical royal tax farmers foreclosing on impoverished peasantry and driving them to migration or starvation, an array of municipal officials grappled with new problems. On the one hand they were engaged in the successful practice of using credit to buy municipal autonomy and invest in the communal economic infrastructure to raise productivity; on the other they were confronted after 1576 by a sustained worsening of the weather that destroyed capital investments and cut output. At the same time, the towns took on debts connected with meeting tax obligations. Towns that had managed to get one set of debts paid before the other set arose did reasonably well; those that sought to do both at once went bankrupt. Although all towns could draw on their democratic tradition of internal governance, the success or failure of individual towns depended on the town council's ability to take advantage of sweeping changes at the national and global levels. A combination of accidents of timing, internal development, political astuteness, and external relations had to be present for any specific new town to survive the natural disasters of the later Habsburg periods.

For the monarchy, the results were temporarily successful. Each military venture abroad sent the Habsburgs back to Castile for more money. While the king's ministers strong-armed popes, city councils, and representatives to the Cortes, treasury officials scrambled to attract new lenders and uncover overlooked assets. The most profitable assets of all turned out to be the small towns and villages of Castile. By transferring hundreds of municipalities from the church's domain and selling town charters to villages formerly ruled by city and town councils, the monarchy gained not only the cash that flowed into (and immediately out of) the royal treasury but also political benefits. The Habsburgs succeeded in their goal of not diminishing the royal domain and in fact enlarged it; many towns and villages eager to escape the rule of the church, a noble lord, or a city council bought charters making them royal towns. Increasing the number of towns and selling them more and more control over their own affairs, though it fragmented administration, cemented loyalties between citizens and monarchs. Eventually, the monarchy exhausted its energies and resources, but for nearly two centuries the sale of town charters enabled the Habsburgs to sustain unpopular foreign policies without arousing Castilians to rebellion.

Appendix A.
Towns and Villages Responding to the
Relaciones Questionnaire, 1575–80

This table comprises the 528 cities, towns, and villages whose responses to the *Relaciones* questionnaire have been published. Throughout the book, I use this list of places as the data set for estimating extent and rates of change. I do not pretend, however, that this list of places or the information in the other categories here is definitive. Many questions and problems arise when handling such a large number of places and changes over several centuries. Not the least of these problems is choosing which subtleties to leave out in order to fit the information into a small space. Out of the thirty-two categories of information for which I gathered data, I have chosen six to present here in five columns. I hope the choices I have made will help readers to get a broad view of the range and pace of changes in small towns and villages, as well as some sense of which jurisdictions suffered or gained the most in different centuries.

I organized the *Relaciones* list into five chronological groups: (1) places that were founded or chartered as cities and towns before the beginning of the Trastamara monarchy in 1369; (2) villages that became towns during the Trastamara monarchy (1369–1516); (3) villages that became towns during the Habsburg monarchy (1516–1700); (4) villages that became towns between the beginning of the Bourbon monarchy in 1700 and the publication of the count of Floridablanca's *Nomenclátor* in 1789; and (5) villages that had not become towns by 1789. I order the places chronologically within each group and, for places that became towns in the same year, I alphabetize by the place-name reported in the *Relaciones*.

Perhaps the most important choice I made was to analyze these 528 places in the *Relaciones* rather than the approximately 270 places whose sales are recorded in the royal treasury ledgers preserved in AGS, and analyzed by Dominguez Ortiz, Guilarte, and Silva. The sales recorded in AGS have the advantage of providing exact sale dates and prices, but these places were not included in the *Relaciones* survey. The *Relaciones* information has the advantage of making a longitudinal analysis possible, because the questionnaire asked specifically whether the place was a city, town, or village and, if it was a town, how it had acquired that status and when. The citizens' often vague answers to the latter question prevent precise dating of township in many cases, but their rich anecdotes more than compensate for the lack of precision.

The columns below contain the following information:

Year of township: The year in which the village became a town. In cases where the sources give only an approximate date for township, e.g., "more than fifty years ago" or "in the reign of King Juan," I list villages under the last possible appropriate date. In cases for which I know the decade but not the exact year, I finish the date with a question mark.

Relaciones *name/modern name:* Each of the places listed under this heading submitted one or more responses to the *Relaciones* questionnaire distributed by King Philip II between 1575 and 1580. I have checked the name and legal status of these places against the list of cities, towns, villages, and *despoblados* in the count of Floridablanca's *Nomenclátor*, published in 1789, and against the place-names on modern maps and census lists.

Former council: The name of the city or town in whose municipal boundary the village was settled. Places originally settled as towns were never in the jurisdiction of another city or town, of course, so this column is not applicable to them and remains blank.

Former lord: Under this heading I list the name or title of the lord of the place on the eve of the Habsburg monarchy, before it was sold or transferred into the royal domain. I use the following abbreviations:

a/ = archbishop of	d/ = duke of	mon/ = monastery of
Al⁰ = Alvaro	J⁰ = Juan	mr/ = marshal of
b/ = bishop of	m/ = marquis of	o/ = military order of
c/ = count of		P⁰ = Pedro

I give the noble title rather than the personal name wherever possible, in order to emphasize the continuity of lineage. Places listed with no former lord were under the jurisdiction of their ruling city or town, listed here as former council.

Year of sale: The year in which the town or village was severed from the jurisdiction of its former lord through transfer, *tanteo,* or sale. Towns and villages that do not have a year of sale remained in the jurisdiction listed here as former lord.

Year of Township	*Relaciones* Name / Modern Name	Former Council	Former Lord	Year of Sale
	Group 1. Places Founded or Chartered before 1369ᵃ			
	Alameda/Alameda de Barajas		c/Barajas	
	Albaladejo		o/Santiago	
	Albalate de Zorita	Zorita	o/Calatrava	1566
	Alcobendas		c/Puñonrostro	
	Alcocer		d/Infantado	
	Alcolea de Almodóvar		o/Calatrava	1575
	Alcolea de Torote		a/Toledo	1578
	Alhambra		o/Santiago	
	Alhóndiga		o/Calatrava	1552
	Almadén		o/Calatrava	
	Almedina		o/Santiago	
	Almodóvar del Campo		o/Calatrava	
	Almoguera		o/Calatrava	1538
	Almonacid de Zorita		o/Calatrava	
	Ambite		a/Toledo	1578
	Archilla	Brihuega	a/Toledo	1579
	Arenas		o/San Juan	
	Argamasilla		o/Calatrava	
	Ballesteros		o/Calatrava	
	Barajas		c/Barajas	1645
	Barcience		c/Cifuentes	
	Belinchón		a/Toledo	1579
	Belmonte		m/Villena	

Year of Township	*Relaciones* Name / Modern Name	Former Council	Former Lord	Year of Sale
	Group 1. Places Founded or Chartered before 1369[a]			
	Buenamesón		o/Santiago	
	Cabezaarados		o/Calatrava	
	Calzada		o/Calatrava	
	Campo de Criptana		o/Santiago	
	Caracuel		o/Calatrava	
	Cardiel		Enrique de Avila	
	Carrión de Calatrava		o/Calatrava	
	Castilseras		o/Calatrava	
	Caudilla		mr/Castilla	
	Chillón		o/Calatrava	
	Daganzuelo	Alcalá	a/Toledo	
	Daimiel		o/Calatrava	
	Espinosa de Henares		d/Infantado	
	Estremera		o/Santiago	1560
	Fuencaliente		o/Calatrava	
	Fuentidueña de Ocaña		o/Santiago	
	Guadalajara			
	Guadamur		c/Fuensalida	
	Gálvez		d/Uceda	
	El Hinojoso de la Orden		o/Santiago	
	El Horcajo de Santiago		o/Santiago	
	Huélamo		o/Santiago	1553
	Jumela		Juan Suárez de Toledo	
	Maqueda		o/Calatrava	
	Miguelturra		o/Calatrava	
	Mohernando		o/Santiago	1564
	Mondéjar		o/Calatrava	1512
	Montarrón	Beleña	c/Montarrón	
	La Mota del Cuervo		o/Santiago	
	Ocaña		o/Santiago	
	Ocentejo		J° Carrillo de Albornoz	
	El Olivar		d/Infantado	
	Orgaz		c/Orgaz	
	Paracuellos/ Paracuellos de Jarama		o/Santiago	1541
	Pedrazuela/ Pedrezuela	Segovia	c/Puñonrostro	
	Picón		o/Calatrava	1564
	Piedrabuena		o/Calatrava	1573
	Polvoranca		c/Orgaz	1550

Year of Township	*Relaciones* Name / Modern Name	Former Council	Former Lord	Year of Sale
	Group 1. Places Founded or Chartered before 1369[a]			
	La Puebla de Montalbán		c/Montalbán	
	Puertollano		o/Calatrava	
	Quintanar de la Orden		o/Santiago	
	Retuerta	Balconete	d/Infantado	
	La Roda		m/Villena	1479
	Sacedón/ Sacedoncillo	Beleña	Pedrarias Dávila	
	Santa Cruz de Mudela		o/Calatrava	1539
	Santorcaz		a/Toledo	
	Los Santos de la Humosa		a/Toledo	
	Segura de la Sierra			
	Socuéllamos		o/Santiago	
	La Solana		o/Santiago	
	Talamanca		a/Toledo	1575
	Talavera de la Reina		a/Toledo	
	Terrinches		o/Santiago	
	La Torre de Juan Abad		o/Santiago	
	Uclés		o/Santiago	
	Valdaracete		o/Santiago	1560
	Valtablado del Río/ Valtablado del Rey		o/Santiago & Al° Carrillo	
	Villaluenga de la Sagra		m/Montemayor	
	Villarejo de Salvanés		o/Santiago	
	Villarrubia de los Ajos/Villarrubia de los Ojos		o/Calatrava	1552
	Villarta/Villarta de los Montes	d/Béjar		
	Villaseca de la Sagra		m/Montemayor	
	El Viso		o/San Juan	
1060	Uceda		a/Toledo	1579
1085	Illescas		a/Toledo	1575
1085	Toledo			
1092	Borox		o/Calatrava	
1100	Cogolludo		o/Calatrava	1377
1124	Casarrubios del Monte	Madrid	c/Casarrubios	1484
1124	Santa Olalla		c/Orgaz	

Year of Township	*Relaciones* Name / Modern Name	Former Council	Former Lord	Year of Sale
	Group 1. Places Founded or Chartered before 1369[a]			
1127	Beleña		Melén Pérez Valdés	1452
1147	Torralba/Torralba de Calatrava		o/Calatrava	
1170	Zorita de los Canes		o/Calatrava	1565
1176	Moratilla/Moratilla de los Meleros		o/Calatrava	
1177	El Castillo de Garcimuñoz		m/Villena	
1178	Illana		o/Calatrava	
1186	Iniesta		m/Villena	
1190	Auñón		o/Calatrava	
1192	Dosbarrios de Ocaña/Dosbarrios		o/Santiago	
1198	Pareja		b/Cuenca	
1199	Hueva		o/Calatrava	
1199	San Silvestre	Maqueda	d/Maqueda	
1207	Villarrubia de Uclés/ Villarrubia de Santiago		o/Santiago	
1220	Cuerva		m/Montealegre	
1220	Manzanares		o/Calatrava	
1224	Miguel Esteban		o/Santiago	
1228	Peñalver		o/San Juan	1552
122?	Hernán Caballero/ Fernáncaballero		o/Calatrava	1553
122?	La Membrilla		o/Santiago	
1250	Valdelloso		mon/Monsalud	1536
1253	Santa Cruz de la Zarza		o/Santiago	
1256	Montiel		o/Santiago	
1260	Cifuentes	Atienza	c/Cifuentes	
1291	Córcoles		mon/Monsalud	
1293	Fuenllana	Montiel	o/Santiago	
1294	San Román	Avila	m/Velada	
1294	Velada	Avila	m/Velada	
1295	Loranca de Tajuña	Guadalajara	m/Mondéjar	1377
1299	Fuentes	Brihuega	a/Toledo	1579
12??	El Provencio		m/Villena	
1305	Viana de Mondéjar	Cuenca		
1317	Malagón		o/Calatrava	1549
1328	Villamayor/ Villamayor de Santiago		o/Santiago	
	Villanueva de Alcardete		o/Santiago	

Year of Township	*Relaciones* Name / Modern Name	Former Council	Former Lord	Year of Sale
	Group 1. Places Founded or Chartered before 1369[a]			
1329	Berninches		o/Calatrava	1572
1338	El Toboso		o/Santiago	
1340	Atanzón	Guadalajara	José Gómez de Mendoza	
1343	La Puebla de Almoradiel	El Corral	o/Santiago	
1347	Villaescusa de Haro	Haro	o/Santiago	
1350	Malpica		m/Malpica	
	Group 2. Villages That Became Towns during the Trastamara Monarchy, 1369–1516			
1369	Fuentelaencina/ Fuentelencina		o/Calatrava	
1369	Pastrana	Zorita	o/Calatrava	1541
136?	Herencia		o/San Juan	
1377	Puebla de Almenara		d/Pastrara	
1385	Cabeza Mesada		o/Santiago	
1393	Castillo de Bayuela	Avila	o/Suan Juan	
1395	Tendilla	Guadalajara	m/Mondéjar	
1399	Puente del Arzobispo	Talavera	a/Toledo	1578
1400	Corral de Caracuel/ Corral de Calatrava[b]		o/Calatrava	
1401	Brea	Almoguera	o/Calatrava	1538
1404	Batres		m/Montealegre	
1404	Villanueva de los Infantes	Montiel	o/Santiago	
1412	Cubas		Alonso de Mendoza	
1412	Griñón		Alonso de Mendoza	
1413	Cobeña	Guadalajara	c/Coruña	
1430	Almuña/Armuña de Tajuña	Guadalajara	m/Mondéjar	
1430	Aranzueque	Guadalajara	m/Mondéjar	
1430	Balconete	Guadalajara	m/Montesclaros	
1430	Fresno de Torote	Alcalá	J°Hurtado de Mendoza	
1430	Lillo	La Guardia	a/Toledo	1575
1430	Meco	Guadalajara	m/Mondéjar	
1430	Pioz	Guadalajara	Jose Gómez de Mendoza	
1430	Pozo de Guadalajara	Guadalajara	P° Gómez de Mendoza	
1430	Serracines	Guadalajara	d/Pastrana	

Year of Township	*Relaciones* Name / Modern Name	Former Council	Former Lord	Year of Sale
	Group 2. Villages That Became Towns during the Trastamara Monarchy, 1369–1516			
1430	Yunquera	Guadalajara	Luís de Mendoza	
1431	Budia	Atienza	d/Infantado	
1434	Bienservida	Alcaraz	c/Paredes de Nava	
1434	Jadraque	Atienza	d/Infantado	
1434	Valdelagua	Atienza	d/Infantado	
1440	Torrenueva		o/Santiago	
1444	Valfermoso de Tajuña	Guadalajara	m/Mondéjar	
1444	Villahermosa	Montiel	o/Santiago	
1445	Cedillo		c/Cedillo	
1445	Huecas		c/Fuensalida	
1445	Peromoro		Pº de Ayala	
1445	San Clemente	Alarcón	m/Villena	
144?	Herrera		d/Béjar	
144?	Santa Maria del Campo/Santa María del Campo Rus	Alarcón	Pº González del Castillo	1578
1457	San Martín de Valdepusa/San Martín de Pusa	Valdepusa	mr/Castilla	
1458	Escariche	Zorita	o/Calatrava	1548
1459	Fuentenovilla		o/Calatrava	1538
1459	Yebra	Zorita	o/Calatrava	
145?	Buendía		c/Buendía	
1461	Saceruela		o/Calatrava	
1461	La Torre de Esteban Ambrán		Pº González de Mendoza	1568
1472	Puebla Don Rodrigo/ Puebla de Don Rodrigo		o/Calatrava	
1474	Villamanrique	Montiel	o/Santiago	
1476	Pesadilla	Alcalá	a/Toledo	1579
1477	Barchín del Hoyo	Alarcón	m/Villena	
1477	El Cañavete	Alarcón	m/Villena	
1477	Las Mesas	Alarcón	m/Villena	
1479	Alberca/La Alberca de Záncara	Alarcón	m/Villena	1628
1479	El Pedernoso	Alarcón	m/Villena	
1479	Pedroneras	Alarcón	m/Villena	
1479	El Peral	Alarcón	m/Villena	
1479	Villanueva de la Jara	Alarcón	m/Villena	
147?	Los Pozuelos		o/Calatrava	
1480	Ajofrín	Talavera	a/Toledo	1575

Year of Township	Relaciones Name / Modern Name	Former Council	Former Lord	Year of Sale
	Group 2. Villages That Became Towns during the Trastamara Monarchy, 1369–1516			
1480	La Cabeza	Segovia	c/Chinchón	
1480	Daganzo/Daganzo de Arriba	Alcalá	c/Coruña	
1480	Quijorna	Segovia	c/Chinchón	
1480	San Agustín		c/Puñonrostro	
1480	Seseña	Segovia	c/Chinchón	
1480	Valdelaguna	Segovia	c/Chinchón	
1482	Alcabón	Toledo	a/Toledo	
1482	Gerindote		b/Segovia	1482
1482	Sacedón	Segovia	c/Chinchón	1482
1482	Torrijos	Talavera	a/Toledo	1482
1485	Méntrida	Segovia	d/Infantado	
1486	Santa Cruz de Retamar		d/Maqueda	
1495	Valdeconcha	Zorita	o/Calatrava	1542
1498	Hontova	Zorita	o/Calatrava	1645
1499	Tembleque	Consuegra	o/San Juan	
1500	Luciana	Almodóvar	o/Calatrava	
1503	Trijueque	Hita	d/Infantado	
1506	Colmenar Viejo	Manzanares	d/Infantado	
1511	Cañada el Moral/ Cañada de Calatrava	Almodóvar	o/Calatrava	
	Group 3. Villages That Became Towns during the Habsburg Monarchy, 1516–1700			
1520	Alocén		mon/Monsalud	1563
1525	Pozo Rubio	Villamayor	o/Santiago	
1531	Argamasilla de Alba	Moraleja	o/San Juan	
1537	Bala de Rey/Vara de Rey	San Clemente	m/Villena	1445
1537	Carrascosa del Campo	Huete		
1537	Fuente de Pedro Naharro	Uclés	o/Santiago	
1537	Horche	Guadalajara		
1537	Tarancón	Uclés	o/Santiago	
1538	Albares	Almoguera	o/Calatrava	1538
1538	Alcubillas	Montiel	o/Santiago	
1538	Valenzuela	Almagro	o/Calatrava	1553
1539	Sayatón	Pastrana	o/Calatrava	1539
1551	Barajas de Melo	Huete		
1552	Leganiel	Huete		
1553	Palomares del Campo	Huete		

Year of Township	*Relaciones* Name / Modern Name	Former Council	Former Lord	Year of Sale
	Group 3. Villages That Became Towns during the Habsburg Monarchy, 1516–1700			
1553	Puebla del Príncipe	Montiel	o/Santiago	
1553	Renera	Guadalajara		
1554	Cózar	Montiel	o/Santiago	
1554	Orusco	Alcalá	a/Toledo	1578
1554	Pezuela/Pezuela de las Torres	Alcalá	a/Toledo	1579
1554	Valdeavellano	Guadalajara		
1554	Villalvilla	Alcalá	a/Toledo	
1555	El Campo Real	Alcalá	a/Toledo	1578
1555	Loeches	Alcalá	a/Toledo	
1556	Valdilecha	Alcalá	a/Toledo	
1557	Almendros	Uclés	o/Santiago	
1557	Camuñas	Consuegra	o/San Juan	
1557	Carabaña	Alcalá	a/Toledo	1578
1557	Enguídanos	Cuenca		
1557	Madridejos	Consuegra	o/San Juan	
1557	Romeral	La Guardia	o/San Juan	
1557	Sahelices	Uclés	o/Santiago	
1557	Villacañas	Consuegra	o/San Juan	
1558	Huelves	Huete		1558
1558	Mazarulleque	Huete		
1558	Rozalén del Monte	Uclés	o/Santiago	
1558	Torrubia del Campo	Uclés	o/Santiago	
1560	Romanones	Guadalajara		
1561	Villar/Villar del Olmo	Alcalá	a/Toledo	
1563	Castellar de Santiago	Montiel	o/Santiago	
1563	Quintanar del Rey	Villanueva de la Jara	m/Villena	
1563	Valdetorres	Talamanca	a/Toledo	1579
1564	El Casar de Talamanca	Talamanca	a/Toledo	1580
1564	Minglanilla	Alarcón	m/Villena	
1564	Ribatajada	Alcolea de Torote	a/Toledo	1578
1564	Romancos	Brihuega	a/Toledo	1579
1564	Usanos	Guadalajara		
1564	Valverde	Alcalá	a/Toledo	
1565	El Olmeda/El Olmeda de las Fuentes	Alcalá	a/Toledo	
1566	Móstoles	Toledo		
1567	Nombela	Escalona	d/Escalona	
1569	Lupiana		mon/Lupiana	
1574	Morata	Alcalá	a/Toledo	

Year of Township	*Relaciones* Name / Modern Name	Former Council	Former Lord	Year of Sale
	Group 3. Villages That Became Towns during the Habsburg Monarchy, 1516–1700			
1574	Tarazona de la Mancha	Villanueva de la Jara	m/Villena	
1574	Villarrubio	Uclés	o/Santiago	1579
1575	Los Hueros	Alcalá	a/Toledo	1585
1575	Menasalbas	La Puebla de Montalbán	c/Montalbán	
1575	Miralcampo	Meco	m/Mondéjar	
1576	Torrejón de Ardoz	Madrid		1575
1577	Valdenuño Fernández	Uceda	a/Toledo	1577
1578	Ajalvir	Alcalá	a/Toledo	1578
1578	Camarma de el Caño/Camarma del Caño	Guadalajara	o/Calatrava	
1578	Escopete	Pastrana		1539
1578	Pozo de Almoguera	Almoguera	o/Calatrava	1538
1578	Pozuelo de Torres/ Pozuelo del Rey	Alcalá	a/Toledo	
1579	Anchuelo	Alcalá	a/Toledo	1581
1579	El Espinoso	Talavera	a/Toledo	
1581	El Cubillo	Uceda	a/Toledo	1581
1581	Fuentelahiguera	Uceda	a/Toledo	1581
1583	Arganda	Alcalá	a/Toledo	
1585	Galápagos	Alcolea de Torote	a/Toledo	1698
1587	Navalcarnero	Segovia		
1591	San Andrés/San Andrés del Rey	Uceda	a/Toledo	1582
1593	Fuente el Fresno	Uceda	a/Toledo	1613
1603	Gascueña	Jadraque	d/Infantado	
1606	Quismondo	Maqueda	d/Maqueda	
1607	Muduex	Hita	d/Infantado	
1616	Valdeaveruelo	Guadalajara		1629
1617	Trillo	Cifuentes	c/Cifuentes	
1625	Iriépal	Guadalajara		1627
1625	La Mierla	Beleña	c/Coruña	
1625	Taracena	Guadalajara		1627
1625	Valdenoches	Guadalajara		1627
1625	Villamanta	Casarrubios	c/Casarrubios	
1626	Alovera	Guadalajara		1626
1626	Aravaca	Madrid		1630
1626	Boadilla del Monte	Madrid		1626
1626	Bolaños		o/Calatrava	1626
1626	Húmera	Madrid		1626
1626	Leganés	Madrid		1641
1626	Portillo	Toledo		1626

Year of Township	Relaciones Name / Modern Name	Former Council	Former Lord	Year of Sale
	Group 3. Villages That Became Towns during the Habsburg Monarchy, 1516–1700			
1626	Las Rozas/Las Rozas de Madrid	Madrid		1626
1627	Burujón	Toledo		
1627	Canillas	Madrid		1627
1627	Canillejas	Madrid		1627
1627	Chamartín	Madrid		1627
1627	Hortaleza	Madrid		
1627	Marchamalo	Guadalajara		17??
1627	Recas	Toledo		1627
1627	Velilla	Madrid		1627
1628	Aldeanueva	Guadalajara		
1628	Cavanillas	Guadalajara		
1628	Pantoja	Toledo		
1628	Ribas/Ribas de Jarama	Madrid		1628
1628	Santo Domingo del Valle/Val de Santo Domingo	Maqueda	d/Maqueda	
1629	Centenera	Guadalajara		1626
1629	Ciruelos	Toledo		
1629	Perales/Perales del Rio	Madrid		1629
1629	Puebla de Guadalajara	Guadalajara		1629
1629	Yélamos de Yuso	Guadalajara		
1630	Arcicollar	Toledo		1630
1630	Azuqueca	Guadalajara		1630
1630	Valdearenas	Hita	d/Infantado	
1630	Yeles	Toledo		
1631	Malaguilla	Guadalajara		1631
1631	Pozuelo de Aravaca/ Pozuelo de Alarcón	Madrid		1637
1634	Yuncos	Toledo		
1635	Navalmoral/ Navalmoralejo	Talavera	a/Toledo	
1638	Yuncler	Toledo		
1640	Quer	Guadalajara		1640
1642	Torralva/Torralva de Oropesa	Oropesa	c/Oreposa	
1644	Camarena	Toledo		1644
1644	Gárgoles de Abajo	Cifuentes	c/Cifuentes	
1644	Gárgoles de Arriba	Cifuentes	c/Cifuentes	
1647	Irueste	Guadalajara		1647
1648	Valderachas/ Valdenoches	Guadalajara		1648

Year of Township	Relaciones Name / Modern Name	Former Council	Former Lord	Year of Sale
	Group 3. Villages That Became Towns during the Habsburg Monarchy, 1516–1700			
1648	Yebes	Guadalajara		1648
1652	Añover/Añover de Tajo	Toledo		
1652	Casasbuenas	Toledo		
1652	La Mata	Santa Olalla	c/Orgaz	
1652	Nominchal/ Lominchar	Toledo		
1653	Alcalá del Río/ Albarreal de Tajo	Toledo		1674
1655	Yunclillos	Toledo		1655
1660	Ugena	Illescas	a/Toledo	
1662	Alamo	Casarrubios	c/Casarrubios	
1665	Villamiel	Toledo		
1669	El Otero	Santa Olalla	c/Orgaz	
1670	Humanes	Mohernando	o/Santiago	1564
1671	Cañizar	Hita	d/Infantado	
1672	Nuez/Noez	Toledo		
1673	Valdesaz	Uceda	a/Toledo	1578
1676	Azaña/Numancia de la Sagra	Toledo		
1678	Valdeverdeja	Puebla de Santiago		
1682	La Despernada/ Villanueva de la Cañada	Segovia		
1692	Chiloeches	Guadalajara		1692
1692	Sevilleja/Sevilla la Nueva	Talavera	a/Toledo	
	Group 4. Villages That Became Towns during the Bourbon Monarchy, 1700–1789^c			
1705	Fuencemillán	Cogolludo	d/Medinaceli	
1728	Ciruelas	Hita	d/Infantado	
1730	Domingo Pérez	Santa Olalla	c/Orgaz	
1734	Valmojado	Casarrubios	c/Casarrubios	
1737	El Carpio	La Puebla de Montalbán	c/Montalbán	
1741	Hontanar/Fontanar	Guadalajara		
1743	Venta de Cabeza Retamosa	Casarrubios	c/Casarrubios	
1744	Olías	Toledo		
1749	Hormigos	Escalona	d/Escalona	
1752	El Pardillo	Galapagar	d/Infantado	
1758	Esquivias	Toledo		

Year of Township	*Relaciones* Name / Modern Name	Former Council	Former Lord	Year of Sale
	Group 4. Villages That Became Towns during the Bourbon Monarchy, 1700–1789[c]			
1789	Alalpardo	Talamanca	a/Toledo	1714
1789	Aleas	Beleña	c/Coruña	
1789	Buges	Guadalajara		
1789	Camarma de Encina	Guadalajara		1578
1789	Camarma de Esteruelas/ Camarma de Esteruelas	Alcalá	a/Toledo	1758
1789	El Canal	Guadalajara		
1789	Carranque	El Viso	o/San Juan	
1789	Carrascosa de Henares	Jadraque	d/Infantado	
1789	Carriches	Santa Olalla	c/Orgaz	
1789	Casa de Uceda	Uceda	a/Toledo	
1789	Casasimarro	Villanueva de la Jara	m/Villena	
1789	Caspueñas	Hita	d/Infantado	
1789	Cendejas de la Torre	Jadraque	d/Infantado	
1789	Cobeja de la Sagra	Toledo		1629
1789	Cobisa	Talavera	a/Toledo	
1789	Drieves	Almoguera	o/Calatrava	1538
1789	Gabaldón	La Motilla		
1789	Gil García	Villanueva de la Jara	m/Villena	
1789	Hornillo	Toledo, Montes de		
1789	Huermeces	Jadraque	d/Infantado	
1789	Madrigueras	Villanueva de la Jara	m/Villena	
1789	Mascaraque	Toledo		
1789	Matarrubia	Uceda	d/Uceda	
1789	Palomeque	El Viso	o/San Juan	
1789	Puebla de Beleña	Beleña	c/Coruña	
1789	Rejas	Madrid		
1789	Rielves	Toledo		1578
1789	Robledo del Mazo	Talavera	a/Toledo	
1789	Sotoca/Sotoca de Tajo	Cifuentes	c/Cifuentes	
1789	Taragudo	Hita	d/Infantado	
1789	Techada	Santa Olalla	c/Orgaz	
1789	Tomelloso	Socuéllamos	o/Santiago	1579
1789	Tribaldos	Uclés	o/Santiago	
1789	Valdeavero	Alcolea de Torote	a/Toledo	
1789	Villaseca de Uceda	Uceda	a/Toledo	1581

Year of Township	Relaciones Name / Modern Name	Former Council	Former Lord	Year of Sale
	Group 4. Villages That Became Towns during the Bourbon Monarchy, 1700–1789ᶜ			
1789	Villaviciosa del Campo/ Villaviciosa de Tajuña	Guadalajara		1579
1789	Viñuelas	Uceda	a/Toledo	1581
	Group 5. Places That Remained Villages in 1789ᵈ			
	Las Abiertas	Talavera	a/Toledo	
	Adovea	Santa Olalla	c/Orgaz	
	Alameda de la Sagra	Toledo		
	Alcaudete	Talavera	a/Toledo	
	Alcañizo	Oropesa	c/Oropesa	
	Alcoba	Toledo		
	Alcorcón	Madrid		
	Alcorlo	Jadraque	d/Infantado	
	Aldeanueva de Barbarroyo	Talavera	a/Toledo	
	Almonacid	Toledo		
	Ambroz	Madrid		
	Angón	Jadraque	d/Infantado	
	Argés	Toledo		
	Arisgotas	Toledo		
	Arroba	Toledo, Montes de		
	Arroyo las Fraguas	Jadraque	d/Infantado	
	Belvis	Talavera	a/Toledo	
	Benalaque	Guadalajara		
	El Bravo	Escalona	d/Escalona	
	Brugel	Talavera	a/Toledo	
	Bujalaro	Jadraque	d/Infantado	
	Burguillos	Toledo		
	Bustares	Jadraque	d/Infantado	
	Cabañas de la Sagra	Toledo		
	Los Cadocos/Los Cortijos	Toledo, Montes de		
	Calera	Talavera	a/Toledo	
	Campillo	Talavera	a/Toledo	
	Carabanchel de Arriba	Madrid		
	Cardeñosa	Jadraque	d/Infantado	
	Carrascalejo	Talavera	a/Toledo	
	Casalgordo	Toledo		
	El Casar de Talavera	Talavera	a/Toledo	
	Casarrubuelos de Madrid	Madrid		

Year of Township	*Relaciones* Name / Modern Name	Former Council	Former Lord	Year of Sale
	Group 5. Places That Remained Villages in 1789[d]			
	Castañal	Talavera	a/Toledo	
	Cazalegas	Talavera	a/Toledo	
	Cendejas de Enmedio	Jadraque	d/Infantado	
	Cerezo	Mohernando	o/Santiago	1564
	Cerralbo	Talavera	a/Toledo	
	Chozas	Talavera	a/Toledo	
	Chueca	Toledo		
	Corralrubio	Talavera	a/Toledo	
	Coslada	Madrid		
	Crespos	Escalona	d/Escalona	
	Erustes	Santa Olalla	c/Orgaz	
	Escalonilla	Toledo		
	Estrella	Talavera	a/Toledo	
	Frexno de Málaga	Guadalajara		
	Fuencarral	Madrid		
	Fuenlabrada	Madrid		
	Fuentelapio	Talavera	a/Toledo	
	Gamonal	Talavera	a/Toledo	
	Getafe	Madrid		
	Las Herencias	Talavera	a/Toledo	
	Hiendelaencia	Jadraque	d/Infantado	
	Hontanar	Toledo, Montes de		
	Hontanarejo/ Fontanarejo	Toledo, Montes de		
	Horcajo/Horcajo de los Montes	Toledo, Montes de		
	Humanejos	Madrid		
	Illán de Vacas	Talavera	a/Toledo	
	Lucillos	Talavera	a/Toledo	
	Magán	Toledo		
	Majadahonda	Madrid		
	Manzaneque	Toledo		
	Marjaliza	Toledo		
	Matillas	Jadraque	d/Infantado	
	Mazarambroz	Toledo		
	Mazuecos	Almoguera	o/Calatrava	1538
	Mañosa	Talavera	a/Toledo	
	Medranda	Jadraque	d/Infantado	
	Membrillar	Santa Olalla	c/Orgaz	
	Membrillera	Jadraque	d/Infantado	
	Mesegar	La Puebla de Montalbán		
	Mesones	Uceda	a/Toledo	1581
	Mocejón	Toledo		
	Molinillo	Toledo		

Year of Township	Relaciones Name / Modern Name	Former Council	Former Lord	Year of Sale
	Group 5. Places That Remained Villages in 1789ᵈ			
	Montearagón	Talavera	a/Toledo	
	Moraleja	Uclés	o/Santiago	
	Muriel	Beleña	c/Coruña	
	Nambroca	Toledo		
	Navahermosa	Toledo, Montes de		
	Navalmoral/Los Navalmorales	Toledo		
	Navalpino	Toledo, Montes de		
	Navas de Esteva	Toledo, Montes de		
	Negredo	Jadraque	d/Infantado	
	Novés	Toledo		
	La Olmeda	Jadraque	d/Infantado	1579
	Pepino	Talavera	a/Toledo	
	Peraleda/Peraleda de San Román	Talavera	a/Toledo	
	La Pueblanueva	Talavera	a/Toledo	
	Puerto de San Vicente	Talavera	a/Toledo	
	Pulgar	Toledo, Montes de		
	Quintería de Santa María de Poyos	Peñalén	o/San Juan	
	Rebollosa	Jadraque	d/Infantado	
	Retuerta	Toledo, Montes de		
	Robledillo de la Jara	Mohernando	o/Santiago	1564
	El Rostro	Toledo, Montes de		
	Ríofrío de Jadraque	Jadraque	d/Infantado	
	San Andrés del Congosto	Jadraque	d/Infantado	
	San Bartolomé de la Raña/San Bartolomé de las Abiertas	Talavera	a/Toledo	
	San Pablo	Toledo, Montes de		
	San Sebastián de los Reyes	Madrid		
	Santa Ana de Bienvenida	San Martín de Pusa	m/Malpica	
	Santiuste	Jadraque	d/Infantado	
	Tiratafuera	Almodóvar	o/Calatrava	
	Torlamora	Talavera	a/Toledo	

Year of Township	*Relaciones* Name / Modern Name	Former Council	Former Lord	Year of Sale
	Group 5. Places That Remained Villages in 1789[d]			
	Torrecilla/Torrecilla de la Jara	Talavera	a/Toledo	
	Torrejoncillo de Illescas/Torrejón de la Calzada	Illescas	a/Toledo	1660
	Totanes	Toledo		
	Valaguera	Illescas	a/Toledo	
	Valdegrudas	Hita	d/Infantado	
	Vargas/Bargas	Toledo		
	Ventas con Peña Aguilera	Toledo, Montes de		
	Vianilla/Viana de Jadraque	Jadraque	d/Infantado	
	Vicálvaro	Madrid		1664
	Villaharta	Consuegra	o/San Juan	
	Villaminaya	Toledo		
	Villanueva de Fuente el Fresno	Madrid		
	Villanueva de Guadalajara	Guadalajara		
	Villanueva del Horcajo	Talavera	a/Toledo	
	Villares	Jadraque	d/Infantado	
	Villaverde	Madrid		
	Yébenes de Toledo	Toledo		
	Zarzuela	Talamanca	a/Toledo	1577
	Zarzuela de Jadraque	Jadraque	d/Infantado	

[a]In group 1, I leave undated and list alphabetically places originally settled as towns in the medieval reconquest—a common practice in the military orders and in seignorial jurisdictions. These places usually had no medieval documents to remind them of the year of their founding.

[b]Alphabetized as Corral de Almodóvar in the published *Relaciones*.

[c]In group 4, I assign the date 1789 to places that described themselves as villages in the *Relaciones*, that were reported as towns in the *Nomenclátor*, and for which I have found no other date of township.

[d]Most of the places in group 5 that were still villages in 1789 achieved township gratis in the late nineteenth century if they comprised more than one hundred households.

Appendix B.
Glossary of Castilian Terms

Abadengo. Territory in ecclesiastical jurisdiction.

Adelantado mayor. Royal appellate judge for municipalities on the Muslim or American frontier.

Alcabala. Royal sales tax, usually set at about 3.5 percent, raised temporarily to 10 percent in 1576.

Alcaide. Commander of a castle or fortification.

Alcalde. Judge.

Alcalde de casa y corte. Judge of the royal court and household, with sovereign jurisdiction over territory within a five-league radius of the monarch's person.

Alcalde mayor. Appellate judge, appointed by the lord or monarch.

Alcalde ordinario. Municipal judge, chosen annually by election, cooption, or sortition.

Alcaldía mayor. Territory subject to the appellate jurisdiction of an *alcalde mayor.*

Aldea. Village established by a city or town in its own municipal territory. The founding citizens of *aldeas* were sent as colonizers, and they and their descendants retained citizenship in the mother city or town.

Alfoz. Municipal territory in Old Castile. The equivalent term in New Castile is *término,* q.v.

Alguacil. Municipal sheriff.

Argolla. Iron ring used as a stockade.

Arras. Bride's portion paid by the groom at the time of marriage.

Arrendamiento. Contract for tax collection through the tax farming procedure. The highest bidder won the contract, paid the total tax and commissions in advance, and in return acquired the power to collect taxes in the contract region.

Arroba. Measure of dry weight and volume. Twenty-five Castilian pounds of 16 ounces or 8 *azumbres,* 11.5 kilograms.

Asiento. Treaty; negotiated settlement.

Audiencia. Royal appellate court.

Averiguación. Verification by a royal accountant of the appraisal of a town's sale price.

Azumbre. Liquid measure divisible into 4 *cuartillos;* 4 pints.

Behetría. Community having the right to choose its lord. The medieval tradition of *behetría* served as a legal precedent for the *tanteo* during the Habsburg period.

Cabeza de partido. Village designated as the meeting place for all the villages in the *partido* for the *repartimiento* of their tax obligations according to their population.

Cacica. Feminine of "cacique," q.v.

Cacique. Native lord of an indigenous town.

Cahiz. Dry measure of volume, divisible into 12 fanegas.

Capítulos. Terms of a municipal charter or other contract.

Carga. Dry measure. One packload. The weight and volume varied.

Carta puebla. Municipal charter.

Caserío. Residential nucleus of a city, town, or village.

Cédula. Decree.

Celemín. Dry measure divisible into 4 *cuartillos,* about 4.625 liters. The weight varied.

Censo. Annuity.

Censo perpetuo enfitéusin. Perpetual leasehold transferring the municipal territory to the council in exchange for the payment of a fixed annuity.

Chancillería. Royal appellate court.

Ciudad. City.

Composición. Negotiated settlement of tax assessment, usually a compromise between a municipal council and the royal treasury.

Concejo. City, town, or village council.

Concejo abierto. Town meeting open to all citizens.

Concejo secreto. Town meeting open only to voting male citizens, usually convened without the knowledge of the town's lord.

Consejo. Royal council.

Constitución. Municipal charter.

Corregidor. Royal judge appointed to preside over a city or royal town.

Corregimiento. Territory subject to the appellate jurisdiction of a corregidor.

Cortijo. Enclosed farmstead exempt from municipal jurisdiction.

Coto. Land exempt from municipal jurisdiction, usually a hunting preserve.

Despoblado. Any municipality deserted or too small to maintain a functioning council.

Dezmería. Land cultivated and therefore subject to the tithe *(diezmo).*

Dismembrar. To alienate a village from its ruling city or town.

Ducado. Money of account worth 11 *reales* or 375 maravedís.

Encabezamiento. Encumbrance of personal property as security for tax collection contract.

Encomienda. Towns making up the seignorial territory of a commander of a military order.

Escribano. Clerk.

Escudo. Gold coin introduced in 1537 worth 350 maravedis; worth 400 maravedis after 1566.

Eximido. Exempted from the jurisdiction of a city or town.

Eximir. To alienate a village from its ruling city or town.

Fanega. Dry measure of volume divisible into 12 *celemines;* 555 liters. The weight varied depending on the item measured. Twelve fanegas made a *cahiz.* Also, the amount of land on which a fanega of grain was sown. The extent varied depending on the region and the quality of the soil. One square fanega was equivalent to about two-thirds of a hectare.

Fuero. Municipal charter granted by the monarch to a city or town.

Gobernador. Royal appellate judge for towns remaining in the military orders after 1560.

Hacienda. Farm; the sum of plowfields belonging to a single owner; estate.

Haza. Plowfield.

Hermandad. Federation of coterminous cities and towns for the pursuit and prosecution of suspected criminals who crossed municipal boundaries and for the settlement of disputes over stock grazing.

Hidalgo. Tax-exempt layman.

Huerta. All the irrigated land of a city, town, or village.

Huerto. Irrigated field or orchard.

Jurado. Representative from a parish to the municipal council.

Juro. Annuity paid from public funds.

Juro de alquitar. Term annuity.
Juro de por vida. Annuity paid for the lifetime of the recipient.
Justicia mayor. Interim royal appellate judge.
Latifundium. Large landed estate under a single ownership and management.
Legua. Linear measure. Castilian league; one hour's walk, about 3.4 miles; 5.6 kilometers.
Liberar. To alienate a village from its ruling city or town.
Libra. Castilian pound; 16 ounces; 460.1 grams.
Librar. To issue (literally to release or let go of) a document, thus allowing it to be executed.
Licenciado. University graduate in law, abbreviated as Lic.
Lugar. Village subject to a town or city.
Lugareño. Villager, citizen of a village.
Maravedí. The smallest unit of money of account. Three hundred seventy-five maravedís were equivalent to one ducado.
Martiniega. Municipal annuity paid on St. Martin's Day.
Mayorazgo. Perpetual trust that removed real property from the partible estate.
Mayordomo. Treasurer; steward.
Mentidero. Place where people gather to exchange news and boasts, usually the marketplace and its column.
Menudos. Miscellaneous crops and wild produce on which the tithe was collected.
Merced. Gift, favor.
Mercedes enriqueñas. Gifts of jurisdiction and land given in perpetuity by King Enrique II to his supporters in the civil war (1366–69) against King Pedro.
Merino mayor. Royal appellate judge over municipalities in Old Castile.
Mero imperio. Authority to make the laws.
Mesa maestral. Income of the master of a military order.
Millones. Royal tax on real and personal property designed to raise 1 million ducados in 1590.
Mixto imperio. Authority to enforce the laws.
Monte. Uncultivated land.
Morador. Noncitizen, usually residing in a city, town, or village to satisfy citizenship requirements.
Notario. Notary.
Orza. Earthenware jug used to store honey; unit of measure for honey.
Partido. Subsection of a municipal territory.
Pechero. Taxpayer.
Pesquisidor. Judge commissioned to investigate reports of wrongdoing by a regular judge.
Picota. Column signifying township, usually surmounted by a point.
Pósito. Granary; seed bank.
Prestamero mayor. Royal appellate judge over municipalities in the Basque country.
Procurador. Representative.
Propios. The corporate assets of a municipality, usually producing cash income.
Pueblo. Any municipality with a functioning council. Generic Spanish term for any indigenous municipality in the Americas.
Quatro. See *Jurado.*
Quintal. One hundred Castilian pounds; 1 hundredweight.
Rastrojo. Stubble left for grazing after the grain harvest.
Real. Silver coin worth 34 maravedís. Royal encampment or headquarters.
Realengo. Territory in royal domain.

Reducción. Town or other municipality returned to royal jurisdiction.

Reducir. To return a town to royal jurisdiction.

Regidor. Councilman.

Reglas de factoría. Rates of conversion, established by the royal treasury to appraise the annual jurisdictional income and market value of towns for sale.

Relación. Report or response.

Repartimiento. Assessment; distribution; apportionment.

Residencia. Audit of an outgoing official.

Residente. Noncitizen resident in a city, town, or village.

Rollo. See *Picota.*

Secano. Nonirrigated land, dependent on rainfall.

Señor. Lord possessing jurisdiction, with the power to make the law as well as enforce it.

Señor de vasallos. Lord of a town.

Señorío. Lordship; proprietary jurisdiction over a city, town, or village and its citizens.

Servicio. Subsidy voted by the Cortes for the monarch's extraordinary expenses of war.

Sesmero. Representative from a *sesmo* to the municipal council.

Sesmo. Segment of the municipal territory, which was traditionally divided into six sectors.

Solariego. Territory in seignorial jurisdiction.

Suq. Muslim market.

Tanteo. Matching bid.

Tercias. Royal share of the tithe, equal to two-ninths of the tithe collected.

Término. Municipal boundary.

Toldo. Awning.

Vara. The staff of office carried by magistrates. Linear measure of length; Castilian yard, about 33 inches or 835 millimeters.

Vara de justicia. See *Vara.*

Varayok. Peruvian boundary guard, carrying a *vara* and responsible for rounding up and redistributing stray livestock.

Vasallaje. Population subject to a specific jurisdiction.

Vasallo. Subject of the monarch or of a lord.

Vasallo del rey. Subject of the monarch by virtue of a personal oath of fealty.

Vecina. Female citizen or head of a citizen household.

Vecindad. Citizenship in a city, town, or village.

Vecino. Citizen of a city, town, or village; head of a citizen household.

Veinticuatro. City councilman in a city having 24 *regidores.*

Villa. Town subject to a lord but free from any other town or city.

Villano. Townsman; citizen of a town.

Villazgo. Charter of township; status of town.

Zoco. Castilian variant of the Arabic *suq*, q.v.

Notes

The following abbreviations identify archives, libraries, and published collections of documents frequently cited in the notes:

ARCHIVES AND LIBRARIES

AGS	Archivo General de Simancas
	Dirección General del Tesoro: DGT
AHN	Archivo Histórico Nacional, Madrid
	Sección Osuna: Osuna
	"Copiador de cartas por el marqués de Mondéjar": Copiador
AMH	Archivo del Ministerio de Hacienda, Madrid
BN	Biblioteca Nacional, Madrid
GAA	Archivo de la Alhambra, Granada
GRAM	Archivo Municipal, Granada
GUAM	Archivo Municipal, Guadalajara
GUAP	Archivo Provincial, Guadalajara
MAHP	Archivo Histórico de Protocolos, Madrid
RAH	Real Academia de la Historia, Madrid

PUBLISHED COLLECTIONS OF DOCUMENTS

Actas	*Actas de las Cortes de Castilla.* 60 vols. Madrid, 1877–1974.
BAE	*Biblioteca de autores españoles.*
BRAH	*Boletín de la Real Academia de la Historia.*
CODIAI	*Colección de documentos inéditos del Archivo de Indias* [title varies]. Edited by Joaquín F. Pacheco, Francisco de Cárdenas, and Luis Torres de Mendoza. 42 vols. Madrid, 1864–84.
CODOIN	*Colección de documentos inéditos para la historia de España.* 113 vols. to date. Madrid, 1842–.
MHE	*Memorial Histórico Español.*
Relaciones Ciudad Real	*Relaciones histórico-geográfico-estadísticas de los pueblos de España hechas por iniciativa de Felipe II: Provincia de Ciudad Real.* Edited by Carmelo Viñas y Mey and Ramón Paz. Madrid, 1971.
Relaciones Cuenca	*Relaciones de pueblos del obispado de Cuenca.* Edited by Julián Zarco Cuevas. 1927. Revised edition by Dimas Pérez Ramírez. Cuenca, 1983.
Relaciones Guadalajara	*Relaciones topográficas de Felipe II: Relaciones de pueblos que pertenencen hoy a la provincia de Guadalajara.* Edited by Juan Catalina García López and Manuel Pérez Villamil. MHE, 41–43, 45–47. Madrid, 1903–5, 1912–15.
Relaciones Madrid	*Relaciones histórico-geográfico-estadísticas de los pueblos de España hechas por iniciativa de Felipe II: Provincia de Madrid.* Edited by Carmelo Viñas y Mey and Ramón Paz. Madrid, 1949.

Relaciones Toledo *Relaciones histórico-geográfico-estadísticas de los pueblos de España hechas por iniciativa de Felipe II: Reino de Toledo.* Edited by Carmelo Viñas y Mey and Ramón Paz. 2 vols. in 3. Madrid, 1951–63.

ARCHIVAL IDENTIFYING INFORMATION

legajo: leg.
libro: lib.
protocolo
título: tit.

A Note on Translation and Place-Names

1. The definition of *villa* as "a town that enjoys by charter certain privileges" provides some idea of the word's earlier legal meaning (Mariano Velázquez de la Cadena et al., *The New Revised Velázquez Spanish and English Dictionary* [Piscataway, N.J., 1985]).

2. See, for example, Juan B. Olaechea, "La ciudadanía del indio en los dominios hispanos," *Cuadernos de Investigación Histórica* 5 (1981): 113–34.

3. An astute French demographic historian, Annie Molinié-Bertrand, solves the problem by placing quotation marks around the word *villa* without translating it (see her "La 'villa' de Linares en la segunda mitad del siglo XVI: Estudio demográfico y socio-económico, según el censo de 1586," *Cuadernos de Investigación Histórica* 2 [1978]: 387–99). In French the confusion extends back into ancient Roman history and archeology (see Philippe Leveau, "La ville antique et l'organisation de l'espace rural: *villa*, ville, village," *Annales: Economies, Sociétés, Civilisations* 38 [1983]: 920–42).

4. See Helen M. Cam, "The Community of the Vill," in *Medieval Studies Presented to Rose Graham,* ed. V. Ruffen and A. J. Taylor (Oxford, 1950), pp. 1–14; and Susan Reynolds, *Kingdoms and Communities in Western Europe, 900–1300* (Oxford, 1984), chap. 5.

5. For a heartrending description of the difficulties these variants pose for Spain's cartographers see José Manuel Casas Torres, *España: Atlas e índices de sus términos municipales,* 2 vols. (Madrid, 1969), 2:18.

Introduction

1. G. R. Elton, *England under the Tudors,* 2d ed. (Cambridge, 1974), chaps. 6 and 7; Robert Tittler, "The End of the Middle Ages in the English Country Town," *Sixteenth Century Journal* 18, no. 4 (1987): 471–87.

2. For a study of the dissolution and expropriation of monastic institutions in the imperial free cities that became Protestant see Anton Schindling, "Die Reformation in den Reichsstädten und die Kirchengüter. Strassburg, Nürnberg und Frankfurt im Vergleich," in *Bürgerschaft und Kirche,* ed. Jürgen Sydow (Sigmaringen, [1980]), pp. 67–88. I am grateful to Thomas Brady for making this article available to me.

3. R. B. Outhwaite, "Who Bought Crown Lands? The Pattern of Purchases, 1589–1603," *Bulletin of the Institute of Historical Research* 44 (1971): 18–33.

4. Gennaro Incarnato, "L'evoluzione del possesso feudale in Abruzzo Ultra dal 1500 al 1670," *Archivio Storico per le Province Napoletane* 89 (1971): 221–87.

5. Modesto Ulloa, *La hacienda real de Castilla en el reinado de Felipe II*, 2d ed. (Madrid, 1977), pp. 75, 95, citing the results of sales in the 1550s; Antonio Domínguez Ortiz, *Política y hacienda de Felipe IV* (Madrid, 1960), 376–85, addressing the same issue in the 1650s.

6. Miguel Angel Ladero Quesada, "El poder central y las ciudades en España del siglo XIV al final del Antiguo Régimen," *Revista de Administración Pública* 94 (1981): 176.

7. "Toda España tiene 32,000 poblaciones y la grandeza del Consejo de Castilla es que acuden a pedir justicia a él 15,760 poblaciones, ciudades, villas, y aldeas" (Julián del Castillo, *Historia de los Reyes Godos que vinieron de la Scythia . . . a España . . . hasta los Católicos Reyes D. Fernando y Da Isabel . . . con adiciones hasta D. Felipe III hechas por Fr. Gerónimo de Castro Castillo, hijo del autor* [Madrid, 1624], p. 489; I am indebted to John H. Elliott for directing my attention to this passage).

8. The remainder of this paragraph is my translation of Villamanta's petition as published in *Actas* 43:190.

9. "Villamanta," *Relaciones Toledo*, 3:696.

10. These passages are extracted from the charter of township that Philip II granted to Linares in 1566, of which both facsimile and transcription have been published in *Privilegio real de Felipe II que concede a Linares el título de villa, haciéndola independiente de Baeza*, Privilegios reales y viejos documentos de las villas, ciudades, y reinos de España, 4 (Madrid, 1969), fol. 10.

11. Particularly critical of the absence of rebellion through most of Castilian history is Antonio Domínguez Ortiz's *Alteraciones andaluzas* (Madrid, 1972). Perhaps as a result of the events of his own lifetime, Domínguez equates the Habsburg monarchy with modern dictatorship and assumes that open opposition is a virtue. He explains the lack of open rebellion in Castile by spotlighting royal measures and aristocratic privileges that he judges to be efficient in suppressing a popular rebellion, which he assumes to be bubbling just below the surface of public life. In pursuit of this interpretation, Domínguez has researched a wide range of economic and social questions in Spain's archives, unearthing documents and whole collections of enormous historical significance. During the past forty years he has published dozens of books and articles bringing these materials and their implications to the attention of scholars. Although a list of these publications is much too long to be included here, his most important interpretations and many of his most significant discoveries can be found in recent books synthesizing his work on the sixteenth, seventeenth, and eighteenth centuries: *Crisis y decadencia de la España de los Austrias* (Madrid, 1969); *The Golden Age of Spain, 1516–1659* (London, 1971); *Política fiscal y cambio social en la España del siglo XVII* (Madrid, 1984); *La sociedad española en el siglo XVII*, 2 vols. (Madrid, 1963–70); *La sociedad española en el siglo XVIII* (Madrid, 1955).

12. This point, demonstrated beyond reasonable doubt by the research of medieval historians, is neatly explicated and summed up by Claudio Sánchez Albornoz in "The Frontier and Castilian Liberties," in *The New World Looks at Its History*, ed. A. Lewis and T. F. McGann (Austin, 1963), pp. 27–46.

13. Claudio Sánchez Albornoz, *Una ciudad hispano-cristiana hace un milenio: Estampas de la vida en León* (Buenos Aires, n.d.). See also José María Font Ríus, *Orígenes del régimen municipal en Cataluña* (Madrid, 1946); Eduardo Hinojosa, *Origen del régimen municipal en León y Castilla: Estudios de historia del derecho español* (Madrid, 1903); José María Lacarra, "Para el estudio del municipio navarro medieval," *Príncipe de Viana* 3 (1941): 50–65; idem, *Panorama de la historia urbana*

en la Península Ibérica (Spoleto, 1958); Juan Ignacio Ruiz de la Peña, "Estado actual de los estudios sobre el municipio asturiano medieval," *Anuario de Estudios Medievales* (Barcelona) 5 (1968): 629–39; and Charles Verlinden, "L'histoire urbaine dans la Péninsule Ibérique," *Revue Belge de Philologie et d'Histoire* 15 (1936): 1142–66.

14. María del Carmen Carlé, *Del concejo medieval castellano-leonés* (Buenos Aires, 1968). A similar institutional approach was taken in the study of the city of Zaragoza by María Isabel Falcón Pérez, *Organización municipal de Zaragoza en el siglo XV* (Zaragoza, 1978). Carlé's work remains the basis for the more recent book by Jean Gautier-Dalché, *Historia urbana de León y Castilla en la edad media (siglos IX–XIII)* (Madrid, 1979).

15. Studies of Castilian municipal government under the Bourbons (i.e., after 1700) are rare, but for an interesting study of the nineteenth-century change from election by town meeting to a system of secondary and tertiary electors see the article by Antonio Palomeque Torres, "Nueva aportación a la historia de la administración local: Elección de magistraturas en una villa toledana antes y despues de la revolución de 1820," *Anuario de Historia del Derecho Español* 31 (1961): 293–305. For Catalan historians, the eighteenth-century municipality holds more interest as the major local institution surviving between the upheavals of Bourbon suppression of the *fueros* and the Napoleonic invasion (see, e.g., Josep M. Torras i Ribé, *Els municips catalans de l'antic règim [1453–1808]: Procediments electorales, òrgans de poder i grupos dominants* [Barcelona, 1983], which covers the sixteenth and seventeenth centuries briefly in order to devote extended attention to the eighteenth century).

16. Henry Kamen cites a 1710 report from the French ambassador in Spain to foreign minister Torcy in Paris that Philip V, the new Bourbon king of Spain, held jurisdiction over "only about 200 of the 700 towns in Castile" (Henry Kamen, *Spain in the Later Seventeenth Century, 1665–1700* [London, 1980], p. 29). Here it is hard to see how the French could have thought that there were only seven hundred towns in the kingdom. Perhaps the ambassador was referring to New Castile, where Philip II had surveyed most of the cities, towns, and villages in the *Relaciones topográficas*. The responses to the *Relaciones* questionnaire were conserved in the Escorial Palace, and even in the modern period their number is usually exaggerated to seven hundred.

17. Philip V reacted first with hostility toward Aragon, Catalonia, and Valencia, which supported his Habsburg rival in the War of the Spanish Succession. He swept away the traditional judicial autonomy of the three Aragonese kingdoms, even before the war ended, by dividing them into twenty-four judicial regions, or provinces. For a brief bibliographic survey of the current debate on the intent and effect of the "Nueva planta" see Jesús Morales Arrizabalaga, *La derogación de los fueros de Aragón (1707–1711)*, Colección de estudios altoaragoneses, 8 (Huesca, 1986).

The preparations and debate that went into the drafting of the constitution of 1978 inspired a rash of retrospective studies of previous reorganizations of Castilian territorial divisions. Most of these historical studies were published by the Instituto de Estudios de Administración Local. Among the most detailed in this series are Adolfo Posada, *Evolución legislativa del régimen local en España 1812–1909* (Madrid, 1982); and Javier Guillamón, *Las reformas de la administración local durante el reinado de Carlos III* (Madrid, 1980).

18. Floridablanca's projected provincial division was published in two volumes: *España dividida en provincias e intendencias y subdividida en partidos* (Madrid, 1789);

and *Nomenclátor; o diccionario de las ciudades, villas, lugares, aldeas, granjas, cotos redondos, etc.* (Madrid, 1789). *España dividida* is organized by projected provinces and lists all the municipalities within each province, noting which municipalities were in royal, ecclesiastical, or seignorial jurisdiction, as well as their status as city, town, village, *despoblado*, etc. The *Nomenclátor* lists all municipalities and jurisdictions in alphabetical order in one column and their projected province in the second column. I am grateful to Richard Herr for allowing me access to his personal copies of these rare volumes.

19. A history of these reforms and their administrative regulations was compiled for the use of the royal treasury by Francisco Gallardo, *Origen, progresos y estado de las rentas de la Corona de España,* 7 vols. (Madrid, 1805–8); see esp. vol. 1, reprinted in 1817.

20. It has taken many years for modern historians to recognize that Florida-blanca's *España dividida* was a proposal rather than a description. Until 1981, specialists in eighteenth-century history and historical geographers believed that the 1789 maps depicted existing provinces (see Amando Melón, "De la división de Floridablanca a la de 1833," *Estudios Geográficos* 71 [1958]: 173–320; idem, "Inmediata génesis de las provincias españolas," *Anuario de Historia del Derecho Español* 27–28 [1957–58]: 17–59; and María Dolores Marcos González, *Castilla la Nueva y Extremadura* [1971], fasc. 6 of *La España del antiguo régimen*, ed. Miguel Artola [Salamanca, 1966]). The definitive death blow to this futile search for older provinces was dealt by the historical geographer who has done most to clarify the territorial divisions of medieval Castile, Gonzalo Martínez Díez, "Génesis histórica de las provincias españolas," *Anuario de Historia del Derecho Español* 51 (1981): 523–93. The dean of eighteenth-century economic history, Miguel Artola, and a colleague published a useful set of maps showing the divisions at the end of the eighteenth century (see Eduardo Garrigós, "Organización territorial a fines del antiguo régimen," in *Instituciones,* ed. Miguel Artola, vol. 4 of *La economía española a fines del antiguo régimen,* ed. Gonzalo Anes [Madrid, 1982], pp. 1–105).

21. "Mando se proceda a su impresion y publicacion, distribuyendo exemplares a todos mis consejos, chancellerías, audiencias y demas tribunales superiores, juntas y juzgados de apelación, y a los pueblos cuyos jueces tengan jurisdiccion y conocimiento en primera instancia, para que procedan en el gobierno de ellos y la administración de justicia por las leyes contenidas en este nuevo código" (*Novísima recopilación de las leyes de España dividida en xii libros,* 6 vols. [Madrid, 1805–7], 1:xlix).

22. See, for example, the sales of township from 1766 through 1803 in AGS, DGT, legs. 310–35.

23. "Constitution of the Cortes of Cádiz," Art. 11, in *Manual of Spanish Constitutions, 1808–1931,* trans. and intro. Arnold R. Verduin (Ypsilanti, Mich., 1941).

24. The proposals and drafts of the 1833 legislation, which Martínez Díez in his 1982 book believed to be lost, have been found and published by Antonio María Calero Amor in *La división provincial de 1833: Bases y antecedentes* (Madrid, 1987). Calero did not study the provincial reforms beyond the publication of the 1833 decree and therefore gives more weight to the decree's effectiveness than the evidence for the next forty years seems to warrant. The constitution of 1833, for example, refers to provinces only in connection with electoral districts for the Cortes: "In case the same individual has been elected a proctor to Cortes for more than one province, he may choose between those that have elected him." The qualifications of a representative were "to have been born in the province that

Notes to Pages 10–12

elects him, or to have resided in it during the previous two years, or to possess in it some rural or urban property or assessed capital equaling one-half of the necessary income for a proctor of the kingdom" (Art. 13:4, *Manual of Spanish Constitutions*).

25. The constitution of 1837 made the first attempt at creating provincial governments. The constitution of 1845 still did not assume provincial loyalties, although it provided in some vague future for a provincial government equal to municipal governments. The constitution of 1856, which was never enacted, provided provinces to represent local interests, and these were also decreed in the constitution of 1869: "In each province there shall be a provincial council composed of the number of members determined by law and elected by the same electors who return deputies to Cortes"; "a law shall determine the organization and powers of the provincial and municipal councils, and their relationship with the delegates of the government" ("Constitution of 1869," Title XI, Arts. 69 and 74, in *Manual of Spanish Constitutions*).

26. Aurelio Guaita, "La división provincial y sus modificaciones," in *3° Symposio Historia de la Administracion (Alcalá de Henares, 1972)* (Madrid, 1974), pp. 309–52; Amando Melón, "Provincias e intendencias en la peninsular España del XVIII," *Estudios Geográficos* 92 (1963): 287–310.

27. Antonio Sacristán y Martínez, *Municipalidades de Castilla y León: Estudio histórico-crítico*, intro. Alfonso María Guilarte, Colección administración y ciudadano, 14 (Madrid, 1981), pp. 324, 545.

28. Cayetano Rosell, ed., *Crónica general de España: Historia ilustrada y descriptiva de sus provincias* (Madrid, 1866–70). Individual volumes appeared in rapid succession: *Segovia* (1866); *Soria* (1867); *Lérida* (1868); *Baleares* (1870).

29. Juan Catalina García López, *El libro de la provincia de Guadalajara* (Guadalajara, 1881); Manuel Martínez Añibarro y Rives, *Intento de un diccionario biográfico y bibliográfico de autores de la provincia de Burgos* (Madrid, 1889); Rafael Ramírez Arellano, *Ensayo de un catálogo biográfico de escritores de la provincia y diócesis de Córdoba*, 2 vols. (Madrid, 1921–23); C. Miguel Vigil, *Asturias monumental: epigrafía y diplomática. Datos para la historia de la provincia*, 2 vols. (1887; facsimile ed., Oviedo, 1987).

30. M.-J. Gounon-Loubens, *Essais sur l'administration de la Castille au XVIe siècle* (Paris, 1860), pp. 217–44. The first goal and most constant royal policy, according to Gounon-Loubens, was to win cities, both by flattering magistrates and through royal privileges. There was a continuous exchange of information between the prince and the communes, he stated, without defining *commune*. "It is to them [i.e., the cities in the Cortes] the kings address themselves, upon their accession, to be proclaimed and recognized as legitimate sovereigns" (p. 225, my translation). This is still about all one can learn from the secondary literature about the administration of Castilian cities.

31. Gounon-Loubens placed great emphasis on the royal corregidor, for example, and wrote approvingly of royal regulations describing in minute detail the duties of corregidores, without seeming to realize how limited in geographical extent were the jurisdictions of the corregidores and how much they depended on local self-administration within their spheres of authority (ibid., p. 222; see also Marvin Lunenfeld, *Keepers of the City: The Corregidores of Isabella I of Castile [1474–1504]* [Cambridge, 1987]).

32. Bartolomé Bennassar, *Valladolid au siècle d'or: Une ville de Castille et sa campagne au XVIe siècle* (Paris, 1967), pp. 23–24. Perhaps because both *ciudad* and *villa* become *ville* in French, Bennassar does not note that Valladolid was a town until the last decade of the century, when it bought the status of city. A

more comprehensive view of Valladolid and its villages in the Middle Ages emerges in the magisterial study by Adeline Rucquoi, *Valladolid en la edad media*, 2 vols. (Valladolid, 1987).

33. Carla Rahn Phillips, *Ciudad Real, 1500–1700: Growth, Crisis, and Readjustment in the Spanish Economy* (Cambridge, Mass., 1979). The city of Segovia and its subject territory have been the subject of a magisterial achievement of historical research and synthesis by María Asenjo González, *Segovia: La ciudad y su tierra a fines del medievo* (Segovia, 1986). The city of Cordoba and its countryside in a later period have received an equally thorough treatment by José Ignacio Fortea Pérez, *Córdoba en el siglo XVI: Las bases demográficas y económicas de una expansión urbana* (Cordoba, 1981). This major study is not to be confused with Fortea's brief thesis defense of the same title, published in Salamanca in 1979.

34. David Vassberg, *Land and Society in Golden Age Castile* (Cambridge, 1984); Michael Weisser, *Peasants of the Montes: The Roots of Rural Rebellion in Spain* (Chicago, 1976).

35. John B. Owens, "Despotism, Absolutism and the Law in Renaissance Spain: Toledo versus the Counts of Belalcázar (1445–1574)" (Ph.D. diss., University of Wisconsin, 1972). The legal and administrative analysis by Owens is enforced in two studies by Antonio Palomeque Torres, "Derechos de Arancel de la justicia civil y criminal en los lugares de los propios y montes de la ciudad de Toledo anteriores al año de 1500," *Anuario de Historia del Derecho Español* 24 (1954): 87–94, and "El fiel del juzgado de los propios y montes de la ciudad de Toledo," *Cuadernos de Historia de España* 55–56 (1972): 323–99; and complemented in the social and economic study by Emilio Cabrera Muñoz, *El condado de Belalcázar (1444–1518): Aportación al estudio del régimen señorial en la baja edad media* (Cordoba, 1977).

36. Salvador de Moxó, *Los antiguos señoríos de Toledo* (Toledo, 1973), p. 116 n. 4. Jurisdictional conflicts between the city and various powerful citizens in the villages within the city's statutory jurisdiction have been described by Jean-Pierre Molénat in "Tolède et ses finages au temps des rois catholiques: Contribution à l'histoire sociale et économique de la cité avant la révolte des comunidades," *Mélanges de la Casa de Velázquez* 8 (1972): 327–77.

37. Hilario Casado, *Señores, mercaderes y campesinos: La comarca de Burgos a fines de la Edad Media* (Valladolid, 1987).

38. Roger B. Manning, "Rural Societies in Early Modern Europe," *Sixteenth Century Journal* 17 (1986): 353.

39. Casado, *Señores, mercaderes y campesinos*, p. 561.

40. Jerome Blum, "The Internal Structure and Polity of the European Village Community from the Fifteenth to the Nineteenth Century," *Journal of Modern History* 43, no. 4 (1971): 541–76.

41. Aristotle *Politics* 1.1.4.

42. Among the most useful and trustworthy of the local histories are Paulino Alvarez-Laviada, *Chinchón histórico y diplomático hasta finalizar el siglo XV: Estudio crítico y documentado del municipio castellano medieval* (Madrid, 1931); Clodoaldo Naranjo Alonso, *Solar de conquistadores: Trujillo, sus hijos y monumentos* (Serradilla [Cáceres], 1929); and Carlos Romero de Lecea, *La comunidad y tierra de Segovia: Estudio histórico-legal acerca de su origen, extensión propiedades, derechos, y estado presente* (Segovia, 1893).

43. Heath Dillard, *Daughters of the Reconquest: Women in Castilian Town Society, 1100–1300* (Cambridge, 1984).

44. The classic for Castile is José María Font Ríus, "Les villes dans l'Espagne

du moyen age: Histoire de leurs institutions administratives et judiciaires," *Recueils de la Société Jean Bodin pour l'Histoire Comparative des Institutions*, vol. 6, *La ville*, pt. 1 (Brussels, 1954), pp. 263–95.

45. Rafael Gibert, *El concejo de Madrid: Su organización en los siglos XII a XV* (Madrid, 1949).

46. Rafael Gibert, "La condición de los estranjeros en el antiguo derecho español," in *Recueils de la Société Jean Bodin pour.l'Histoire Comparative des Institutions*, vol. 10, *L'étranger* (Brussels, 1958), pp. 158–68; idem, "Libertades urbanas y rurales en León y Castilla durante la edad media," in *Les libertés urbaines et rurales du XI au XIVe siècle*, Collection histoire, 19 (Paris, 1968), pp. 187–218.

47. Social anthropologists have studied individual towns in the twentieth century—they are the standard item of their investigation—but they emphasize social and cultural structures and do less with the town as a political unit within the larger state. When they turn their attention to the premodern background of these institutions, they do so through the prism of social science models that focus on national and regional institutions. When the municipality comes in, it is as the lowest unit looked at from above, with little attention to its internal development and its interests.

48. A similar disparity between administrative history focused on the central government and social and economic studies limited to local history in Italy has been noted by C. J. Wickham in *The Mountains and the City: The Tuscan Apennines in the Early Middle Ages* (Oxford, 1988).

49. Noël Salomon, *La vida rural castellana en tiempos de Felipe II*, trans. Francesc Espinet Burunat (Barcelona, 1973); Carmelo Viñas y Mey, *El problema de la tierra en la España de los siglos XVI–XVII* (Madrid, 1941). See also F. Javier Campos y Fernández de Sevilla, *La mentalidad en Castilla la Nueva en el siglo XV: Religión, economía y sociedad según las 'Relaciones topográficas' de Felipe II* (Madrid, 1986), which surveys all the responses question by question.

50. Miguel Artola, *Antiguo régimen y revolución liberal* (Barcelona, 1978), p. 45 and n. 9; Moxó, *Antiguos señoríos*, pp. 168–70.

51. Salvador de Moxó, *La disolución del régimen señorial en España*, (Madrid, 1965); idem, "Las desamortizaciones eclesiásticas en el siglo XVI," *Anuario de Historia del Derecho Español* 31 (1961): 327–61.

52. Salvador de Moxó, "El señorío, legado medieval," *Cuadernos de Historia* 1 (1967): 105–18; idem, *La alcabala: Sobre sus orígines, concepto y naturaleza* (Madrid, 1963); idem, "La nobleza castellana en el siglo XIV," in *La investigación de la historia hispánica del siglo XIV: Problemas y cuestiones* (Barcelona, 1973); idem, "Los orígenes de la percepción de alcabalas por particulares," *Hispania* 72(1958):307–39; idem, "Los señoríos: En torno a una problemática para el estudio del régimen señorial," *Hispania* 24(1964):185–236, 339–430; idem, "Sociedad, estado y feudalismo," *Revista de la Universidad de Madrid* 20, no. 78(1971):171–202.

53. Salvador de Moxó, *La incorporación de señoríos en la España del antiguo régimen* (Valladolid, 1959); idem, *La disolución*.

54. In addition to Moxó, *La incorporación*, see also Francisco J. Hernández Montalbán, "La cuestión de los señoríos en el proceso revolucionario burgués: El Trienio Liberal," in *Estudios sobre la revolución burguesa en España*, by Bartolomé Clavero, Pedro Ruiz Torres, and Francisco J. Hernández Montalbán (Madrid, 1979), pp. 113–58.

55. This led him, for example, to speak of "un señorío jurisdiccional impropio para los estados creados ya bajo los Austrias y faltos de anténtico dominio solariego

de signo tradicional, como veremos ciertamente en señoríos toledanos del siglo XVII" (Moxó, *Antiguos señoríos*, p. 171).

56. See, for example, Artola's struggle to discard the idea of large landed estates during the medieval centuries, *Antiguo régimen*, esp. pp. 100–109.

Chapter 1: The Constitution of Town and Land

1. The relationship between town council and municipal territory has been accepted as a fundamental characteristic of medieval Castilian law and urban history since Rafael Gibert first systematically demonstrated its legal evolution in the case of Madrid (see Gibert, *El concejo de Madrid*, esp. chap. 8, "La villa y la tierra"). Gibert used the phrase "patrimonio de la villa y tierra" to describe the relationship between the town council and its municipal territory. A much harsher picture of the relationship between the city council of Toledo and its municipal territory emerges in the article by Jean-Pierre Molénat, "Tolède et ses finages au temps des rois catholiques." A more recent study of Old Castile in the Middle Ages uses the phrase "comunidad de villa y tierra," which implies an equitable relationship between town and land without demonstrating it (see esp. the introduction to Gonzalo Martínez Díez, *Las comunidades de villa y tierra de la Extremadura Castellana: Estudio histórico-geográfico* [Madrid, 1983]). Typically, studies of medieval Castile stop at about the year 1500, while studies of modern Castilian history seem to ignore the lessons of the medieval legal historians demonstrating the legal structure of the realm at the beginning of the modern period. The most important recent study of Castilian agriculture in the sixteenth century, for example, does not address the legal underpinnings of the municipal commons at the beginning of the Habsburg period and speaks of the commons as discrete sections of land rather than the entirety of the municipal territory (see Vassberg, *Land and Society in Golden Age Castile*). An older study that has gained wide recognition, Michael Weisser, *Peasants of the Montes*, skips the distinction between municipal commons and corporate assets altogether. This leads the author to mistakenly generalize from the peculiarly oppressive legal condition of the villagers in the Montes de Toledo to the legal status of Castilian villages in general. Weisser's confusion arose when he failed to realize that the Montes de Toledo was not part of the city's statutory municipal territory but a neighboring section of land purchased as a corporate asset (*propio*) by the city council. The sweeping conclusions that Weisser draws from his uniquely disadvantaged sample cannot be taken seriously as a description of Spanish rural society.

2. "Qual lavor aya de defender la rayz. Et conviene saber, que la lavor con el aradro fecha, o con el açadon et tanxiere la tierra de sulco fasta el sulco, puede defender el heredamiento: otra presa non vala" (*Fuero de Zorita de los Canes, según el códice 217 de la Biblioteca Nacional* [siglo XIII al XIV]: Sus relaciones con el fuero latino de Cuenca y el romanceado de Alcázar, Art. 31, MHE, 44, ed. Rafael de Ureña y Smenjaud [Madrid, 1911], p. 57). On the importance and management of the commons see Vassberg, *Land and Society in Golden Age Castile*.

3. See Sánchez Albornoz, "The Frontier and Castilian Liberties."

4. "Otorgo vos otro que si, que tod aquel que rayz oviere, ayala firme, et estable, et valecedera por sienpre assi que de ella, et en ella pueda fazer qual se quier cosa quel ploguiere; et aya poderío de darla, et de venderla, et de camiarla, et de enprestarla, et de enpennarla, et de testamentarla, si quiere sea sano, si quiere

enfermo, si quiere aya voluntad de se yr, o de aqui fincar" (*Fuero de Zorita*, Art. 18, MHE 44, 57).

5. "Parecieron presentes Juan de Pioz alcalde del lugar de Miralcanpo ques del muy magnífico señor conde de Tendilla e Alonso de Viñuelas alguazil e Alonso de Chiloeches e Pedro de Pinilla rexidores e Pasqual Sánchez de Galves e Juan de Sancho Garçia e Diego Prieto e Pedro Prieto e Pedro Nuñez de Corpa e Diego Delgado y Alfonso de Yeves hijo de lá de Bartolomé de Yeves difunto e Diego de Pinilla hijo de lá de Juan de Pinilla difunto e Fernando Pastor . . . vecinos de Miralcanpo e los que no somos casados por nosotros y en nonbre de nuestras madres" ("Capitulación echa entre el señor marqués de Mondéjar y el consejo y becinos de su lugar de Mira el canpo," AHN, Osuna, leg. 2983, fol. 500).

6. During his previous visit to Meco, in 1509, the count had been incensed to find the Meco town council enclosing some of its commons land and building a fortified tower, thus squandering the money intended for a church bell tower and antagonizing its powerful neighbor, the town of Alcalá de Henares. Now, in this 1512 visit, he was pleased to discover that the Meco farmers who rented the only piece of private property that he owned in the town of Meco, the farm of Moneder, were occupying the farm all year, building permanent houses, and raising their families at some distance from Meco's residential nucleus.

7. "Vesamos las manos de vuestra señoría a la qual suplicamos le plega darnos a censo por perpetuo ynfituosin para sienpre jamás el dicho su lugar de Miralcanpo con las dichas casas y eredades y otros edificios que en él están hechos fasta agora e con toda la heredad de Monedero e soto redondo y dehesas y exidos y qualquier otro derecho vuestra señoría perteneziente poseydo e posee e nosotros avemos poseydo e posehemos en nonbre de vuestra señoría y como sus renteros hasta agora así en el término juridizión de vuestra señoría como en los términos e juridizión de Guadalajara, y si algun derecho vuestra señoría tiene a la pesca del rio que sea para nosotros y todas las otras cosas que a vuestra señoria pertenezen e a poseydo e poseemos en nonbre de vuestra señoría" ("Capitulación," fols. 500–500v).

8. "Con las dichas condiçiones damos a vuestra señoría nosotros e los que despues de nosotros vinieren para agora e para sienpre jamas de çenso perpetuo ynfetuosin seisçientas fanegas de pan por mitad trigo y çevada de pan vueno linpio y enjuto e no volazo tal que sea de dar y tomar e un par de gallinas buenas e vibas por cada vecino de los dichos diez y seis veçinos o de los de que mas oviere de manera que no seamos obligado a pagar por todo lo arriba contenido mas de las dichas seisçientas fanegas de pan trigo e çevada como dicho es e los dichos un par de gallinas por cada un veçino y si cada un año no pagaremos el dicho pan que sea en mano de vuestra señoría tomar el dicho lugar con todas las cosas e mejoramientos e aprovechamientos por comisas" (ibid., fols. 501–501v).

9. "Que seamos libres y esentos de pagar sisas y provisiones de lanas y corambres e sevos e que qualquier veçino del dicho lugar sea libre para poder vender su pan e lanas e coranbres e sevos e otras qualesquier que tenga sin penas e achaques ningunos a do quisieren e por vien obieren e que vuestra señoría ni sus subçesores no nos puedan echar en préstidos de pan ni de maravedís ni de cosa alguna mas de lo que aqui diremos que damos a vuestra señoría . . . que vuestra señoría no pueda tomar ni tome ni sus herederos ni subçesores pan alguno por preçio alguno que sea salvo que nosotros lo podamos vender a quien quisiéremos" (ibid., fol. 501).

10. "Otrosí que vuestra señoría e sus subçesores sean obligados a poner un mayordomo en el dicho lugar para reçibir el pan que oviéremos de dar en el tienpo que se coxiere e si vuestra señoría no lo pusiere no seamos obligados a proproçión

ninguna que contra nosotros se hiçiere e que el dicho pan que oviéremos de dar que nosotros no seamos obligados a lo llevar a parte ninguna que sea salvo a los graneros o cámaras o silos de vuestra señoría en el dicho lugar. . . . Otrosí que vuestra señoría no ponga por mayordomo a ninguno de los veçinos del dicho lugar si ellos no quisieren" (ibid., fols. 501–501v).

11. "Otrosí que de quales quier cosas que se vengan a vender de fuera parte que se venda en el dicho lugar que no aya alcavala alguna ni se lleve y si vuestros ofiçiales o mayordomo o recavdador vendiere qualquier pan que quisiere o otras cosas que no paguen alcavala ninguna de lo que así vendieren" (ibid., fol. 501).

12. "Primeramente que en el dicho lugar seamos obligados de tener continuamente diez y seis vecinos e moradores con sus casas pobladas e que menos no podamos tener e si caso fuere que algun vecino se fuere o su casa se despoblare que tengamos quatro meses de plazo para poder traer otro" (ibid., fol. 500v).

13. "Otrosí que de quinze en quinze años seamos obligados a renovar esta escritura" (ibid., fol. 501).

14. "Vuestros umildes vasallos e servidores vesamos las manos de vuestra señoría . . . e damos poder a vuestra señoría e a vuestros oficiales e a otros qualesquier justicias así eclesiásticas como seglares que nos hagan ansí tener e guardar e cunplir e pagar haziendo e mandando hazer entrega o execución en nuestros bienes con las costas que sobre ello se hizieren si remisos e neglixentes o rebeldes fuéremos" (ibid., fols. 500, 502v).

15. "Otrosí que los dichos diez y seis veçinos y mas quantos oviere en el dicho lugar en adelante para agora e para sienpre jamás seamos y sean libres que no paguemos ni paguen alcavala ninguna de qualesquier cosas que vendiéremos e vendieren los que adelante fueren en el dicho lugar e sus términos ni nos sea demandada la dicha alcavala por vuestra señoría ni por otro ninguno y si fuere pedida por alguna persona que vuestra señoría nos saque a paz y a salvo çerca dello de tal guisa que nosotros seamos libres y esentos della. . . . Otrosí caso fuere que por los reyes nuestros señores que sea o fueren pedidos o demandados servicio o servicios o ballesterías que los veçinos e moradores que agora somos o fueren al tienpo en el dicho lugar que vuestra señoría nos saque a paz y salvo de los dichos pedidos o monedas e serviçios e ballesterías sin nos fueren demandados de qualquier persona que los vengan demandando" (ibid., fol. 500v).

16. "Otrosí que no seamos obligados a dar ni pagar a vuestra señoría otros maravedís algunos ni pagues ni otra cosa alguna sino esso que avajo se dirá . . . que seamos libres y esentos de todas la fazenderas lievas y belas e ballesterías e que no seamos obligados a las hazer ni en ellas contribuyr y por el consiguiente de llevar a vuestra señoría ni dar paja . . . que no seamos obligados a tomar vino ni pan ni por consiguiente a lo dar" (ibid., fols. 500v–501).

17. "Otrosí que vuestra señoría nos dé de limosna para reparo de la yglesia del dicho lugar e otros hornamentos veynte mill maravedís. . . . E suplicamos a vuestra señoría que nos mande otorgar e otorgue todo lo suso dicho e cada una cosa e parte dello prometiendo como quien es de lo tener guardar e cunplir e de no yr ni venir contra ello ni contra parte dello agora ni en ningun tienpo que sea dando sobre ello a vuestra fee e todo ello firmado de vuestro nonbre e sellado con vuestro sello" (ibid., fols. 501v–502).

18. "E ansí leydo por mi el dicho escrivano en presencia de todos los susodichos conçejo e honbres buenos e testigos de yuso escritos y todos los dichos capítulos y petición de suso contenidos todos los suso dichos dijeron que otorgavan e otorgaron todo lo que en la dicha petición y capítulos es contenido . . . e rogaron a mi el dicho escrivano que signase dos escrituras dello de un tenor la una para que

tobiese el dicho señor conde e la otra para el dicho conçejo e honbres buenos . . .
e por que ninguno de todos los suso dichos no savía rogaron al dicho Gastón de
Torres e a Juan de Valdepeñas e Françisco Nuñez Montero que firmasen por ellos
de sus nonbres" (ibid., fol. 502).

19. "Yo don Yñigo López de Mendoça conde de Tendilla señor de las villas de
Mondéjar e Balhermoso capitán general del reyno de Granada alcayde de la dicha
çiudad de Granada y su Alanbra e fortalezas por la reyna nuestra señora vi la
petiçión que vos los sobredichos alcalde e alguaçil e regidores e otros omes vuenos
de mi lugar de Miralcanpo me distes e la obligaçión que en ella e en los dichos
capítulos me haçéis . . . e vos prometo y doy mi fee como quien soy por mi e por
mis herederos e subçesores" (ibid., fol. 502v).

20. In the seventeenth century, the lord's descendants wrote a history of their
family estates, but neither they nor their secretaries and paleographers could locate
this farm or figure out how to spell its name. They sometimes spelled it *Monedero*,
Monester, or *Monasterio*, apparently confusing it with a town north of Guadalajara
that the family had owned in the fifteenth century. They had no trouble with the
name Miralcampo or Miralcanpo, which appears in the seignorial records until
the town became depopulated and was reintegrated into Meco in the early eighteenth century.

For an introduction to the single-entry bookkeeping practices of the seignorial
accountants see Patti A. Mills, "Financial Reporting and Stewardship Accounting
in Sixteenth Century Spain," *Accounting Historians Journal* 13, no. 2 (1986): 65–
76.

21. "Miralcampo," *Relaciones Guadalajara*, 42:303–7.

22. "Del escaso número y reducida extensión de las plazas existen algunos
testimonios directos y los muy expresivos, reveladores de una radical diferencia de
concepto urbano entre las ciudades hispanomusulmanes y las cristianas. . . . Dentro
del recinto murado no existían grandes espacios libres. En la red de calles y
callejuelas tortuosas y desiguales, el frecuente y caprichoso ensanchamiento o el
cambio de dirección de una calle, daban lugar a pequeñas plazoletas y rinconadas
de reducida superficie" (Leopoldo Torres Balbas, *Resúmen histórico del urbanismo
en España* [Madrid, 1954], p. 32; reprinted in "Dos tipos de ciudades," in *Resúmen
histórico*, 2d ed. [Madrid, 1968], pp. 67–96. See also Pedro Chalmeta, *El "señor
del zoco" en España: edades media y moderna. Contribución al estudio de la historia
del mercado* [Madrid, 1973]).

23. This pattern of development, which starts with the town or city and then
spawns villages within the municipal boundaries, was a distinguishing characteristic
of the conquest society from the Duero River basin south. North of that line two
patterns of settlement prevailed. In Asturias, Galicia, and the Basque country—
the regions not abandoned by the Christians during the Muslim occupation—
villages and hamlets came first. Each village or parish had a council, and a large
number of councils that had a lord in common or some historical ties formed
themselves into a federation, or *hermandad*. The *hermandad* had no capital city or
town, but the councils traditionally met under a large tree in an open field, or a
large tree in the plaza of one council. The tree in Guernica, for example, was the
traditional meeting place for the assembly of councils from one of the Basque
hermandades. South of the region of *hermandades*, kings in the tenth and eleventh
centuries built strings of castles along the frontier with the Muslims and established
a system of *alfoz* and *aldea* around each castle. The *alfoz* was the countryside under
the protection of the royal commander of the castle, and the king appointed a

royal judge to exercise jurisdiction over the *alfoz*. King and royal judge alike encouraged settlers to move into the *alfoz* by granting them the right to form a municipal government, or *aldea*, under the jurisdiction of the royal judge and protected by the castle commander. No *aldea* had precedence over the others, and each *aldea* was linked vertically to the judge and commander but not with the other *aldeas* of the *alfoz*. The regions of *hermandad* and *alfoz* and *aldea* lost their central importance during the reconquest of the eleventh and twelfth centuries, when Christian settlers moved into the Tagus River basin. The *comunidad de villa y tierra* pattern of settlement in the Tagus and Andalusia has not received much attention from historians, although the demographic and administrative homogeneity and importance of the region known as New Castile exercised a normative force on the older regions. By the end of the fifteenth century, Old Castile, Galicia, and Asturias were converting to the *comunidad de villa y tierra* structure (Martínez Díez, *Las comunidades de villa y tierra*, pp. 9–22).

24. "Todas las poblaciones que en vuestros términos fechas fueren, non sean estables, si el concejo plaziente non fuere; mas que las derrueque el conceio sin calonna" (*Fuero de Zorita*, Art. 6, MHE, 44:49).

25. AHN, Osuna, leg. 2983, fols. 504–6.

26. "Los mui magníficos señores Melchior Pinilla y Juan Serranos, alcaldes ordinarios de la dicha villa" ("Miralcampo," *Relaciones Guadalajara*, 42:303).

27. Both the boundary and the territory it encloses are called *término* in New Castile. In Old Castile the municipal territory was usually called *alfoz*.

28. Miguel Angel Ladero Quesada estimates that in the sixteenth century about 20 percent of the Castilian population lived in the cities ("El poder central y las ciudades en España," p. 176).

29. The terminology for these islands of land not incorporated in the surrounding municipality differs from region to region. Because they were not populated or had no legal standing, they produced no documents of their own. We know of their existence because of references to them in the documents of the surrounding or neighboring municipalities. They are nearly impossible to study because of the lack of documentation, but Hilario Casado has been able to locate thirty-six in the region around Burgos, where they were known as *granjas*. Casado argues convincingly that they are remnants of previously inhabited towns or villages that had become almost entirely depopulated by the end of the fifteenth century (*Señores, mercaderes y campesinos*, pp. 72–82).

30. "Hay noticia y fama que antes que este pueblo se poblase había una venta junto a la plaza principal la cual llamaban La Venta de la Cruz por ser cruz de lo sobredicho [several roads] y hacer noche en ella todos los dichos pasageros en la cual venta hay fama que solían saltear y matar" ("Villanueva de Alcardete," *Relaciones Toledo*, 3:742).

31. "Doña María Carrillo muger del dotor Ybarra y doña Catalina Carrillo viuda de Manuel Gómez de Andrada vecinas de Alcalá de Henares" (AHN, Osuna, leg. 2268, Alcalá, 1580); "Sepan quantos esta carta de censo vieren como yo Francisco Paredes vecino de la noble villa de Madrid . . . tomo a censo . . . de vos el honrrado Alonso Ruys clérigo cura de la yglesia de San Ginés de la dicha Madrid" (MAHP, protocolo no. 1, 23 Sept. 1508, fols. 312–13); "Alonso de Garabaxales y Alonso de Garabaxales el mozo y María de Garabaxales y Beatriz de Garabaxales hijos del dicho Alonso Garabaxales vecinos de Mondéjar otorgan" (AHN, Osuna, leg. 2268, Mondéjar, 1601); "Juan Blela, Juan Nigo, Luis Laragaldia, tratantes de géneros de ropa y otras cosas estantes en Estremera de nación franceses . . . a

Joseph Plugeant tanbien de nación francés y residente en Tembleque que por hacernos merced y buena obra nos a dado y prestado para ayuda a nuestro comercio y trato de tales tratantes de ropas" (MAHP, protocolo no. 29.776, 2 Mar. 1770).

32. "En la villa de Paracüellos Antón Ruiz cura de la villa de Paracüellos y Alonso Bartolomé Ruiz vecino de la villa de Vayona su hermano se convinieron y trocaron cierta hacienda" (AHN, Ordenes Militares, Paracúellos, carpeta no. 117, 13 Mar. 1513). The modern name of the town of Vayona is Titulcia.

33. AGS, Contadurías generales, leg. 3072, 29 Oct. 1555 and 9 Apr. 1556, published in Tomás González, *Noticia histórica documentada de las célebres minas de Guadalcanal desde su descubrimiento en el año de 1555, hasta que dejaron de labrarse por cuenta de la real hacienda*, 2 vols. [Madrid, 1831], 1:56, 129.

34. John H. Elliott, *The Count-Duke of Olivares: The Statesman in an Age of Decline* (New Haven, 1986), pp. 166, 671–72; Antonio Herrera García, *El Aljarafe sevillano durante el antiguo régimen: Un estudio de su evolución socioeconómica en los siglos XVI, XVII, y XVIII* (Seville, 1980), pp. 14–15, 69.

35. Juan Manuel's great grandson sold the Infantado in 1371 for thirty thousand gold francs to pay his ransom after being captured by the Black Prince at the Battle of Nájera ("Alcocer," *Relaciones Guadalajara*, 1:162, n. 1).

36. "Carta real nombrando alcalde mayor para los asuntos entre cristianos y moros en el arzobispado de Sevilla con el obispado de Cádiz," cited in Filemón Arribas Arranz, *Un formulario documental del siglo XV de la cancillería real castellana* (Valladolid, 1964), p. 76.

37. Ramón Carande, *Sevilla, fortaleza y mercado: Las tierras, las gentes y la administración de la ciudad en el siglo XIV*, 2d ed. (Seville, 1975), pp. 79–81. The Castilian monarch wrote to the "duque e ancianos de la magnífica comunidad de Genova" to impose sentence on a convicted Genoese whose property was in Genoa ("Commo se escrive a los consoles de los genoveses que estan en Sevilla," published in Arribas Arranz, *Un formulario documental*, p. 36). The notarial register (*protocolo*) kept by the Genoese community in Seville has provided a rich source for a history of that community and its business dealings with local Castilians (see Ruth Pike, *Enterprise and Adventure: The Genoese in Seville and the Opening of the New World* [Ithaca, 1966]).

38. "Carta de naturaleza o nacionalidad castellana a un extranjero," cited in Arribas Arranz, *Un formulario documental*, p. 48.

39. The complaint is a frequent theme in petitions for the status of town, as we will see below in chapters 4 and 5.

40. "Pezuela," *Relaciones Madrid*, p. 472.

41. "Vecindad, Diego Hernández de Ulloa, 17 agosto 1498," GRAM, Actas, vol. 1, fol. 52. The procedure is very informal compared with that for the granting of citizenship in Italian cities described in Julius Kirshner, "Paolo di Castro on 'Cives ex Privilegio': A Controversy over the Legal Qualifications for Public Office in Fifteenth-Century Florence," in *Renaissance Studies in Honor of Hans Baron*, eds. A. Molho and J. Tedeschi (DeKalb, Ill., 1971), pp. 227–64; see also idem, "*Civitas Sibi Faciat Civem:* Bartolus of Sassoferrato's Doctrine on the Making of a Citizen," *Speculum* 48 (1973): 694–713.

42. See below, chap. 5.

43. See above, n. 5.

44. Thomas Capuano, "Vignettes of Daily Life in Alonso de Herrera's *Agricultura general*" (Paper presented at the annual meeting of the Sixteenth Century Studies Conference, St. Louis, October 1988).

45. Juan Fernández de Oviedo y Valdés, *Las quinquagenas de la nobleza de España* (Madrid, 1880), pt. 1, estancia 8, p. 108.

46. "Dejadme entrar, que bien puedo, / en consejos de los hombres; / que bien puede una mujer, / si no a dar voto, a dar voces" (Felix Lope de Vega, *Fuenteovejuna*, act 3, lines 61–64).

47. "Vuestros umildes vasallos e servidores Juan de Pioz alcalde e Alonso de Vinñuelas alguazil e Juan de Chiloeches e Pedro de Pinilla rexidores e Pasqual Sánchez de Galve e Juan de Sancho Garzía e Martín de Polo e Miguel de Sancho Garzía e Diego Prieto e Pedro Prieto e Pedro Nuñez de Corpa e Diego Casaldo e Alonso de Yeves hijo de lá de Bartolomé de Yebes defunto y Diego de Pinilla hijo de lá de Juan Sanz de Pinilla defunto e Fernando Pastor, vecinos de Miralcanpo e los que no somos casados por nosotros e en nonbre de nuestras madres" (AHN, Osuna, leg. 2983).

48. "Sepan quantos esta carta de venta e censo vieren como yo Juan de Villamayor vecino de Madrid y yo Catalina Alvarez su mujer . . . otorgamos e conoscemos por esta presente carta que vendemos . . . a vos el noble cavallero Diego de Luxán hijo del comendador Juan de Luxán vecino de la dicha villa de Madrid" (MAHP, protocolo no. 1, 1508, fols. 475v–477v).

49. This paragraph is my translation of Stephen/Stephanie's story related by the town's expert witnesses in "Valdaracete," *Relaciones Madrid*, pp. 630–31.

50. GRAM, Reales cédulas, leg. 1.

51. Francisco Layna Serrano, *Historia de Guadalajara y sus Mendozas en los siglos XV y XVI*, 3 vols. (Madrid, 1942), 2:520.

52. "Chamartín," *Relaciones Madrid*, p. 218.

53. "Humanejos," ibid., p. 333.

54. "Los Hueros," ibid., pp. 325–26.

55. "Hordenanzas de la villa del tienpo que no avya rregidores en ella" (Layna Serrano, *Historia de Guadalajara*, 2:519).

56. Seville's resident, as opposed to transient, population has been the object of solid and wide-ranging studies that have demonstrated that the city's greatest period of growth occurred in the fifteenth century and that the population movement occurred in two phases, with immigrants from farther north settling in the city's countryside first and then their descendants several generations later moving into the city proper (Antonio Collantes de Terán, *Sevilla en la baja edad media: La ciudad y sus hombres* [Seville, 1977]: Antonio Domínguez Ortiz, "La población del reino de Sevilla en 1534," *Cuadernos de Historia* 7 [1974]: 337–55).

57. Layna Serrano, *Historia de Guadalajara*, 2:519–20.

58. "Que se lean las escripturas del concejo y estas ordenanzas tres veces cada año" (AHN, Osuna, leg. 2004/4).

59. "Este día pareció en el cabildo Diego Aljaemy vecino de Alhendín y presentó una cédula del Rey nuestro señor por la qual su alteza le hizo merced del oficio de alguazil del dicho lugar. Obedeciéronla y mandáronla cumplir y recibieron juramiento del dicho Diego Aljaemy" (GRAM, Actas, 2, 12 Oct. 1512).

60. "Juan de Luz se despide del marqués de Mondéjar; Juan de Añasco se despide del marqués de Mondéjar" (GRAM, Personal, leg. 930, Alhambra de Granada, 9 Aug. 1516).

61. "Yten que no se elijan juntamente en una elecion padre y hijo ni yerno ni dos hermanos ni dos cuñados ni suegro a suegro y que no sean arrendadores de alcavalas ni de monedas ni personas que devan maravedis algunos a la iglesia ni al concejo de deuda liquida de trezientos maravedis arriva hasta que realmente

ayan pagado ni el que oviere rescivido ni resciviere corona ni los mesoneros ni texedores ni carpinteros ni bohoneros ni carnizeros ni zapateros ni cortidores ni albañiles ni atondidores ni barneros ni sastres ni reneros ni zurradores ni honbre que acude a jornal ni los que usan de otros semejantes o mas bajos oficios o los usaron el año antes de la elecion" (AHN, Osuna, leg. 2005–2/1–46).

62. "E esto en quanto a alcaldes y regidores pero que para los demas oficios del dicho concejo puedan ser elegidos los susodichos con que no avian rescivido o resciviere corona" (ibid.).

63. Salomon, *La vida rural castellana*, pp. 38–39.

64. The officers had to explain each lawsuit, whom it was against, before which tribunals, secretaries, and notaries it was being litigated, what the status of each was, what documents and privileges were at issue, which lawyers and attorneys the town had hired for each lawsuit, and what the salary of each was. "Hordenanzas echas en el año de 1593 por el conçejo de la villa de Estremera para el buen rexímen govierno de dicha villa y guarda de sus campos" (AHN, Osuna, leg. 2004/4).

65. "Muchos veçinos desta villa en las capellanías memorias y aniversarios y otras obras pías que fundaron para el servicio de Dios nuestro señor y bien de sus ánimas dexaron por patrones a los alcaldes hordinarios desta villa para que las hagan cumplir y cada día otros van haciendo lo mismo y es justo que los dichos alcaldes tengan dello mucho cuydado y cumplan con la confianza que dellos hicieron los fundadores lo qual no podrían hacer si no saven de que memorias y obras pías son patrones y para que lo sepan ordenamos que en la sala del ayuntamiento desta villa en lugar publico y claro que se pueda leer aya una tabla donde se escriban todas las memorias y obras pías de que an quedado y quedaren por patrones los dichos alcaldes" (ibid.).

66. "Dotó el Autor de la Naturaleza a la Patria de cierta peregrina y tan oculta calidad que olvidados de nuestro proprio ser nos llama y arrastra con notable eficacia y virtud, confesandola dulce imán de nuestro corazón. Es su afición cadena de oro, en que gustosamente cautiva la voluntad se dexa sentir, mas no se sabe ponderar. Nos inclinamos a su adoración, qual si fuesse verdadera Deidad, o como ponderó Herocles, como si fuera otro Dios; porque la Patria en cierto modo nos da el ser y aún la materia para la conservación" (Juan de Talamanco, *Historia de la ilustre y leal villa de Orche, señora de sí misma, con todas las prerogativas de señorío y vassallaje* [Madrid, 1748], ed. Alberto García Ruiz, 2d ed. [Guadalajara, 1986], p. 1).

67. "Pasé diez leguas adelante e poblé en un valle que se llama Mapocho doce leguas de la mar la ciudad de Santiago del Nuevo Extremo a los 24 de hebrero de 1541 formando cabildo y poniendo justicia" (Pedro de Valdivia, "Relación hecha por Pedro de Valdivia al emperador, dándole cuenta de lo sucedido en el descubrimiento, conquista y población de Chile y en su viaje al Perú," in *CODIAI*, 4:7).

68. Francisco Domínguez Compañy, *Ordenanzas municipales hispanoamericanas* (Madrid, 1982), p. 6.

69. Samuel Eliot Morison, "The Earliest Colonial Policy toward America: That of Columbus," *Bulletin of the Pan American Union* 76, no. 10 (1942): 543–55; Charles Verlinden, *Cristóbal Colón y el descubrimiento de América*, trans. Florentino Pérez-Embid (Madrid, 1967); Demetrio Ramos, "Colón y el enfrentamiento de los caballeros: Un serio problema del segundo viaje, que nuevos documentos ponen al descubierto," *Revista de Indias* 39 (1979): 9–88; idem, *La revolución de Coro de*

1533 contra los Welser y su importancia para el régimen municipal (Caracas, 1965).

70. John V. Lombardi, *People and Places in Colonial Venezuela* (Bloomington, 1976), p. 47.

71. Prudencio de Sandoval, *Historia de la vida y hechos del Emperador Carlos V*, ed. Carlos Seco Serrano, BAE, 82 (Madrid, 1956), p. 473.

72. Lombardi, *People and Places in Colonial Venezuela*, 47–48.

73. Bernal Díaz del Castillo, *Historia verdadera de la conquista de la Nueva España*, 5th ed., 2 vols. (Mexico City, 1960), p. 85.

74. "Como yo sembré unas pepitas de naranja junto a otra casa de ídolos, y fue de esta manera: que había muchos mosquitos en aquel río, fuimonos diez soldados a dormir en una casa alta de ídolos, y junto a aquella casa las sembré, que había traído de Cuba, porque era fama que veníamos a poblar, y nacieron muy bien porque los papas de aquellos ídolos las beneficiaban y regaban y limpiaban desque vieron que eran plantas diferentes de las suyas: de allí se hicieron de naranjos toda aquella provincia" (ibid., 1:77, n. 14).

75. "Mando dar pregones y tocar trompetas y atambores en nombre de s. m. y en su real nonbre Diego Velázquez y el por su capitan general, para que cualesquiera personas que quisiesen ir en su compañía a las tierras nuevamente descubiertas a conquistarlas y poblarlas les darían sus partes del oro y plata y requezas que hubiere y encomiendas de indios despues de pacificadas" (ibid., 1:84).

76. Ibid., 1:58.

77. The book was completed about 1568, and the first edition was published at Madrid in 1632. There have since been fifteen Spanish editions.

78. Diego Gutiérrez de Salinas, *Discursos del pan y del vino del niño Jesús* (Alcalá, 1600); Juan Catalina García López, "Diego Gutiérrez de Salinas," *Biblioteca de escritores de la provincia de Guadalajara y bibliografía de la misma hasta el siglo XIX* (Madrid, 1899).

79. "Bernal Díaz del Castillo, vecino y regidor de la muy leal ciudad de Santiago de Guatemala, uno de los primeros descubridores y conquistadores de la Nueva España y sus provincias y Cabo de Honduras e Higüeras, que en esta tierra asi se nombra; natural de la muy noble e insigne villa de Medina del Campo, hijo de Francisco Díaz del Castillo, regidor que fue de ella, que por otro nombre le llamaban el Galán, y de María Díez Refón, su legítima mujer" (Díaz del Castillo, *Historia verdadera*, 1:39).

80. "Estando para dar su ánima a Dios un rico y hidalgo que se decía Villalpando, ayudándole a bien morir diciéndole que se acordase de Dios y como estaba en lo ultimo 'todo lo que me decis creo, mas bueno es Xetafe.' Y así se trae por comun hablar entre muchos, 'Acordaos de Dios, Villarpando. Bueno es Xetafe' y aunque ha que pasó mas de cincuenta años, está tan fresco como si hubiera un año" ("Getafe," *Relaciones Madrid,* p. 303).

81. "El no sé qué de esta simpatía cortó la pluma para bosquexar algunos recuerdos de Orche mi Patria, que si no iguala a otras en grandeza hace su figura reparable sobre Repúblicas de menos glorias; pero aunque fuesse menor, la de cada uno se lleva la primacia; porque en estilo de Seneca, no se debe estimar la propria por grande, ni por chica, sino por suya" (Talamanco, *Historia de la villa de Horche,* p. 1).

Chapter 2: Lord of Land and Subjects

1. The most recent biographers of Alba and Olivares both emphasize that their subject's surviving correspondence does not address matters of estate management. Both authors attribute the silence in part to a massive destruction of records, although Alba's biographer, William Maltby, assures me in private conversation that the duke's intact correspondence from abroad does not mention his estates in Spain (William S. Maltby, *Alba: A Biography of Fernando Alvarez de Toledo, Third Duke of Alba, 1507–1582* [Berkeley and Los Angeles, 1983]; Elliott, *The Count-Duke of Olivares*).

2. Gerónimo de Zurita y Castro, *Anales de la corona de Aragón*, bk. 6 [Zaragoza, 1585], chap. 54, fol. 157.

3. Ibid., fols. 150–150v. The depleted and depopulated villages and the number of settler households to be brought in were as follows: Almayater, 60; Almuñécar, 150; Berja, 300; Bicar, 150; El Buñol, up to 30; Estepona, 100; Maro, 60; Mijas, 150; Motril, 350; Oxen, 60; and Torrox, 200.

4. Zurita quotes a 1508 document from the royal archives as reporting: "Mas esto con otras cosas que ocurrían entonces, al parecer, de mayor importancia, y necessidad, no se pudo poner en esecución: y hoy no está aquello a menos costa, y peligro" (ibid., fol. 150v). The grant, issued in Seville in October 1508, is published as appendix 5, "Merced de los bienes de Almayater," in *Correspondencia del conde de Tendilla: Biografía, estudio y transcripción*, ed. Emilio Meneses García, Archivo Documental Español, vol. 31 (Madrid, 1973), pp. 303–4.

5. "Antes creo que os vere yo a vos señor alla que vos a mi aca que quiero ir a ver esa merced que su alteza me hizo y otros me quisieran quitar" (Tendilla to Iñigo Manrique, *alcaide* of Málaga, 18 Jan. 1509, *Correspondencia*, 31:461).

6. The best account of Ferdinand's policy on the Granada coast is still Zurita y Castro, *Anales*, chap. 54, fols. 150–150v. For the financing of the defense of the coast see Alfonso Gámir Sandoval, "Las 'fardas' para la costa granadina (siglo XVI)," in *Carlos V (1500–1558): Homenaje de la Universidad de Granada*, ed. Antonio Gallego Morell (Granada, 1958), pp. 293–330; idem, "Las fortificaciones costeras del Reino de Granada al occidente de la ciudad de Málaga hasta el Campo de Gibraltar," *Miscelánea de Estudios Arabes y Hebraicos*, 9, no. 9 (1960): 135–56; and "Organización de la defensa de la costa del reino de Granada desde su reconquista hasta finales del siglo XVI," *Boletín de la Universidad de Granada* 73 (1943): 259–337.

7. Tendilla to Gutierre Gómez de Fuensalida, 3 Nov. 1508; see also Gaspar Ibáñez de Segovia, "Historia de la casa de Mondéjar; y sucesión de la Baronía de Moncada," BN, ms. 3315, fol. 188.

8. The eight veterans received their houses, garden plots, and fields between November 1490 and May 1497. The grants are catalogued in Miguel Angel Ladero Quesada, "Mercedes reales en Granada: Catálogo y comentario," in *Granada después de la conquista: Repobladores y mudéjares* (Granada, 1988), pp. 147–55, nos. 657, 662, 674, 682, 685, 697, 714, 739, 745.

9. "Que se pierde Almayater quel año pasado no se labraron las viñas y si este queda asi la mejor renta esta para perderse a para sienpre y la seda no criandose ogaño no valdra de renta veinte mill maravedis el lugar" (Tendilla to the marquis of Denia, 6 Mar. 1509, *Correspondencia*, 31:519).

10. "A lo que dezis que los mios pregonaron franquezas no era menester que para tan poca cosa hicieran tanto estruendo pero en fin pareceme que yo no hago a nadie injuria si porque los que alli van me labren mis heredades quiero pagar

por ellos lo que devieren de pechos y otras cosas" (Tendilla to the council of Málaga, 3 Jan. [1509], ibid., 31:450).

11. "Porque la voluntad del rey nuestro señor es que Almayater se avezinde de Christianos nuevos enbio esta cedula que os mostrara Juan de Cordova mi mayordomo. Pidos de mucha gracia ayudeis en que se haga bien como se que lo aves de hazer y lo hazes en todas las cosas que me tocan pues todo lo tenes tan cierto para lo que os cunpliere como vuestras propias haziendas que alli o donde quieran que esten son todos vasallos de la reina nuestra señora y vuestros y aun tanbien iran de aca los mas que se an de avezindar alli" (Tendilla to the council of Vélez-Malaga, 19 Dec. 1508, ibid., 31:437–38).

12. "Aves de saber que los de Vélez . . . se enbian a quexar que yo defiendo el termino de Almayater. Vos sabes que aquello no es asi que yo no deiendo sino que no destruyan las heredades con los ganados, que la yerva ni la defiendo ni tengo por que" (Tendilla to Captain Gonzalo de Buitrago, 17 Feb. 1509, ibid., 31:488).

13. "Hablad en esto a Caravajal y a Aguirre y a Polanco y a Zapata y teneldos prevenidos para si se quejaren y a Vargas no dexes de hablar que como hasta aqui eran las heredades del rey comianse las viñas y cortavan los olivos y los arboles y estava todo destruido. Porque no les consientes esto quexasen" (ibid.).

14. Tendilla to King Ferdinand, 18 Jan. 1509, ibid., 31:459.

15. "Pedro de Madrid ha torrnado a loquear y a querer enbiar los soldados a Almayater de manera que ha estorvado que no se vengan alli muchos y de los que avia se han ido algunos tanto que recelo que se an de perder grand parte de las heredades de aquel lugar porque quedan por labrar las viñas y si vos tardais o mensajero vuestro con el despacho perderse a la cria de la seda" (Tendilla to Buitrago, [9 Mar. 1509], ibid., p. 523).

16. In a report to Charles V on the members of the royal council, Dr. Lorenzo Galíndez de Carvajal wrote that Vargas was "cobdiciosísimo" (CODOIN, 1:124).

17. "Dize en unos escriptos que presenta que valen las casas que no entran en los diez e ocho meses quatro cuentos y los que me dieron a mi otros tantos todo por hazer alla bulto y porque parezca ques grand cosa lo que se me dio y lo peor es y de lo que mas me pesa quel señor lic. de Vargas ge lo manda por su carta lo qual yo no creeria aunque lo dixese el angel quanto mas que lo dize el diablo" (Tendilla to Buitrago, [9 Mar. 1509], Correspondencia, 31:524).

18. Tendilla, letters dated 7–10 April 1509, ibid., 31:555–57.

19. "Lo quel rey n. s. me dio son las casas y heredades de Almayater exepto ocho casas que se fueron primero de que estava hecha merced a unos escaladores y a otros. Dizenme que es buena cosa. No querria dezir quanto dizen que rentara pero los dos tercios de lo que dizen querria que fuese" (Tendilla to the bishop of Málaga, 11 Apr. 1509, postscript, ibid., 31:562).

20. "Licencia a los nuevamente convertidos que vayan a Motril a labrar las viñas y la seda," 17 Mar. 1509, ibid., 31:533.

21. "Ay tenes preso un Hernando Madravi que se tomo creyendo que era salteador porque traya espada. Sy por el proceso que contra el se hizo no parece que tiene culpa en aver sydo salteador o averse juntado con los que en esto andan, por lo de la espada no merece pena que yo le puse por guarda de Agron y para eso le di lugar que la truxese y una vallesta porque me cortavan los razimos, y sy no es culpado como digo en mas desto, soltaldo luego" (Tendilla to Juan de Baena, 26 Feb. 1513, ibid., 32:207). "Yo el marques etc. doy licencia a vos Alonso el Corty, vecino de Alhamba, para que podays tener una ballesta en el cortijo de Saylon cerca de Montexicar que tenes a rrenta para guardar los panes de los puercos

y otras alimañas que vienen a hacer daño en ellos" ("Licencia a Alonso el Corty," 9 May 1513, ibid., 32:307).

22. "Tengos en muchas gracias con todo el cuydado que tenes de lo que toca a esa hazienda. Yo os seguro que por mucha seda que aya ogaño no me den a mi mas seda que me suelen dar" (Tendilla to Captain Luis de Paz, 9 May 1513, ibid., 32:308).

23. Tendilla to mosén Soler, captain of the sea, with Jaime de Murcia, 4 Oct. 1509, ibid., 31:803.

24. Guadahortuna, at an altitude of twelve hundred meters, was a *despoblado* in 1503, when Queen Isabella instructed the city council of Granada to establish a new town there (see below, chap. 3).

25. Tendilla to Luis de Mendoza, 7 Oct. 1509, *Correspondencia*, 31:799. Antonio de Mendoza, the future viceroy of New Spain and Peru, would have been about eighteen years old in 1509.

26 Ibid., 31:804–5.

27. "Perdoname señor que quebranto la regla del escrevir de otra mano que porque no me alcançe la señora marquesa de Pliego que viene detras a ver a su marido no puedo esperar a que venga quien me escriva y yo no voy para ver señoras aunque voy sano loado Dios" (Tendilla to the treasurer Francisco de Vargas, 17 Oct. 1509, ibid., 31:809).

28. "Una tienen la mas bonita que nunca vi. No se si lo haze que a todos paresçen bien sus nietos" (Tendilla to the marquis of Denia, 12 Oct. 1509, ibid., 31:810).

29. [25] Oct. 1509, ibid., 31:815. He was probably sincere in this praise, for four years later he sent one of his sons, Francisco, to study at the college.

30. Tendilla to the corregidor of Málaga, 20 Jan. 1513, ibid., 32:149–50.

31. "Por una cedula del rey n.s. veres como su al. manda que en su fortaleza deys lugar para que se ponga los frutos que yo tengo en Almayater a cada año y como quier que vos de buena voluntad hareys lo que os enbio a rrogar, acorde de os enbiar la dicha cedula la qual os notificara el capitan Luys de Paz. Pidos de gracia que los ayays por bien y que seys para poner todos los frutos que ay se cojen mios en su fortaleza en el palacio que tiene Salzedo, que bien creo que sy en aquel no oviere hueco para donde se pongan que dares otro para que puedan estar a rrecabdo" (Tendilla to the *alcaide* of Almayater, 5 May 1513, ibid., 32:298); "Ay os enbio una cedula del Rey n.s. para quel alcayde de la fortaleza de Almayater de en ella donde pueda poner los esquilmos que en esta villa se cojen. Requerelde con ella y que de el palacio en que esta Salzedo y sy mas fuere menester mas, que aunque el tiene buena voluntad a las cosas que yo le rruego lo hazed como digo y avleos con el dulcemente y lo que rrespondiere con el rrequerimiento que vos le hizierdes enbiadme lo y con el que membiardes el rrequerimiento membiad la cedula que os enbio" (Tendilla to Captain Luis de Paz, 5 May 1513, ibid.).

32. "Una cedula ha deber en que mande s. a. a los contadores mayores que me libren de los años de xiii y xiiii y xv y xvi en los recaudadores de Malaga xv mil cada año que montan la alcabala de los renteros que tienen cargo de mi hacienda que por otra parte pagan los que no son mis vecinos renteros otros xi mil y si pena pareciere por alla el os dira donde se habra el libramiento pero aquel no querria yo que paresciese que engañaron me en una cedula que me dieron alli cuyo traslado envio porque la hicieron de manera que parece que no me hacia la merced sino por cuatro años y al marques de Denia prometio ge la para siempre sino que se havia de librar de cuatro en cuatro años y si esto no se libra hace cuenta que es

perdida Almayater y despoblada" (Tendilla to Francisco Ortiz, 10 Mar. 1514, Copiador).

33. "El encabezamiento de Almayater querria que librasedes y dizeme Alonso Serrano el Gazil que llaman que vino de alla que sy yo le do poder de Almayater quel lo encabezara pero haziendose por esta via de alla es mejor. Respondeme a esto lo que podes hacer y sy esto y lo de Azañon y Viana y lo de la fortaleza de Almayater se pudiese acabar" (Tendilla to Francisco Ortiz, 12 May 1515, ibid.); "Lo del encabezamiento de Almayater para my lo querria yo sy lo podes despachar pues me esta hecha la merced de los quinze mill pero quanto esto no oviere remedio saquese para el concejo aunque sy los Turcos asoman aca bien creo que no aya vuestro concejo ni encabezamiento ni apeamiento" (Tendilla to Francisco Ortiz, 12 June 1515, ibid.).

34. "Ese libramiento de Almayater avia de decir doce y trece y catorce y quince. Haceldo emendar que no vale nada asy porque no ha de llegar al año de 16 y enbialdo luego que mas tengo que hacer con Hernando de Cordova sobre el que sy fuese otra gran cosa en el mismo dice que se puede emendar" (Tendilla to Francisco Ortiz, 7 July 1515, ibid.).

35. AGS, Cámara de Castilla, leg. 92, "Almayate." I am indebted to Bernard Vincent for generously making available to me his notes on this legajo.

36. "Pues aca nos dixeron que os davan a Estepa para Espejo y holgue por lo vuestro y por lo mio que tengo esperanza de aver unos lugarejos de la orden a troque que estan juntos a lo mio en Castilla" (Tendilla to the *alcaide de los donzeles*, 29 Jan. 1513, *Correspondencia*, 32:159). The count may have been thinking of trying to trade some of his Andalusian properties for the towns of Estremera and Valdaracete, which were in the Order of Santiago and bordered his town of Mondéjar, or for the town of Peñalver, which was in the Order of San Juan and just north of his town of Tendilla.

37. Tendilla to his son Luis, 26 Apr. 1513, ibid., 32:282.

38. He succeeded in buying a *despoblado*, Meniar, in the Alpujarras Mountains, and began settling it in early 1513: "Pidos de mucha gracia que a ell alguacil de Meniar que va a poblar el y sus hijos y otros vecinos de Turon los ayays rrecomendados en qualquiera cosa que por ellos pudierdes hacer porque en ello rrecibire yo muy buena obra" (Tendilla to *teniente* and *alguacil mayor* of the Alpujarras, 8 Jan. 1513, ibid., 32:118; for further information see Tendilla to Juan Hurtado de Mendoza, 10 April 1514, Copiador).

39. AHN, Osuna, leg. 291/3; transcription (from an imperfect notarial copy) in Angel González Palencia and Eugenio Mele, eds., *Vida y obras de don Diego Hurtado de Mendoza*, 3 vols. (Madrid, 1941–43), 3:253–70.

40. See above, n. 35.

41. "Carta de venta a favor del señor don Luis Hurtado de Mendoza de la hazienda de Almayate que es en termino de Belez Malaga que compro de Christoval de Rueda y su muger año de 1564," AHN, Osuna, leg. 277, no. 6; Ibáñez de Segovia, "Historia de la casa de Mondéjar," fol. 321.

42. His permanent absence from New Castile was a consequence of service to the monarchy, as a commander in the military conquest of Granada from 1482 to 1492, as royal ambassador to Pope Innocent VIII in 1486 and 1487, and as military governor of the Kingdom of Granada from 1492 to his death in 1515. The count's position as captain general of the Kingdom of Granada required him to reside in the Alhambra Palace—which he called "this honorable prison"—while the turbulent Granadine situation, with its religious divisions, raids by

Muslim pirates from North Africa, banditry by mountain holdouts, and economic dislocation, demanded his constant attention and activity.

43. RAH, Salazar y Castro, M 23, fol. 121.

44. "Traslado del privilegio rodado escripto en papel que dio el señor rey don Enrique 3° al señor don Diego Hurtado de Mendoza, señor de La Vega y almirante de la Mar, por la qual le hace merced de la villa de Tendilla," Dec. 1395 AHN, Osuna, leg. 2983/1.

45. The village of Tendilla is not mentioned in the medieval Guadalajara documents that were still available to the historian Juan Catalina García at the beginning of the twentieth century. Juan Catalina believed that the documentary silence indicated that Tendilla was not settled until late in the fourteenth century, despite the claims of the citizens that their town was won from the Muslims by the Cid ("Tendilla," *Relaciones Guadalajara*, 43:61, n. 2; "Aumentos," ibid., 43:90–109). In the face of this paucity of early documentation, Juan Catalina made good use of local oral tradition in Tendilla. Nearly a century later, I was no more successful than he in discovering new local archival sources. Eighteenth-century writers, such as Juan de Talamanco, accused the French armies of deliberately destroying archival materials in the Alcarria region during the War of the Spanish Succession. In Tendilla, another possible cause of losses may be the dampness that pervades the town. I have begun to think that the oldest seignorial towns, including Tendilla, simply did not produce many documents, because their internal affairs were administered orally, as was the custom in both justice and economic transactions until the advent of municipal notaries in the early sixteenth century, while their relations with other jurisdictions were the prerogative of the lords, who kept few written records other than royal privileges and occasional account ledgers. The original royal privileges remain in the possession of the family's descendants, the dukes of Infantado. The account ledgers, legal briefs and depositions, notarized copies of the royal privileges, and all the rest of the estate records are housed in AHN, Osuna.

46. See above, n. 44.

47. Bartolomé Yun Casalilla, *Sobre la transición al capitalismo en Castilla: Economía y sociedad en Tierra de Campos (1500–1830)* (Valladolid, 1987), pp. 182–83.

48. For the commercial importance of this Valencia-Castile trade see Miguel Angel Ladero Quesada, "La hacienda castellana de los Reyes Católicos, 1493–1504," *Moneda y Crédito* 103 (1967): 107.

49. "Tendilla," *Relaciones Guadalajara*, 43:67.

50. Modesto Ulloa, *Las rentas de algunos señores y señoríos castellanos bajo los primeros Austria* (Montevideo, 1971). The same proportion of commercial to agricultural income was apparently characteristic of other noble estates developed in the fifteenth century (see Yun, *Sobre la transición*, p. 125).

51. "Tendilla," *Relaciones Guadalajara*, 43:67. Quotations in the next several paragraphs are taken from ibid., 43:65–71.

52. Ibid., 43:65. In addition to making charcoal from the olive tree prunings, it is customary around the Mediterranean to mix the ground olive pits with a binder and to use this mixture to form bricks for use as fuel. I have not been able to discover whether this custom was followed in Tendilla.

53. Notarial transcript of the 1430 grant, in AHN, Osuna, leg. 1873/21:1–2. The 1458 partition is in ibid., leg. 1762.

54. Apart from the repartition of the marquis's estate by his sons, during the fifteenth century the estate was the object of a prolonged lawsuit between the marquis of Santillana and his heirs, on the one hand, and the heirs of the admiral's

daughter from his first marriage (see L. J. Andrew Villalon, "The Law's Delay: The Anatomy of an Aristocratic Property Dispute (1350–1577)" (Ph.D. diss., Yale University, 1984).

55. Traslado de la fundación del mayorazgo instituido por Iñigo Lopez de Mendoza y Elvira de Quiñones hecho Guadalajara, 1474, 1478," AHN, Osuna, leg. 291/1–2.

56. Sixteenth-century notarial transcripts of the founding documents in AHN, Osuna, leg. 291/1–2.

57. "Tendilla," *Relaciones Guadalajara,* 43:91; "Aumentos," ibid.

58. "Iñigo López de Mendoza me hizo relación que algunos vasallos suyos han entrado en lo publico desa dicha cibdad a labrar panes e vinos e otras labranzas e que les demandais cierto tributo e quereis poner emposicion sobre ello por razon de las dichas tierras e porque mi merced es que los dichos sus vasallos que en las dichas tierras comunes e publicas entraron e labraron sean quitos e esentos e non paguen el tal tributo e imposicion que les avedes puesto e queredes poner yo vos mando que ge lo non demandedes nin consentades demandar agora nin en algund tiempo nin por alguna manera" (Ibáñez de Segovia, "Historia de la casa de Mondéjar," fol. 137v).

59. AHN, Osuna, leg. 2983/1. On seasonal provisioning efforts in the fair towns of the Tierra de Campos see Yun, *Sobre la transición,* p. 103.

60. Tendilla to the marquis of Denia, 21 May 1509, *Correspondencia,* 31:601.

61. Tendilla to the marquis of Denia; the count of Cifuentes; the royal secretary, Zapata; the royal treasurer, Cazalla; the duke of Alba; the marquis of Denia; the count of Benavente; and King Ferdinand, 18–21 May 1509, ibid., 31:599–606.

62. "Si no hiziera hazer lo que hizieron los de Guadalajara no me diera nada sino a cartas cartas mas aver hecho ir alcalde de Guadalajara que bive con el con vara a mi tierra y a Tendilla dentro y rebolverme pleitos que tenga que hazer para hazerme torcedor sintolo a par de muerte y entiende si puedo vengarme y con setenas" (Tendilla to the marquis of Denia, 20 May 1509, ibid., 31:601).

63. "Yo estoy en ponerle otros pleitos mas rezios que aquel y creo con ayuda de Dios que le hare hincar la rodilla en muchas cosas de las que le tocan. Asentado lo de la paz dell enperador, los grandes y los menores todos ternemos el juego igual para lo que fuere justicia" (Tendilla to his son Luis, 24 May 1510, ibid., 3223–24).

64. Ibáñez de Segovia, "Historia de la Casa de Mondéjar," fol. 176; AGS Diversos de Castilla, 22 Dec. 1486, leg. 41/27. The count's brother, Diego Hurtado de Mendoza, archbishop of Seville and president of the Council of Castile, carried out the transactions for him.

65. Tendilla to the duke of Terranova, 8 Feb. 1513, *Correspondencia,* 2:183; Tendilla to the bishop of Mondoñedo, 27 Feb. 1513, ibid., 2:209–10.

66. The litigation and final disposition of the case are described in Ibañez de Segovia, "Historia de la Casa de Mondéjar," fol. 252; AGS, Patronato real, 11 and 26 Apr. 1511, leg. 1119; and AHN, Osuna, leg. 1983, no. 16/31/33/34.

67. "Esto señor os suplico quanto puedo y no ay que dezir sino que esto a la olla para botar a mi tierra por un pesquisidor que me aves enbiado a Tendilla" (Tendilla to Lic. Vargas, 27 Feb. 1513, *Correspondencia,* 32:208).

68. "Ved si es bien que agora se sentencie lo del vino de Tendilla. Esto me parece a mi que se avia de hazer alcanzando a saber en la sentencia pasada que votos ovo por nos si se pudiese saber y quantos votos ovo contra porque creo yo que los del consejo consultaran con sus señores por no trabajar en ver el proceso" (Tendilla to Lic. Berrio, 13 Apr. 1513, ibid., 32:248).

69. A few years earlier Zomeño had been the royal commissioned judge in boundary and usage disputes between the city of Toledo and some of the villages over which the city claimed jurisdiction (see Molénat, "Tolède et ses finages au temps des rois catholiques," p. 350).

70. The count's letters from February 1513, when this incident occurred, through the following summer are full of accusations and pleading about this case (see esp. Tendilla to the treasurer Vargas, 15 July 1513, *Correspondencia*, 32:451–56).

71. Tendilla to his son Luis, [Apr. 1513,] ibid., 32:208–400.

72. As the count had predicted, the salaries and fees owing to the royal secretaries amounted to fifty thousand maravedís and were discounted from the amount returned to the citizens. The count reimbursed them. "Ya avras visto la sentencia que dio Zomeño mas monta de CC mill maravedís aquellas penas y con salarios y costas mas de CCL mill maravedís. Ay se nos iran las ayudas de costa si avemos de pedir merced dellas y si no la pedimos he las yo de pagar pero con todo la sentencia en lo del pazer y cortar fue buena" (Tendilla to his son Luis, [4 July 1513,] ibid., 32:420). The royal order to the treasury was issued on September 23, 1513, according to Gaspar Ibáñez de Segovia ("Historia de la casa de Mondéjar," fol. 280v).

73. In February 1513 he began negotiating for a horse owned by the commander of the Castilian fortress in Ceuta because he had recently sold most of his herd and found himself "con dineros y syn cavallos" (Tendilla to Juan Hurtado de Mendoza, 1 Feb. 1513, ibid., 32:162). In April, irritated by the long negotiations and still waiting for delivery of the stud he had bought, he wrote, "Quedo señor suplicandoos que el cavallo mande vuestra merced dar ques del señor don Juan hijo del señor conde de Coruña dias ha y señalado cuyo fue y la color y aun el sabor" (Tendilla to Antonio de Cordova, 21 Apr. 1513, ibid., 32:260).

74. See, e.g., his refusal to lower the rent on these pastures, which he had received as payment for his war services during the Granada campaign, for a young relative, Pedro Laso de la Vega (older brother of the poet Garcilaso de la Vega) (Tendilla to Pedro Laso de la Vega, 10 Apr. 1514, Copiador).

75. "Unas puertas que faltan de las casas que yo tengo en la dicha alcaria [Meniar] se haga pesquisa dellas y de cierta madera que asy mismo falto porque todo mandes que se buelva" (To the *teniente* and *alguacil mayor* of the Alpujarras, 8 Jan. 1513, *Correspondencia*, 32:118).

Chapter 3: The Emergence of Absolute Monarchy and Town Liberty

1. The reconquest and settlement of the Duero and Tajo basins and of Andalusia have been the focus of many disputes among medieval historians. The latest scholarship tends to abandon the military aspects and treat the reconquest as a population movement and an urban phenomenon. Especially influential in focusing attention on the urban organization of the reconquered territory has been the work of Carlé, *Del concejo medieval castellano-leonés*. The population movement as a resettlement of abandoned territory has been brought into the foreground by Julio González, *Repoblación de Castilla la Nueva*, 2 vols. (Madrid, 1975–76). González makes a strong argument that the present population of Andalusia is descended, not from the Muslims, who abandoned the land after the reconquest, but from Christian colonists who immigrated from the north (idem, "Reconquista y repoblación de Castilla, León, Extremadura y Andalucía [siglos XI a XIII]," in *La reconquista española y la repoblación del país: Conferencias del curso celebrado en*

Jaca en agosto de 1947 [Zaragoza, 1951] pp. 163–206). For a restatement of the debate over whether the municipal council became a closed oligarchy see Carlos Astarita, "Estudio sobre el concejo medieval de la Extremadura castellano-leonés: Una propuesta para resolver la problemática," *Hispania* 42 (1982): 355–413.

2. A recent work of historical geography by Gonzalo Martínez Díez clarifies the spatial and administrative relationships in this region of Old Castile. The kings granted most of these castles in Old Castile and their *alfoces* to private persons who, as proprietary lords (*señores*), appointed the judges. All these *aldeas* were abandoned as the castles fell to the Muslim general Almanzor between 976 and 1002. After Almanzor's death, the settlers reoccupied and reconstituted the towns north of the Duero River. Those *aldeas* that were not subject to a lord were under the jurisdiction of a royal judge (*merino del rey*), whose jurisdiction consisted of several *aldeas* collectively known as a *merindad*. By the mid-fourteenth century this repopulated region north of the Duero was made up of nineteen *merindades* under the king's appellate judge for the region, the *merino mayor de Castilla* (Martínez Díez, *Las comunidades de villa y tierra*, pp. 9–22).

3. One of the liveliest debates in medieval Castilian history has been over the question whether the Castilian municipality was continuous from Roman to Visigothic or Muslim times or from Muslim to Christian. Claudio Sánchez Albornoz believed that the Leonese municipality rose as the fruit of the social, economic, and political organization of the country after the reconquest. In his rotund rejection of continuity from earlier societies, he includes a chapter on Muslim cities headed "Not even a semblance of municipal government" (*Ruina y extinción del municipio Romano en España e instituciones que le reemplazan* [Buenos Aires, 1943], p. 117). This conclusion accords with traditional views of Muslim cities in Spain, which present no evidence of municipal self-government other than mention of the ubiquitous but ill-defined "council of notables." The relationship between the city proper and its surrounding territory, however, is well attested in the most recent survey, Rachel Arié's *España musulmana (siglos VIII–XV)* (Barcelona, 1982), pp. 26–27.

4. In the mid-fourteenth century, when the city of Toledo sent representatives to the Cortes for the first time, because the monarchy was imposing a sales tax (*alcabala*) on all cities and citizens of the realm, a dispute arose between Toledo and León over which city should have precedence. In the first of many royal attempts to resolve this dispute, King Alfonso XI ordered a compromise that reveals the normal procedures of communication between royal and local administration: documents issued by the king, his chancery, and the judges of his court addressed to the cities, towns, and villages of the king's dominions should mention León before Toledo; in those documents to be delivered to Toledo and the towns and villages of the notariate for the Kingdom of Toledo, however, Toledo would be listed before León (*Novísima recopilación de las leyes*, lib. 3, tit. 4, ley 1).

5. Martínez Díez, *Las comunidades de villa y tierra.*

6. Lacarra compared the *fuero* and ordinances of a single town, Estella, and concluded that the *fueros* tended to be general and almost theoretical in nature, while the municipal ordinances reveal a wealth of specific detail, because they were written in response to local conditions and by the councils actively engaged in the town's administration (José María Lacarra, "Ordenanzas municipales de Estella, siglos XIII y XIV." *Anuario de Historia del Derecho Español* 5 [1928]: 434–45; idem, "Fuero de Estella," ibid., 4 [1927]: 404–51).

7. For a detailed description of the city councils in action as courts of law see Dillard, *Daughters of the Reconquest.*

8. A standard catalogue of documents related to public ceremonies, for example, lists no royal entry ceremonies for Madrid, which remained a royal town and did not become a city even when it became the capital of the monarchy (Jenaro Alenda y Mira, *Relaciones de solemnidades y fiestas públicas de España* [Madrid, 1903]).

9. In the rest of Europe, except England, a similar multiplication of grants of local autonomy occurred, with old settlements receiving the same sort of privileges as new (Susan Reynolds, *Kings and Communities in Western Europe, 900–1300* [Oxford, 1984], pp. 131–32).

10. On the harsh terms imposed by ecclesiastical lords in France, England, and Italy see ibid., p. 134.

11. Pegerto Saavedra, *Economía, política, y sociedad en Galicia: La provincia de Mondoñedo, 1480–1830* (Madrid, 1985).

12. As a matter of courtesy and protocol, many documents were addressed first to members of the royal family and nobles as individuals, then to the prelates, royal judges, and military officers as administrators of their respective jurisdictions. Whereas this usage was not consistant, all documents intended for the entire realm were consistantly addressed to the municipalities as the administrative units of the taxpaying citizens, who made up over 95 percent of the monarchy's subjects. The full formula, for example, would begin "Al ilustrísmo príncipe don Carlos mi muy caro e muy amado fijo e a los ynfantes, perlados, duques, marqueses, condes, ricos ommes, maestres de las órdenes, e a los del mi consejo, presidente e oydores de las mis abdiencias, alclldes de la mi casa e corte e chancillerias e a los priores, comendadores e subcomendadores, alcaydes de los castillos e casas fuertes y llanas" before arriving at "todos los concejos, corregidores, govenadores e asistentes, alcalldes, alguaziles, merinos, prestameros, rregidores, veynte e quatros, cavalleros, escuderos, oficiales e ommes buenos de *todas cibdades e villas e lugares de los mis Reynos*" (*Documentos del archivo general de la villa de Madrid*, ed. Timoteo Domingo Palacido, 5 vols. [Madrid, 1888–1932], 4:195–96, emphasis added).

13. Moxó, *Antiguos señoríos*, pp. 29–67. Enrique II made equally extensive grants during the war in the northern parts of the modern provinces of Madrid and Guadalajara. In 1368 he granted the towns of Hita and Buitrago, which commanded the routes south from Burgos into the Tajo River basin, to his new adherent, Pedro González de Mendoza. At the time of the grant the two towns were supporting King Pedro, and Mendoza assumed the responsibility for conquering and then controlling Hita and Buitrago (see Helen Nader, *The Mendoza Family in the Spanish Renaissance, 1350–1550* [New Brunswick, N.J., 1980], pp. 38–44).

14. Moxó, "Los señoríos," pp. 400–404.

15. "La excesiva prodigalidad de los Monarcas de la Casa de Trastámara, cuyas liberales donaciones han convertido el término 'merced enriqueña' en sinónimo de merced caprichosa o inadecuada, entregó al señorío solariego de los nobles muchas villas y lugares, antes realengos" (Moxó, *La incorporación*, pp. 13–14).

16. Moxó: *La alcabala; La disolución; La incorporación*; "Las desamortizaciones"; *Antiguos señoríos*; "Los orígenes."

17. [Petri Bellugae Valentini], *Speculum Principum ad Alphonsium Siciliae et Aragoniae regem* [1439] (Antwerp, 1657).

18. The terminology, concepts, and historical context of these documents have been elucidated by Luis Sánchez Agesta in "El 'poderío real absoluto' en el testamento de 1554: Sobre los orígines de la concepción del estado," in *Carlos V*

(*1500–1558*): *Homenaje de la Universidad de Granada*, ed. Antonio Gallego Morell (Granada, 1958), pp. 439–67.

19. A few years later he used the same language to justify executing Alvaro de Luna for violating the royal prerogatives!

20. Moxó, "El señorío," pp. 110–13. In 1480 Cabrera and Bobadilla received the villages of Chinchón, Ciempozuelos, San Martín de la Vega, Valdelaguna, Seseña, Villaconejos, Odón, Moraleja de Enmedio, Moraleja la Mayor, Serranillos, Tiracentenos, Sacedón, and Cienvallejos, all alienated from the city of Segovia (Marqués del Saltillo [Miguel Lasso de la Vega], *Historia nobiliaria española*, 2 vols. [Madrid, 1951], pp. 131–33). In 1482 the chief royal accountant, Cárdenas, received the villages of Gerindote, Alcabón, and Torrijos, alienated from the bishopric of Segovia, as well as the property that later would become the estate of Maqueda, alienated from the cathedral of Toledo. In 1484 Gonzalo Chacón received the village of Casarrubios del Monte, alienated from the royal town of Madrid.

21. Rafael Ramírez Arellano, "Rebelión de Fuenteovejuna contra el comendador mayor de Calatrava, Fernán Gómez de Guzmán (1476)," *BRAH* 39 (1901): 446–512.

22. "Sean deputados alcaldes, conviene a saber, sy el lugar fuere de treynta vezinos o dende ayuso un alcalde, e sy fuere de treynta vezinos arriba dos alcaldes, puestos por el concejo e oficiales del tal lugar" ("Cortes de Madrigal de 1476," *Cortes de los antiguos reinos de León y Castilla*, 5 vols. [Madrid, 1861–1903], 4:6).

23. "Todo logar de cinquenta vezinos abaxo sea avido por yermo e despoblado tanto que sea logar sin cerca para en estos casos" (ibid., 4:5).

24. "Parescionos ser el mas cierto e mas syn costa vuestra que para entre tanto se hiziessen hermandades en todos vuestros rreynos, cada cibdad e villa, con su tierra entre sy e las unas con las otras" (ibid., 4:3).

25. Cited by Moxó in "El señorío," p. 113, and by many others.

26. Antonio Matilla Tascón made a penetrating analysis of the monarch's intentions and frustrations in his introduction to *Declaratorias de los reyes católicos sobre reducción de juros y otras mercedes* (Madrid, 1952).

27. The *marquesado* de Villena was associated with two important literary figures. The infante Juan Manuel had been lord of Villena in the thirteenth century. Enrique de Villena, the fifteenth-century author of several treatises and poetic works and translator of classics, was a politically inept member of the royal family who often managed to make the wrong choice at the moment it would cost him the most. He received the town of Villena from Juan II of Castile and took the traditional title of marquis of Villena, but he joined the side of the infantes of Aragon. Juan II stripped him of the Villena estate and title, leaving him with just a commandery in a military order, but Enrique continued to claim the *marquesado* and used the name by which he is still known, Enrique de Villena.

28. "Los dichos pueblos son de la corona real de los reducidos y que no estan sujetos a señor alguno" ("Gil García," *Relaciones Cuenca*, p. 270); "Esta villa cae y esta en el reino de Castilla dentro del reino de Toledo en la provincia que dicen del marquesado de Villena en la Mancha de Aragon, de lo reducido a la corona real" ("Tarazona de la Mancha," ibid., p. 509).

29. For the political and military history of the siege of Alarcón see Manuel Torres Fontes, "La conquista del marquesado de Villena en el reinado de los Reyes Católicos," *Hispania* 13 (1953): 37–151. Events within the fortress of Alarcón were described by its commander, Pedro de Baeza (see "Carta que Pedro de Baeza

escrivió a el marques de Villena sobre que le pidió un memorial de lo que por el avia fecho," *Documentos relativos al reinado de Enrique IV*, MHE 5, pp. 485–510).

30. Ladero Quesada, "El poder central y las ciudades en España."

31. Francisco Bejarano Robles, *Los repartimientos de Málaga* (Málaga, 1985), pp. 6, 17.

32. Julio Caro Baroja, *Los Moriscos del Reino de Granada* (Madrid, 1957), p. 7. The new marquis of Villena, Tendilla's brother-in-law, received two towns, Serón and Tixola, to compensate for the difference between what his father had lost in the *marquesado* of Villena and what he had been given in Escalona. Tendilla's uncle, the cardinal of Spain, received the largest grant in the Kingdom of Granada and placed it in a perpetual trust for his son in the form of the *marquesado* of Zenete. This young cousin of Tendilla's also received newly elevated towns in other parts of the kingdom.

33. "Carta para que el corregidor de Granada vaya al término de Guadahortuna para que se haga allí un lugar," GRAM, Cédulas reales, Alcalá de Henares, 10 Mar. 1503, fols. 512–512v.

34. Ibid., fols 465–465v

35. GRAM, Actas del Cabildo, 2: 18 Feb.–20 May 1513, fols. 5, 29, 34, 41, 45v, 47, 51v, 52, 52v, 54, 55.

36. Ibid., 18 Feb. 1513, fol. 34, and 13 Sept. 1513, fol. 84.

37. AGS, DGT, leg. 281, fol. 115.

38. For population estimates of the cities at the beginning and end of the sixteenth century see Ladero Quesada, "El poder central y las ciudades en España."

39. The Spanish Constitution of 1978 proclaims: "La capital del Estado es la villa de Madrid" (*Constitución española*, Tit. 1, Art. 5).

40. Ramón Carande, *Carlos V y sus banqueros: La hacienda real de Castilla*, 2d ed., 3 vols. (Madrid, 1965–68), 2:527.

41. Weisser, *Peasants of the Montes*.

42. Miguel Angel Ladero Quesada, "La repoblación del reino de Granada anterior al año 1500," *Hispania* 28 (1968): 489–563.

43. The following is extracted from GRAM, Actas del Cabildo, leg. 2. There are no published proceedings for this meeting of the Cortes, if it did actually meet.

44. José Peraza de Ayala, "Los antiguos cabildos de las Islas Canarias," *Anuario de Historia de Derecho Español* 4 (1927): 225–97.

45. For a description of these European factories in the eastern Mediterranean, Africa, and Southeast Asia and their resonance in Columbus's letters see Charles Verlinden, *The Beginnings of Modern Colonization*, trans. Yvonne Freccereo (Ithaca, 1970).

46. Instructions to Columbus and Antonio de Torres about settlers, supplies, and provisions for the island of Hispaniola, 15 June 1497, in Christopher Columbus, *Libro de los privilegios del almirante don Cristóbal Colón (1498)*, ed. and trans. Ciriaco Pérez-Bustamante (Madrid, 1951), doc. 8.

47. Authorization for Columbus to apportion land on the island of Hispaniola among the settlers, 22 July 1497, ibid., doc. 22.

48. For these complaints see Ramos, "Colón y el enfrentamiento de los caballeros."

49. For Columbus's itinerary in Castile see Juan Manzano Manzano, *Cristóbal Colón: Siete años decisivos de su vida, 1485–1492* (Madrid, 1964).

50. For the litigation to regain titles and income see Antonio Muro Orejón, Florentino Pérez-Embid, and Francisco Morales Padrón, eds., *Pleitos colombinos*, vol. 1, *Proceso hasta la sentencia de Sevilla (1511)* (Seville, 1967).

51. The seven Spanish towns and cities founded by Velázquez were: Baracoa, Bayamo, Trinidad, Sancti Spiritus, Havana, Camagüey, and Santiago de Cuba (Irene Wright, *The Early History of Cuba, 1492–1586* [New York, 1916], p. 59; see also map 3).

52. Manuel Giménez Fernández, "Hernán Cortés y su revolución comunera en la Nueva España," *Anuario de Estudios Americanos* 5 (1948) 1–144; Richard Konetzke, "Hernán Cortés como poblador de la Nueva España," *Revista de Indias* 9 (1948): 341–81; Robert S. Chamberlain, "La controversia Velázquez-Cortés sobre la gobernación de la Nueva España, 1519–1522," *Anales de la Sociedad de Geografía e Historia de Guatemala* 19 (1943): 23–56.

53. "Despues que hubimos hecho liga y amistad con mas de treinta pueblos de las tierras que se decian los Totonaques que entonces se rebelaron al gran Montezuma y dieron la obediencia a Su Majestad y se profirieron de nos servir" (Díaz del Castillo, *Historia verdadera,* 1:151).

54. "Porque secretamente Diego Velázquez enviaba a rescatar y no a poblar, segun despues pareció por las instrucciones que de ello dio y aunque publicaba y pregono que enviaba a poblar" (ibid., 1:81–82).

55. "¿Pareceos, señor, bien que Hernando Cortés asi nos haya traido engañados a todos y dio pregones en Cuba que venia a poblar y ahora hemos sabido que no trae poder para ello sino para rescatar y quieren que nos volvamos a Santiago de Cuba con todo el oro que se ha habido y quedaremos todos perdidos y tomarse ha el oro Diego Velazquez como la otra vez? Mirad, señor, que habeis venido ya tres veces con esta postrera, gastando vuestros haberes y habeis quedado empeñado, aventurando tantas veces la vida con tantas heridas; hacemoslos, señor, saber porque no pase esto mas adelante y estamos muchos caballeros que sabemos que son amigos de vuestra merced para que esta tierra se pueble en nombre de su majestad" (ibid., 1:137–38).

56. "Hernando Cortes en su real nombre y en teniendo que tengamos posibilidad, hacerlo saber en Castilla a nuestro rey y señor y tenga, señor, cuidado de dar el voto para que todos le elijamos por capitan, de unanime voluntad, porque es servicio de Dios y de nuestro rey y señor" (ibid., 1:138).

57. Hernando Cortés, *Hernán Cortés: Letters from Mexico,* trans. Anthony Pagden, 2d ed. (New Haven, 1986), p. 26. Pagden's translation is superior in every respect to the currently available Spanish editions, as well as to other English translations; however, I have substituted my own translations for the names of municipal offices.

58. Díaz del Castillo, *Historia verdadera,* 1:138.

59. Ibid.

60. Cortés, *Letters from Mexico,* p. 26.

61. Díaz del Castillo, *Historia verdadera,* 1:139.

62. Cortés, *Letters from Mexico,* p. 27.

63. Ibid.

64. Díaz del Castillo, *Historia verdadera,* 1:151–52.

65. The most extensive and perceptive discussion of the central role of municipalities in the Castilian mentality and of the process of founding Spanish towns in the New World is in Lyle N. McAlister, *Spain and Portugal in the New World, 1492–1700* (Minneapolis, 1984), pp. 133–52.

66. "Real cédula de población otorgada a los que hicieran descubrimientos en tierra firme," Burgos, 1521, *CODIAI,* 2:558–67; *Recopilación de leyes de les reynos de las Indias,* 4th ed., 3 vols. (Madrid, 1791; facsimile ed., 1943), vol. 2, bk. 4, title 7, p. 19. Manuel Fábila finds the origins of these later orders in the 1513

instructions for settlers that were incorporated into the royal order of 1523 (*Cinco siglos de legislación agraria*, 1493–1940 [Mexico City, 1941]).

Chapter 4: The Habsburg Sale of Jurisdiction

1. "Testamento 1554," in Sandoval, *Historia de la vida y hechos del emperador Carlos V*, BAE, 80:536–39. See the discussion of this will in the context of earlier royal wills by Luis Sánchez Agesta, "El "poderío real absoluto."

2. Moxó, "Las desamortizaciones"; Carande, *Carlos V y sus banqueros*, 2:367–433.

3. AGS, Patronato real, leg. 26, fol. 12. Papal and royal documents use the verb *dismembrar* to describe the transfer of towns from the military orders to the royal domain, probably because nearly all municipalities in the orders were already towns and therefore did not need to be "exempted" or "liberated" from another municipality before being transferred (Moxó, "Las desamortizaciones," p. 330). The geographical extent of the towns dismembered from the orders was the Tajo River basin—New Castile and Extremadura—and western Andalusia. The official documents describe the affected area as "Castilla y León" because a group of towns northwest of Seville belonging to the Order of Santiago were grouped as a single commandery whose income belonged to the High Commander of León (*comendador mayor de León*). This commandery in Andalusia was called by the Order the Provincia de León. The procedures followed in this census are described in Felipe Ruiz Martín, "Demografía eclesiástica hasta el siglo XIX," in *Diccionario de historia eclesiástica de España*, ed. Quintín Aldea Vaquero, Tomás Martínez, and José Vives Gatell, 3 vols. (Madrid, 1972), 2:684. "Carta del emperador a la emperatriz, Borgo San Donnino, May 18, 1536," cited in J. M. Jover, *Carlos V y los Españoles* (Madrid, 1963), p. 411.

4. The Almoguera appraisal and sale process are described in detail in Ibáñez de Segovia, "Historia de la Casa de Mondéjar," chap. 3. See also Moxó, "Las desamortizaciones," pp. 316–17, 336; "Almoguera," *Relaciones Guadalajara*, vol. 42; "Albares," "Drieves," "Fuentenovilla," "Mazuecos," and "Pozo de Almoguera," ibid., vol. 47; "Brea," *Relaciones Madrid*.

5. Luis Hurtado de Mendoza (d. 1566), third count of Tendilla and second marquis of Mondéjar, was the son of the count of Tendilla who gave the village of Miralcampo its municipal territory in 1512 (see above, chap. 1). Luis himself carried on a long and bitter legal battle against the city of Guadalajara to clear Miralcampo's title to the land, and his son, the third marquis of Mondéjar, gave a charter of township to Miralcampo in 1575.

In an early article on the finances of the marquises of Mondéjar I tried to figure out how Luis could have raised the forty-seven thousand ducados for this purchase, when his salary as captain general of the Kingdom of Granada had not been paid for more than twenty years (Helen Nader, "Noble Income in Sixteenth-Century Castile: The Case of the Marquises of Mondéjar, 1480 to 1580," *Economic History Review*, 2d ser. 30 [1977]: 411–28). I now suspect that Charles gave Almoguera and Fuentenovilla to Luis in lieu of arrears.

6. The council of Almoguera resisted giving up control over its former villages. After litigation with the marquis and the town of Albares, all agreed that the new towns would submit two lists of nominees to the Almoguera council in the annual elections for municipal office. The commons continued to have its headquarters in Almoguera, where the commons judge was elected annually in a meeting

attended by representatives from all the towns in the commons ("Albares," *Relaciones Guadalajara*, vol. 47).

7. Antonio Domínguez Ortiz, "Ventas y exenciones de lugares durante el reinado de Felipe IV," *Anuario de Historia del Derecho Español* 34 (1964): 163–207; Moxó, "Las desamortizaciones"; José Gentil da Silva, *En Espagne: Développement économique, subsistance, déclin* (Paris, 1965). See also Saltillo, *Historia*, 2:296–99.

8. The towns were Almendralejo, Calzadilla, Fuente de Cantos, Monasterio, and Montemolín. Fuente de Cantos bought its liberty from the city of Seville in 1587 but was unable to pay its creditor, whose heirs took possession of the town's jurisdiction in 1615. The other four towns were repossessed by King Philip III in 1608 and sold again by Philip IV in 1628 (Saltillo, *Historia*, 2: 278–79).

9. Carrión de los Ajos was in the commandery that the Order of Calatrava called Casas de Sevilla y Niebla. Unless otherwise noted, the appraisal, sale, and transfer of Carrión described below is excerpted from "Carrión de los Ajos: Asiento sobre su venta a Gonzalo de Céspedes," AGS, DGT, leg. 282, fol. 31.

10. Juan Infante-Galán, *Los Céspedes y su señorío de Carrión, 1253–1874* (Seville, 1970), p. 35. Infante-Galán reports that no premodern documents survive in the Carrión municipal archives. He did not have access to the marterials in AGS. He based his monograph on local ecclesiastical and genealogical documents and on the archives of the military orders in the AHN.

11. Moxó, *La incorporación*, pp. 12–17; Herrera García, *El Aljarafe sevillano*, pp. 60–61.

12. Zárate had gone to Peru in 1544, returned to Spain by 1547, accompanied Philip II to England in 1554, and in 1555 was appointed to administer the new Guadalcanal silver mines north of Seville, because "as a result of having lived some time in the Indies he had seen the mines that were worked there." By early 1560 Zárate had a new post as the first royal administrator of the north coast customs tax, which Philip II had just confiscated from its proprietary administrator, the constable of Castile. Zárate audited the accounts, recommended reforms, and claimed that the royal customs collectors in Laredo had collected as much in five months as the constable's administrators had in the previous year. When the treasury decided to reorganize the administration of salt revenues, Zárate was posted back to Seville. While administrator of the royal salt revenues for all of Andalusia, he acted as the royal commissioner in alienating and selling the towns of Carrión de los Ajos and Rianzuela. According to James Lockhart, "perhaps the most consistently informative and generally trustworthy chronicler is Zárate, who combines direct personal experience with good education and judgement" (Lockhart, *Men of Cajamarca: A Social and Biographical Study of the First Conquerors of Peru* [Austin, 1972], p. 186n). A telling measure of Zárate's skill as historian is the fact that an English translation of his work by J. H. Cohen was published in paperback by Penguin Books as *The Discovery and Conquest of Peru* (Baltimore, 1968). For his correspondence with other aspiring historians during the late 1540s see Manuel Miguélez, *Catálogo de los códices españoles de la biblioteca del Escorial. I: Relaciones histórico-geográficas de los pueblos de España, 1574–1581* (Madrid, 1917), pp. 105, 110. For his activities as royal commissioner in alienating Rianzuela from the diocese of Seville and selling it to Hernando de Solís see Herrera García, *El Aljarafe sevillano*, pp. 444–47. For Zárate's career in Peru and Spain see Teodoro Hampe Martínez, "Agustín de Zárate: Precisiones en torno a la vida y obra de un cronista indiano," *Caravelle (Cahiers du monde hispanique et luso-bresilien)* 45 (1985): 21–36; and idem, "La misión financiera de Agustín de Zárate, Contador General

del Perú y Tierra Firme (1543–1546)," *Ibero-Amerikanisches Archiv* 12, no. 1 (1986): 1–26.

13. Carrión's area was small for its population, even in the rich Aljarafe region. At the other end of the scale, San Andrés del Rey, alienated from the diocese of Sigüenza in 1579, was appraised at forty-five households and more than one square league in area ("San Andrés del Rey," *Relaciones Guadalajara*, 41:301–7).

14. These twenty-four folios form the middle portion of "Carrión de los Ajos: Asiento sobre su venta a Gonzalo de Céspedes" (see above, n. 12); the document is not paginated.

15. Gonzalo did not live long to enjoy his status as a lord. On May 19, 1580, doña Inés de Nebreda, widow of "don Gonzalo de Céspedes, señor de la villa de Carrión y veinticuatro" of Seville, acknowledged receipt of Gonzalo's quarterly payment on an annuity drawn on the customs tax *(almojarifazgo)* of the Indies. Their son Pedro inherited the lordship of Carrión, which later passed to a collateral descendant who was lord of Villafranca and acquired the noble title marquis of Villafranca in 1609. A later descendant, Francisco Manuel de Céspedes, marquis of Villafranca and lord of Carrión, would shine as a star of Seville's eighteenth-century Enlightenment (Infante-Galán, *Señorío*, pp. 34, 43–61).

16. AGS, DGT, leg. 491.

17. The 1574 bull was confirmed in 1604 by Clement VIII for Philip III, who agreed to restore some of the alienated jurisdictions to the church (Domínguez Ortiz, "Ventas y exenciones," p. 165). For the juridical foundations for sales of ecclesiastical jurisdictions, with lists of specific sales of monastic lands, see Alfonso María Guilarte, *El régimen señorial en el siglo XVI* (Madrid, 1962), p. 52 and app. 24. A clergyman's objection to the sales is reported in Nicolás López Martínez, "La desamortización de bienes eclesiásticos en 1574," *Hispania* 86 (1962): 230–50.

18. John H. Elliott, *Imperial Spain, 1469–1716* [London, 1963], p. 227.

19. For the most erudite and lively description of the *Relaciones topográficas* questionnaire, the parallel *Relaciones geográficas* questionnaire in the Americas, and modern editions of the questions and responses see Howard F. Cline, "The Relaciones geográficas of the Spanish Indies, 1577–1648," in *Guide to Ethnohistorical Sources*, ed. Howard F. Cline, vol. 12, pt. 1, of *Handbook of Middle American Indians*, gen. ed. R. Wauchope (Austin, 1972). The genesis, authorship, and purposes of the *Relaciones* have been a favorite topic for speculation among historians. Alfonso María Guilarte pointed out the link between the *Relaciones* and the alienation of jurisdiction (*Régimen señorial*, p. 52). For a sensible discussion of the debate, as well as a bibliography on it, see the introductory remarks in Salomon, *La vida rural castellana*, pp. 14–15.

20. The royal administrators used the verb *eximir* throughout the documentation related to the alienation of episcopal and monastic jurisdictions. Here, the instruction is referring to the towns in the archdiocese already dismembered *(eximidos)* from the military orders and other ecclesiastical jurisdictions. The instructions to corregidores are printed at the beginning of the modern editions of the *Relaciones* for Ciudad Real, Cuenca, Madrid, and Toledo provinces. I cite here the transcription in Manuel Miguélez, "Las relaciones histórico-geográficas de los pueblos de España hechas por orden de Felip II," in *Catálogo*, pp. 262–63.

21. The word *relación* generally refers to an informational report or declaration to a superior. Current usage refers to the sixteenth-century questionnaires and responses for Castile as *Relaciones topográficas* and to those for the New World as *Relaciones geográficas*.

22. Juan López de Velasco, "Memorial de Juan López de Velasco, Madrid, October 26, 1583," in *Bibliografía madrileña, ó descripción de las obras impresas en Madrid,* ed. Cristóbal Pérez Pastor, vol. 3 (Madrid, 1907), p. 422; *Relaciones Cuenca,* pp. 26–27 n. 15.

23. "Relacion de los lugares eclesiasticos que su magt. ha mandado que no se enajenen," AGS, DGT, leg. 282.

24. The twenty-two new towns exempted from Alcalá were Torres, El Pozuelo, Los Hueros, Loeches, El Campo, Tielmes, Carabaña, Orusco, El Olmeda, Corpa, Villalvilla, Torrejón de Ardoz, Arganda, Valdelecha, Ambite, El Villar, Pezuela, Valverde, Anchuelo, Camarma de Esteruelas, Loranca, and Camarma del Caño (BN, ms. 13061).

25. Ibid.

26. The towns exempted from the cathedral of Seville were Cantillana, Breves, Rianzuela, Almonaster, and Albaida (Quema), according to Diego Ortiz de Zúñiga, as cited by Herrera García in *El Aljarafe sevillano,* pp. 58–59, 104.

27. María Isabel López Díaz, "Las desmembraciones eclesiásticas de 1574 a 1579," *Moneda y Crédito* 129 (1974): 135–52.

28. Alfonso Menéndez González, "La desamortización eclesiástica en Asturias en la época de Felipe II," *Instituto de Estudios Asturianos* 37, nos. 109–10 (1983): 489–515; 38, no. 111 (1984): 55–79.

29. Moxó, *La incorporación,* pp. 12–14; and more explicitly, idem, *La disolución,* pp. 1–12.

30. I have analyzed all the published *Relaciones,* which generally include the modern provinces of Ciudad Real, Cuenca, Guadalajara, Madrid, and Toledo. The total number of towns and villages responding to the *Relaciones* questionnaires is lower than most counts indicate, for several reasons. Some responses were published in the volumes of two or three provinces because their editors did not take into account the fact that the provincial boundaries have changed several times since the first *Relaciones* were published at the beginning of this century. Some places submitted more than one response; variations in their name made them appear to be different towns. Other places, between their responses to the first questionnaire in 1575 and the second in 1580, changed their names when they became towns.

31. For Philip III's agreements with the popes on the issue of raising money see Francisco Fernández Izquierdo, "Las ventas de bienes de las órdenes militares en el siglo XVI como fuente para el estudio del régimen señorial: La Provincia de Calatrava de Zorita," *Hispania* 42 (1982): 422–23.

32. For the sale of offices during the reigns of Charles and Philip II see Margarita Cuartas Rivero, "La venta de oficios públicos en Catilla-León en el siglo XVI," *Hispania* 44 (1984): 495–516. For the reigns of Philip III and Philip IV see Alfonso Menéndez González, "La venta de oficios públicos en Asturias en los siglos XVI y XVII," *Instituto de Estudios Asturianos* 38, no. 112 (1984): 678–707, esp. p. 682; and Antonio Domínguez Ortiz, "La venta de cargos y oficios públicos en Castilla y sus consecuencias económicas y sociales," *Anuario de Historia Económica y Social* 3 (1970): 105–37.

33. David Vassberg, *La venta de tierras baldías: El comunitarismo agrario y la corona de Castilla durante el siglo XVI* (Madrid, 1983).

34. Vassberg, *Land and Society in Golden Age Castile.*

35. During the early Middle Ages the *behetrías* had enjoyed the privilege of deciding which lord they would accept, but by the end of the thirteenth century they became, in effect, royal towns. They claimed exemption from the royal head

tax (*servicio* or *pecho*) in exchange for supplying men or cash for the royal galleons. For a brief review of these conditions and privileges in the *behetrías* see Pedro Fernández Martín, "Las ventas de las villas y lugares de behetría y su repercusión en la vida económico-social de los pueblos y de Castilla," *Anuario de Historia Económica y Social* 1 (1968): 261–64.

36. For the following information about the sales to Lerma I have drawn on the relevant excerpts published by Pedro Fernández Martín in ibid., pp. 267–75.

37. The eleven towns and their populations in 1608, as reported in ibid., p. 275, were: Boadilla de Rioseco, 440; Capillas, 253; Fuentes de Don Bermudo, 462; Mahamud, 315; Mazuecos, 236; Palacio de Meneses, 236; Pozo Durama, 97; Presencio, 339; Santa María del Campo, 585; Torquemada, 686; and Villa Vaquerín, 186, with a total population of 3,835. The true number of households cannot be calculated from the appraisal, because it counted as half-households an unknown number of households headed by hidalgos and widows.

38. The story of San Lorenzo de los Negros, based on the account of one of the bandits' Spanish captives, has been published by D. M. Davidson as "Negro Slave Control and Resistance in Colonial Mexico, 1519–1650," *Hispanic American Historical Review* 46 (1966): 235–53, and is neatly summed up and analyzed in William D. Phillips, Jr., *Slavery from Roman Times to the Early Transatlantic Trade* (Minneapolis, 1985), pp. 213–14.

39. *Actas* 43:126.

40. Ibid., 43:197–98.

41. For the origins and course of the debate on "absolute royal power" in Spain see Sánchez Agesta, "El 'poderío real absoluto.'"

42. For Baeza see below, chap. 5; for Seville see Herrera García, *El Aljarafe sevillano*, p. 105, n. 27.

43. AGS, DGT, leg. 281, fol. 113. In this sale, carried out in 1561, Guadalajara sold about ninety-eight *yuntas* of its commons land to the neighboring towns of Horche, Lupiana, Loranca, Yebes, Atanzón, Centenera, Valbueno, Husanos, Camarma, La Puebla, and Villanueva and to the monastery of La Piedad.

44. "Fuentes para la historia de Guadalajara," *Relaciones Guadalajara*, 46:200–201; *Actas* 10:467.

45. *Actas* 43:125–32, 190–91.

46. The conditions of 1626 are summarized in Saltillo, *Historia*, 2:296–99.

47. The negotiations between the Cortes and the king's ministers leading to the new subsidy of 1625 are described by Charles Jago in "Habsburg Absolutism and the Cortes of Castile," *American Historical Review* 86 (1981): 307–26. The financial background and consequences of the seventeenth-century alienations and sales are described in Domínguez Ortiz, "Ventas y exenciones," pp. 163–207.

48. Domínguez Ortiz, "Ventas y exenciones," p. 170.

49. The treasury accounts published by José Gentil da Silva indicate that 275 jurisdictions, with a total of 52,306 households, were alienated from cities between 1628 and 1668.

50. John H. Elliott and José Francisco de la Peña, *Memoriales y cartas del conde duque de Olivares*, 2 vols. (Madrid, 1978), 1:16.

Chapter 5: In Pursuit of Justice and Jurisdiction

1. "Yo Gomez de Frias escrivano del concejo de la villa de Linares doy fee e verdadero testimonio como el dicho dia de San Juan se pregono el dicho previlejo y exencion desta villa a altas e yntelejibles bozes, por boz de Juan Catalan pregonero

publico, estando el susodicho subido en los corredores de las casas de cabildo desta villa que salen a la plaça estando presentes los dichos señores alcaldes y algunos de los dichos señores rejidores en presencia de mucha gente e antes que se començase de pregonar" (*Privilegio real*, fol. 10).

2. "Despues de acabado se tocaron en los dichos corredores las trompetas y el dicho dia uvo en la dicha plaça la dicha musica de trompetas y ministriles que muchas e diversas vezes las tocaron en la plaça por la dicha fiesta e ouo procession por la mañana desde la yglesia maior al monesterio de San Juan Baptista y en la dicha procesion ovo danças y antes de ella reguzijo de jentes de a cavallo y se lidiaron seis toros e ovo juegos de cañas y otros reguzijos" (ibid.).

3. "Y por que es verdad di este escrito en publica forma. Testigos Francisco de la Cruz y Francisco Alvares y Juan Gomez, vezinos desta villa, y otra mucha gente de ella y de la cibdad de Baeza e de otras partes. E fize aqui este mio segno en testimonio de verdad" (ibid.).

4. Dillard, *Daughters of the Reconquest*, p. 188.

5. Juan Sánchez Caballero, "Historia de la independencia de Linares," *Oretania* 4, no. 11 (1962): 186. Unless otherwise noted, the following section on Linares is based on Sánchez Caballero's article, which appeared in six issues of *Oretania* between 1962 and 1966. The article includes photo reproductions of most of the medieval royal documents still extant in the Linares municipal archives.

6. Ibid., p. 190.

7. Ibid., 5, no. 13 (1963): 5.

8. "Por quanto el emperador mi señor que santa gloria aya en veynte y dos de otubre del año pasado de mill y quinientos y treynta y siete fundado en la relacion que la dicha ciudad de Baeça le hizo y afirmado que traeria ynconvenientes exhimir y apartar de la jurisdicion della a la dicha villa de Linares y los otros lugares de su tierra y que dello se seguirian pleytos y debates y desasosiegos le concedio una su carta por la qual prometio de no exsimir ni apartar de la jurisdicion de la dicha ciudad de Baeça la dicha villa de Linares ni se haria nouedad en quanto a la jurisdicion de como entonzes estaba por ciertas quantias de maravedís con que por ello le sirvieron" (ibid., 5, nos. 14–15 [1963]: 57–58).

9. Molinié-Bertrand, "La 'villa' de Linares," p. 390.

10. "Somos ynformado que despues aca por tener la dicha ciudad entendido que a la dicha villa no se le podia conceder la dicha jurisdicion les han hecho e hazen mucho e muy malos tratamientos y se consumen las haziendas de sus vezinos en pleytos y diferencias lo qual a sido y es caussa no solo para no aumentarse la dicha villa pero para se despoblar y disminuyr sino se remediase de donde resultaria disminucion en nuestras rentas y patrimonio real" (*Privilegio real*, fols. 1v–2v).

11. "Por las quales caussas justamente pudieramos rebocar la dicha carta y concesion pero por algunos otras consideraciones que para ello se an tenido visto y platicado por los del nuestro consejo de la hazienda e con nos consultado fue acordado que declarando y modificando la dicha carta e concesion e quedandose la dicha villa de Linares en el corregimiento de la dicha ciudad de Vaeça para las cossas y cassos que adelante seran declarados deviamos concederle juridicion cevil y criminal en primera ynstancia por lo qual y por les hazer bien y merced e remediar los dichos dañõs e ynconvenientes y porque nos sirvieron y socorrieron para ayuda a nuestras grandes necesidades con siete mill y quinientos maravedis por cada vno de los vezinos que ay en la dicha villa en los quales fecha la quenta dellos se montaron ocho quentos y quinientas y veynte mill maravedis . . . es nuestra merced y voluntad de exsimir y apartar a vos la dicha villa de Linares con todo vuestro termino e dezmeria segund que agora lo teneys" (ibid., fols. 1v–2v).

12. "Como quiera que por ser o começar a ser la dicha carta tan nociba e perjudicial a la dicha villa de Linares por pribarlos de la esperança que tenian de se libertar e apartar de la jurisdicion de la dicha ciudad y dexarlos en perpetua subjecion" (ibid., fol. 1).

13. AGS, DGT, leg. 281, fol. 131.

14. For the following section on the *repartimiento* see Manuel Sánchez Martínez and Juan Sánchez Caballero, *Una villa giennense a mediados del siglo XVI: Linares* (Jaén, 1975), pp. 37–41. Their analysis utilizes eleven packets of documents in the Archivo Municipal de Linares containing the three censuses and assessments, the council's deliberations, the memorials presented to the council by Pedro de Jaén, and the autograph letter from Philip II authorizing the council to raise the money by encumbering its *propios* and imposing an assessment.

15. This Pedro de Jaén may be the person of the same name who appears in the tax census of 1586 as an "escudero" (military officer) whose income derived from grainlands and annuities (see Molinié-Bertrand, "La 'villa' de Linares," p. 399).

16. "En la villa de Linares dia de señor San Juan Baptista veinte e quatro dias del mes de Junio año del nascimiento de nuestro salvador Jesu Christo de mill e quinientos e sesenta e seis años los muy magníficos señores Linares conviene a saber el doctor Luis Barba e Alonso Lopez de Javalquinto allcaldes hordinarios de la dicha villa por su magestad e Luis Maroto e Juan Diaz de la Donzella e Francisco Perez Barragan, Juan Cobo, Rodrigo Pretel, Miguel Gascon, regidores de la dicha villa, mandaron pregonar el previlejio que su magestad a la dicha villa concedio dandole jurisdicion alta e baxa, mero misto ynperio, ques el de suso contenido e para celebrar la dicha fiesta en memoria dello mandaron lidiar toros y que oviese jente de a cavallo y sus tronpetas y otros regocijos y asi lo proveieron e mandaron y lo firmaron los señores allcaldes e rejidores comissarios de la dicha fiesta" (*Privilegio real*, fol. 10).

17. "Que el sennor de la villa ni otro non meta mano sobre ningun vezino" (*Fuero de Zorita* 16, MHE, 44:55).

18. Castilian summary justice was carried to the Americas, where its processes have been described by Woodrow W. Borah in *Justice by Insurance: The General Indian Court of Colonial Mexico and the Legal Aides of the Half-Real* (Berkeley, 1983).

19. Dillard, *Daughters of the Reconquest*, p. 181.

20. The *rollo* of Linares remained as a symbol of the town's independence and jurisdiction until 1813. In that year the Cortes of Cádiz ordered this monument of municipal jurisdiction torn down in the most important towns because it was imposing a system of provincial governments, which failed with the Cortes itself.

21. The *mentidero* was any public outdoor space where the veterans of Spain's foreign wars gathered to petition for pensions as a reward for their (inflated claims of) military service. The most famous *mentideros* were the Puerta del Sol in Madrid and the Spanish Steps in Rome. Carmelo Viñas y Mey, "La asistencia social a la invalidez militar en el siglo XVI," *Anuario de Historia Económica y Social,* 1 (1968): 598–605.

22. The history of these columns and of their destruction in the nineteenth century, first by order of the Cortes of Cádiz and later by the centralizing Cortes of the Bourbon monarchy, is related by Constancio Bernaldo de Quirós, *La picota: Crímenes y castigos en el país castellano en los tiempos medios* (1907; reprint, Madrid, 1975).

23. Fernando Jiménez de Gregorio, "Notas geográfico-históricas de los pueblos

de la actual provincia de Madrid en el siglo XVIII," *Anales del Instituto de Estudios Madrileños* 8 (1972): 288, 6 (1970): 399, 11 (1975): 91.

24. Ibid., 8 (1972): 292.

25. "Cada uno dellos durante el dicho tienpo pueda traer e trayga en poblado e despoblado vara, e que sea tennida de verde porque aya diferencia" ("Cortes de Madrigal de 1476," *Cortes de los antiguos*, 4:8). The monarchs also appointed "ad hoc" judges to preside over tax and accounting protests. The count of Tendilla called these judges "juezes de vara que entienden en cosas de rentas y de cuentas" (Tendilla to Francisco Ortiz, 4 June 1513, in *Correspondencia*, 2:416).

26. "Cédula de la reina doña Juana y en su nombre el rey, para que las justicias del reino de Granada no embaracen al marqués de Mondéjar en el conocimiento de las causas criminales de los componentes del ejército a su mando" (9 Feb. 1519, RAH, Salazar y Castro, M 131, fols. 215–215v). "Avia tres varas en el Alhanbra" (Tendilla to Lazaro de Padilla, 4 July 1513, in *Correspondencia*, 2:415).

27. "Luego su señoría por ser ya noche, e porque en las dichas minas haya recaudo y se cumpla lo mandado por su Magestad, mandó a Pedro de Valencia Guerra, vecino de Llerena, que es persona de confianza, que con dos alguaciles y el con vara de justicia, se quede en las dichas minas esta noche presente" (González, *Noticia histórica*, 1:37).

28. "Manzaneque," *Relaciones Toledo*, 2:24–25.

29. The U.S. canes and their importance to the functioning of each pueblo are described in Alfonso Ortiz, ed., *Southwest*, vol. 9 of *Handbook of North American Indians*, gen. ed. William C. Sturtevant (Washington, D.C., 1979), pp. 183–489 passim.

30. Charles issued a number of prospecting licenses to private individuals during his first visit to Spain (see Tomás González, *Noticia histórica*, 1:1–7).

31. Molinié-Bertrand, "La 'villa' de Linares," pp. 390, 395.

32. Sánchez Caballero, "Historia de la independencia," *Oretania* 6, nos. 16–18 (1964): 127.

33. At the end of the seventeenth century the council owned twelve pastures. Its citizens sowed about 16,500 *cuerdas* of grain annually on their arable property and owned terracing with 49,000 olive trees, 49 irrigated vegetable and fruit gardens, and 379 *cuartas* of vineyard (ibid., p. 128).

34. Ulloa, *La hacienda real*, p. 430.

35. For the historic development of the corregidor from an ad hoc appointment to a regular feature of royal participation in city government see Agustín Bermúdez Aznar, *El corregidor en Castilla durante la baja edad media, 1348–1474* (Murcia, 1974). Marvin Lunenfeld has culled from published materials a handy list of corregidores during the reign of Isabella (see Lunenfeld, *Keepers of the City*).

36. Thus the modern maps that simply show dots for the cities that were the headquarters of *corregimientos* illustrate the number of corregidores but do not show the shrinking territory over which they held jurisdiction (see, e.g., Bartolomé Bennassar, *Un siècle d'or espagnole* [Paris, 1982], p. 62).

37. For a survey of the location of the *corregimientos* in the first decade of the seventeenth century see Jean Marc Pelorson, *Les letrados, juristes castillans sous Philippe III: Recherches sur leur place dans la société, la culture, e l'état* (Le Puy-en-Velay, 1980), pp. 122–33. Pelorson discusses neither the geographical extent of the individual *corregimientos* nor changes in the authority of the corregidores.

38. "Pezuela," *Relaciones Madrid*, pp. 464–65.

39. "Villarrubia," *Relaciones Toledo*, 3:751.

40. For these royal decrees and the material that follows on Almodóvar see

Manuel Corchado Soriano, *La orden de Calatrava y su campo,* 3 vols. (Ciudad Real, 1984), 1:102–4.

41. The dismemberment of the cities is such a vast subject that I am handling it in a second volume, on Castilian cities and the royal domain.

42. Layna Serrano, *Historia de Guadalajara,* 3:36.

43. AHN, Osuna, leg. 1825–24/1–2.

44. AGS, DGT, leg. 281, fol. 85.

45. "Carta real nombrando alcalde mayor para los asuntos entre cristianos y moros en el arzobispado de Sevilla con el obispado de Cádiz," cited by Arribas Arranz in *Un formulario documental,* p. 76.

46. Sandoval, *Historia de la vida y hechos del Emperador Carlos V,* p. 255.

47. *Real* at that time meant "the royal encampment during a field campaign." In the twentieth century the name has succumbed to folk etymology and been reversed to Manzanares el Real. I do not find this *corregimiento* in Pelorson's listing of corregidores in the reign of Philip III.

48. "Colmenar Viejo," *Relaciones Madrid,* p. 198.

49. "Executoria despachada por los señores de la real chancillería de Valladolid . . . en favor del consejo justicia y reximiento de la villa de Meco" (AHN, Osuna, leg. 2983, pp. 504–6).

50. Luis Cervera Vera, *La villa de Lerma en el siglo XVI y sus ordenanzas de 1594* (Burgos, 1976); Adrián Arcaz Pozo, "La ordenanza de Colmenar Viejo (1575) como fuente de investigación para su historia local," *Anales del Instituto de Estudios Madrileños* 18 (1980): 513–24; Enrique Omero de Torres, "Ordenanzas de la villa de Alcalá de los Gazules, dadas por don Fadrique de Rivera, marqués de Tarifa, en el año de 1513," *BRAH* 56 (1910): 71; "Ordenanzas que el año de 1569 hizieron por la justicia y regimiento de la villa de Saldaña para la guarda y conserbación de los montes de los Villahanes" AHN, Osuna, leg. 1825/34; "Ordenanzas que se hizieron en la villa de Herrera del Rio de Pisuerga, 1569," ibid., leg. 2268/2; "Hordenanzas echas en el año de 1593 por el concejo de la villa de Estremera para el buen reximen govierno de dicha villa y guarda de sus campos," ibid., leg. 2004/4.

51. Jerónimo Castillo de Bobadilla, *Política para corregidores y señores de vasallos* (Madrid, 1597; Antwerp, 1704; facsimile, Madrid, 1978).

52. "Yo ¡para qué traigo aqui / este palo sin provecho?" (Lope de Vega, *Fuenteovejuna,* act 2, lines 482–83).

53. Pedro Calderón de la Barca, *El alcalde de Zalamea,* act 3: "Sobre mí no habéis tenido / jurisdicción: el consejo / de guerra enviará por mí" (lines 542–44); "Vos no debéis de alcanzar, / señor, lo que en un lugar / es un alcalde ordinario" (lines 764–66); "Toda la justicia vuestra / es sólo un cuerpo no más; / si éste tiene muchas manos, / decid, ¿qué más se me da / matar con aquesta un hombre / que esotra había de matar?" (lines 917–22); "Bien dada la muerte esté; / que errar lo menos no importa, / si acertó lo principal" (lines 938–40).

54. Castillo de Bobadilla, *Política,* bk. 2, chap. 16, art. 12.

55. Ibid., bk. 2, chap. 16, arts. 13–14.

56. See, for example, Michael Weisser, "Crime and Punishment in Early-Modern Spain," in *Crime and the Law: The Social History of Crime in Western Europe since 1500,* ed. V. A. C. Gatrell, B. Lenman, and G. Parker (London, 1980).

57. "Peñalver," *Relaciones Guadalajara,* 41:249–63.

58. The population of Peñalver in fact declined before the Valladolid judges gave their final ruling in November 1597. In the 1560s the bishop responded to

the lawsuit, alleging that he had provided many benefits to the town and that its population had grown under his jurisdiction to over 400 households. In 1580 the council reported that the population had declined to 365 households because of the crop failures of recent years.

59. See, e.g., the opening statements by Weisser in "Crime and Punishment in Early-Modern Spain," p. 76.

Chapter 6: The Economic Pleasures and Perils of Liberty

1. "Esta villa no se entiende que sea mui antigua sino nueva a lo menos el crescimiento de vecindad porque fue aldea de Guadalaxara" ("Horche," *Relaciones Guadalajara,* 43:436).

2. "Escritura de donación," Guadalajara, 12 May 1399, Archivo Municipal de Horche, published in Talamanco, *Historia de la ilustre y leal villa de Orche.* This is the oldest document in the municipal archive and the earliest reference to the town in a written record.

3. The citizens of the seignorial town of Tendilla, just east of Horche, experienced even more violent disputes with the city of Guadalajara in the same years (see above, chap. 3).

4. For an excellent history of Horche's agricultural and economic development see Jesús García Fernández, "Horche," *Estudios Geográficos* 14 (1953): 198–237.

5. "La villa de Orche abra quarenta y dos años que es villa por privilegio del emperador don Carlos dado en Valladolid a veinte dias del mes de diciembre del año de mil e quinientos e treinta y siete años que por servicios que la villa hizo a su magestad le dio juridicion sobre si y eximio de la ciudad de Guadalaxara en todo ansi en primera instancia como en grado de apelacion y visita y residencia" ("Horche," *Relaciones Guadalajara,* 43:437; the "Privilegio de la villa" is published in Talamanco, *Historia de la ilustre y leal villa de Orche,* pp. 55–62).

6. The municipal ordinances of Horche were approved by royal order on December 5, 1551, and were published in Talamanco, *Historia de la ilustre y leal villa de Orche,* pp. 66–72.

7. The stage lumber survived until it was burned by the English forces in 1710 (ibid., p. 64).

8. Guadalajara was not able to pay its taxes in the late 1550s and finally agreed to raise eight thousand ducados for the royal treasury by selling 92.5 *yuntos* of its municipal territory to eleven of its former villages. Horche's bloc of 46 *yuntos* and 5 fanegas was by far the largest purchase, (AGS, DGT, leg. 281, fol. 113).

9. Ibid., fols. 113, 725; Talamanco, *Historia de la ilustre y leal villa de Orche,* p. 64.

10. The practice in Spain of creating new offices in order to extract one-time payments from local government has received little attention from historians, though its existence in the Americas has been mentioned (see J. H. Parry, *The Sale of Public Office in the Spanish Indies under the Habsburgs* [Berkeley, 1953], pp. 1–5).

11. "Constitucion de la villa de Estremera, August 8, 1568," AHN, Osuna, leg. 2003/5.

12. Mathías Escudero, "Relación de casos notables que an sucedido en diversas partes de la Christiandad, especialmente en España . . . con algunas cosas que sucedieron en la tierra del auctor," Biblioteca Pública, Toledo, MS 64, n.p.

13. "Romanones," *Relaciones Guadalajara,* 45:264; "Pezuela," *Relaciones Madrid,* p. 426; "Santorcaz," ibid., p. 591.

14. Escudero, "Relación de casos notables," 1571; "Tendilla," *Relaciones Guadalajara*, 43:65. The Alcarria is the northern limit of olive production in Castile. On the economic geography of the Alcarria see Demetrio Ramos, "Notas sobre la geografía del bajo Tajuña," *Estudios Geográficos* 26 (1965): 41–154; on the production ceiling in grain, wine, and wool during the last half of the sixteenth century see Modesto Ulloa, "La producción y el consumo en la Castilla del siglo XVI: Sus reflejos en las cuentas de la hacienda real," *Hispania* 31 (1971): 5–30; on the erratic weather of the late sixteenth century see Fernand Braudel, *The Mediterranean and the Mediterranean World in the Age of Philip II*, trans. Sian Reynolds, 2 vols. (New York, 1975), 1:272–75.

15. Archivo Municipal de Almonacid de Zorita, legs. 1, 13; see the fine catalogue of this archive edited by Francisco Fernández Izquierdo, María Teresa Santos Carrascosa, and María Angeles Yuste Martínez, "Catálogo del Archivo Municipal de Almonacid de Zorita (Guadalajara), siglos XIIIXIX," *Wad-al-Hayara* 8 (1981): 85–214.

16. "Leganés," *Relaciones Madrid*, p. 343; "Miralcampo," *Relaciones Guadalajara*, 42:519; "Torralba," *Relaciones Ciudad Real*, p. 519.

17. AHN, Osuna, leg. 2003/12/1.

18. Unless otherwise noted, all of the information about Almonacid de Zorita is taken from the unpaginated manuscript of Escudero, "Relación de casos notables."

19. The name Francisco Ortiz was so common in the sixteenth century that it is difficult to identify this person. He may have been the Francisco Ortiz who was "ayuda de cámara" to Philip II (RAH, Salazar y Castro, MS. 300, "Tablas genealógicas, Vargas," fol. 136v; I am indebted to Linda Martz for this information).

20. Escudero, "Relación de casos notables," n.p.

21. Francis Brumont, *La Bureba à l'époque de Philippe II: Essai d'histoire rurale quantitative* (New York, 1977), pp. 20–21. For the history of Spain's epidemics in this period see the important work of Vicente Pérez Moreda, *Las crisis de mortalidad en la España interior, siglos XVIXIX* (Madrid, 1980).

22. "Madridejos," *Relaciones Toledo*, 2:4; "Sacedón," *Relaciones Madrid*, p. 546.

23. "Talamanca," *Relaciones Madrid*, p. 615; "Córcoles," *Relaciones Cuenca*, p. 243. "Aqui ha cogido el catarro a todos, y a los que no ha cogido hasta ahora andan temerosos . . . yo soy solo en mi posada, porque todos los que hay en ella están en el suelo, que camas no tienen, y es de manera que en ella y en muchas no hay quien dé a otro una jarra de agua, y lo mismo acontece ya por la casa del duque y todas las demás de la ciudad y fuera della" (Gerónimo de Arceo to Gabriel de Zayas, Lisbon, 21 Sept. 1580, *Correspondencia del duque de Alba con Felipe II y otros personajes sobre la conquista de Portugal en 1580*, in CODOIN, 33:63–64).

24. Brumont, *La Bureba*, p. 22.

25. "Berninches," in *Diccionario geográfico-estadístico-histórico de España y sus posesiones de ultramar*, ed. Pascual Madoz, 16 vols. (1845–50; reprint, Madrid, 1959).

26. By 1786 Serracines was reduced to fifteen households, and a few years later it incorporated itself into the town of Fresno de Torote (Jiménez de Gregorio, "Notas geográfico-históricas de los pueblos," *Anales del Instituto de Estudios Madrileños* 11 [1975]: 90).

27. "Romancos," *Relaciones Guadalajara*, 42:101–4.

28. Valdesaz remained a village under the jurisdiction of the town of San Andrés for nearly a century, buying its township in 1673, when it paid twelve ducados per household by agreement with Barrionuevo's descendants.

29. The following account of Valenzuela's struggle for autonomy is drawn from "Valenzuela," *Relaciones Ciudad Real*, pp. 547–55.

30. "Dicho pueblo e villa de Valenzuela es tan antiguo y por tal tiene nombre y esta puesto en el catalogo de los lugares del Campo de Calatrava en el archivo del convento porque tiene este nombre antes que Almagro tuviese nombre de Almagro. . . . La dicha villa de Valenzuela como dicho tiene antiguamente se halla por escrituras y procesos causados que es villa por si y sobre si sin que tuviese sujecion a ninguna governacion . . . . Ansi se halla por cartas de justicia que se enviaban a los alcaldes de la villa de Almagro a los alcaldes de la villa de Valenzuela para haber de pedir justicia" (p. 547).

31. "El avecindamiento duro poco tiempo porque los de Almagro les fueron quebrantando y no cumpliendo con los capitulos y asientos que tenian hecho cuando les dio la jurisdicion por lo que el concejo de Valenzuela se desavecindo de la dicha villa e tornaron a poderarse en su villadgo y usar de su jurisdicion como antes solia" (pp. 547–48).

32. "La villa de Valenzuela queriendo defenderse enviaron un propio a responder a la demanda a la real chancilleria de Granada y para defensa de su derecho dicese que llevo los privilegios y fuerzas que esta villa tenia y en el camino los perdio y la mas comun opinion que en esta villa hay, que personas de Almagro de industria le emborracharon . . . . Nunca mas siguieron su justicia porque se dice que en el dicho año de siete no quedaron en la dicha villa sino trece vecinos por la mucha pestilencia y hambre y estos quedaron en tan poca calor que no pudieron seguir el pleito y ansi condenados que fuese aldea de Almagro" (p. 548).

33. "Ansi fueron condenados que fuese aldea de Almagro y lo fue hasta el año de mil y quinientos y treinta y ocho que la dicha villa sirvio a la majestad real del emperador don Carlos de gloriosa memoria con dos mil ducados por tornar a su libertad y les dio carta de previlegio a diez de noviembre del dicho año desde el cual dicho tiempo goza de su juridicion alta y baxa, mero mixto imperio como antes solia" (p. 548).

34. "Hay en esta villa mas de treinta huertas. Hay en muchas dellas arboles como son almendros, granados, y algunas olivas y higueras y hay hortalizas y todas legumbres, navos, verengenas, melones, pepinos, rabanos, lechugas, coles y para sus ganados alcaceres y todo esto se riega con anorias que las hay con abundante agua a dos o tres estados" (p. 550).

35. "Crianse buenos ganados de lana y cabrio, muy buenas mulas de yeguas, y los ganados vacunos que se crian hacen gran ventaja para labor mas que en otras partes" (p. 551).

36. "La villa de Almagro se quexo de los alcaldes de la villa de Valenzuela diciendo que les quebrantaban su jurisdicion. . . . Hasta hoy dura el pleito e se han dado tres sentencias en favor de esta villa declarando que la villa de Valenzuela tiene sus terminos conforme a una mojonera que partia los restrojos entre esta villa y la villa de Almagro" (pp. 552–53).

37. The royal treasury agreed to the sale on July 10, 1552, and the appraisals, price negotiations, and installment payments were finally completed on October 2, 1556 (see AGS, DGT, leg. 280, fol. 13).

38. "Un juez de comision el año de mil y quinientos y setenta y cuatro para dar la jurisdicion y señalarla partio y quito mas de la mitad de los restrojos y todas las dehesas a la villa de Valenzuela y las dexo fuera de su jurisdicion de lo cual tiene suplicado esta villa y en ello recibe agravio porque esta privado de la juris- dicion que antes tenia hasta que su majestad mande otra cosa" ("Valenzuela," *Relaciones Ciudad Real*, p. 553).

39. "Las armas que esta villa tenia en su ayuntamiento antes que se vendiese figuraba por lo alto dos cabezas de aguilas con sus alas y una cruz de Calatrava y un castillo y el tuson como lo tiene la villa de Almagro e que despues que de señorio se derribo el ayuntamiento porque estaba viejo y de presente hacen otro y no se han puesto armas ningunas hasta agora" (ibid., p. 548).

40. "Este pueblo es de hasta ciento y sesenta vecinos y que cada uno vive en su casa por si y que cuando se vendio al dicho Diego Alfonso se le contaron mas de ciento y ochenta vecinos y el haberse disminuido ha sido que muchos se han ido del pueblo y otros se han muerto y otros no se quieren casar en este pueblo por ser de señorio" (ibid., p. 552).

41. See above, chap. 3.

42. "Perales," *Relaciones Madrid*, p. 438. This is the present Perales del Río, not to be confused with Perales de Tajuña, which does not appear in the *Relaciones*.

43. Ramón Esquer Torres, "Lugares de las cinco leguas: Madrid y sus aldeas," *Anales del Instituto de Estudios Madrileños* 5 (1970): 121–25.

44. "Campo Real," *Relaciones Madrid*, p. 140.

45. "En tiempo de los Catolicos Reyes don Fernando y doña Isabel, que estan en gloria, siendo señor de la villa de Alcobendas don Juan Arias de Avila tuvo necesidad de que el concejo de la dicha villa de Alcobendas saliese por su fiador de ciertos paños y sedas que saco fiado de ciertos mercaderes y el dicho concejo de la dicha villa de Alcobendas salio por su fiador. Llegado el plazo y no pagando el dicho don Juan Arias la deuda los mercaderes a quien se debia dieron a executar a el concejo de la dicha villa de Alcobendas ante la justicia de la villa de Madrid" ("San Sebastián de los Reyes," ibid., p. 574; the following account of events in San Sebastían is drawn from this source).

46. "Y como la villa de Alcobendas no tenga mas juridicion y termino de tan solamente el asiento del pueblo y todos los vecinos de la dicha villa de Alcobendas como martiniegueros que son a la dicha villa de Madrid y la pagan cierto tributo de martiniega en cada un año por razon de gozar los pastos con sus ganados de la dicha villa de Madrid y su tierra, tiniendo como tenian los dichos sus ganados en tierra de Madrid la justicia de la dicha villa de Madrid hizo entrega y execucion en los ganados de los vecinos de la dicha villa de Alcobendas por los maravedis que ansi se debian a los mercaderes, los cuales dichos ganados se depositaron en la dicha villa de Madrid. . . . Y visto por los señores de los dichos ganados que fueron Pedro Rodriguez el viejo y Martin Garcia y Andres Rodriguez y otros vecinos de la dicha villa de Alcobendas que tenian sus ganados depositados y que no los podian sacar sin pagar se juntaron y acordaron que diesen como dieron vecindad en la villa de Madrid, y se saliesen como salieron fuera del señorio y dominio del dicho don Juan Arias de Avila, señor de la dicha villa de Alcobendas" (p. 574).

47. "En el contorno de este dicho lugar hay la iglesia de Santa Maria de Dos Casas y Nuestra Señora de Mesones que son lugares despoblados y no saben certificadamente por que se despoblaron mas de que oyeron decir a sus antepasados que por grandes enfermedades se habian despoblado" (p. 572). "En el distrito y termino de este dicho lugar hay tres dezmerias de lugares despoblados, que la una se dice Doscasas y esta a la orilla del rio de Jarama una legua de este dicho lugar, y la otra se dice Mesones media legua de este dicho lugar, y la otra se dice Fuentidueña y en aquesta dezmeria esta la iglesia, que es una ermita muy devota, que se llama Nuestra Señora de la Paz, y estos tres pueblos se despoblaron por lo que se ha sabido de las personas antiguas en tiempo de peste puede haber noventa años. . . . Y hiciesen y fundasen este dicho lugar por estar en termino e juridicion

de la dicha villa de Madrid y por cierta dispusicion de podelles hacer en el sitio y asiento donde esta puesto y por estar en el dicho sitio una ermita que tenia por nombre San Sebastian fue dada la dicha vecindad en la dicha villa de Madrid y sacado sus ganados libremente como personas que ya no eran vasallos del dicho don Juan Arias de Avila comenzaron de hacer en este dicho sitio y asiento unas cabañas de retama y carrasca que en el dicho sitio habia y comenzaron de hacer su habitacion y morada en ellas" (p. 579).

48. "Que es tierra de labranza ordinaria que no es fertil, y ordinaria de ganados ovejuno y vacuno. . . . Los vecinos del dicho lugar gozan con sus ganados de todo el pasto comun de la dicha villa de Madrid y su tierra y el real de Manzanares libremente" (p. 570). "Los enmaderamientos de pino y saz se proveen de las sacedas que se han plantado de doce años a esta parte en la ribera del rio de Jarama" (p. 577).

49. "Esta dicha villa de Alcobendas tiene al presente hasta trescientos vecinos pocos mas o menos e que de mas de sesenta años a esta parte la dicha villa no ha crecido ni menguado el numero de los dichos trescientos vecinos en diez vecinos mas o menos" ("Alcobendas," *Relaciones Madrid*, p. 25).

50. "La gente del dicho lugar es la mayor parte de el muy pobre y necesitada porque no tienen granjerias ni tratos mas de ser jornaleros y labradores pobres porque los venados y caza del Pardo de Su Magestad les han puesto en mucha miseria y detrimento por comer como se han comido y comen el fruto de las heredades de pan y vino que es el fruto que en este lugar se acostumbra coxer y no tienen otros frutos ni granjerias" ("San Sebastián de los Reyes," ibid., p. 570).

51. "El primero honbre que en el se bautizo es vivo y se llama Sebastian Perdiguero el viejo, el cual es un hombre alto, enhiesto de cuerpo y rostro, que en todo este tiempo no se ha conocido haber tenido enfermedad ninguna hasta agora, que puede haber tres meses o cuatro que esta enfermo de un cuartanario y es de edad de mas de setenta y seis años y ha sido un hombre no regalado y del campo" (ibid., p. 575).

52. "En el dicho lugar hay una casa pobre donde los pobres se acogen, y Maria Marcos, mujer de Martin Garcia, doto a el dicho hospital hasta diez fanegas de tierras, que rentan un año con otro diez hanegas de pan por mitad trigo y cebada, y no tienen otro aprovechamiento ni renta mas de algunas limosnas de ropa para camas a los pobres" (ibid., p. 572).

53. William A. Christian, Jr., *Local Religion in Sixteenth-Century Spain* (Princeton, 1981).

54. "Agora nuevamente se ha hecho y edificado una iglesia en el dicho lugar donde primero estaba una ermita la cual se hizo y reedifico de limosnas en dos años que tiene noventa pies de largo y sesenta de ancho, que tiene cuerpo y dos naves, los pilares de piedra barroqueña y las vueltas de los arcos de ladrillo, todo de madera de Cuenca, y se ha adornado de cruz y manga y ciriales y palio para el Santisimo Sacramento, que todo ello se ha hecho dende a seis dias del mes de abril del año de setenta y seis hasta agora [23 Dec. 1579], que se ha gastado en ello mas de ocho mil ducados todo de limosnas" ("San Sebastián de los Reyes," *Relaciones Madrid*, pp. 577–78).

55. "Se fue . . . un vecino de este dicho lugar que se llamaba Portazguero solo a fin de comer carne en la dicha villa de Alcobendas el cual comio y ceno aquel dia en la dicha villa de Alcobendas, siendo venida la noche vino a este dicho lugar a su casa y se sento en una silla y hallo que su mujer y hijos y criados comian nabos guardando el voto hecho y les dixo a modo de hacer poca cuenta y escarnio

del voto que buenos se andaban comiendo sus nabos que el venia harto de comer carne y se quedo muerto en la dicha silla supitamente sin hablar mas palabra" (ibid., pp. 578–79).

Chapter 7: War and Taxes

1. García de Toledo to Philip II, in Cesáreo Fernández Duro, *Armada española desde la unión de los reinos de Castilla y de Aragón*, 9 vols. (Madrid, 1972–73), 2:413–15.

2. Francisco de Mendoza was the son of the viceroy Antonio de Mendoza and Catalina de Vargas. Francisco's paternal grandparents were the same count of Tendilla who was the lord of Miralcampo and the countess of Tendilla, Francisca Pacheco, sister of the marquis of Villena. His maternal grandparents were the royal treasurer Francisco de Vargas and María de Lago (on Francisco de Vargas as royal treasurer see María Antonia Varona García, *La chancillería de Valladolid en el reinado de los reyes católicos* [Valladolid, 1981], pp. 317–18).

3. Dionisio de Alcedo y Herrera, *Aviso histórico*, cited in Marcos Jiménez de Espada, "Antecedentes," *Relaciones geográficas de Indias: Perú*, 3 vols., BAE, 183–85 (Madrid, 1965), 183:271.

4. The second of Antonio's brothers, Bernardino de Mendoza (d. 1557), had made his naval career as galley commander and was then in Naples as lieutenant of the viceroy; Antonio's youngest brother, Diego Hurtado de Mendoza (1503–75), had recently returned to Castile in disgrace after years of service in Italy as the emperor's ambassador to Venice, the papacy, and the Council of Trent.

5. Commission and instruction to Mendoza, 26 Apr. 1556, printed in González, *Noticia histórica*, 1:205. As general administrator of the Guadalcanal mines, he received an annual salary of two thousand ducados.

6. Instruction to Torregrosa, 21 June 1556, in ibid.

7. Francisco de Mendoza to Francisco de Eraso, Valladolid, 26 Apr. 1557, AGS, Estado, Correspondencia de Castilla, no. 124, in ibid., 1:391–92.

8. The town meeting in which the royal commissioned judge, Antonio Alvarez de Zamudio, dismembered the town from the military order took place on January 19, 1560, but several complications in the financing of the transfer delayed full possession for two years (see AHN, Osuna, leg. 2010–3).

9. Ibid., leg. 2739.

10. Ibid., legs. 2003/8, 2739.

11. Deed of sale, Estremera and Valdaracete, 1562, ibid., leg. 3104/9. For the election of officials in Estremera, 1562, see ibid., leg. 2005/2/1; for resignations tendered by Estremera clerks to Francisco de Mendoza, 1561, see ibid., leg. 2005/8/1a-e.

12. "Instruction given by his majesty to don Juan de Mendoza, captain general of the Spanish galleys," San Quentin, 19 Aug. 1557. This and the documents for the following section on the western Mediterranean campaign are printed in "Sucesos marítimos desde 1547 hasta 1564 con las relaciones de las jornadas al Peñón de Vélez año 1563 y 1564, del sitio que puso el rey de Argel a Orán y Mazalquivir, socorro que introdujo en equella plaza don Francisco de Mendoza, y del cegamiento del Rio de Tetuán por don Alvaro Bazán," in Martín Fernández Navarrete, comp., *Colección de los viages y descubrimientos que hicieron por mar los españoles desde fines del siglo XV, con varios documentos inéditos concernientes a la historia de la marina castellana y de los establecimientos españoles en Indias*, 5 vols.

(Madrid, 1829–59; reprint, Buenos Aires, 1945–46), 4:343–433; and in Fernández Duro, *Armada española*, vol. 4.

13. Peter Pierson, *Philip II of Spain* (London, 1975), p. 152.

14. On November 10, 1561, Francisco's agents in Seville mortgaged another 3,600,000 maravedís of the seignorial income from Estremera and Valdaracete to Catalina de Mendoza, citizen of Panama and widow of Balthasar Díaz de Avila, at 8.33 percent, and on January 16, 1562, 1,500,000 maravedís to Juana de Ribera, widow of Hernando de Orejón. In January 1562 Francisco's agents in Seville, Pedro Luis de Torregrossa and three partners, borrowed 3,450,000 maravedís from Juan de Guzmán at an interest rate of 6.67 percent and used part of it to pay off the loan to the chapel, again assigning the seignorial income from the towns of Estremera and Valdaracete as security. Juan de Guzmán was a citizen of the city of Santiago de Guatemala, residing in Seville and acting as broker for several New World investors (Annuity on Estremera and Valdaracete, AHN, Osuna, leg. 2739).

15. The resounding triumph of Bernardino's career had been to save Charles's 1541 expedition against Algiers, including the duke of Alba, by moving the fleet to La Herradura. This incident is succinctly described in Maltby, *Alba*, p. 46.

16. Navarrete, *Colección de los viages*, 4:390; Fernández Duro, *Armada española*, 2:52–59; González, *Noticia histórica*, 2:93.

17. Navarrete, *Colección de los viages*, 4:397.

18. Phillips, *Ciudad Real*, 1500–1700, pp. 76–94.

19. "Este dicho lugar de San Pablo acude a la dicha cibdad de Toledo la que habla en cortes por el dicho lugar, y a la dicha cibdad acude a los repartimientos que se hicieren" ("San Pablo," *Relaciones Toledo*, 3:389).

20. "Hay opiniones que unos dicen cae en el reino de Aragón, y que ansí comunmente se dice estar en la Mancha de Aragón y casi de la raya de Sierra de Cuenca, otros ser del reino de Toledo" ("Iniesta," *Relaciones Cuenca*, p. 302).

21. "Al octavo capítulo dixeron que no lo saben" ("Albaladejo," *Relaciones Ciudad Real*, p. 3). "No se tiene claridad ni certinidad qué ciudad hable en cortes por la dicha villa, si es Toledo o Cuenca" ("Tarancón," *Relaciones Cuenca*, p. 499). "Cae este pueblo en el distrito de Cuenca y Huete e que las dichas ciudades, o cualquiera de ellas que tienen voto de hablar en corte, hablará por este pueblo" (ibid., "Valdeloso," pp. 546–47). "Entienden, pues esta villa entra en el reino de Toledo, Toledo hablara por el en los repartimientos que se le hicieren porque alli esta villa acude a pagar el servicio a Su Majestad perteneciente" ("Arenas," *Relaciones Ciudad Real*, p. 82). "No tiene voto en cortes Illescas, ni menos acude a ninguna parte a dar voto, y menos para tratar cosa alguna de las que le convengan y sus repartimientos el pueblo los hace sin junta de otro concejo" ("Illescas," *Relaciones Toledo*, 1:493).

22. "Para los repartimientos que en esta villa se hacen no se acude a parte alguna, sino que se hacen en ella, conforme a las cédulas que del Consejo de contaduría se traen, así en lo del pecho como en lo del alcabala, conforme a la costumbre que la villa tiene" ("Villaescusa de Haro," *Relaciones Cuenca*, p. 567; virtually the same statement appears in "Villarrubio," ibid., p. 613). "No tiene voto en cortes ni se sabe donde ha de acudir para las cosas que el capítulo dice, si a Toledo o a Cuenca" ("El Toboso," ibid., p. 517).

23. "En los repartimientos que esta villa hace que en la Corte o en Granada se provee por S[u] M[agestad] y por petición de procurador de esta villa" ("La Puebla de Almoradiel," *Relaciones Cuenca*, p. 419). "Por ella y las demas de su reino

habla Toledo y propone y negocia, y en lo tocante a repartimientos de alcabalas y servicios pertenecientes a Su Majestad se acude a encabezonar por alcabalas al Real Consejo de Hacienda, y a los servicios y pechos reales a la villa de Almagro" ("Almodóvar del Campo," *Relaciones Ciudad Real*, p. 65). "Al consejo de las Ordenes acude por sus repartimientos o al contador que está puesto para el efecto por S[u] M[agestad]" ("Santa Cruz de la Zarza," *Relaciones Cuenca*, p. 482).

24. Carande, *Carlos V y sus banqueros*, 2:520.

25. Salvador de Moxó accepted as self-evident these claims by royal attorneys and treated the private collection of the sales tax as if the lords were actually keeping the tax themselves (see Salvador de Moxó, "Los orígenes"; and the broader study of the sales tax by the same author, *La alcabala*). Discrepancies between seignorial account records and royal treasury accounts for the same tax, however, suggest that the matter may be less straightforward: that lords claimed as a seignorial prerogative the right to collect the royal taxes and keep a portion as a service fee, just as the monarchy kept the *tercias* on the tithe collection, or that high bidders paid a premium for winning the right to collect the tax and then recouped this expense by collecting more from the taxpayer town.

26. The treasury accounts for the sale of this tax collection were entered in the same ledgers as the accounts for the sale of township, i.e., the fifty-six legajos catalogued as "Ventas de lugares, alcabalas y oficios, 1541–1803," AGS, DGT, legs. 230–335.

27. During the summer and fall he operated a lumber camp in the forested mountains of Anguix; during the winter months he left the camp in the care of two forest rangers, who manufactured charcoal which the count sold in the city of Guadalajara.

28. "Relacion de la hazienda que vuestra señoria tiene en Extremadura," AHN, Osuna, leg. 469–40.

29. AHN, Osuna, leg. 469–5.

30. Ibid., leg. 469–6.

31. On the tax collection in 1579 see ibid., leg. 469–7; on the 1580 settlement see ibid., leg. 469–8.

32. Yun Casalilla, *Sobre la transición*, p. 230; see also Phillips, *Ciudad Real, 1500–1750*, p. 78.

33. For the three-year struggle between the monarchy and the Cortes that finally resulted in the tax increases of 1576 see Charles Jago, "Philip II and the Cortes of 1576," *Past and Present* 109 (1985): 24–43.

34. AHN, Osuna, leg. 469–9.

35. Ibid., leg. 469–58.

36. The Mondéjar contract and subsequent legal claims are contained in ibid., leg. 2268.

37. Ulloa, *Las rentas*.

38. AHN, Osuna, leg. 3788.

39. Phillips, *Ciudad Real, 1500–1750*, pp. 76–94.

40. "Son muchas las vejaciones y molestias que reciben los naturales destos Reynos que residen en los lugares que no tienen encavezadas las alcavalas y tercias, y los salarios y costas que elevan los administradores y ministros que tienen, con que se disminuye la becindad y el trato y comercio y respetivamente el valor de las dichas alcavalas y tercias por irse muchas personas a otros lugares que estan encavezados" (*Actas* 44:64).

41. "Y porque para conseguir el privilegio y separacion, villazgo y asignacion de termino que pretendeis es necesario mi consentimiento lo he tenido por bien,

pues todo lo referido no es en perjuicio mio, ni de mis subcesores" (AGS, DGT, leg. 310, fol. 34). "Se me ha suplicado por parte del dicho lugar sea servido de prestar mi consentimiento para con el ganar privilegio de Su Magestad y de su real consejo en camara para hacerse villa con jurisdicion civil y criminal, mero misto imperio que se han de usar y egercer las personas que para ello nombraren en primero de enero de cada un año asi para administrar justicia como para los demas oficios concegiles que son dos alcaldes ordinarios, dos regidores, un procurador general, mayordomo de posito y propios, alguacil maior, segund y en la forma que os acostumbra la dicha mi villa de Peñaranda y las demas de su partido y suelen haver, que es nombrando para cada uno de los dichos oficios dos personas que sean vecinos para que yo y mis subcesores podamos elegir y proveher en cada una de ellas la que mas aproposito y conveniente nos parezca para su egercicio" (ibid.).

42. "Por quanto estoy bien informado de los pleytos y diferencias que ha havido y hay entre la villa de Peñaranda y el lugar [de San Juan] jurisdicion de ella y de lo costoso que es el hir la justicia de la dicha villa hallarse a los inventarios almonedas y particiones de las personas que mueren en el dicho lugar en daño y perjuicio de los menores y obras pias que quedan fundadas y otros muchos inconvenientes que se estan experimentando" (ibid.).

43. "El unico remedio de todo es el separar y dividir el dicho lugar de la jurisdiccion civil y criminal de la dicha mi villa de Peñaranda . . . para que se eximirse de la dicha jurisdicion y se hiciese villa de por si y sobre si" (ibid.).

44. "Preciviendo vos el referido lugar de San Juan del Monte las fatales resultas que necesariamente havia de producir la nueva esclavitud que se os imponia con esta expecie de venta" (ibid.).

45. "No tubo efecto la dicha exempcion por cierta puja que la dicha villa hizo sirviendo a Su Magestad con maior cantidad de la que havia ofrecido el dicho lugar por su exempcion" (ibid.).

46. "Que la misma experiencia os acreditó mui brebe no eran vanos vuestros temores pues apenas se declaró y ejecutorió no haver lugar el tanteo intentado por vuestra parte quando comenzó la villa a trataros y a vuestros vecinos con cierto ayre de tiranía" (ibid.).

47. "Porque me haveis servido con tres mil quinientos y treinta ducados de vellon que haveis entregado en mi tesoreria general, por la presente de mi propio motu, cierta ciencia, y poderio real absoluto de que en esta parte quiero usar y uso como rey y señor natural, eximo, saco, y libero a vos el dicho lugar de San Juan del Monte de la jurisdicion de la expresada villa de Peñaranda y os hago villa de por si y sobre si" (ibid.).

Bibliography

The most abundant sources of information about the transformation from village to town come from the estate records of noble lords. A vast collection of these records survives in the Sección Osuna of the Archivo Histórico Nacional (AHN) and in the Colección Salazar y Castro of the Real Academia de la Historia (RAH). Partly because the library of the RAH has very restricted hours for public use and has been closed to the public during reconstruction during the past few years, the AHN collection proved to be more accessible. Manuscript and some printed materials in the Osuna section are numbered and tied into bundles, commonly known in Spanish archives as legajos. Extent of cataloguing varies. Sometimes one number is assigned to the entire legajo; in other cases a separate number stands for each individual document in the legajo or, alternatively, for each packet in the legajo, with or without a subsidiary number for each document within the packet. In citing these documents, I duplicate the numbers as they existed when I did my research, without trying to standardize them.

Without some insight into motives and objectives, even the most extensive accounts cannot illuminate town and village decisions. The documents that lend themselves to quantitative analysis—estate records, notarial registers, litigation records, and royal treasury accounts—record the consequences of the system but are not particularly revealing of how towns actually functioned internally and what motivated citizen decisions as the town developed. At first glance, it may seem that such information could not exist for the ordinary taxpayer, but Castile possesses a unique source of information gathered in the late sixteenth century: the *Relaciones topográficas* express the aspirations of the citizens in their own words. Philip II created the *Relaciones* in 1575 when he sent a questionnaire to the city, town, and village councils in the archdiocese of Toledo, which encompassed most of New Castile, La Mancha, and Extremadura and parts of the modern provinces of Cuenca, Jaén, and Albacete.

The 1575 questionnaire comprised fifty-seven questions and was followed in 1578 by a revised questionnaire of forty-five questions. The first three questions on the 1575 questionnaire (numbered 1, 3, and 4 in the 1578 revision) often elicited a spontaneous narrative of the community's history and ambitions. The first question asked the name of the town past and present. The second asked when the place had been settled and by whom. The third asked specifically whether it was a city, town, or village. If it was a city or town, how long had it enjoyed that status and by what authority? If it was a village, in which city or town jurisdiction did it lie? Question 7 (numbered 8 in 1578) asked who the lord or owner of the pueblo was, whether the king, a private lord, or one of the military orders or autonomous towns (*behetrías*); and why and when it had been alienated from the royal domain and come to belong to someone else. These pointed questions often evoked from the citizens of newly chartered towns tales of struggle, frustration, and victory. They provide an invaluable picture of local history in the words of the citizens themselves.

More than six hundred original, notarized responses to the *Relaciones* questionnaire are preserved in the library of the Escorial Palace, and an eighteenth-century copy exists in the library of the RAH in Madrid. The first *Relaciones* to be published were those from the towns and villages in the modern province of Guadalajara. The editor, Juan Catalina García López, performed an invaluable service to later historians by appending to each *Relación* an essay entitled "Aumentos," which incorporates the results of his own research in the relevant municipal archive and often includes long transcriptions of documents now lost. Although his *Relaciones* transcriptions relied on the eighteenth-century copies rather than the originals, his "Aumentos" were a remarkable accomplishment by a prolific, perceptive, and absolutely devoted historian of the province. Noël Salomon, the modern historian who has studied the whole corpus of original *Relaciones*, found that both the eighteenth-century copies and the transcriptions by Juan Catalina García were perfectly reliable except for minor lapses in spelling and punctuation. An archivist of the Escorial library, Julián Zarco y Cuevas, published transcriptions of the *Relaciones* for his home province of Cuenca, which have recently been corrected and revised in a new edition. The great bulk of the remaining *Relaciones*, for the modern provinces of Madrid, Toledo, and Ciudad Real, have been transcribed and published in recent years by Carmelo Viñas y Mey and Julián Paz. In citing the responses, I abbreviate the published title to the one word by which they were known in the sixteenth century—*Relaciones*—and the name of the modern province in the published title— *Madrid*, say, or *Guadalajara*—followed by the name of the municipality— "Almodóvar del Campo," for example—and volume and page numbers.

The number of responses to the *Relaciones* questionnaire is variously estimated to have been between 550 and 700. For reasons I have noted in appendix A, however, there are duplicate responses among the original and published responses. I believe that the published *Relaciones* comprise the responses from 528 cities, towns, and villages, and I estimate annual rates of change and total extent of change on this data set.

For the sale of towns outside the geographical scope of the *Relaciones*, the royal treasury kept regular ledgers to record the bids and payments. These royal treasury accounts are preserved in the Archivo General de Simancas (AGS). The appraisals are deposited in several sections of the archive, principally in Contaduría Mayor de Cuentas. The audited ledgers of completed sales eventually found their way into that section of the AGS known as the Dirección General del Tesoro (DGT) and are catalogued by place-names in its massive Inventario 24. Again, the numbering of legajos and folios depends on the nature of the documents themselves. Each folio contains a separate packet, usually comprising a single legal document ranging from two pages to hundreds of pages of manuscript or print. The entire documentation for the sale of Carrión de los Ajos, for example, is catalogued as a single folio, "Carrión de los Ajos: Asiento sobre su venta a Gonzalo de Céspedes," AGS, DGT, leg. 282, fol. 31.

For systematic accounts of local events the most informative sources are memoirs and records of litigation. One of the most engaging memoirs of the sixteenth century was written by Mathías Escudero, a citizen and town councilman of Almonacid de Zorita. His "Relación de casos memorables" attempts to chronicle all the events in Europe during his lifetime, including monstrous births and earthquakes, but is most satisfyingly detailed and pungent when describing the history of his own town. A more self-conscious history of the town of Horche was published in the eighteenth century by a native son, Juan de Talamanco, preserving in loving detail the particulars of local tradition. Both of these narrative sources were exploited by Juan Catalina García López, who possessed an admirable instinct for the telling detail.

For statements about the aspirations of lords, we are dependent on the fortuitous preservation of memoirs, letters, and legal briefs. The letters dictated by Iñigo López de Mendoza, second count of Tendilla, were recorded by his secretary in four bound legajos. Two legajos in the Biblioteca Nacional (BN), "Registro de cartas referentes al gobierno de las Alpujarras," Mss. 10230 and 10231, contain letters dictated in 1508–9 and 1510–13. These were transcribed and published by Emilio Meneses García as *Correspondencia del conde de Tendilla: Biografía, estudio y transcripción*. Two more legajos in the Osuna section of the AHN contain letters dictated in 1504–6 and 1513–15. The latter legajo also contains letters dictated by his eldest son, Luis, third count of Tendilla and second marquis of Mondéjar, from 1515 to 1518. These two legajos, never published, are catalogued as "Copiador de cartas por el marqués de Mondéjar," AHN, Osuna, legs. 3406, 3407. I cite the letters published in *Correspondencia* by addressee, date, and volume and page number. For letters in "Copiador," which was not paginated when the archive microfilmed it for me, I cite addressee and date.

Additional material for all levels of the society exists in city and town council minutes, in royal decrees and privileges preserved in municipal archives, and in litigation appealed to the royal appellate courts. In this book, I draw heavily from unpublished documents in the Granada city archives (Archivo Municipal, or GRAM), because the counts of Tendilla were Granada city councilmen. Their letters commenting on partisan maneuvering within the council meetings illuminate the rather dry official minutes (Actas), providing valuable insights into the procedures and vocabulary of Castilian municipal administration.

Most towns still preserve their town charters and royal privileges in the municipal archives—cupboards, trunks, and even suitcases—in the town hall. A few towns having a long tradition of litigation and record keeping can produce documents that go back to the twelfth century. Paradoxically, the oldest municipal archives reveal the least information about town formation, because places originally founded as towns did not have to litigate the issue. Their municipal archives filled up instead with records of litigation against other towns, annual bids for leases on the *propios*, and resolutions and actions of the town council. Villages, in contrast, did not accumulate municipal archives. Their municipal records were carried off for audit by the ruling town council and usually never returned, though once the village became a town, its records were its own to keep. Most municipal archives, in other words, contain records beginning at the time of township, whether the place was originally founded as a town or was elevated from village to town by royal grant or sale. Town records, therefore, have been used only sparingly here. To do justice to the archival riches of those towns that have the longest series and greatest volume of documentation would take up too much space without changing the conclusions, while events leading up to the granting of town charters either were not recorded by the village council or were not preserved by the ruling town.

The growth and decline of towns continues in the modern age, and each change affects how and where archives are preserved. Most towns lost their commercial character after the railroads changed Spain's transportation network in the nineteenth century, a devastating blow to the economic prosperity and civic life of most farm towns. Towns without thriving commerce have little call for municipal archives, though they strive with varying success to maintain the symbols of their former autonomy and prosperity. It is not unusual to find a town with a huge marketplace reduced to a population of seven or eight widows and widowers still keeping the plaza, fountains, and municipal laundry clean and beautiful. In Budia, where only one man still farms, the mayor and councilmen are stonemasons who travel widely to find building contracts and have recently restored the town's column of justice to its former elegance. The municipal archive is usually the last town symbol to go, and it is a poignant moment when the handful of citizens confess that their archive has been moved to the next town—the town from which their ancestors achieved liberty in the Habsburg centuries.

Actas de las Cortes de Castilla. 60 vols. Madrid, 1877–1974.
Alba, duque de [Fernando Alvarez de Toledo]. Correspondencia del duque de Alba con Felipe II y otros personajes sobre la conquista de Portugal en 1580 CODOIN, 32–35. Madrid, 1859.
Alenda y Mira, Jenaro. Relaciones de solemnidades y fiestas públicas de España. Madrid, 1903.
Alvarez-Laviada, Paulino. Chinchón histórico y diplomático hasta finalizar el siglo XV: Estudio crítico y documentado del municipio castellano medieval. Madrid, 1931.
Arcaz Pozo, Adrián. "La ordenanza de Colmenar Viejo (1575) como fuente de investigación para su historia local." Anales del Instituto de Estudios Madrileños 18 (1980): 513–24.
Arié, Rachel. España musulmana (siglos VIII–XV). Barcelona, 1982.
Arribas Arranz, Filemón. Un formulario documental del siglo XV de la cancillería real castellana. Valladolid, 1964.
Artola, Miguel. Antiguo régimen y revolución liberal. Barcelona, 1978.
Asenjo González, María. Segovia: La ciudad y su tierra a fines del medievo. Segovia, 1986.
Astarita, Carlos. "Estudio sobre el concejo medieval de la Extremadura castellano-leonés: Una propuesta para resolver la problemática." Hispania 42 (1982): 355–413.
Atienza Hernández, Ignacio. "El poder real en el siglo XV: Lectura crítica de los documentos de donación de villas y lugares. La formación de los estados de Osuna." Revista Internacional de Sociología, 2d ser. 48 (1983): 557–91.
Atlas Nacional de España. Mapa de base municipal: Límites de término municipal puestos al día por el Servicio de Deslindes del Instituto Geográfico y Catastral hasta 12 de mayo 1972. Madrid, 1972.
Ayusa y de Iriarte, F. D. de. Fundación, excelencias y grandezas y cosas memorables de la antiquísima ciudad de Huesca. Introduction by F. Balaguer Sánchez. 5 vols. 1619. Facsimile ed. Huesca, 1987.
Aznar Vallejo, Eduardo. La integración de las Islas Canarias en la Corona de Castilla 1478–1526): Aspectos administrativos, sociales y económicos. Madrid, 1983.
Baeza, Pedro de. "Carta que Pedro de Baeza escrivió a el marques de Villena sobre que le pidió un memorial de lo que por el avia fecho." Documentos relativos al reinado de Enrique IV. MHE, 5:485–510. Madrid, 1853.
Bejarano Robles, Francisco. Los repartimientos de Málaga. Málaga, 1985.
[Bellugae Valentini, Petri.] Speculum Primcipum ad Alphonsium Siciliae et Aragoniae regem. [1439.] Antwerp, 1657.
Bennassar, Bartolomé. Un siècle d'or espagnole. Paris, 1982.
———. Valladolid au siècle d'or: Une ville de Castille et sa campagne au XVIe siècle. Paris, 1967.
Bermúdez Aznar, Agustín. El corregidor en Castilla durante la baja edad media, 1348–1474. Murcia, 1974.
Bermúdez de Pedraza, Francisco. Antigüedad y excelencias de Granada. Madrid, 1608.
———. Historia eclesiástica, principios y progressos de la ciudad, y religión católica de Granada, corona de su poderoso reyno y excelencias de su corona. Granada, 1638.
Bernáldez, Andrés. Memorias del reinado de los reyes católicos. Edited by Manuel Gómez-Moreno and Juan de Mata Carriazo. Madrid, 1962.
Bernaldo de Quirós, Constancio. La picota: Crímenes y castigos en el país castellano en los tiempos medios. Madrid, 1907. Reprint. Madrid, 1975.

Blázquez y Delgado-Aguilera, Antonio. "El itinerario de don Fernando Colón y las relaciones topográficas." *Revista de Archivos, Bibliotecas y Museos* 10 (1904): 83–105.

Blum, Jerome. "The Internal Structure and Polity of the European Village Community from the Fifteenth to the Nineteenth Century." *Journal of Modern History* 43, no. 4 (1971): 541–76.

Borah, Woodrow W. *Justice by Insurance: The General Indian Court of Colonial Mexico and the Legal Aides of the Half-Real.* Berkeley, 1983.

Braudel, Fernand. *The Mediterranean and the Mediterranean World in the Age of Philip II.* Translated by Sian Reynolds. 2 vols. New York, 1975.

Brumont, Francis. *La Bureba à l'époque de Philippe II: Essai d'histoire rurale quantitative.* New York, 1977.

Cabrera Muñoz, Emilio. *El condado de Belalcázar (1444–1518): Aportación al estudio del régimen señorial en la baja edad media.* Cordoba, 1977.

Cabrillana, Nicolás. "Los despoblados en Castilla la Vieja." *Hispania* 31 (1971): 485–550.

———. "Villages désertés en Espagne." In *Villages désertés et histoire économique XI–XVIII siècle,* edited by Georges Duby, pp. 461–512. Paris, 1965.

Calero Amor, Antonio María. *La división provincial de 1833: Bases y antecedentes.* Madrid, 1987.

Cam, Helen M. "The Community of the Vill." In *Medieval Studies Presented to Rose Graham,* edited by V. Ruffen and A. J. Taylor, pp. 1–14. Oxford, 1950.

Campos y Fernández de Sevilla, F. Javier. *La mentalidad en Castilla la Nueva en el siglo XV: Religión, economía y sociedad según las 'Relaciones topográficas' de Felipe II.* Madrid, 1986.

Capítulos de corregidores de 1500. Facsimile of the incunable in the Biblioteca Colombina, Seville. Edited by Antonio Muro Orejón. Seville, 1963.

Capuano, Thomas. "Vignettes of Daily Life in Alonso de Herrera's *Agricultura general.*" Paper presented at the annual meeting of the Sixteenth Century Studies Conference, St. Louis, October 1988.

Carande, Ramón. *Carlos V y sus banqueros: La hacienda real de Castilla.* 2d ed. 3 vols. Madrid, 1965–68.

———. *Sevilla, fortaleza y mercado: Las tierras, las gentes y la administración de la ciudad en el siglo XIV.* 2d ed. Seville, 1975.

Carlé, María del Carmen. *Del concejo medieval castellano-leonés.* Buenos Aires, 1968.

Caro Baroja, Julio. *Los Moriscos del Reino de Granada.* Madrid, 1957.

Carretero Zamora, Juan Manuel. *Cortes, monarquía, ciudades: Las Cortes de Castilla a comienzos de la época moderna (1476–1515).* Madrid, 1988.

Casado, Hilario. *Señores, mercaderes y campesinos: La comarca de Burgos a fines de la edad media.* Valladolid, 1987.

Casas Torres, José Manuel. *España: Atlas e índices de sus términos municipales.* 2 vols. Madrid, 1969.

Castillo, Julián del. *Historia de los Reyes Godos que vinieron de la Scythia . . . a España . . . hasta los Católicos Reyes D. Fernando y Da Isabel . . con adiciones hasta Felipe III hechas por Fr. Gerónimo de Castro Castillo, hijo del autor.* Madrid, 1624.

Castillo de Bobadilla, Jerónimo. *Política para corregidores y señores de vasallos.* Madrid, 1597. Antwerp, 1704. Facsimile. Madrid, 1978.

Cavillac, Michel. Introduction to *Amparo de pobres,* by Cristóbal Pérez de Herrera [1598]. Madrid, 1975.

Ceballos, Jerónimo de. *Arte real para el buen govierno de los reyes y príncipes y de sus vasallos.* Toledo, 1623.

Cepeda Adán, Jose. "Desamortizaciones de tierras de las Ordenes Militares en el reinado de Carlos I." *Hispania* 40 (1980): 487–528.

Cervera Vera, Luis. *La villa de Lerma en el siglo y sus ordenanzas de 1594.* Burgos, 1976.

Chalmeta, Pedro. *El "señor del zoco" en España: edades media y moderna. Contribución al estudio de la historia del mercado.* Madrid, 1973.

Chamberlain, Robert S. "La controversia Velázquez-Cortés sobre la gobernación de la Nueva España, 1519–1522." *Anales de la Sociedad de Geografía e Historia de Guatemala* 19 (1943): 23–56.

Christian, William A., Jr. *Local Religion in Sixteenth-Century Spain.* Princeton, 1981.

Cline, Howard F. "The Relaciones geográficas of the Spanish Indies, 1577–1648." In *Guide to Ethnohistorical Sources,* edited by Howard F. Cline, pp. 184–242. Vol. 12, pt. 1, of *Handbook of Middle American Indians,* general editor R. Wauchope. Austin, 1972.

Cohn, Henry J. "Church Property in the German Protestant Principalities." In *Politics and Society in Reformation Europe: Essays for Sir Geoffrey Elton on his Sixty-fifth Birthday,* edited by E. I. Kouri and Tom Scott, pp. 158–87. London, 1987.

Colección de documentos inéditos del Archivo de Indias [title varies]. Edited by Joaquín F. Pacheco, Francisco de Cárdenas, and Luis Torres de Mendoza. 42 vols. Madrid, 1864–84.

Colección de fueros municipales y cartas pueblas de los reinos de Castilla, León, corona de Aragón y Navarra. Edited by Tomás Muñoz y Romero. Madrid, 1847.

Collantes de Terán, Antonio. *Sevilla en la baja edad media: La ciudad y sus hombres.* Seville, 1977.

Columbus, Christopher. *Libro de los privilegios del almirante don Cristóbal Colón (1498).* Edited and translated by Ciriaco Pérez-Bustamante. Madrid, 1951.

Constitución española. Madrid, 1978.

Corchado Soriano, Manuel. *La orden de Calatrava y su campo.* 3 vols. Ciudad Real, 1984.

Cortés, Hernando. *Hernán Cortés: Letters from Mexico.* Translated by Anthony Pagden. 2d ed. New Haven, 1986.

Cortes de los antiguos reinos de León y Castilla. 5 vols. Madrid, 1861–1903.

Cuartas Rivero, Margarita. "La venta de oficios públicos en Catilla-León en el siglo XVI." *Hispania* 44 (1984): 495–516.

Davidson, D. M. "Negro Slave Control and Resistance in Colonial Mexico, 1519–1650." *Hispanic American Historical Review* 46 (1966): 235–53.

Díaz del Castillo, Bernal. *Historia verdadera de la conquista de la Nueva España.* 5th ed. 2 vols. Mexico City, 1960.

Diccionario de historia eclesiástica de España. Edited by Quintín Aldea Vaquero, Tomás Marín Martínez, and José Vives Gatell. 4 vols. Madrid, 1972–75.

Dillard, Heath. *Daughters of the Reconquest: Women in Castilian Town Society, 1100–1300.* Cambridge, 1984.

Documentos del archivo general de la villa de Madrid. Edited by Timoteo Domingo Palacio. 5 vols. Madrid, 1888–1932.

Domínguez Compañy, Francisco. *Ordenanzas municipales hispanoamericanas.* Madrid, 1982.

———. *Política de poblamiento de España en América: La fundación de ciudades.* Madrid, 1984.

Domínguez Ortiz, Antonio. *Alteraciones andaluzas.* Madrid, 1972.

———. "La población del reino de Sevilla en 1534." *Cuadernos de Historia* 7 (1974): 337–55.

———. *Política fiscal y cambio social en la España del siglo XVII.* Madrid, 1984.

———. *Política y hacienda de Felipe IV.* Madrid, 1960.

———. *La sociedad española en el siglo XVII.* 2 vols. Madrid, 1963–70.

———. *La sociedad española en el siglo XVIII.* Madrid, 1955.

———. "La venta de cargos y oficios públicos en Castilla y sus consecuencias económicas y sociales." *Anuario de Historia Económica y Social* 3 (1970): 105–37.

———. "Ventas y exenciones de lugares durante el reinado de Felipe IV." *Anuario de Historia del Derecho Español* 34 (1964): 163–207.

Elliott, John H. *The Count-Duke of Olivares: The Statesman in an Age of Decline.* New Haven, 1986.

———. *Imperial Spain, 1469–1716.* London, 1963.

Elliott, John H., and José Francisco de la Peña. *Memoriales y cartas del conde duque de Olivares.* 2 vols. Madrid, 1978.

Elton, G. R. *England under the Tudors.* 2d ed. Cambridge, 1974.

Escudero, Mathías. "Relación de casos notables que an sucedido en diversas partes de la Christianidad, especialmente en España . . . con algunas cosas que sucedieron en la tierra del auctor." Biblioteca Pública, Toledo. MS 64.

España dividida en provincias e intendencias y subdividida en partidos. Madrid, 1789.

Esquer Torres, Ramón. "Lugares de las cinco leguas: Madrid y sus aldeas." *Anales del Instituto de Estudios Madrileños* 5 (1970): 121–25.

Estow, Clara. "The Economic Development of the Order of Calatrava, 1158–1366." *Speculum* 57 (1982): 267–91.

Fábila, Manuel. *Cinco siglos de legislación agraria, 1493–1940.* Mexico City, 1941.

Falcón Pérez, María Isabel. *Organización municipal de Zaragoza en el siglo XV.* Zaragoza, 1978.

Fernández de Oviedo y Valdés, Gonazalo. *Las quinquagenas de la nobleza de España.* Madrid, 1880.

Fernández Duro, Cesáreo. *Armada española desde la unión de los reinos de Castilla y de Aragón.* 9 vols. Madrid, 1972–73. Vols. 2 and 4.

Fernández Izquierdo, Francisco. "Las ventas de bienes de las órdenes militares en el siglo XVI como fuente para el estudio del régimen señorial: La Provincia de Calatrava de Zorita." *Hispania* 42 (1982): 419–62.

Fernández Izquierdo, Francisco, María Teresa Santos Carrascosa, and María Angeles Yuste Martínez, eds. "Catálogo del Archivo Municipal de Almonacid de Zorita (Guadalajara), siglos XIII–XIX." *Wad-al-Hayara* 8 (1981): 85–214.

Fernández Martín, Pedro. "Las ventas de las villas y lugares de behetría y su repercusión en la vida económico-social de los pueblos y de Castilla." *Anuario de Historia Económica y Social* 1 (1968): 261–80.

Font Ríus, José María. "Les villes dans l'Espagne du moyen age: Histoire de leurs institutions administratives et judiciaires." In *Recueils de la Société Jean Bodin pour l'Histoire Comparative des Institutions,* vol. 6, *La ville,* pt. 1, pp. 263–95. Brussels, 1954.

———. *Orígenes del régimen municipal en Cataluña.* Madrid, 1946.

Fortea Pérez, José Ignacio. *Córdoba en el siglo XVI: Las bases demográficas y económicas de una expansión urbana.* Cordoba, 1981.

Fuero de Baeza. Edited by Jean Roudil. Utrecht, 1962.

Fuero de Zorita de los Canes, según el códice 217 de la Biblioteca Nacional (siglo XIII al XIV): Sus relaciones con el fuero latino de Cuenca y el romanceado de Alcázar. MHE, 44. Edited by Rafael de Ureña y Smenjaud. Madrid, 1911.

Gallardo, Francisco. Origen, progresos y estado de las rentas de la Corona de España. 7 vols. Madrid, 1805–8.

Gámir Sandoval, Alfonso. "Las 'fardas' para la costa granadina (siglo XVI)." In Carlos V (1500–1558): Homenaje de la Universidad de Granada, edited by Antonio Gallego Morell, pp. 293–330. Granada, 1958.

——. "Las fortificaciones costeras del Reino de Granada al occidente de la ciudad de Málaga hasta el Campo de Gibraltar." Miscelánea de Estudios Árabes y Hebraicos 9, no. 9 (1960): 135–56.

——. "Organización de la defensa de la costa del reino de Granada desde su reconquista hasta finales del siglo XVI." Boletín de la Universidad de Granada 73 (1943): 259–337.

García de Cortázar y Ruiz de Aguirre, J. A. La historia rural medieval: Un esquema del análisis estructural de sus contenidos a través del ejemplo hispanocristiano. Santander, 1982.

García Fernández, Jesús. "Horche." Estudios Geográficos 14 (1953): 198–237.

García López, Juan Catalina. Biblioteca de escritores de la provincia de Guadalajara y bibliografía de la misma hasta el siglo XIX. Madrid, 1899.

——. El libro de la provincia de Guadalajara. Guadalajara, 1881.

——. La Alcarria en los dos primeros siglos de su reconquista. Guadalajara, 1973.

Garçon, Maurice. "Les tribulations des hermaphrodites." Histoire de la Médecine (Paris) 12, no. 2 (1962).

Garrigós, Eduardo. "Organización territorial a fines del antiguo régimen." In Instituciones, edited by Miguel Artola, pp. 1–105. Vol. 4 of La economía española a fines del antiguo régimen, edited by Gonzalo Anes. Madrid, 1982.

Gautier-Dalché, Jean. Historia urbana de León y Castilla en la edad media (siglos IX–XIII). Madrid, 1979.

Gerbert, Marie-Claude. La noblesse dans le royaume de Castille: Etude sur ses structures sociales en Estrémadure, 1454–1516. Paris, 1979.

Gibert, Rafael. El concejo de Madrid: Su organización en los siglos XII a XV. Madrid, 1949.

——. "La condición de los extranjeros en el antiguo derecho español." In Recueils de la Société Jean Bodin pour l'Histoire Comparative des Institutions, vol. 10, L'étranger, pp. 158–68. Brussels, 1958.

——. "Libertades urbanas y rurales en León y Castilla durante la edad media." In Les libertés urbaines et rurales du XI au XIVe siècle, pp. 187–218. Collection histoire, 19. Paris, 1968.

Giménez Fernández, Manuel. "Hernán Cortés y su revolución comunera en la Nueva España." Anuario de Estudios Americanos 5 (1948): 1–144.

González, Julio. "Reconquista y repoblación de Castilla, León, Extremadura y Andalucía (siglos XI a XIII)." In La reconquista española y la repoblación del país, pp. 163–206. Zaragoza, 1951.

——. Repoblación de Castilla la Nueva. 2 vols. Madrid, 1975–76.

González, Tomás. Censo de población de las provincias y partidos de la corona de Castilla en el siglo XVI con varios apéndices para completar lá del resto de la península en el mismo siglo. Madrid, 1829.

——. Noticia histórica documentada de las célebres minas de Guadalcanal desde su descubrimiento en el año de 1555, hasta que dejaron de labrarse por cuenta de la real hacienda. 2 vols. Madrid, 1831.

González Herrero, Manuel. *Segovia: Pueblo, ciudad y tierra: Horizonte histórico de una patria.* Segovia, 1971.

González Jiménez, Manuel, and Antonio González Gómez, eds. *Libro del repartiiento de Jerez de la Frontera.* Cádiz, 1980.

González Palencia, Angel, and Eugenio Mele, eds. *Vida y obras de don Diego Hurtado de Mendoza.* 3 vols. Madrid, 1941–43.

Gorges, Jean-Gérard. *Les villas hispano-romaines: Inventaire et problématique archéologique.* Paris, 1979.

Gounon-Loubens, M.-J. *Essais sur l'administration de la Castille au XVIe siècle.* Paris, 1860.

Grice-Hutchinson, Marjorie. *Early Economic Thought in Spain, 1177–1740.* London, 1978.

Grupo '77. *La legislación del antiguo régimen.* Salamanca, 1982.

Guaita, Aurelio. "La división provincial y sus modificaciones." In *3° Symposio Historia de la Administración (Alcalá de Henares, 1972),* pp. 309–52. Madrid, 1974.

Guilarte, Alfonso María. *El régimen señorial en el siglo XVI.* Madrid, 1962.

Guillamón, Javier. *Las reformas de la administración local durante el reinado de Carlos III.* Madrid, 1980.

Gutiérrez de Salinas, Diego. *Discursos del pan y del vino del niño Jesús.* Alcalá, 1600.

Hampe Martínez, Teodoro. "Agustín de Zárate: Precisiones en torno a la vida y obra de un cronista indiano." *Caravelle (Cahiers du monde hispanique et lusobresilien)* 45 (1985): 21–36.

———. "La misión financiera de Agustín de Zárate, Contador General del Perú y Tierra Firme (1543–1546)." *Ibero-Amerikanisches Archiv* 12, no. 1 (1986): 1–26.

Hernández Montalbán, Francisco J. "La cuestión de los señoríos en el proceso revolucionario burgués: El Trienio Liberal." In *Estudios sobre la revolución burguesa en España,* by Bartolomé Clavero, Pedro Ruiz Torres, and Francisco J. Hernández Montalbán, pp. 113–58. Madrid, 1979.

Herrera, Gabriel Alonso de. *Obra de agricultura.* Edited by José Urbano Martínez Carreras. BAE, 235. Madrid, 1970.

Herrera García, Antonio. *El Aljarafe sevillano durante el antiguo régimen: Un estudio de su evolución socioeconómica en los siglos XVI, XVII, y XVIII.* Seville, 1980.

Hinojosa, Eduardo. *Origen del régimen municipal en León y Castilla: Estudios de historia del derecho español.* Madrid, 1903.

———. *El régimen señorial y la cuestión agraria en Cataluña durante la edad media.* Madrid, 1905.

Ibáñez de Segovia, Gaspar [marqués de Mondéjar]. "Historia de la casa de Mondéjar; y sucesión de la Baronía de Moncada." BN. Ms. 3315.

Ibn Khaldun. *The Muqaddimah: An Introduction to History.* Translated by Franz Rosenthal. 3 vols. New York, 1958.

Incarnato, Gennaro. "L'evoluzione del possesso feudale in Abruzzo Ultra dal 1500 al 1670." *Archivio Storico per le Province Napoletane* 89 (1971): 221–87.

Infante-Galán, Juan. *Los Céspedes y su señorío de Carrión, 1253–1874.* Seville, 1970.

Jago, Charles. "Habsburg Absolutism and the Cortes of Castile." *American Historical Review* 86 (1981): 307–26.

———. "Philip II and the Cortes of 1576." *Past and Present* 109 (1985): 24–43.

Jiménez de Espada, Marcos. *Relaciones geográficas de Indias: Perú*. 3 vols. BAE, 183–85. Madrid, 1965.

Jiménez de Gregorio, Fernando. *Diccionario de los pueblos de la provincia de Toledo hasta finalizar el siglo XVIII*. 5 vols. Toledo, 1962–83.

——. "La población en la zona sur-occidental de los Montes de Toledo." *Estudios Geográficos* 94 (1964): 51–88; 98 (1965): 85–126; 104 (1966): 451–94; 108 (1967): 319–56.

——. "Notas geográfico-históricas de los pueblos de la actual provincia de Madrid en el siglo XVIII." *Anales del Instituto de Estudios Madrileños* 2 (1967): 275–90; 4 (1969): 247–66; 5 (1970): 125–42, 277–301; 6 (1970): 397–416; 7 (1971): 313–32; 8 (1972): 279–308; 9 (1973): 357–448; 11 (1975): 89–122; 13 (1976): 129–52; 14 (1977): 261–86.

Jover, J. M. *Carlos V y los Españoles*. Madrid, 1963.

Kagan, Richard L. *Lawsuits and Litigants in Castile, 1500–1700*. Chapel Hill, 1981.

Kamen, Henry. *Spain in the Later Seventeenth Century, 1665–1700*. London, 1980.

Kellenbenz, Herman. "El valor de las rentas de las encomiendas de la Orden de Calatrava en 1523 y en 1573." *Anuario de Historia Económica y Social* 1 (1968): 584–98.

Kirshner, Julius. "*Civitas Sibi Faciat Civem*: Bartolus of Sassoferrato's Doctrine on the Making of a Citizen." *Speculum* 48 (1973): 694–713.

——. "Paolo di Castro on 'Cives ex Privilegio': A Controversy over the Legal Qualifications for Public Office in Fifteenth-Century Florence." In *Renaissance Studies in Honor of Hans Baron*, edited by A. Molho and J. Tedeschi, pp. 227–64. DeKalb, Ill., 1971.

Konetzke, Richard. "Hernán Cortés como poblador de la Nueva España." *Revista de Indias* 9 (1948): 341–81.

Lacarra, José María. "Fuero de Estella." *Anuario de Historia del Derecho Español* 4 (1927): 404–51.

——. "Ordenanzas municipales de Estella, siglos XIII y XIV." *Anuario de Historia del Derecho Español* 5 (1928): 434–45.

——. *Panorama de la historia urbana en la Península Ibérica*. Spoleto, 1958.

——. "Para el estudio del municipio navarro medieval." *Príncipe de Viana* 3 (1941): 50–65.

Ladero Quesada, Miguel Angel. "El poder central y las ciudades en España del siglo XIV al final del Antiguo Régimen." *Revista de Administración Pública* 94 (1981): 173–98.

——. *El siglo XV en Castilla: Fuentes de renta y política fiscal*. Barcelona, 1982.

——. *España en 1492*. Historia de América Latina: Hechos, Documentos, Polémica, 1. Madrid, 1978.

——. *Granada después de la conquista: Repobladores y mudéjares*. Granada, 1988.

——. "La hacienda castellana de los Reyes Católicos, 1493–1504." *Moneda y Crédito* 103 (1967): 81–112.

——. "La repoblación del reino de Granada anterior al año 1500." *Hispania* 28 (1968): 489–563.

——. "Les finances royales de Castille à la veille des temps modernes." *Annales: Economies, Sociétés, Civilisations* 25 (1970): 775–88.

Layna Serrano, Francisco. *Historia de Guadalajara y sus Mendozas en los siglos XV y XVI*. 3 vols. Madrid, 1942.

Leveau, Philippe. "La ville antique et l'organisation de l'espace rural: *villa*, ville, village." *Annales: Economies, Sociétés, Civilisations* 38 (1983): 920–42.

Lockhart, James. *Men of Cajamarca: A Social and Biographical Study of the First Conquerors of Peru.* Austin, 1972.

Lomax, Derek W. *La Orden de Santiago (1170–1275).* Madrid, 1965.

———. *The Reconquest of Spain.* New York, 1978.

Lombardi, John V. *People and Places in Colonial Venezuela.* Bloomington, 1976.

López de Velasco, Juan. "Memorial de Juan López de Velasco, Madrid, October 26, 1583." In *Bibliografía madrileña, ó descripción de las obras impresas en Madrid,* edited by Cristóbal Pérez Pastor, 3:422. Madrid, 1907.

López Díaz, María Isabel. "Las desmembraciones eclesiásticas de 1574 a 1579." *Moneda y Crédito* 129 (1974): 135–52.

López Martínez, Nicolás. "La desamortización de bienes eclesiásticos en 1574." *Hispania* 86 (1962): 230–50.

Lorente Toledo, Enrique. *Gobierno y administración de la ciudad de Toledo y su término en la segunda mitad del siglo XVI.* Toledo, 1982.

Lunenfeld, Marvin. *Keepers of the City: The Corregidores of Isabella I of Castile (1474–1504).* Cambridge, 1987.

McAlister, Lyle N. *Spain and Portugal in the New World, 1492–1700.* Minneapolis, 1984.

MacKay, Angus. "Ciudad y campo en la Europa medieval." *Studia Historica* 2, no. 2 (1984): 27–33. Reprinted in MacKay, *Society, Economy and Religion in Late Medieval Castile.* London, 1987.

Madoz, Pascual, ed. *Diccionario geográfico-estadístico-histórico de España y sus posesiones de ultramar.* 16 vols. Madrid, 1845–50. Reprint. Madrid, 1959.

Maltby, William S. *Alba: A Biography of Fernando Alvarez de Toledo, Third Duke of Alba, 1507–1582.* Berkeley and Los Angeles, 1983.

Manning, Roger B. "Rural Societies in Early Modern Europe." *Sixteenth Century Journal* 17 (1986): 353–60.

Manual of Spanish Constitutions, 1808–1931. Translated and introduced by Arnold R. Verduin. Ypsilanti, Mich., 1941.

Manzano Manzano, Juan. *Cristóbal Colón: Siete años decisivos de su vida, 1485–1492.* Madrid, 1964.

Marcos González, María Dolores. *Castilla la Nueva y Extremadura.* 1971. Fasc. 6 of *La España del antiguo régimen,* edited by Miguel Artola. Salamanca, 1966.

Martín, José Luis. *Orígenes de la orden militar de Santiago (1170–1195).* Barcelona, 1974.

Martínez Añibarro y Rives, Manuel. *Intento de un diccionario biográfico y bibliográfico de autores de la provincia de Burgos.* Madrid, 1889.

Martínez Díez, Gonzalo. "Génesis histórica de las provincias españolas." *Anuario de Historia del Derecho Español* 51 (1981): 523–93.

———. *Las comunidades de villa y tierra de la Extremadura castellana: Estudio histórico-geográfico.* Madrid, 1983.

Martz, Linda. *Poverty and Welfare in Habsburg Spain: The Example of Toledo.* Cambridge, 1983.

Matilla Tascón, Antonio, ed. *Declaratorias de los reyes católicos sobre reducción de juros y otras mercedes.* Madrid, 1952.

Melón, Amando. "De la división de Floridablanca a la de 1833." *Estudios Geográficos* 71 (1958): 173–320.

———. "Inmediata génesis de las provincias españolas." *Anuario de Historia del Derecho Español* 27–28 (1957–58): 17–59.

———. "Provincias e intendencias en la peninsular España del XVIII." *Estudios Geográficos* 92 (1963): 287–310.

Menéndez González, Alfonso. "La desamortización eclesiástica en Asturias en la época de Felipe II." *Instituto de Estudios Asturianos* 37, nos. 109–10 (1983): 489–515; 38, no. 111 (1984): 55–79.

———. "La venta de oficios públicos en Asturias en los siglos XVI y XVII." *Instituto de Estudios Asturianos* 38, no. 112 (1984): 678–707.

Miguélez, Manuel. *Catálogo de los códices españoles de la biblioteca del Escorial. I: Relaciones histórico-geográficas de los pueblos de España, 1574–1581.* Madrid, 1917.

Mills, Patti A. "Financial Reporting and Stewardship Accounting in Sixteenth-Century Spain." *Accounting Historians Journal* 13, no. 2 (1986): 65–76.

Molénat, Jean-Pierre. "Tolède et ses finages au temps des rois catholiques: Contribution à l'histoire social et économique de la cité avant la révolte des comunidades." *Mélanges de la Casa de Velázquez* 8 (1972): 327–77.

Molinié-Bertrand, Annie. "La 'villa' de Linares en la segunda mitad del siglo XVI: Estudio demográfico y socio-económico, según el censo de 1586." *Cuadernos de Investigación Histórica* 2 (1978): 387–99.

Morales Arrizabalaga, Jesús. *La derogación de los fueros de Aragón (1707–1711).* Colección de estudios altoaragoneses, 8. Huesca, 1986.

Morison, Samuel Eliot. "The Earliest Colonial Policy toward America: That of Columbus." *Bulletin of the Pan American Union* 76, no. 10 (1942): 543–55.

Moxó, Salvador de. "El señorío, legado medieval." *Cuadernos de Historia* 1 (1967): 105–18.

———. *La alcabala: Sobre sus orígines, concepto y naturaleza.* Madrid, 1963.

———. *La disolución del régimen señorial en España.* Madrid, 1965.

———. *La incorporación de señoríos en la España del antiguo régimen.* Valladolid, 1959.

———. "La nobleza castellana en el siglo XIV." In *La investigación de la historia hispánica del siglo XIV: Problemas y cuestiones.* Barcelona, 1973.

———. "Las desamortizaciones eclesiásticas del siglo XVI." *Anuario de Historia del Derecho Español* 31 (1961): 327–61.

———. *Los antiguos señoríos de Toledo.* Toledo, 1973.

———. "Los orígenes de la percepción de alcabalas por particulares." *Hispania* 72 (1958): 307–39.

———. "Los señoríos: En torno a una problemática para el estudio del régimen señorial." *Hispania* 24 (1964): 185–236, 399–430.

———. "Sociedad, estado y feudalismo." *Revista de la Universidad de Madrid* 20, no. 78 (1971): 171–202.

Muro Orejón, Antonio, Florentino Pérez-Embid, and Francisco Morales Padrón, eds. *Pleitos colombinos.* Vol. 1, *Proceso hasta la sentencia de Sevilla (1511).* Seville, 1967.

Nader, Helen. *The Mendoza Family in the Spanish Renaissance, 1350–1550.* New Brunswick, N.J., 1980.

———. "Noble Income in Sixteenth-Century Castile: The Case of the Marquises of Mondéjar, 1480 to 1580." *Economic History Review*, 2d ser. 30 (1977): 411–28.

Naranjo Alonso, Clodoaldo. *Solar de conquistadores: Trujillo, sus hijos y monumentos.* Serradilla (Cáceres), 1929.

Navarrete, Martín Fernández, comp. *Colección de los viages y descubrimientos que hicieron por mar los españoles desde fines del siglo XV, con varios documentos inéditos concernientes a la historia de la marina castellana y de los establecimientos españoles en Indias.* 5 vols. Madrid, 1829–59. Reprint. Buenos Aires, 1945–46. Vol. 4:

Nomenclátor; o diccionario de las ciudades, villas, lugares, aldeas, granjas, cotos redondos, etc. Madrid, 1789.

Novísima recopilación de las leyes de España dividida en xii libros. 6 vols. Madrid, 1805–7.

O'Callaghan, Joseph. "Don Pedro Girón, Master of the Order of Calatrava, 1445–1466." *Hispania* 21 (1961): 342–90. Reprinted in O'Callaghan, *The Spanish Military Order of Calatrava and Its Affiliates.* London, 1975.

——. *A History of Medieval Spain.* Ithaca, 1975.

Olaechea, Juan B. "La ciudadanía del indio en los dominios hispanos." *Cuadernos de Investigación Histórica* 5 (1981): 113–34.

Omero de Torres, Enrique. "Ordenanzas de la villa de Alcalá de los Gazules, dadas por don Fadrique de Rivera, marqués de Tarifa, en el año de 1513." *BRAH* 56 (1910): 71.

Ortiz, Alfonso, ed. *Southwest.* Vol. 9 of *Handbook of North American Indians,* general editor William C. Sturtevant. Washington, D.C., 1979.

Outhwaite, R. B. "Who Bought Crown Lands? The Pattern of Purchases, 1589–1603." *Bulletin of the Institute of Historical Research* 44 (1971): 18–33.

Owens, John B. "Despotism, Absolutism and the Law in Renaissance Spain: Toledo versus the Counts of Belalcázar (1445–1574)." Ph.D. diss., University of Wisconsin, 1972.

Palomeque Torres, Antonio. "Derechos de Arancel de la justicia civil y criminal en los lugares de los propios y montes de la ciudad de Toledo anteriores al año de 1500." *Anuario de Historia del Derecho Español* 24 (1954): 87–94.

——. "El fiel del juzgado de los propios y montes de la ciudad de Toledo." *Cuadernos de Historia de España* 55–56 (1972): 322–99.

——. "Nueva aportación a la historia de la administración local: Elección de magistraturas en una villa toledana antes y despues de la revolución de 1820." *Anuario de Historia del Derecho Español* 31 (1961): 293–305.

Parry, J. H. *The Sale of Public Office in the Spanish Indies under the Habsburgs.* Berkeley, 1953.

Pelorson, Jean Marc. *Les letrados, juristes castillans sous Philippe III: Recherches sur leur place dans la société, la culture, e l'état.* Le Puy-en-Velay, 1980.

Pérez de Ayala, José. "Los antiguos cabildos de las Islas Canarias." *Anuario de Historia del Derecho Español* 4 (1927): 225–97.

Pérez Moreda, Vicente. *Las crisis de mortalidad en la España interior, siglos XVI–XIX.* Madrid, 1980.

Pescador del Hoyo, María del Carmen. "Los orígines de la Santa Hermandad." *Cuadernos de Historia de España* 55–56 (1972): 403–43.

Phillips, Carla Rahn. *Ciudad Real, 1500–1750: Growth, Crisis, and Readjustment in the Spanish Economy.* Cambridge, Mass., 1979.

Phillips, William D., Jr. *Slavery from Roman Times to the Early Transatlantic Trade.* Minneapolis, 1985.

Pierson, Peter. *Philip II of Spain.* London, 1975.

Pike, Ruth. *Enterprise and Adventure: The Genoese in Seville and the Opening of the New World.* Ithaca, 1966.

Posada, Adolfo. *Evolución legislativa del régimen local en España, 1812–1909.* Madrid, 1982.

Privilegio real de Felipe II que concede a Linares el título de villa, haciéndola independiente de Baeza. Facsimile ed. and transcription. Privilegios reales y viejos documentos de las villas, ciudades, y reinos de España, 4. Madrid, 1969.

Ramírez Arellano, Rafael. *Ensayo de un catálogo biográfico de escritores de la provincia y diócesis de Córdoba.* 2 vols. Madrid, 1921–23.

———. "Rebelión de Fuenteovejuna contra el comendador mayor de Calatrava, Fernán Gómez de Guzmán (1476)." *BRAH* 39 (1901): 446–512.

Ramos, Demetrio. "Colón y el enfrentamiento de los caballeros: Un serio problema del segundo viaje, que nuevos documentos ponen al descubierto." *Revista de Indias* 39 (1979): 9–88.

———. *La revolución de Coro de 1533 contra los Welser y su importancia para el régimen municipal.* Caracas, 1965.

———. "Notas sobre la geografía del bajo Tajuña." *Estudios Geográficos* 26 (1965): 41–154.

"Real cédula de población otorgada a los que hicieran descubrimientos en tierra firme, Burgos, 1521." In *CODIAI,* 2:558–67. Madrid, 1864.

Recopilación de leyes de los reynos de las Indias. 4th ed. 3 vols. Madrid, 1791. Facsimile ed. 1943.

Relaciones histórico-geográfico-estadísticas de los pueblos de España hechas por iniciativa de Felipe II: Provincia de Ciudad Real. Edited by Carmelo Viñas y Mey and Ramón Paz. Madrid, 1971.

Relaciones histórico-geográfico-estadísticas de los pueblos de España hechas por iniciativa de Felipe II: Provincia de Madrid. Edited by Carmelo Viñas y Mey and Ramón Paz. Madrid, 1949.

Relaciones histórico-geográfico-estadísticas de los pueblos de España hechas por iniciativa de Felipe II: Reino de Toledo. Edited by Carmelo Viñas y Mey and Ramón Paz. 2 vols. in 3. Madrid, 1951–63.

Relaciones de pueblos del obispado de Cuenca. Edited by Julián Zarco Cuevas. 1927. Revised edition by Dimas Pérez Ramírez. Cuenca, 1983.

Relaciones topográficas de España: Relaciones de pueblos que pertenecen hoy a la provincia de Guadalajara. Edited by Juan Catalina García López and Manuel Pérez Villamil. *MHE,* 41–43, 45–47. Madrid, 1903–5, 1912–15.

Reynolds, Susan. *Kingdoms and Communities in Western Europe, 900–1300.* Oxford, 1984.

Rivera, Milagros. *La encomienda, el priorato y la villa de Uclés en la edad media (1174–1310): Formación de un señorío de la orden de Santiago.* Madrid, 1985.

Romero de Lecea, Carlos. *La comunidad y tierra de Segovia: Estudio histórico-legal acerca de su origen, extensión propiedades, derechos, y estado presente.* Segovia, 1893.

Rosell, Cayetano, ed. *Crónica general de España: Historia ilustrada y descriptiva de sus provincias.* Madrid, 1866–70.

Ruano, Eloy Benito. "Aportaciones de Toledo a la guerra de Granada." *al-Andalus* 25 (1960): 41–70.

Rucquoi, Adeline. *Valladolid en la edad media.* 2 vols. Valladolid, 1987.

Ruiz de la Peña, Juan Ignacio. "Estado actual de los estudios sobre el municipio asturiano medieval." *Anuario de Estudios Medievales* (Barcelona) 5 (1968): 629–39.

Ruiz Martín, Felipe. "Demografía eclesiástica hasta el siglo XIX." In *Diccionario de historia eclesiástica de España,* edited by Quintín Aldea Vaquero, Tomás Nartínez, and José Vives Gatell, vol. 2, pp. 682–89. Madrid, 1972.

Saavedra, Pegerto. *Economía, política, y sociedad en Galicia: La provincia de Mondoñedo, 1480–1830.* Madrid, 1985.

Sacristán y Martínez, Antonio. *Municipalidades de Castilla y León: Estudio histórico-crítico.* Introduction by Alfonso María Guilarte. Colección administración y ciudadano, 14. Madrid, 1981.

Salomon, Noël. La vida rural castellana en tiempos de Felipe II. Translated by Francesc
Espinet Burunat. Barcelona, 1973.
——. Recherches sur le thème paysan dans la 'Comedia' au temps de Lope de Vega.
Bordeaux, 1965.
Saltillo, Marqués del [Miguel Lasso de la Vega]. Historia nobiliaria española. 2 vols.
Madrid, 1951.
Sánchez Agesta, Luis. "El 'poderío real absoluto' en el testamento de 1554: Sobre
los orígines de la concepción del estado." In Carlos V (1500–1558): Homenaje
de la Universidad de Granada, edited by Antonio Gallego Morell, pp. 439–67.
Granada, 1958.
Sánchez Albornoz, Claudio. Despoblación y repoblación del valle del Duero. Buenos
Aires, 1966.
——. "The Frontier and Castilian Liberties." In The New World Looks at Its History,
edited by A. Lewis and T. F. McGann, pp. 27–46. Austin, 1963.
——. Ruina y extinción del municipio romano en España e instituciones que le reem-
plazan. Buenos Aires, 1943.
——. Una ciudad hispano-cristiana hace un milenio: Estampas de la vida en León.
Buenos Aires, n.d.
Sánchez Caballero, Juan. "Historia de la independencia de Linares." Oretania 4,
no. 11 (1962): 186; 5, no. 13 (1963): 5–8; 5, nos. 14–15 (1963): 55–66; 6,
nos. 16–18 (1964): 125–28; 7, no. 20 (1965): 97–101; 8, no. 22 (1966): 185–
89.
Sánchez Martínez, Manuel, and Juan Sánchez Caballero. Una villa giennense a
mediados del siglo XVI: Linares. Jaén, 1975.
Sandoval, Prudencio de. Historia de la vida y hechos del Emperador Carlos V. Edited
by Carlos Seco Serrano. BAE, 80–82. Madrid, 1955–56.
Schindling, Anton. "Die Reformation in den Reichsstädten und die Kirchengüter.
Strassburg, Nürnberg und Frankfurt im Vergleich." In Bürgerschaft und Kirche,
edited by Jürgen Sydow, pp. 67–88. Sigmaringen, 1980.
Silva, José Gentil da. En Espagne: Développement économique, subsistance, déclin.
Paris, 1965.
Solano Ruiz, Emma. La orden de Calatrava en el siglo XV: Los señoríos castellanos
de la orden al fin de la edad media. Seville, 1978.
Talamanco, Juan de. Historia de la ilustre y leal villa de Orche, señora de sí misma,
con todas las prerogativas de señorío y vassallaje. Madrid, 1748. Edited by Alberto
García Ruiz. 2d ed. Guadalajara, 1986.
Tendilla, conde de [Iñigo López de Mendoza]. "Copiador de cartas por el marqués
de Mondéjar." AHN, Osuna. Legs. 3406, 3407. Cited by addressee and date.
——. "Registro de cartas referentes al gobierno de las Alpujarras." BN. Mss.
10230, 10231. Published as Correspondencia del conde de Tendilla: Biografía,
estudio y transcripción. Edited by Emilio Meneses García. 2 vols. Archivo Documental Español, 31–32. Madrid, 1973–74.
Thompson, I. A. A. "The Purchase of Nobility in Castile, 1552–1700." Journal
of European Economic History 8, no. 2 (1979): 313–60.
Tittler, Robert. "The End of the Middle Ages in the English Country Town."
Sixteenth Century Journal 18 (1987): 471–88.
Toledo, García de. "Discurso de d. García de Toledo sobre los inconvenientes
que tienen cargos de generales de galeras." In Armada española desde la unión de
los reinos de Castilla y de Aragón, edited by Cesáreo Fernández Duro, vol. 2, pp.
409–11. Madrid, 1972.

Torras i Ribé, Josep M. *Els municips catalans de l'antic règim (1453–1808): Procediments electorales, òrgans de poder i grupos dominants*. Barcelona, 1983.

Torres Balbas, Leopoldo. *Resúmen histórico del urbanismo en España*. Madrid, 1954. Reprinted in "Dos tipos de ciudades." In *Resúmen histórico*, 2d ed., pp. 67–96. Madrid, 1968.

Torres Fontes, Manuel. "La conquista del marquesado de Villena en el reinado de los Reyes Católicos." *Hispania* 13 (1953): 37–151.

Ulloa, Modesto. *La hacienda real de Castilla en el reinado de Felipe II*. 2d ed. Madrid, 1977.

———. "La producción y el consumo en la Castilla del siglo xvi: Sus reflejos en las cuentas de la hacienda real." *Hispania* 31 (1971): 5–30.

———. *Las rentas de algunos señores y señoríos castellanos bajo los primeros Austria*. Montevideo, 1971.

Valdeón Baruque, Julio. *Enrique II de Castilla: La guerra civil y la consolidación del régimen (1366–1371)*. Valladolid, 1966.

———. "Un despoblado castellano del siglo XIV: Fuenteungrillo." In *Estudios en memoria del professor D. Salvador de Moxó*, 3:705–16. Madrid, 1982.

Valdivia, Pedro de. "Relación hecha por Pedro de Valdivia al emperador, dándole cuenta de lo sucedido en el descubrimiento, conquista y población de Chile y en su viaje al Perú." In *CODIAI*, 4:7–8. Madrid, 1865.

Varona García, María Antonia. *La chancillería de Valladolid en el reinado de los reyes católicos*. Valladolid, 1981.

Vassberg, David. *Land and Society in Golden Age Castile*. Cambridge, 1984.

———. *La venta de tierras baldías: El comunitarismo agrario y la corona de Castilla durante el siglo XVI*. Madrid, 1983.

Velázquez de la Cadena, Mariano, et al. *The New Revised Velázquez Spanish and English Dictionary*. Piscataway, N.J., 1985.

Verlinden, Charles. *The Beginnings of Modern Colonization*. Translated by Yvonne Freccereo. Ithaca, 1970.

———. *Cristóbal Colón y el descubrimiento de América*. Translated by Florentino Pérez-Embid. Madrid, 1967.

———. "L'histoire urbaine dans la Péninsule Ibérique." *Revue Belge de Philologie et d'Histoire* 15 (1936): 1142–66.

Vigil, C. Miguel. *Asturias monumental: epigrafía y diplomática. Datos para la historia de la provincia*. 2 vols. 1887. Facsimile ed. Oviedo, 1987.

Villalon, L. J. Andrew. "The Law's Delay: The Anatomy of an Aristocratic Property Dispute (1350–1577)." Ph.D. diss., Yale University, 1984.

Viñas y Mey, Carmelo. *El problema de la tierra en la España de los siglos XVI–XVII*. Madrid, 1941.

———. "La asistencia social a la invalidez militar en el siglo XVI." *Anuario de Historia Económica y Social* 1 (1968): 598–605.

Vincent, Bernard, and Antonio Domínguez Ortiz. *Historia de los Moriscos: Vida y tragedia de una minoría*. Madrid, 1978.

Weisser, Michael. "Crime and Punishment in Early-Modern Spain." In *Crime and the Law: The Social History of Crime in Western Europe since 1500*, edited by V. A. C. Gatrell, Bruce Lenman, and Geoffrey Parker, pp. 76–96. London, 1980.

———. *Peasants of the Montes: The Roots of Rural Rebellion in Spain*. Chicago, 1976.

Wickham, C. J. *The Mountains and the City: The Tuscan Apennines in the Early Middle Ages*. Oxford, 1988.

Wright, L. P. "The Military Orders in Sixteenth- and Seventeenth-Century Spanish Society: The Institutional Embodiment of a Historical Tradition." *Past and Present* 43 (1969): 34–70.

Wright, Irene. *The Early History of Cuba, 1492–1586.* New York, 1916.

Yun Casalilla, Bartolomé. *Sobre la transición al capitalismo en Castilla: Economía y sociedad en Tierra de Campos (1500–1830).* Valladolid, 1987.

Zárate, Agustín de. *The Discovery and Conquest of Peru.* Translated by J. H. Cohen. Baltimore, 1968.

Zurita y Castro, Gerónimo de. *Anales de la corona de Aragón.* Book 6. [Zaragoza, 1585].

Index

Index